Praise for

EGGSHELL SKULL

'Brutal, brave and utterly compelling, Bri Lee's extraordinary memoir shines a light on the humanity and complexity of our justice system and the limitless courage victims of crime must summon in a legal process stacked against them at every turn. In the age of #MeToo, *Eggshell Skull* is a prescient personal account of a young woman's fierce and unflinching battle against her abuser. I can't remember a book I devoured with such intensity, nor one that moved me so profoundly.'

Rebecca Starford,
author of *Bad Behaviour* and co-founder of *Kill Your Darlings*

'An illuminating meditation on society's complicity in sexual assault, told through one woman's pursuit of justice in a system that has failed women and survivors for too long. Powerful as it is timely, *Eggshell Skull* is a courageous, heartbreaking and ultimately hopeful memoir from one of Australia's sharpest young writers.'

Liam Pieper, author of *The Toymaker*

'*Eggshell Skull* is as finely wrought as its name suggests—a sensitive and clear-eyed account of childhood sexual abuse that ripples out to encompass both its psychic aftershocks and the gruelling work of seeking legal redress. Lee doesn't flinch from the ugliness of the crime, but her eye for detail is always compassionate, never gratuitous. This is a book that honours its survivors, and one that should establish Lee as a serious name in Australian nonfiction.'

Jessica Friedmann, author of *Things That Helped*

'*Eggshell Skull* is a page-turner of a memoir, impossible to put down . . . A great book with which to open a conversation about sexual assault and the way in which the legal system has let women down for too many years. If you are confused or disturbed by the sudden upsurge of #MeToo accusations, *Eggshell Skull* will give you an insight into the anger and vitriol of many survivors.'

Krissy Kneen, author of *An Uncertain Grace*

ABOUT THE AUTHOR

Bri Lee is a writer and editor whose work has been published in *The Guardian, Griffith Review,* the VICE network and elsewhere, and she regularly appears on ABC Radio. In 2016 Bri was the recipient of the inaugural Kat Muscat Fellowship, and in 2017 was one of *Griffith Review's* Queensland writing fellows. She is the founding editor of the quarterly print periodical *Hot Chicks with Big Brains,* which has published nonfiction about women and their work since 2015. In 2018 Bri received a Commonwealth Government of Australia scholarship and stipend to work on her second book at the University of Queensland.

EGGSHELL
SKULL

A memoir about standing up,
speaking out and fighting back

BRI LEE

ALLEN&UNWIN
SYDNEY·MELBOURNE·AUCKLAND·LONDON

This book is a personal account based on real events and features a mix of both transcribed and reconstructed dialogue. Assertions of innocence or guilt are occasionally expressed merely as the author's opinion, independent from court rulings. It has been necessary to obscure identifying features of some individuals for both legal and moral reasons, and so dates, locations and other identifiers have been changed where required. Every single name has been changed, therefore any correlation to real individuals is purely coincidental.

First published in 2018

Allen & Unwin
83 Alexander Street
Crows Nest NSW 2065
Australia
Phone: (61 2) 8425 0100
Email: info@allenandunwin.com
Web: www.allenandunwin.com

A catalogue record for this book is available from the National Library of Australia

ISBN 978 1 76029 577 6

Set in 12/17 pt Fairfield Light by Bookhouse, Sydney
Printed and bound in Australia by Griffin Press

10 9 8 7 6 5 4 3 2 1

The paper in this book is FSC® certified. FSC® promotes environmentally responsible, socially beneficial and economically viable management of the world's forests.

The eggshell skull rule applies in many common law juris-dictions in both civil and criminal law. The premise is that if Person A were to have a skull as thin as an eggshell, and Person B struck them on the head, intending only to punch them, but in fact killed them, B is responsible for the damage they cause A. In criminal law the maxim was first stated by Lord Justice Lawton: a defendant must 'take their victims as they find them'.

PROLOGUE

ONE AFTERNOON WHEN I WAS about ten, my dad drove me to get a pie for lunch as a treat. As his big red ute pulled into the carpark in front of the bakery, we saw a man and woman yelling at each other.

'Stay in the car,' my dad said, roughly pulling up the handbrake and getting out. The rusty door whined and banged shut behind him.

I sat still and looked forward through the dusty front windscreen as though I was watching television with muffled sound. The yelling got louder and the woman raised her arms, gesturing, and the man raised his arms and shoved her, hard.

My father reached them in a few measured strides, and it was as if I saw him transform. He became tall and strong, transcending his daggy, three-quarter cargo pants and floppy leather sandals. I saw the woman had also transformed, but in the opposite way: she looked tiny and terrified. I think she was clutching her face.

With one hand Dad reached into his pocket and pulled out his badge, and with the other, keeping his palm open and down, he gestured for the man to step back. The situation de-escalated quickly. The three of them stood there, my father with his legs planted wide and firm, the other two shifting their weight, while he took down something in his notebook and they left. Later I would learn that the woman didn't want to make a complaint and refused further police assistance. Dad waited until they were well on their way to the train station across the road before he looked back at me in the ute, beckoning for me to come out. I fought the urge to run to him, brimming with questions, my curiosity about this adult occurrence making me feel naughty.

We went into the bakery. 'Tell the lady which kind of pie you would like,' he said in front of the hot box, his hand on my shoulder.

⌒

I know plenty of people hate cops. I'm young and blessed to be friends with lots of creative people, left-wing political activists, and older friends who remember Queensland under Premier Joh Bjelke-Petersen when unions saved both livelihoods and lives. I've met bad cops who misuse their power, and I know there are lazy cops who make life difficult—and of course I wonder who guards the guards—but I can't think of cops without thinking of my dad. For most of my life, I'd been blinded by anecdotal evidence full of love and sacrifice. The cop I know best was admired for his calm, non-violent approach. The cop I know best launched me, squealing, from his shoulders into sparkling pools on birthdays. He helped me grow a veggie garden and watered it every morning when I lost interest. He raised me on an addictively binary vision of right and wrong. His uniform was crisp. He got up early in the morning without an alarm clock. People in the neighbourhood called on him, asking for advice. When he moved from patrol work to prosecution he had to take a pay cut of about 20 per cent because he was no longer in danger on a daily basis, but I remember sometimes he would notice cars following us home from school and we'd have to double around dead-end streets until they knew he'd seen them and tore off. Stranger danger was real.

After he'd spent a few years in prosecution, some rich barristers offered him a job at about double his wage. Mum and Dad fought about it because the money would have made things a lot more comfortable at home, but neither of them wanted him to work for defence. I'll never forget my brother and me agreeing that our dad would never go 'dark side'. He was our hero.

Dad often came home with stories about the best and worst in human beings. We talked about why people did bad things. Life was understood as a series of choices, actions and consequences.

Later, friends and people at work asked me all the time if I went into law to follow in my father's footsteps, but it was never that literal. If anything he tried to direct me away from the pursuit. 'Never look for justice,' he'd say when he'd finished unloading on Mum after days at domestic violence callover in Holland Park Magistrates Court. Sometimes I was allowed to listen to these discussions, and sometimes I'd be shooed from the room, forced to eavesdrop.

'What is rape?' I remember asking him once, as he took off his boots. I was in my primary school uniform, young enough to be asking the definitions of words as I heard them for the first time.

'Cameron,' my mum said, frowning at him as she exhaled loudly and left the room.

'Rape is when one person has sex with another person, but the other person doesn't want to,' Dad explained.

I thought quite clearly, *That's weird*, and dismissed the word as being entirely irrelevant to me.

Another time my father came home after visiting someone in the neighbourhood and told me that I was to 'get a man drunk' before I married him because some men 'become very nasty', and you wouldn't be able to tell until they drank.

When I finished high school, being young and dumb, I presumed that only particular jobs could offer significance and humanity. I fantasised about dying young as a wiry doctor with Médecins Sans Frontières, but didn't get the grades for medicine. Not smart enough to be a martyr, and with Agatha Christie-style 'lady detectives' apparently not really existing, I started a journalism course at university. I thought an internal compass that pointed toward 'truth and justice' would be enough, but I also believed that *I* wasn't enough. There was a mince grinder inside my mind, pulverising my self-esteem, manifesting in all kinds of masochistic quirks. I would run cross-country until I vomited, take exhaustive lists of my physical faults, reject invitations to events where I might be made to experience happiness.

'I think I'm going to change across to law,' I announced at the dinner table one night, having just turned eighteen.

My mum tried to talk me out of it, sensing it would make me unhappy. 'I always thought you'd make a wonderful tour guide—why not study tourism and hospitality? You could travel the world and have your adventures that way!'

I rolled my eyes. Mum was an artist and ran a wonderful art supplies store. I was harsh on her, confused by why she didn't want to watch the world news every day and boycott Nestlé with me. I was that kind of youth: the angsty, self-important, skinny white girl with an XXL 'Make Trade Fair' T-shirt and a clarinet exam every six months. If I'd been eighteen in 1986 I would have been one of those poor suckers who walked out of seeing *Top Gun* at the cinema and straight into the US Air Force recruitment booth— blind to my own cliché, craving heroism, secretly longing to make a sacrifice of myself.

Looking back on all this is bittersweet. I wanted a battle but rather got sucker-punched and almost didn't get back up.

'Never look for justice,' my dad said to me that night, and then time and time again.

I didn't listen.

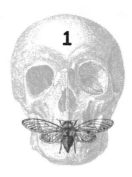

1

IT WAS A SWELTERING JANUARY in Brisbane, my first day at my new job, and my tweed pencil skirt no longer clipped up at my waist so I had to keep my jacket on as I walked from the bus stop to the Supreme and District Courts building. I had finished law school at the end of 2014 and returned to Queensland in the new year after two months on a graduation trip eating hotdogs and drinking Budweiser around the USA. New stretch marks at my hips were itchy from my fast increase in weight over the holidays. Sweat was soaking into the underarms of the shirt I had just ironed that morning. Things were off to a bad, and late, start. I hadn't got all my things ready the night before for the same reason I never bought more tampons when I finished a period—an absurd optimism rendered me perpetually unprepared for anything I didn't really want to happen.

As I was heading down George Street I passed a bakery, and as the smell of pies washed over me in a blast of heat I remembered The Pie Incident. Thirteen years had passed and my father was semiretired, leaving the law just as I was entering it.

Yayoi Kusama's *Eyes are Singing Out* mural sits opposite the smooth cement and glinting chrome courts building. The work is a huge row of black and white eyes set on a diagonal so that people walking past can see it, but so that the eyes clearly look upward toward the courts. Sunlight streamed through the colossal panes of glass that rose from the ground to the third storey. It was all very open plan. Very heels-click-on-marble.

I stepped into an elevator hoping for a moment to myself but a dozen people pooled in after me and I got stuffed at the back. My collar was tight at my throat, stockings cutting into my waist, and my toes were being crushed into my stiff high heels. I felt a kind of claustrophobia inside my own sweaty body. I couldn't catch the breath I needed in that elevator; it was as though I was in a clothes dryer, tumbling around, getting hot and disoriented. I had no moment of calm before being thrown into the first-impressions competition—I felt big and round and everything about the room I stepped into seemed trim and square. It was day one of a full year of everything about that place sanding off my edges.

⌒

I found the other associates milling around our training room in the Supreme Court Library and tried to act cool while my eyes darted about, searching their faces for someone I'd recognise. Most of them had gone to the University of Queensland—as usual—but I hadn't moved in the right circles to know them. Hadn't studied enough, hadn't sat at the right dinner tables with the right gown.

Someone waved to me, and I was relieved to see it was Evelyn. She and I had known each other since taking an acting class together in high school. I liked to joke that I spent my life following in her footsteps, in her slim shadow, doing everything she did, just a little bit shitter. Not wanting to break that trend, I had been appointed to the District Court and she to the Supreme Court. The distinction was important: everything in this new world needed to be measured. Everyone sat somewhere in the hierarchy.

Within moments of stepping into that room and being confronted with that new peer group, I lost perspective. To get a job as a judge's associate—at any level of court—is a prestigious and significant achievement. Of all the graduate positions a young law student can hope for, an associateship is the dream most of us don't dare to tell anyone we've dreamed, let alone applied for. I had posted in fifty individual applications. We were to be assistants, clerks, mentees, travelling companions, and foot soldiers to judges. With only one associate to each judge, the tradition effectively bottlenecked entry-level jobs in the judicial segment of the industry and encouraged rampant nepotism. Several associates in the room literally shared last names with judges and Queen's Counsel. I didn't doubt their merit—I envied it.

As I approached Evelyn's group, I stared at her hair. A shiny, dark, long-yet-professional bob. It was a visual representation of how perfect I imagined her whole life to be. Once, years ago, I'd found out that her parents paid for her to get it cut regularly at Oscar Oscar, and I'd never felt so simultaneously vindicated and inferior; my mum cut my hair for most of my life. Evelyn was chatting to others in the group about the graduate position she had lined up at a top-tier law firm for the following year. I smiled and nodded but thought I caught someone looking at the pimple above my lip and tried not to draw attention to myself. I didn't have a job lined up and didn't want to be asked the same question. Couldn't we all just have celebrated the achievement of being an associate a little longer? I zoned out, imagining what would happen if the chip on my shoulder manifested itself into an *actual* wound: it'd be like that scene in *Kill Bill* where an arm is chopped off and the blood gushes out like a spectacular column of water from a busted fire hydrant.

Someone else joined the conversation, and I leaned back on my heels and scanned the room again. So many handsome young men in R.M. Williams boots, so many stunning young women in Rhodes & Beckett suits.

'I'll bet you brought a suitcase full of incredible clothes home from the States?' Evelyn asked me.

'Oh, dude, it's fucking amazing—the consignment stores are like Lifeline on crack,' I replied, flinching at how crass I sounded. I tried to start talking about the Press Museum in Washington, DC, wanting to make a better impression on the beautiful strangers, but one of the judges came into the room, and we all hushed and took our seats.

Three hours flew by as we were reminded of the importance of discretion in our roles as assistants and confidantes to judges. We heard horror stories of how previous associates had fucked up. We were the public faces of our judges: we were not to say, do or even *think* anything that could ever possibly be considered bias. There were to be no emotions on our faces, regardless of how intense testimony or the return of a verdict might be. We could never speak to the media. Our Facebook profiles needed to be trim and respectable; the mood in the room stiffened as we all catalogued the Halloween costumes and beer kegs of undergraduate years. I'd already done a bit of a purge. It would not be unheard of for *The Courier-Mail* to trawl through an associate's profile if their judge was in a high-profile trial. This was the new rule of thumb for us all: how would something look in *The Courier-Mail*? Similarly, expressing political opinions was inappropriate. A Federal Court associate had written an open letter about political preferences to *The Australian* one year, and his legal career dried up in front of his eyes despite his family name. He was the cautionary tale of pride, the Icarus none of us could afford to forget.

But it was easy to lose track, in a room like that one—with so many brilliant minds, beacons of success—that we were still the smallest fish. In the months that followed I saw our status sour people I'd previously called friends. I would watch how some judges mentored their associates with great generosity and care, and how others slowly crushed their optimism and trust. It was a different world, up there in that tower made of glass: blindingly ivory.

After the training session I texted my judge. I was nervous to see him again because we hadn't met in person since my afternoon of training with his previous associate, Rebecca, six months earlier. *Good morning, Judge. Training has finished for the morning, if you are free I can come up to chambers otherwise I'll lunch with the associates and see you at three.*

I started heading to the bathroom when one of the associates I'd just met called out to me. 'Bri, come join us for coffee, we're going to plan a dinner for next week,' Alexandra said. She and I had done a summer clerkship at Corrs Chambers Westgarth the previous year. I didn't know if she'd got a graduate offer with them, but I sure hadn't and it had been a sting to see her that morning and be reminded of my rejection. Alexandra did marathons, spoke a bunch of languages and did volunteer legal work for something environmental.

My phone buzzed with a response from Judge: *Good morning, come up to chambers please.*

'Nah, I'm right, thanks,' I replied. 'Gonna pop up and see Judge. Besides, I'll be in Gladstone next week!'

'Circuit already!?' Alexandra asked, as she jumped into the elevator with a group of Supremes and waved goodbye.

'I know!' I waved back.

'Eew, Gladstone,' came an unfamiliar voice from inside the elevator as the doors closed.

I swiped my brand-new security pass and the elevator slowly took me up to level thirteen. I felt completely out of my depth. This space belonged to the Evelyns and Alexandras of the world. It belonged to people like my boyfriend, Vincent, more than me. The beautiful, bilingual people whose parents had gone to university.

I took a deep breath and knocked on Judge's door, and he looked and gave me a big smile. He invited me to take a seat and I remembered how nervous I'd been a year earlier, sitting in the same chair for the job interview, but as we chatted I also remembered how much we'd laughed together, how much I admired his lack of pretension.

'Rebecca showed me some of your updates from America,' he began. 'It looks like you had a fantastic trip.'

'Oh, absolutely,' I replied. 'I can't believe how different all the states are. New York was magic, though. I went to the Frick, like you suggested, and was blown away.'

'Fantastic, isn't it!' Judge said. He collected art, I'd learned the last time I was there. 'But I'm afraid we've got a bit of work to do before we can chat more. As you know, we're heading off to Gladstone this Sunday.'

'Yes, Rebecca has shown me all the preparations.'

'But before that, I need to deliver a judgment I reserved from a pre-trial hearing last week.'

'Oh,' I said, instantly nervous again.

He got up and walked to his desk, collecting a wad of stapled paper. 'I'd like you to proofread this and set up a time tomorrow for me to deliver it. You'll have to contact all the parties and make sure we have a courtroom booked.'

'Sure.' I took the documents from his outstretched arm and stood up, noticing he hadn't sat back down.

'You'll be alright to organise all that?' he asked.

'Absolutely,' I lied.

'Great,' he said, turning to sit at his desk, 'let me know how you go.'

I left his room and took a seat in my new office, just outside his chambers. It was clean and simple, a small square with a large calendar on the wall, beside my computer, that Rebecca had prepared for me. The calendar colour-coded the eight towns that Judge and I would be travelling to on circuit. It noted that of all the weeks in the year we had for work, only two would consist of civil law: the rest were criminal. Gladstone came first—two weeks beginning Sunday, then only two weeks back home before Bundaberg. After that, three weeks in Brisbane, then off to Warwick, and it continued on.

I grew anxious as I stared at the year in front of me, so I brought my attention to the present: to the proofreading. I scanned down the page and identified it as an s590AA application with catchwords listed: *ADMISSIBILITY OF SIMILAR FACTS—indecent treatment of a child—rape—admissibility of previous similar sexual conduct.* My stomach clenched, and I pushed back from the desk. I knew what it would be—I remembered it from law school. Prosecution had testimony from someone else, not the complainant, that the defendant liked certain things during sex, and this would go a long way in convincing a jury that the complainant was telling the truth. It was for Judge to decide if the probative value of this evidence outweighed its prejudicial value. The outcomes of pre-trial hearings like this were critical, often determining the outcome of a trial before it even began. I rummaged in the desk for a red pen and took a deep breath in, rolling my chair back around to face the document.

The defendant was accused of sexually assaulting and raping his girlfriend's young daughter. She'd been in primary school when the offending took place and was now a teenager. In her police statement she listed several occasions when the defendant had tied her up before assaulting her, the severity of the bondage and penetration increasing over time until she complained to her mother. The critical incident in question was when the defendant allegedly tied the girl to the Hills hoist in his backyard before raping her. Prosecution had found one of the defendant's previous sexual partners who was willing to testify that while they were together he liked bondage, and that she had ended the relationship because his sexual desires grew in intensity until she no longer felt comfortable with them. I read on and on, forgetting to check for spelling or citations, gripped by morbid curiosity.

'He wanted to tie me up to the Hills hoist outside and have sex with me there,' the defendant's ex-girlfriend testified.

I flipped to the end of the document. Judge allowed the reference to the Hills hoist but excluded the general bondage content. The Hills hoist was a detail so unusual, so specific, that its probative weight could not be denied.

I checked my watch and went for a walk down the length of the building to the ladies' room. It was quiet here on the higher levels where the judges had their chambers, with frosted-glass walls and grey couches, wide and low. I had known on a theoretical level that this would be a *Law & Order: SVU* kind of job, but I hadn't thought I would encounter this side of it on my first day. It seemed odd that the floor was quiet. Wasn't anyone outraged? Judge was acting completely normal. Was this the new normal? Already?

There was a Hills hoist in the backyard of my grandparents' house. I conjured the image of it, remembering the smell of fresh laundry and my grandmother's cigarette smoke. But now I saw a child tied to it, crying, being raped. I saw the reality in my mind, the manicured grass and the blue pool just beyond it. The warm Queensland afternoon and the sun-weathered plastic pegs. It was the only Hills hoist I knew of, so I couldn't move the imagery of the offending elsewhere. It hit too close to home—literally, my grandparents' home just down the road from where I grew up, where I still lived. The heinous snapshot had slid in through a crack between the layers of my life, like a slippery ghost, and something else tweaked inside me. A memory from my own backyard in grass green and sky blue. In the ladies' room, my head flicked involuntarily, as though trying to shake the thought. I turned the taps on and watched the water flow over my hands, focusing on the sound it made and the coolness of my skin. I didn't look at myself in the mirror before going back to work. I couldn't have looked myself in the eye.

That afternoon all of the new associates got taken on a short tour of the cells under the building. It was cold down there, and everything seemed large, but it wasn't shiny like upstairs. Cement instead of marble, grey bars instead of chrome arches. At the end of the tour, the security officer asked if we had any questions, and someone asked if all these temporary holding cells had filled up after the G20 protests; the government had panicked about it.

'Not even close,' the officer said with a laugh.

I raised my hand next. 'I read a newspaper article yesterday that said the prisons at Wacol are too full and we need more facilities. Is that true?'

'It's not a problem of not enough space at the correctional facilities,' he said, shaking his head, 'it's that we're sending too many people to gaol for too long. The longer they're in, the less likely they are to ever truly get out, and it's expensive to keep them incarcerated and pretty awful for them too.'

We all nodded as though we, the children from the top of the tower, could even come close to understanding that dungeon.

Back up on level thirteen I looked out over Brisbane bathed in hot yellow sunlight and thought about how all the people in the top levels were university-educated, white-collar overachievers. Far beneath us, fifteen stories down, under the ground, near where the cars were parked, we kept the criminals. We even kept the alleged criminals down there, away from the sun. My career in the clouds was built on the misfortune and misconduct of the people way below. The chrome impossible without the concrete. I made $50,000 my first year out of university, and I made it from a system that is funded by necessity because people keep doing awful things to each other.

From the window where I stood, I saw a group of Indigenous Australians gathering in Roma Street Parkland, laughing and sharing food. Following years of invasion and genocide Australia's First Nations people made up 3 per cent of our population—but almost a third of our prison population identified as Aboriginal or Torres Strait Islander. According to the president of the Queensland Law Society, not a single District or Supreme Court judge identified as Aboriginal or Torres Strait Islander.

When I turned from the window, I noticed that artworks hung on most of the walls, accompanied by plaques and explanations, and many pieces were by Indigenous Australian artists. The courts building struck me as a freakishly physical manifestation of Australia's social dichotomy. Way up there, we liked looking as though we liked acknowledgement. We liked the words we could copy and paste to the beginnings of speeches, the box we could tick at the beginning of events, to show we cared, before we went ahead and didn't. We made large corporate orders to absurdly expensive florists to match our acquisitions of acknowledgement, and those paintings sat silently beside the lilies, well behaved, where we could keep an eye on them.

⌒

For the first few days of work, I thought that view from level thirteen was beautiful. On one side of the building, out through Judge's windows, we saw the river and the hills, and on the other, near the elevators, a glinting expanse of modern infrastructure. It only took a couple of weeks for me to turn from the windows. After enough trials and sentences, I realised I was looking out over a constellation of crime scenes. Spots that seemed tiny from way up there were locations, chosen through significance or circumstance, for rapes and bashings. It quickly became hard for me to look at all the ant-sized people bustling to-and-fro and keep my mind from wandering between them, wondering which ones were the criminals, which ones were the victims, and which ones might be any day now. It seemed impossible that many people would go through that city, or along that river, or through those mountains, lucky enough to be neither. Perhaps this was because I knew that at the end of the day, when I was walking home among them, I wasn't one of the lucky untouched.

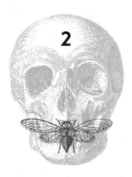

2

IN THAT FIRST WEEK BACK in Brisbane, my first week at work, I spent most evenings with Vincent. We had skyped during my two months away, but something vulnerable inside me had calcified over again. He was the one person to have ever reached me, and the one man I'd somehow opened up to, but I'd only been gone a fortnight when I realised that how much I missed him was inhibiting my happiness, and I resented it. I didn't know how to be in love with him and not be with him, so I tried to push him from my mind by reaching back to behaviours and feelings I'd once had when travelling alone. By the end of the trip I had finally shaken the impulse to reach for him when I saw something wonderful.

Being back was full-on. I had somehow forgotten how handsome he was in real life: strong features, thick dark hair, slim and tall. Inhaling the smell of his neck as he held me at Brisbane Airport gave me a head rush. I'd never voiced my wondering if he would even really wait for me, or still want me when I returned. We had been together for three years since meeting at law school, and I panicked that my life was moulding to his. Connection to someone seemed to necessitate a loss of independence. Being in a relationship meant compromising on things I'd barely finished fighting for. But my hard-won comfort in solitude had turned into missing his company. Despite how relaxed he was, I second-guessed ordering at restaurants and didn't know when to wear high heels anymore. There were so many moments of bartering my autonomy for his affection. I oscillated between convincing myself he didn't really love me and feeling terror at the prospect that he did. I didn't know how to just be in love.

Lying in his arms after dinner on the Thursday night of my first week back, a few nights before I'd have to leave for Gladstone, I did an appalling job of articulating my thoughts. 'Sometimes I feel like when I don't see you for a while I can't keep this love open, like it's too hard, and now I'm home it's like I'm trying to crack my ribs open to let you at my heart again.' I started crying at my failure to explain myself. 'And now I have to go away again.'

Vincent kissed my cheeks, my forehead and my lips, his quiet blessing, 'I'll be right here when you get back.'

He wasn't listening to what I was trying to say. Perhaps it made even less sense to him than it did to me. Maybe he thought I was just stressed, and maybe he was right.

⌐

The next morning at work, Judge and I held a callover ahead of going to Gladstone. At callovers the judge goes through the list of every outstanding matter—every active file—at a courthouse. The prosecutor needs to know the details of these matters and which ones the Department of Public Prosecutions (DPP) wants to prioritise. Defence lawyers need to be ready to advise the court how their client intends to plead when their matter is mentioned. Among what felt like a million other tasks, it was my job to take note of every piece of information that might be relevant later. The following week Judge might ask me why a certain matter couldn't be listed for trial and I would need to be able to remind him the defendant was in hospital, or that a witness was unavailable.

I began seeing how human the system was. Matters that had been waiting on the list at Gladstone for years might have to wait six more months if a certain lawyer was on long service leave. Expert witnesses needed to be able to take time off work to testify. Sometimes, I would learn, we just couldn't make it to the end of the list in two short weeks. The towns and cities we travelled to on circuit weren't big enough to justify having a judge sit there permanently, but they needed to have their matters dealt with locally, and so judges would travel out west and up north for two weeks at a time. My judge had the most circuits scheduled out of all the District Court judges.

'Did you see that barrister's cufflinks?' I asked Judge later in the private elevator after court adjourned.

'No.'

'They were big shiny dollar signs,' I said, grinning, 'the size of fifty cent pieces, glinting in the light.'

'Really!?' Judge gave a light laugh and shook his head. We were off to a good start.

Back in my office I prepared us for the coming trials. The bulk of the court list was child sex offences, and when I remarked upon this to Judge he agreed and we commiserated.

'Unfortunately it's the bread and butter of the District Court,' he said, 'but sometimes you get a good bit of old-fashioned violence, like that second trial.'

I laughed.

'You know,' he said, 'two adults going at each other, fisticuffs, the occasional chainsaw—it becomes a welcome reprieve from the child sex stuff.' He was smiling now, but it was a knowing, tainted smile I would come to recognise.

That evening at home over dinner, my mum asked me about circuit.
'And it's always for two weeks at a time?'

'Yep,' I replied. 'Sometimes we come back in the middle weekend
and sometimes we don't.'

'Depends on the location,' my dad added between mouthfuls.

'Nope,' I said, pointing my fork at him, 'it depends on the judge.'
He nodded. 'Mm.'

'Everything depends on the judge,' I said.

'And where do you live while on circuit?' Mum asked.

I shrugged. 'A hotel or motel or apartment thingo. I do all the
bookings but I've never heard of any of the places before. I have
to research and print out maps so I know how to drive us from
the airport to the accommodation. I'm really nervous about it all.'

'You'll be fine, sweetie,' she said, smiling, 'you're good at all
that stuff.'

'Now that you've got a job,' Dad said, changing the subject, 'you
should think about saving up for a deposit.'

My older brother, Arron, was almost thirty, an electrical engineer,
and had just bought a place out in Donnybrook—a two-hour drive
from Brisbane—because even on his great wage the worst house
on the worst street was all he could afford. Dad was over the
moon: both kids had finished university, and one out of two had
real estate. He'd get the Baby Boomer Gold Star once I was also
up to my eyeballs in a mortgage, and then he'd be able to wipe his
hands on his pants and crack a light beer.

After the large meal I went to my bedroom and closed the door,
cherishing the white shaggy carpet under my feet and the quiet
hum of the cooking show my mum was watching on the other
side of the wall. I took some things out of my American suitcase,

still not fully unpacked, and replaced them with others, trying on some of the pantsuits I'd bought before leaving and finding that many wouldn't button at my hips. I had to dig around my cupboard for clothes Mum had bought me from op shops in previous years; things I'd hated when she'd brought them home because I couldn't believe that she'd thought I was so big. I looked at the mirror, the grey dresses and black slacks fitting me, and to quell my rising anxiety I resolved to do better.

The spaghetti bolognese Mum had lovingly prepared for me that night, because she knew it was my favourite, because she knew I was stressed, pooled in a clumpy mash on top of the shower drain, and I swirled it around with my fingers, pushing it down. Tears came out as the food came out and it felt good. The hot water felt good. I would do better. Be better.

⌒

I waved to Judge as I saw him walk toward the Qantas check-in area at Brisbane Airport, and was relieved to see him also in casual clothes. I heard stories of other judges requiring their associates be in formal workwear at all times, even on Sundays when flying out for circuits. Not for the first or last time, I considered how lucky I was to be paired with him in particular. We went up to the Qantas Lounge and I swore under my breath, looking out across the free bar and buffet area. The 'other half' milled around.

Later on in the plane Judge saw two fashion magazines sticking out of my tote bag. 'Did you take those from the Lounge?' he asked, and I panicked before I looked up and saw he was smiling.

'Maybe?' I answered with a grin, and the plane took off.

We chatted and I asked him all kinds of questions about circuit. He told me some towns were different from others, that juries did and didn't respond to different things in different areas. In some regional places it was extremely difficult to get guilty verdicts, while in a few others being charged practically meant convicted. Some communities had particularly tense relationships with the local police—powderkeg style—whereas some were brimming with mutual respect and cooperation.

I had asked for the window seat and I looked down at Gladstone, thinking that the huge rusty aluminium refinery beside the town seemed like a giant, inflamed pimple. I didn't know if I could make that kind of joke with Judge. After six years of university and a couple of months travelling, I found it difficult to avoid swearing in front of him. I didn't even know if I could ask him about the political news I'd read in the paper that morning, or about his weekend. He wasn't only my boss, but an extremely intelligent and important man as well, and it was the beginning of our year together. My eyelids were drooping but I fought the fatigue, embarrassed at how it would look for me to fall asleep—it was exhausting not knowing quite how to behave.

I thought back to what I'd researched about Gladstone. Previously home to the Gureng Gureng and Bayali Aboriginal tribes, then at various stages 'discovered and named', the town was now home to almost 50,000 people. It was one of Queensland's granite-belt towns that had benefited greatly from the mining boom and grown into a city, but that golden tide had receded. The big shipping port I'd read about stretched out beneath the plane window, spoiling what would otherwise be a beautiful coastline.

When we landed and picked up the hire car, I remembered I would have to drive it, and my knuckles went white as I gripped the steering wheel. It would be one thing to make a conversational faux pas, but I couldn't imagine rear-ending someone with my judge riding shotgun.

We pulled into a supermarket to pick up supplies for the week, and he passed me in the magazine aisle. 'You know you have to pay for these ones?' he said, walking past me, and we laughed.

I messed up a lot on my first day in court. It was overwhelming. I made a note in my diary to make sure I trained my associate better than I had been trained. Rebecca, my predecessor, had already known how to do the job when she'd started working for Judge, and given he was a relatively new appointment to the District Court judiciary, he'd never had to work with someone who so fully had no idea what they were doing. To make things worse, I was the only associate that year to be sent on circuit in their first week. I couldn't pop into another associate's office and ask for help. Even with all the posturing and competition among associates I had presumed we'd share a certain level of camaraderie, but I was marooned. The prosecutor's name was Eric and he seemed to take pity on me, but I couldn't be seen to be talking to him too much or asking for his help.

During another callover first thing in the morning, I spoke aloud in court when I wasn't supposed to. Afterwards, in chambers, Judge had to tell me things I should have known already. I forgot to pick up a jury list in the morning and didn't tell the court transcribing service that we needed daily transcripts. I took hours to process files at the end of the day, knowing each one should have needed only a few minutes' attention from an intelligent mind. If I made any mistakes there could be grave consequences for real people's lives. It slapped me in the face with every new case. *Wake up, little girl!* the job yelled at me.

Nearly a hundred matters were on the list and I was fortunate— or unfortunate, depending on how you look at it—to be working for a man who took the responsibility of his job seriously.

'If we don't bring this matter on in these sittings,' he said to a lawyer asking for an adjournment that week, 'these people won't have their case heard for another three months.' Time was a warped concept in court. People's liberties hung in the balance every single day, and juries deliberated for hours that felt like years, yet matters would be adjourned for months on end. I didn't know how or why things worked the way they did, and our time in Gladstone was hell because of it. We stayed back at work every day until well after the sun set.

The courtroom in Gladstone was obviously much older than the ones in Brisbane, but not old enough to be nice in an antique way. The ceilings were low, the bricks speckled and the carpets mustardy. As always, Judge sat up on a raised platform at one end of the room behind a huge closed-in desk. He faced outward toward everyone except me. In every courtroom, the associate has a small desk in front of the judge's; normally the height of Judge's desk started after the top of my head when seated. We could pass things to each other and whisper to the exclusion of all others if we needed to, and together we faced the rest of them: the public in the pews right down the back, the prosecutors and defence counsel at the bar table directly opposite us, the jurors in two rows of six along one wall, and the defendants in the specially separated dock, normally somewhere between the bar table and the public. All those basic elements are consistent in courtrooms across Queensland and Australia.

Sometimes the dock is open to the air in the middle of the room with just a wooden balustrade, at others it's off to the side and enclosed in glass, as in Gladstone. I'd read studies about different types of docks having prejudicial effects on juries' perceptions, but nobody talked about this that year. I would see over ten different kinds of docks, and it seemed like the cherry on top of a sundae of reasons why juries got things wrong.

Once callover was finished that first morning, Judge adjourned so the group of potential jurors could be brought to the court. I was in overdrive preparing. I found the old wooden barrel I would pull the jurors' name cards from, and the form I needed to fill out and then place with the records of the trial. Cheryl, the extremely friendly bailiff, was trying to chat to me about her weekend and I was short in response. I felt as if I was sandbagging my house for a cyclone and Jehovah's Witnesses came knocking—just not the right time. She had multicoloured hair and an inability to match the volume of her voice to her quiet surroundings. By the end of the day I knew all kinds of private information about her. I had managed to dodge most of her extremely personal questions.

'So the first trial is this indecent treatment one, right?' I asked her, picking out a folder from the fifty or so others, trying to bring the focus back to work. 'James Williams?'

'Probably! Another stepdad?'

'Huh?' I asked, confused, panicking I'd missed something.

'You'll see,' she replied cheerily, swinging her courthouse keys around her fingers, 'I'm just off to the loo!'

When everything was ready, I made the short walk from the courtroom to the doorway of Judge's chambers. 'They're ready for you, Judge,' I said, and he stood and followed me out.

'Good morning, Judge,' Cheryl said to him brightly in the hallway, 'all ready to go?'

'Yes, let's get to work.' He adjusted his wig; one of the little white curly tails was stuck in the collar of his jabot and I fought the urge to adjust it for him. I wondered if one day I would feel comfortable doing that.

My pondering was cut short by Cheryl dramatically bursting open the courtroom door. 'Silence, all stand,' she boomed, and it began.

The associate is the one who stands up at the beginning of the trial, in front of the whole courtroom, and arraigns the defendant. I read out the document telling Williams what he was charged with, who he'd allegedly done it to, and when. The bailiff had called for silence and Judge offered an official welcome, but my voice was the one that levelled each heinous accusation, the one that made clear why we were all gathered. My fingertips left sweat dots on the pages. Williams stood up and I asked him if he pleaded guilty or not guilty to three counts of indecent treatment of a child under sixteen, each with a circumstance of aggravation that she was under his care.

'Not guilty,' he said assuredly, three times. He was a balding man in his forties or fifties. *An ordinary-looking dude,* my notes said.

I pulled twelve name cards, one after the other, from the old wooden barrel, and watched the unlucky Gladstone residents huff, inch past each other, and take their seats in the jury stands when I called their names. Prosecution and defence called out challenges to some of the names I called. Normally defence don't want too many highly educated people, and nobody wants a lawyer or a priest in the jury room because people defer to their opinions too much.

The next step is the prosecutor's job—to read out a list of witness names so that jurors can raise their hands and speak to the judge if they recognise any names and might have a conflict of interest.

'The third witness,' the prosecutor called out while I was busy scribbling down minutes and keeping up, 'is Breanne-Leigh Stowers.'

My head snapped to attention because of the involuntary way our minds betray us when our names are called. I was to spend the afternoon of the following day hearing my name in among testimony about a sex offender.

A woman from the jury raised her hand, and Judge asked her to approach his bench. I heard them whispering but nobody else in the court was close enough.

'What is your reason for requesting excusal?' he asked her.

'Well,' she whispered very softly, 'I had something like this happen to me, and I just, I mean . . . I don't want to listen to this.'

'I see,' Judge said, 'and you feel that your personal circumstance means you would not be able to be a fair and impartial juror in this trial?'

'Ah,' she hesitated, 'yes?'

'Very well, you are excused,' Judge said to her, and directed me to pick a replacement from the barrel.

I lost count, throughout the year, of the number of women who excused themselves from sex crime trials because they themselves were survivors.

We adjourned for a short break so that the jury could get acquainted over Nescafé Blend 43 and Monte Carlos. Judge addressed counsel to make sure everything was in order, and then we took a break as well.

I made Judge a cup of coffee and we sat in the armchairs in his chambers, chatting about Gladstone for a few nice moments until it was time to go back in.

First, the complainant gave evidence through a prerecording. She didn't want to be in the same courtroom as Williams—who we soon learned, as per the bailiff's prediction, was her mum's ex-boyfriend. She'd been thirteen when, allegedly, he began touching her and saying inappropriate things to her, then fourteen when his behaviour allegedly escalated.

'He would say weird things to me,' she said. 'Like he would say to me "Who taught you how to do that so well?" and "Oh, how'd you get so good at that?" while he was doing stuff.'

I shifted in my seat, a strange tightness coming across my chest and belly. I looked up at Williams and he was just watching the screen, a calm disdain on his face, his thin lips pursed. I didn't recognise the words, or his face, but something in her mimicry of his tone rang true and evoked something familiar to me. A saccharine and filthy way of speaking to someone who is terrified.

When the prosecutor had finished stepping the girl through her evidence-in-chief, she underwent three hours of cross-examination. We had to break for lunch in the middle of it, and I was incredulous—three hours of crying and reliving trauma.

'We don't even expect young people to sit through three-hour-long nature documentaries!' I said to Judge.

A defence barrister's job is to make the jury question the credibility and reliability of a complainant, and this barrister was good at his job. He poked holes in her stories, reminding her of inconsistencies between afternoon and night-time incidents. He accused her and her mother of colluding to bring Williams—the 'evil ex'—down. Eventually the barrister was asking her how much she knew about sex, and where she'd learned the names and slang for certain acts that she was alleging happened to her. He made a big deal out of how she knew the difference between a flaccid or erect penis. Sixteen was apparently too old to claim innocence, even though the alleged acts began when she was just thirteen. She got upset and cranky. She said she hated Williams. It was horrible.

The next day we heard from the witness whose name sounded just like mine. Breanne-Leigh was the complainant's best friend, and was recounting times when she had visited the home where Williams lived. She told the court what she knew about the offending and how Williams made her feel.

I told myself the sick feeling in my belly was just a symptom of the anxiety I had about the new job. I was still making mistakes every hour. Learning the ropes was always going to be a bit tough. I just had to get settled. Back in my room that night, after dinner, I paced around with a warm beer, wondering if I could call Vincent. What would I tell him? *I mean, it's really messing with me that I keep hearing my name in and around this kind of stuff, like, it's bringing shit up.* I practised trying to sound casual about it. What would he say? What did I even want him to say? I just wanted someone to talk to about what was happening to me. A change in my body, a discomfort, a drywall in my mind being scratched at, a darkness leaking into my life.

I stepped out onto my balcony and looked over the lights of Gladstone. A man way down on the street staggered home. Where the fuck was I? How had I got myself there, so alone yet in the middle of so many people's stories and crimes? It was only the beginning of the year; what if things got worse? I had to tell Vincent. *You're going to finish this beer, and then you're going to rip the bandaid off.* I stepped inside, sliding the door closed behind me with purpose, and I sat at the foot of the bed and necked the last of the beer, and found his name in my phone. My blood was pounding in my ears, my head lolling back slightly, my eyes shut tight, as I listened to the dial tone.

'Beep. Beep. Beep. Beep. Beep. Beep. The number you have dialled is unavailable. Please leave a message after the tone.'

I hung up fast, before the recording began. It was time for another beer and another cigarette.

Later in the evening I ate a whole packet of chocolate-coated Scotch Finger biscuits then threw them all up. We were staying in serviced apartments and after vomiting in the shower, washing my hair and brushing my teeth, I slipped into the tightly made bed, exhausted but clean.

⌒

At the end of the next day the defendant took the stand. His barrister stepped him through all the dates on which the allegations had taken place, producing a business work diary that suggested Williams had been out on painting jobs on a number of occasions his girlfriend's daughter said he'd cornered her. The barrister remarked that Williams worked a lot; Williams replied that he was just trying to support his family, and that he was saving for a boat. Some of the jury nodded. In the break, Judge told me how rare it was for a defendant to give evidence.

'But he's got a relaxed, normal-guy kind of manner, doesn't he?' Judge said.

'Well, they don't always *look* like monsters, do they?' I replied.

'But he's just a regular guy like you, you know?' He grinned, teasing me. 'He goes fishing on the weekends sometimes, he's saving for a boat. Just a regular guy like the jury.'

The prosecutor did an okay job cross-examining Williams, but I knew that this was one matter out of a fortnight of work he had listed ahead of him. He might not have even known that Williams intended to take the stand. Prosecution have to put their whole case forward to give defence a chance to prepare, but the same isn't true of defence needing to alert prosecution to their intentions.

Williams wasn't afraid to look across to the jury when he answered questions. He shrugged a lot, offering a kind of sad surprise that he was sitting in court. He intimated that his ex was a little 'unhinged', that this accusation could be her elaborate plan to get back at him for leaving her for a younger, more beautiful woman.

～

The jury went out to deliberate but took less than an hour.

'We've got a verdict, Judge,' I said to him, and saw surprise flicker across his face.

'How long is that!?' he asked, gathering his robes from where he'd just put them away.

'Almost forty minutes.'

'I think that might be a record,' he replied, putting on his wig.

'Does it mean anything?' I asked.

'Yes,' he said, pausing to look at me, 'they normally take a little longer to decide if they're going to lock someone away.'

A few jurors were laughing as they entered the courtroom. I glared at them but they didn't look in my direction until Judge entered and sat at his bench behind me. Then they all sat quietly, at attention.

'Would the speaker please stand up,' Judge asked, and a man got to his feet. 'Have you reached a verdict?'

'Yes, we have,' the man said. He was in a flannel shirt and jeans, with a brown belt and boots.

'Very well,' Judge nodded and turned his face to me, 'please take the verdict.'

I stood up, holding the arraignment sheet I'd sweated onto just two days earlier, and felt myself shrink at the absurdity of the room, of us sitting there to determine the truth about such a shitty thing. In his summing up before the jurors had begun deliberating, Judge had reminded them that he made decisions about the law, while they made decisions about the facts. It offended me. Who were these people to decide such a thing? How are they not chosen more carefully? How often did they get it wrong? And me! I still had pimples and lived at home eating my mum's spaghetti—why the fuck was I the one standing there taking the verdict?

'Do you find the defendant guilty or not guilty of count one, indecent treatment of a child, under sixteen, under care?' I asked the speaker.

'Not guilty,' he replied.

I asked again, and again, and the verdict was the same on each count: *not guilty, not guilty.*

Judge formally announced that Williams was acquitted on all charges. Court adjourned and Williams was let out of the dock.

He started shaking hands with people, beaming. The complainant was somewhere else, waiting for her mobile to go off, and I looked up at Eric, the prosecutor, pitying him having to make that call. I pictured her crying. I was familiar with that image: I'd seen it replaying on the screens in court for hours.

With the verdict coming so fast and no sentence to carry out, Judge and I had a few hours free in the afternoon. I should have started on my pile of overdue paperwork but I was twitchy. My skin was hot and it felt as though I had bindi-eyes in my blood, or that I'd breathed in too much of the fibreglass insulation my dad once made me help him put in our roof. Dry grass outside the courthouse crunched under my feet and pebbles came loose from the hot, black bitumen road.

I called Vincent, raging to him about how cavalier the jurors had seemed. How they'd thought the complainant wasn't trustworthy because she was sixteen and knew what an erection was.

'How could it only take them half a fucking hour!? Did they run out of fucking biscuits!?'

Vincent listened patiently.

'Did I tell you the jurors were complaining about Subway?' I asked him at one point.

'No,' he said.

'They get lunch during the trial, and they didn't want to have to eat sandwiches again.'

'Wow.'

'Subway is good food! I get Subway as a treat sometimes when I don't pack lunch!'

I asked him how he was doing, and we chatted for a little while until the inevitable pause before we said goodbye. The words I really wanted to say wouldn't come out. The sun was too bright and I didn't know what I wanted from him. We told each other we loved each other and hung up, then I sat on a bench and picked at my fingernails for a while, feeling even more alone than before I'd called him.

⌒

Back in chambers I found Judge, hoping to share some vitriolic confusion with him as well, but he had already moved on to preparations for the sentences he had to deliver the following day.

Too freshly outraged to move on, I logged on to my computer in the empty courtroom and started researching child sex offences. The line of defence for Williams, unofficially, was that he just *wasn't* a child sex offender—he was a normal man, working hard, saving for a boat. He was just a bloke, and he liked women the way a bloke was supposed to. Definitely not a paedophile.

It didn't take long for me to find what I was looking for: a 2011 report by the Australian Institute of Criminology clarifying commonly held mistaken beliefs about sex offenders.

It is a common misconception that all child sex offenders are paedophiles, the subheading went on, when in the majority of cases sex offences against children are opportunistic and carried out by people who are also attracted to adults. The offending most commonly takes place in the home, without the use of a weapon, and the perpetrator is an older male, known to the victim.

I then found a comment thread on a website where thousands of women reported the age they were when they first noticed men looking at them in a sexual way. The average was between eleven and thirteen depending on location. It was some kind of unspoken phenomenon in the collective unconscious: girls were being sexualised to the point that it made them self-conscious, at ages so young as to be illegal if acted upon, and yet society still labelled a man who was attracted to a twelve-year-old a paedophile. A paedophile is someone who is consistently sexually attracted to prepubescent children. If a man is attracted to adult women, but molests or rapes his thirteen-year-old stepdaughter because he is also attracted to her—and has the opportunity and believes he'll get away with it—does that make him a paedophile? And what difference does that make? Where does our almost world-wide historical obsession with virginity and purity fit into all this? In Australia, where more than one in ten women have been sexually assaulted before they turn fifteen, perhaps that makes a whole lot of men kind-of paedophiles.

Where does this leave the pitiable man-who-can't-help-it trope— the misunderstood and unfortunate soul who wishes he didn't have forbidden fantasies about children? The AIC says those men, those 'real' paedophiles, are a fraction of the population. It seemed to me to be the difference between 'true' psychopathic killers, so rare as to be an anomaly, and the average murderer. I was more interested in the men like Williams. He had convinced twelve people that he wasn't 'that kind of man', but it panicked me that the jury didn't believe his stepdaughter. That she wasn't worth even a full hour of their consideration if it meant they might have to eat sandwiches for lunch again.

The Williams case planted a fear inside me. A spore that would fester and grow with each trial I sat in. If people didn't believe these women, why would they believe me?

⌒

I cried in the shower most nights we spent in Gladstone, throwing up dinner a few times too, as the sentences we heard stacked up. A few drug matters and a couple of assaults and robberies broke up the waves of sex offences. I went for a walk one night and almost felt afraid for my safety before I catalogued each assault and rape and remembered that every single one had happened in a domestic setting. Out on the street, walking to Maccas at half past ten, was perfectly safe compared to being a girl whose mum brought home a new boyfriend. I was also already a decade older than the average victim. The more I drank the more it all bled together.

When we were finally on our flight home, Judge took a moment to ask me how I felt, at the end of our first busy period.

'I'm angry at everything,' I said, 'and it just feels like a lot of crime, and a lot of bad guys, and I don't understand where they all come from and where they all go.'

Judge smiled.

'And I think my father has accidentally raised a daughter for the Crown,' I added, and he laughed.

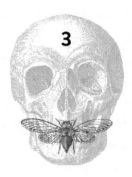

3

IN HINDSIGHT, IT WASN'T A coincidence that of all the associates in that building, Megan and I became good friends. We worked for judges with similarly gentle temperaments and senses of humour. Hers and mine both got lumped with a huge portion of the sex offence trials and sentences, and we both saw plenty of regional Queensland on circuit. She and I were both stumbling through our first serious relationships, grappling to reconcile our independence with the romance arcs we'd been drip-fed since birth. We both loved travelling, we often swore, we even got adult acne at around the same time. She, a petite blonde, and me the giant ginger, spent the year trying to make each other laugh, or at least smile, in the face of overwhelming sadness. When Megan and I got beers and pizza after work, I didn't long to be a different person like I did with Evelyn. Megan helped me see what I might eventually learn to like about myself.

We emailed each other sitting in court when barristers said particularly ridiculous things, or when jurors asked ludicrous questions, or when other associates got reputations for behaving as though they shat golden eggs.

OMG, I emailed her from the courtroom computer when I was back in Brisbane Monday morning, *I've just come down to prepare court for a sentence, and there are twenty boys in the back rows from a visiting school, and a barrister has just come in and dropped all his stuff down at the bar table, turned to the DPP prosecutor and clerk, and said: 'I've got a hot date at lunch, boys, so let's not fuck around.'*

Holy shit, what!? she replied within a minute.

And it's a male prosecutor, and a male clerk, and the barrister's instructing solicitor is a man, and Judge is a man, and there are all these teenage boys in the back row, and we're about to start a rape sentence. Do you ever get tired of being the only woman in court who isn't the complainant? Am I being too sensitive? Now they're talking about Call of Duty.

The next day we started another trial. The defendant, Mr Baker, was a big man—both tall and wide—with a white beard. He gave the overall impression of a Santa Claus impersonator in the off-season, especially because of how confused and sad he seemed. It was another child sex trial, though, so I was fresh out of sympathy.

It had only been a couple of weeks and I'd already stopped giving these men the benefit of the doubt. But had I ever presumed them innocent? I was too close to see any of it properly. I knew about damning yet inadmissible evidence, having proofread or seen many pre-trial arguments where evidence that could almost certainly secure a guilty verdict is deemed inadmissible. I'd been researching how widespread sexual assault against girls is. At law school the first and most sacred principle they teach you comes from Blackstone: that it is better that ten guilty men go free, than for a single innocent man to be imprisoned. Benjamin Franklin said it was 100. I doubted that Franklin had been confronted with the rapes of one hundred girls, but my tally was stacking up. I also started seeing more clearly how men were given the benefit of the doubt outside of the courtroom. Debate about quotas for hiring and boards was raging in the press, while some commentators were denying the existence of the wage gap. It was all connected in a big sticky web that I couldn't see past.

Every case felt like a David and Goliath battle. 'There's no evidence apart from the complainant's story,' they kept saying, but what evidence was she supposed to bring? So many of them were terrified, submitting to intercourse to avoid the punches or cuts that, ironically, would have helped them secure a conviction. So many took months or years to come forward—then, despite showing monumental strength in making a report, they were cross-examined about their 'inexplicable' delay.

My opinion on a defendant's guilt or innocence had no effect on the outcome of a case, so while I was forced to sit mute, observe and document, at least my mind was free to indulge in whatever trains of thought helped me through the day.

I looked across at the twelve people whose names I'd just called out, who now sat at attention for *R v Baker* listening to Judge's opening address. Had they come in with clean eyes and ears? How much evidence would they actually hear and how much would be confirmation bias? Sex crime trials have higher rates of conviction where weapons are involved and where people of colour are the defendants. Mr Baker was big enough not to have needed even a butter knife against a small girl, and he was Caucasian. It was a farcical idea that my selection of individuals from the wooden barrel would turn them, miraculously, from average Australians full of fear and misunderstanding into truly objective arbiters of truth.

Thinking about all that for too long made the wigs and robes seem gaudy. The pomp and rigmarole was a pantomime. The more I learned of the huge, 'blind' justice system, the more I learned that it was just as human and fallible as everything and everyone that created and preceded it. I didn't know how to reconcile its festering belly with the righteous image of my father. Disillusioned was an understatement.

The prosecutor stood up and welcomed the jury, resting one arm on his podium and taking a relatable, calm approach to stepping them through the horrors Mr Baker was accused of perpetrating. The jury was going to hear about two occasions that Maggie, the complainant, and her mother took the train to visit Mr Baker. Once they arrived at his house, they all shared a cup of tea and had a chat. After the tea, on both occasions, Maggie's mother suddenly felt sleepy and lay down for a long nap. Baker had a room full of model aeroplanes, and one time he took Maggie there, and another time he took her into a white van he'd parked out the back of his house.

While Maggie presented her evidence-in-chief from the witness box, I heard her mention that Mr Baker's house was near Yeronga Train Station, and my gut dropped. That was my train station, in the suburb I'd been born into, grown up in, still lived in. I'd be getting the train home to Yeronga that afternoon. Had I walked past Mr Baker's house before? Had he been in line behind me at the bakery before? Another light in the constellation of crimes had flickered on.

The second time, in the white van, Maggie had fought back. She said that both times she had been terrified of Mr Baker, and that she had 'frozen', but somehow in the back of that van, with his body so huge and terrible, she'd screamed and kicked and escaped. I looked at her properly then. She wore a white blouse, and her long brown hair was still slightly wet from being washed that morning; a beautiful, gentle cowlick sat just to the left of where she parted it. A gold chain sat lightly at her neck. Maggie had managed the impossible: Maggie had fought The Freeze. And she sat there in court, just metres from Baker! Maggie was my heroine.

‿

At lunchbreak I got coffee with Dad. I thought my mum had probably told him to keep an eye on me at work, because we would meet up every other week.

'What's with this mum-falling-asleep thing?' I asked him after briefly explaining the trial. 'She's just given evidence—the mother, that is—and she clearly thinks that her tea was spiked, but they kind of dance around it, even though the suggestion is blatant.'

'They must have decided they couldn't charge him for it,' Dad said, 'and so they can't make an accusation of criminal conduct in a trial that they have no evidence to support.'

'But everybody knows that's what happened—or at least what the Crown is suggesting happened—so what difference does it make to say it out loud instead of dancing around it?'

'They're just the rules, my dear.' He smiled and took a sip of his flat white.

'The rules suck.'

'Yep, sometimes they do.' We were sharing a slice of lemon tart and started talking about plans for Easter when he asked me, 'And how are you doing?'

I laughed. 'This is like when I text your phone and Mum texts me back, pretending to be you, but I can tell it's her because of the kisses at the end.'

I told him I was just tired, and felt like a liar.

As I walked back to my office, a wave of sadness hit me, topped with guilt, and I nearly burst into tears. How could I tell him what was actually eating at me, rotting on the inside? How could I do that to my mother and father—make them as sad as I knew they'd be? At least if I carried my secret alone, there would be only one casualty. Camera crews were pooling around the doors to the courts building and I kept my face down. So many awful things were happening in the building, I didn't even know which one had made the news.

⤙⤚

Judge had been wondering about Maggie's mother's sleepiness too, and after lunch we convened court with counsel only.

'What's this about the mother being sleepy after having tea, then, gentlemen?' Judge asked.

'Yes, your Honour,' the prosecutor stood up, taking the lead, 'we have advised the witness not to make any criminal allegations about that aspect of the narrative, as we're not in a position to go into it.'

'Well, be careful then,' Judge said sternly. 'It's getting a bit messy, and I don't want a mistrial.'

'Of course, your Honour.'

'Very well, let's get the jury back in.'

As usual, there was barely any other 'evidence'. It was painful sometimes to see the looks on the jurors' faces when they realised they wouldn't get any CCTV footage or *CSI*-style DNA tests. It is the absolute catch-22: people feel they need certain types of evidence to feel comfortable convicting a defendant of a crime, but crimes against women and children are usually committed inside homes, by people they know. Mr Baker's fingerprints would be all over that house and that van because they were his property, and there wouldn't be any footage of the inside of his home. Without Baker ejaculating and then Maggie going straight to get a rape kit, there were no DNA test results to reveal in court. Maggie's testimony was evidence, but defence had spent several hours telling the jury how unreliable it was. The defence barrister had the usual explanations to offer: that the mother had some ulterior motive, while the girl had an overactive imagination and was only too ready to go along with a wicked deception.

Crimes against men often have the kind of evidence that juries can easily accept—a black eye or a smashed window—but the justice system we uphold comes from the olden days. Queensland legislation says that a complainant's lack of physical protest can't be held as evidence that she consented, but without any broken ribs or split lips, defence barristers will tell the jury they 'don't have anything else to go on'. In order for the jury to find a defendant guilty, they often have to perceive a complainant as being particularly virtuous. It's so easy for them to say that 'her word alone' wasn't enough to overcome their reasonable doubts. The alternative is a little terrifying—that if one in five women are assaulted, one in five men might be assaulters.

That day, the jury were sent out to deliberate, and within an hour they'd replied with a note. My heart sank, thinking it would be Gladstone all over again, but it was a question: *Please define reasonable doubt?*

We reconvened court and Judge read out the prescribed paragraphs from the Queensland benchbook: a compendium of resources that tell judges what to tell juries about certain issues, infamous for confusing the matter further rather than clarifying it.

'You know what they do in New Zealand?' Judge asked me as we returned to chambers, after I'd made a joke about tallying the number of times we'd be asked that question.

'What?'

'When the jury asks, "What does reasonable doubt mean?", they just tell them, "You have to be sure,"' he said, smiling.

'Wow! But that's so—'

'So simple!'

'I know!'

'And it works,' he said, gesturing excitedly. 'Here we get all caught up in sounding smart and using big words. Jurors don't care about legal words, they just want to know how to do their job. If you tell them they need to be sure, they'll tell you what they really believe.'

I wondered, yet again, why Judge had only made it to the District Court. I imagined how differently that building might run if he was at the top. He'd been on the Fitzgerald Inquiry—the commission of inquiry into police corruption in Queensland in the 80s that got a premier deposed and several very powerful men jailed—and spent years in both prosecution and defence. He researched childhood development and designed rules for when barristers were cross-examining kids in court. He actually cared about the justice system. But he'd have to retire in a couple of years. What part of the game hadn't he played right?

Dad had told me plenty about how political the appointing of magistrates and judges was. I thought again of his refrain, 'Never look for justice.' Apparently not even within the justice department itself. I couldn't hide my loathing of the judges whose religious and 'moral' beliefs influenced the way they ran court. Perhaps the power-parties took place after Church on Sundays—it was as likely an explanation as any.

⌒

As I walked to work the next morning, I felt like shit. It didn't help when I spotted Evelyn as she strode into the glass sliding doors ahead of me. Did she straighten her hair every day? Was she one of those rare and miraculous creatures who remembered to moisturise their elbows in winter? My pitiable state was unsurprising, given my smoking, drinking and purging the night before, but I was grateful that the jury were out deliberating. It gave me time to catch up on feeling human.

I made a coffee and sat by the window on level thirteen. Dark clouds were threatening rain nearby, but in the clearer distance an aeroplane made its way slowly across the skyline. I wondered if Maggie would be triggered, for the rest of her life, whenever she saw a model aeroplane. A harmless—even fun—object for most people might sit dormant in her mind, ready to explode her brain in an unsuspecting moment. Horrific memories of screaming and trauma would shatter through her life like shrapnel. I read once that the human body slowly pushes shrapnel back out through the skin. That a shard of metal can take years to reach the surface and finally, truly be expelled. Veterans get bits coming out of them decades after wars. Could the same thing happen to memories? Perhaps that was what I was feeling: an itchy, irksome thing, a foreign object inside me, moving just millimetres every year, tearing through me until it breached.

'He told me I was beautiful,' Maggie had said.

I wanted to go find her, to hug her and tell her that she'd be okay, but I wasn't yet at a time in my own life where I could walk past a trampoline and not think about what had happened to me, so I'd have been lying. What would I really have told her? That she was braver than me, for a start. That I was so proud of her—in awe of her, even. But I'd also have had to tell her that her memories would be with her forever. That they might walk silently alongside her, like giant spiders nobody else could see. That some people might be afraid of them when she tried to explain it all. That she might find them grotesque.

'Hey, hey,' Megan sat down beside me, 'what's up?'

'Ugh, just the same shit, you know. The mum's friend. They're deliberating. It's already been overnight so I'm hopeful.'

'That's good.'

'What about you?'

'I'm in a child exploitation material sentence,' she said with a sigh.

'Oh, shit, again!? How many of these gross dudes are out there?'

'Too many, I guess,' she said. 'We've had to break for lunch because there's literally so much material to go through.' We both sat quietly looking out the window to the city below. 'Lizzie was in my office crying this morning,' Megan told me.

'Shit, I didn't realise it was that bad,' I replied.

'Her judge told her that she wasn't the first choice for the job,' Megan said very quietly.

'What!?' I stage-whispered, 'what good does it do to tell someone that?'

'I know, it's just cruel.' She shook her head.

Judge called out to me from his office and I jumped up, waving goodbye to Megan.

'I left my evidence law material down in court,' Judge said to me, sitting at his desk, pen in hand.

'I'll grab it!' I smiled. 'Are you checking about this tea-drugging business?'

'Yes, I'm a bit nervous about a mistrial,' he said. 'I need to know how to direct the jury, or if I should just leave it.'

I nodded. We hadn't had a mistrial yet but Megan had told me how painful it was. One of the counsel makes an error, or a witness says something about the defendant's criminal history, or a juror asks a stupid question about having googled the defendant, and the whole trial goes down the drain. Cancelled. It takes at least another six months to schedule a retrial, the complainant has to go through the whole horrific process again, and the defendant is either out on bail or locked up in the meantime. Nobody wins.

I'd only ever heard stories about defendants calling for a retrial after being found guilty because they rightly suspected that the complainant just wouldn't be able to go through the whole process again.

Retrials were a huge problem in the system, and one I was keen to avoid happening on my watch. Not to Maggie.

⌒

I took the internal judges' elevator down to level ten and grabbed all his materials, then exited the courtroom through the normal doors to go back up to our offices. But I was stopped mid-stride, disturbed.

Outside the courtroom, the stark, open foyer was silent, but Mr Baker may as well have been screaming. Or maybe his soul was screaming and I could hear it because I also belonged to his awful world. As he sat looking out the huge glass window, such terrible sadness emanated from him that I couldn't tear my eyes away. He was like a beacon for a black hole. I let an empty elevator open and close in front of me, staying where I was at the end of the room, quietly watching his obese, slumped figure. Baker would wait the next two days to find out if he was about to go to prison. He had his hands clasped in his lap, and the skin on them was thin and covered in age spots.

I thought about those ancient hands moving over a young girl's backside and flinched.

The rain was coming down so hard, Baker couldn't even see anything out the window. Just a huge glass pane of rippling grey. On another day I had stood watching the effect of a real Queensland downpour on the large cold windows, marvelling at the beauty of the dappled light and how protected I was from nature, ten storeys high in a marvellous human invention. I didn't know what Baker was thinking while he sat there, but probably it wasn't about how fantastic glass skyscrapers were.

Baker should have gone outside and walked around a bit, got a fresh flat white, enjoyed the rain on his thin skin, because it seemed likely he would be looking at large grey walls every day for the next eight years.

It must be an awful time for a defendant, waiting for a verdict. Perhaps if I was a more selfless or mature person I'd say something like, 'I wouldn't wish it on my worst enemy', but of course I knew one person in particular I would wish it on.

In the elevator back up to Judge, with my arms full, I pressed my forehead against the cool chrome panels. Would I? Could I?

Maggie had. Maggie's mum believed her. I felt sure that my family would believe me. Maggie wasn't old enough to have a boyfriend, though.

I looked at the greasy stain my cheek had left on the elevator wall and exited quickly as the doors opened on level thirteen, thinking of how disgusting my body was, wondering how Vincent could want me if he knew what had happened to me, let alone if I told him properly about this stuff or tried to deal with it in some way that meant telling other people and talking about it a lot. It could alter something between us; it could shift our tectonic plates. He might not want to be intimate with me again. Maybe it was best I not tell anyone, ever. I was fine, after all. I had a law degree, I was in a good job, I had friends and a boyfriend. Why would I light a fire under all that?

'Thank you,' Judge said to me as I placed all the material on his desk. 'I also need you to proofread this judgment for me, please,' and he passed me a thick document. It was another pre-trial hearing about the admissibility of evidence he must have heard before I'd started. A friend of the family had allegedly molested three young girls—all cousins—when they were in the swimming pool, and the defendant's family had enough money to fight the allegations at each stage. I sat back at my desk and thought about my own pool in Yeronga, out the back of our house, right next to the trampoline. Perhaps the fire had already been lit.

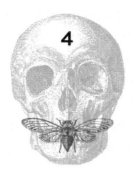

4

BUNDABERG WAS BEAUTIFUL. JUDGE AND I were staying at Bargara, a beachside outcrop of houses on stilts and sleek apartments that converged at a jetty with some single-storey shops attached to the shoreline. Each morning Judge and I met at the car, and I drove us for twenty minutes through sugarcane fields to the courthouse further inland. The sky was bright blue and the fields of rich green grew up around us at least ten feet high. In his luxurious, silent car we slid along the long, flat road, only catching a glimpse of the horizon at one point in the journey where the road gave a slight rise. I remember looking out for that vision, remembering to be grateful for the blue and the green, the cool leather seats. It was the one time that entire year when I enjoyed driving for Judge. The one time my nervousness behind the wheel was overcome by the beauty of our surroundings.

It was only when we reached the courthouse and had to buzz ourselves into the carpark through the barbed-wire fence, and I could see the men waiting on the cement out the front of the Magistrates Court, and the police officers milling around with their heavy utility belts, that I was brought back to reality. We'd step out of the car into the humidity that was normal for a tropical autumn and enter the old brick building, and I would walk past a filing system of current matters and a huge storage room full of floor-to-ceiling shelves of old cases. I wondered if there had been a crime in Bundaberg for every sugarcane plant that grew in Bundaberg. How many women and children needed to be processed—churned through the system—before change would come?

The Bundaberg courts building was unremarkable but for its odours. The old building had a mould problem, so chlorine in the air stung my eyes as though I was in a public swimming pool. Somehow the pong from the ancient carpets still reached my nose, though. The courtroom itself had few features of note, but the dock was new. It sat apart like an implant, with its glass panels and sleek metal lock, from the wood and linoleum of the rest of the room. The seats for the public were reminiscent of church pews.

I hung my robes in my little office annexed to Judge's and thumbed through the fresh stack of files on my desk, practising the pronunciation of names, ready to read them out in the courtroom when I arraigned each one of them.

The word 'arraignment' came from an old French word that meant 'to call to account'. At the beginning I had thought the arraignment was a meaningful, significant moment in court, but by Bundaberg I knew better. That feeling had been conjured by my own ego because I happened to have a role in that part of the process, but Judge and counsel were rarely surprised by anyone's plea, and even less surprised to hear about their offending. Very few criminals were original, neither in their crimes nor in the way they tried to evade responsibility for them.

At that moment I remembered a funny story my father had told my family about a break-and-enter where the burglars posted pictures of themselves and their stolen loot on Facebook, tagging the McDonald's carpark they were in. The police pulled the CCTV footage, tracked them right back to their rental property around the corner, and arrested them within twenty-four hours. 'They're not criminals because they're smart!' Dad had said, and we'd all laughed. It was less funny now. So many defence submissions for sentencing stated that their clients were 'below average intelligence'. Maybe we could make jokes about intelligence for punch-ups down the pub, but I felt quite sure that the 'smarter' sex offenders were simply more educated and wealthy and therefore less likely to be brought to court.

Judge once wondered aloud to me about what he was supposed to make of the submission. 'Technically half the population is of below-average intelligence, but I don't think 50 per cent of people would agree, would they? And what does defence even mean when they say it? Intelligence comes in all different shapes and forms. If they're trying to tell me he lacks a formal education, then they should just tell me that. Maybe I could make an order that makes it easier for him to find certain kinds of work.' Judge was holding his wig in his hand, waving it around, frustrated. 'Don't just tell me he's stupid.'

A magpie on a branch near the window cried out, bringing me back to the present. Its throat caught the sunlight as it bobbed to warble its beautiful song. Every new town would have another new stack for me. Towns I would never go to in my whole life would have stacks waiting for someone else.

⌒

I found the file for the trial that was to start that morning. *R v Kevin Donny Reester*. The indictment listing the charges against Reester was the biggest I'd ever seen. It stretched over five pages and painted a picture of offending that escalated as it spanned almost a decade. Multiple counts of *indecent treatment of a child* were followed by counts of *rape* in the double digits. Two counts of *maintaining a sexual relationship with a child* finished things off with a horrific flair. Every count carried multiple circumstances of aggravation—communicating to the reader that yes, things got worse.

Many indicated that the complainant was under twelve or under ten, and all showed that the child was 'under the care' of Reester at the time. I got to the end of the long list of allegations before I realised that there were actually three complainants. I hadn't noticed initially because they shared their last name; they were sisters.

The courtroom was empty and silent as I set up my workspace in front of Judge's bench. I finished preparing things but couldn't shake a bad thought: I'd never seen multiple complainants in a single criminal trial before. *That's right*, I remembered from university, *joinders*. I slumped back into my chair and looked at the dust motes floating through the still space. There are extremely strict rules about putting a single defendant on trial for offences against multiple complainants; history shows that it's just too overwhelmingly prejudicial to the accused. Juries can't get past it—can't resist a conviction. We are social animals. We groupthink. Normally the Crown has to make an application to the court to allow a joinder, but that day my anxiety rose when I couldn't see any record of that happening on the file. The case painted against Reester by the indictment document alone was overwhelming. I felt sure he would plead guilty if things went to trial like this—with all three sisters together.

A door at the opposite end of the court opened, and I pretended I was busy but watched two men walk in. I didn't need to see that one of them was a security officer to guess the other was Reester—the space, previously still and quiet, hummed with tension. They took their places: Reester in the dock and the security officer sitting in front of it. Reester wasn't just slim, he was skinny, and I estimated he was much shorter than me. I glanced from the balding man behind the glass to his file on my desk. It had manifested in front of me. From a case note in class to something dirty and real. I didn't even want to touch it. My stomach had begun churning.

I knew that Reester's lawyer would challenge the joinder application. He'd be an idiot not to. And if those girls couldn't bring their case together then maybe none of them would even testify. The offending had occurred over a decade ago so there was unlikely to be any evidence aside from their memories. They weren't children anymore either, and juries aren't kind to women unless they're 'perfect victims'.

I returned to my little office and looked out the window, but the magpie was gone. The palm trees stood out against the vast blue sky vista, and I fumbled trying to fasten my jabot around my neck. The little white tie with its two starched tails felt utterly ridiculous. A tightness was spreading across my chest and I ripped it back off, panting for air. I fumbled with the window but it was sealed shut, so I put my forehead on the cool glass and tried to imagine feeling the breeze I could see moving the palm fronds. I willed the magpie to return, humming his song, my fingers at my neck, and counted to five breathing in, and counted to five breathing out. I needed a break but someone knocked at my door. There was no rest for those who worked with the wicked.

⌒

Callover finished about an hour later and Judge announced that the court would move on to the listed trial—to Reester.

'Sorry to delay proceedings, your Honour,' the prosecutor stood up as she spoke, adjusting her wig, 'but there needs to be some further pre-trial discussion.'

I wrote in my notes: *I knew it.*

'How long will you need?' Judge asked. I had heard him ask that question to counsel countless times before and thought I detected a hint of disappointment. Of course he knew they'd be splitting the charges; he was always a step ahead of everyone else in the courtroom. He had probably picked up on this a week ago at the preliminary callover back in Brisbane while I was scrambling around making other notes.

'Well, that depends on Mr Crane,' she replied with a hint of attitude, glancing toward the defence counsel.

Crane got up. 'Well, your Honour, it doesn't *depend on me*, it depends on—'

'What are we talking about here?' Judge cut in.

'Whether the complainants should be tried separately or if the current indictment is really suitable for a joinder application.' The prosecutor pursed her lips. Her name was Marie Goode and she was lovely, but I yearned for someone quicker and meaner to fight for the sisters. All her sentences came out as questions, as those of so many perfectly intelligent women tend to do.

'Very well, we'll adjourn,' Judge announced, 'but please keep in mind that the people called for the jury are waiting on us.'

Goode nodded. 'Of course, your Honour.'

I looked over at Reester, sitting up straight with a pressed grey shirt. His eyes were a very pale blue, almost white, and he was still and calm, like a crocodile, just waiting.

⌒

We waited on counsel for an hour before Judge sent me out to get an update. It was all part of the strange system, that I could pop my head into the chambers of the prosecutors and defence counsel, asking for updates. Judge couldn't be seen to do it himself, but everyone knew I was asking in order to report back to him. I would scuttle along the corridors of some of these shabby old regional courthouses, ferrying messages, imagining myself to be a little carrier rat. There's no real job description for a judge's associate but by then I had realised that if nobody notices you and everything runs smoothly, then you can rest assured you're good at your job.

I knocked on the prosecutor's door and when the clerk opened it by just a crack, I caught a glimpse of a woman crying. Her shoulders were hunched over and long black hair fell in front of her face.

'Hi,' I said gently to the clerk, 'I'm just wondering if you have an update for his Honour?'

The crying woman pulled another tissue out of a box beside her, and I realised she must be one of the three sisters. The absurd little remaining hope I had for a joined trial was waning.

'Yes, we'll be about another ten minutes and then we'll present a new indictment,' the clerk replied in a vaguely apologetic tone.

'Sure—the eldest sister?' I asked.

'Yes, Clare,' the clerk said. We nodded to each other and as the clerk stepped back from the door to shut it, I saw Clare's face when she tucked her hair behind her ear. She was nodding but her eyes were swollen and her nose was a raw red.

I stood for a moment, alone in the dark corridor, absorbing the information and all its implications. Reester wouldn't plead now. No way.

I considered the kind of women Clare and I were. Perhaps we'd both had the same night terrors or sinusoidal guilt trips. If the way we stayed silent was the same, would the way we fought be the same? Then I considered the kind of men Kevin Reester and Samuel were. I didn't think Samuel would plead either. He had once tried to bully my brother into investing in a pyramid scheme. Samuel and Kevin were both top-notch dickheads. Would Clare go through with everything and give evidence alone? I was afraid for her.

I waited for a sign in each complainant, a warning with every new defendant. Was this trial my omen?

⌒

I pulled twelve names out of the barrel after lunch that afternoon, and once the jury took their seats the trial finally started. When I read out the indictment, count by count, and Kevin Donny Reester stood up straight and calm, and protested his innocence, count by count, I watched the faces of the people selected to decide his fate. The accusations were so horrific and so numerous I was angry at them for giving him the benefit of the doubt at all. As I read out each rape count I saw one of the women shift uncomfortably in her seat. *You haven't heard shit yet, lady,* I wanted to snarl, *buckle up,* but when I sat down again and looked at her face, and saw her sadness, my anger turned to sadness too.

Goode stood up slowly, turning her body to face the jurors, and began the painful process of introducing them to the precise nature of the offending they'd be listening to for the next three days.

As it turned out, Reester had a very specific modus operandi. He had encouraged Clare's mother to move into his house with her daughters because he could provide for them, which was true. He would sit under the house at night once his partner and the girls had gone to bed and drink for hours while he listened to all his favourite country music. Then, on random evenings, when he decided it was time, he would put on a particular record—a Slim Dusty record—and as it played he would drag his heavy feet up the stairs, and Clare would start crying in her bed. She came to know the smell of Jack Daniel's as a precursor to her tiny child's body being violated.

For years and years it was the same: the Slim Dusty and the Jack Daniel's and the footsteps. The offending started tentatively, with touches as Reester glanced nervously at the door and she pretended to be asleep, but with time the violations developed until she was crying out loud, her body ripped and bleeding. The culmination of these bedroom visits was Clare being covered in his ejaculate, too young to have any idea what the sticky, smelly substance was.

The jury heard this was the last time Reester came into her room at night. They did not hear that she was the eldest—by then around thirteen—of three sisters, and that one possibility for the cease in his offending was that he had moved on to her younger sisters' tiny bodies. If the joinder application had been made and succeeded, the jury would have heard those allegations too.

By the time the prosecutor finished her opening address, a feeling of filth had settled around the room. I imagined it emanating from Reester like a gas, slowly poisoning us all.

As Crane took his turn to address the jury with opening remarks, I lamented the missed opportunity for the whole thing to have gone straight to sentence. Perhaps if Goode had pushed a little harder, Reester would have pleaded. I wanted to believe this so badly, but when I looked over to the dock at his face, only a few metres from where I sat, I realised that it never would have happened. Reester wasn't even tense. He was less anxious than I was. I suppose the word 'frustrated' best describes the attitude of that short, square-chinned man. He shook his head when certain facts were alleged, and rolled his eyes as the complainant was quoted. Crane was already picking apart the inconsistencies in her story.

I looked at Reester's nose and wondered if he smelled things the same way I did. How could both of us be human and yet have so little understanding of each other's brains? I fantasised about cracking his skull open, imagining that maggots and cockroaches would come pouring out. *Aha!* I would say. *It's alright, he's just a rotten thing.* An image of Samuel's face sprang to mind, his head cracked open, and huge brown locusts swarmed out and toward my face. I felt myself flush and start sweating, and my eyes went soft around the edges. I picked up my pen and scribbled in my notebook just to keep my head down. *On the weekend I will go and see some turtles.* It wasn't working, I couldn't breathe, I could feel tears coming. I took a plastic ruler and dug the pointy corner of it deep into my thigh, under the desk, and focused on the feeling. I breathed in, and I breathed out.

Court adjourned after defence's opening address, then the jury were dismissed to their tearoom after being warned not to tell anyone about the proceedings. It was a small town, though, and while I didn't think any of them would *know* if he was guilty, I thought it was likely some of them had already made up their minds one way or the other.

In the week before Bundaberg I had bought a Fitbit, a food diary planner, and hired a personal trainer. I felt that amazing sense of skinny potential, daydreaming about how awesome the future Bri would be because the present-day one was so crap. On Tuesday morning the only personal trainer in Bargara met me by the beach, and I explained that I was the biggest I'd ever been and that I wanted to get 'back in shape'. I was fishing for a compliment but she didn't bite.

In the middle of some particularly awkward lunge manoeuvre, where I lifted a heavy ball over my head while I took ridiculous big steps, a man further along the path came around a corner toward us. I saw his head turn to look at me. I kept my gaze straight ahead but I felt his eyes on me and it was uncomfortable. I kept lunging and lifting as he got closer, the unnatural movement making me feel silly, and when he was finally alongside me, his attention unbroken as I panted, he said brightly, 'Keep it up!'

'Yeah, you too, buddy,' I barked back. *Fucking idiot*. Lunge. *Fucking*. Lift. *Male*. Lunge. *Gaze*. If I hadn't been so red in the face from the exercise, the PT would have seen me blush. She rolled her eyes and shrugged: universal baby boomer language for 'boys will be boys'.

Later that morning when I met Judge at the car, he inquired how my morning was and I replied that it was fine.

'A good workout with that lady, then?' he asked.

Fuck. That man had been Judge, offering actual-happy-morning encouragement to a friend and colleague. I stood there by the car with my mouth open for a moment too long before bumbling out some apologies, and he laughed it off. As we drove to work he inquired about my exercise and asked if I enjoyed any particular sports. I remembered how the people in this world of success like understanding each other. I think Judge was comforted by the fact that I had a personal trainer. That I was *that kind of person*: someone who woke up early to look after her body. It's a Type A personality thing. A presumption that a lifestyle work ethic translates to a broad intelligence; a recognition that all hard work is good; healthy body, healthy mind. Perhaps he felt reassured that he'd made the right choice in hiring me.

Once when I did some work experience at an exceptionally boring commercial law firm in Brisbane I met their best employee, Elizabeth. She went to bed every night before nine so that she could wake up every morning before five because she and her husband did marathons . . . or maybe it was triathlons. Whatever it was, it was most weekends too. And I remember thinking, *You'll make partner.* I also remember thinking, *If I ever work here, I will gouge my eyes out.* The memory of Elizabeth made me afraid that I'd turn into a boring person, so I replied to Judge that the only sport I ever truly took an interest in was dodgeball.

'Just feels good to chuck stuff at people sometimes, you know?' I said, and he laughed.

⌒

Clare had pre-approved status as a 'special witness', which allowed her to give evidence via videolink. She was in some other random room in the old courthouse, and she could see counsel and Judge on a screen. In court her face appeared on old TV screens in front of us and the jurors. The rig was set up so that she didn't have to see

Reester, the prosecutors having convinced the court that she was too distressed to be in his physical presence. It was a good thing too, because even with Goode's gentle questioning it took a full day to get through evidence-in-chief. Clare had almost fainted twice when pressed, again, to differentiate the specifics of the offending from one night to another. A bucket sat beside her chair and she reached over to dry-retch into it many times, the audiovisual link quickly shutting off, followed by a short adjournment. Judge had offered, twice, to finish for the day, but Clare insisted she wanted to get it over with.

'I want it done,' she'd said, and I felt myself nodding.

She had to remember back and forth to which times she bled or didn't, which times there was penetration or not, what the ejaculate smelled like, which Slim Dusty song. I have the word *torturous* in my notes.

'Now I want to ask you about the very last time you remember Kevin coming into your room at night, Clare,' Goode said to the screen. We had all just returned from yet another break to allow Clare a moment to gather herself. The jurors were solemn when they took their seats in court again. I saw a woman stuffing a wet tissue up the sleeve of her blouse and a man looking embarrassed as he brushed biscuit crumbs from his protruding belly.

'Yes,' Clare replied, taking a sharp breath, 'okay.'

'So can you please tell me everything you remember from that night?'

Christ almighty. I could feel the room brace itself. I watched Clare on the screen take a deep breath now as though she were about to dive.

'Well it was the same thing again,' she started, and her hand made a rolling motion on the word *again*, 'and I was in bed and he was under the house listening to his records, and then the Slim Dusty song came on, and ah—' her voice rose, and she took another sharp breath in, 'and I knew—' her voice broke, 'that he was coming for me—' and tears poured down her face again and she cried out, trying to finish her sentence, 'and so I remember I got all my teddies and all my toys and I put them all around the edge of my bed on top of my sheets and I tucked myself in as tight as I could!' she screamed, continuing as though exorcising the memory, 'but he didn't care!' She wailed so loudly the speakers on the screen hummed.

The courtroom sat absolutely still and silent, all eyes transfixed on Clare's body rocking back and forth, all ears listening to her cries. It seemed as though she was battling to stay conscious.

She gripped the edge of the table again. 'But he didn't care! He ripped the sheets off the bed and grabbed me by my ankles and dragged me on my belly to the edge of the bed.'

To Crane's credit, he was gentle in cross-examination. I didn't think it came from a place of kindness—he would have skewered himself in front of the jury if he'd made Clare shed a single extra tear—but it was still a relief. It seemed almost merciful, the way he stepped through small inaccuracies, putting the case forward only as far as he was legally bound to do.

The defence approach was one of complete denial, and without the corroborating testimony of her sisters, Clare's racked recollections wouldn't necessarily be enough to remove the 'reasonable doubt' we were all supposed to carry. Reester's silence and refusal to give evidence seemed stark, if only for how loud and pained the complainant's testimony was. The scales of justice felt difficult to weigh with such a palpable imbalance.

At the end of it all, when Judge thanked her and told her she could go, I watched the monitor showing her standing up and exiting the room. She moved slowly, retreating from battle, exhausted but alive, and she would wait another two days and nights to hear the outcome of the war.

⌒

The only other Crown witness was Clare's mother, and this would not be the last time I was disappointed in a mother's testimony. Every time, it seemed, it was the same story of domestic violence and emotional manipulation. It would be far too easy—a gross oversimplification—to ask those mothers why they didn't know or why they didn't do more to protect their children.

Clare's mother told the court that Reester was the first man in years who had provided a stable home for them. She described him as occasionally 'unpleasant', but added that she hadn't felt she could uproot her children again.

'What other man would take me and three girls under ten?' she asked. 'We'd already shifted three times since my youngest was born.'

'Did your daughter ever tell you about what Reester was doing?' Goode asked the witness.

'No, never.'

⌒

My own mum was arriving in Bargara that night for a couple of days before the weekend. She was the light at the end of the Reester tunnel. I was exhausted and wanted to spend time with someone I didn't have to put on a show for, but I was also nervous because I wouldn't be able to throw up after dinner anymore.

For weeks if I'd eaten dinner and then tried to go straight to sleep, I would just lie in bed thinking about all the fat inside me, until I would cry and tell myself awful things, and finally get up and purge. I slept so soundly after I'd emptied my stomach. It was meaningful. At once an assurance that I couldn't get bigger, and a difficult act of strength and determination, and a good dose of punishment. I liked the way the heaving made my abs work. *I will do better*, I said to myself. *Just one more time, then you can go to bed.* I would brush my teeth again. *Good girl.*

'Isn't this lovely!' Mum remarked about my room when she arrived on Thursday afternoon.

I didn't know how to tell her I'd rather be in a crappy motel than hearing any more about Kevin Donny Reester. She was right, though: it was the kind of apartment we'd stay in for a special family holiday. The ocean crashed loudly just outside the big windows and you could sit in the bath with a cold beer watching the waves roll in at sunset. We walked to the shops to get fish and chips for lunch, and my hair whipped around my face when we took a selfie to send to Dad. I tried not to talk about work, but I felt as if I didn't have anything else to say. No hobbies anymore, no books I'd read in a long while.

The inconsistencies in dates and complaints that Crane had pointed out made me anxious overnight, but—to my surprise and relief—Goode's closing address the next morning was amazing. It would be the only time in the whole year that I saw the sorrow and anguish expressed by a complainant accurately and respectfully used to convince the jury of her testimony. My hope for a conviction fluttered back to life in the prosecutor's oration.

Defence had the right of final reply, though, because they hadn't given any evidence, and there is something to be said for having your voice be the last in the minds of the jury before they retire to consider a verdict. I watched the twelve people rise and shuffle out, and I took note of the time for the meticulous minutes I was required to keep. The next four hours felt like hell to me, and I could only imagine what the wait was like for Clare, or for Reester himself.

I was selfish, though, of course. I was waiting for *my* sign. Waiting for a hope that justice might be done.

On Friday afternoon Judge's wife joined him for the weekend so I booked a restaurant for the four of us to have dinner together. Before we left to meet them, Mum started asking me a lot of questions. What kind of car did they drive? What kind of restaurant? How should she address Judge? I was having a hard time pretending I wasn't nervous she'd say something wrong.

'Are you worried I'll say something wrong?' she asked.

'Yes,' I replied, grinning. She laughed and I laughed too.

We spent the weekend eating gelati and sitting by the ocean and lying on the couch watching television. We went to an op shop and a second-hand bookstore, and I felt as though an older, happier version of me was coming home into my skin again.

A few times I thought to tell Mum about Samuel, but I realised while we were chatting to my dad on the phone that I would need to wait and tell them together. Not for any symbolic or meaningful reason, but just because I wasn't sure I'd be able to get it out twice.

The staff at the courthouse were friendly and chatty. It would turn out to be the same at all of the regional centres I visited—cakes and slices always in the tearoom, and a deputy registrar who talked about the local buildings and sport teams, or bitched about the local solicitors whom they'd grown up with. It was lovely for a little while, but inevitably I became impatient.

'I've decided to call it the "circuit shuffle",' I said to Judge while we waited in chambers for a note from the jury, 'where they chat to me so much I have to start walking backwards out of the room to escape without being rude.' He laughed.

One of the associates in Brisbane whom I wasn't even really friends with had gone out of her way to warn me about an older male staff member at the Bundaberg registry getting 'a little too close' to her. The story was corroborated by a third associate. 'Nothing to report officially,' she said to me subtly, 'but something to be aware of.'

I was trying to keep busy while waiting for Reester's verdict and so carried some files downstairs to be processed, but I tripped on my heel and almost fell forward. The man I had been warned of was behind me, and as I fell he put his hand low on the small of my back just above my butt.

I whipped around in shock and loudly rejected his help. 'I'm *fine*, thank you!' It came out aggressively and I saw surprise register on his face and immediately I felt stupid that I would presume his assistance was sinister. But when he laughed and shrugged it off, walking back to his desk, I felt even *more* stupid. *If I was falling forwards why the fuck did you put your hand on me like that?* I stared at the back of his head, furious, but still second-guessing myself. *Am I losing it?*

All the dickheads swam into my mind, multiplying like in an Escher painting: Reester, Samuel, this handsy man, all in the foreground, no perspective.

I dumped the files on a nearby desk and felt my phone vibrate— the bailiff was calling.

'Yeah it's just me,' the bailiff said. 'We've got a verdict.'

My Fitbit buzzed at me with encouragement, reading my increased heart rate as a sign I was exercising.

⌇

The fifteen minutes it took to bring everyone back into the courtroom were awful. I was practising the script I had to read out to take the verdicts. There were so many different counts I had to be extremely careful to follow procedure. I always felt as if I was trespassing somehow, when I stood and took the verdicts, like a baby in adult dress-ups.

'Silence, all stand,' the bailiff finally announced as Judge entered.

Then the jury came in, standing in a row, shuffling anxiously.

'Yes,' Judge said, looking at me from up on his bench, nodding and sombre, 'please take the verdict.'

'Speaker, have the jury reached their verdicts?'

'Yes, we have.'

'And do you find the defendant, Kevin Donny Reester, guilty or not guilty of count one, rape?'

'Guilty.'

'So says your speaker, so say you all?'

The chorus of twelve voices said 'yes' and they continued to say 'yes' for every count.

When I eventually sat down again the pressure of tears was building behind my eyes and I shut them tightly. I couldn't show any emotion lest the defence team think the impartial arbitration of justice had been compromised. The prosecutor's clerk ducked out of the courtroom, probably to go find Clare, to tell her the 'good news'. I pictured her face, crying, and I imagined her sisters crying with her, terrified of their own trials ahead, but emboldened by the strength of the eldest. I wondered if their mother embraced them, and how many times she might have said she was sorry. I pretended to drop a pen under my desk, frantically wiping my eyes and slapping my cheeks as I hid for a moment. We adjourned for a short break before sentence, and Reester was taken away in handcuffs.

⟶⟵

When I went back into court to prepare for the sentence I saw a woman and child sitting at the back of the room in the public seats next to the dock. I don't know much about kids and how big they are at what ages, but this one looked to be at the stage of life where his school backpack would still comically swamp him. A child in a courtroom is always a curious sight, like a live lamb in a butcher's. He had little jeans on and his long blond hair was clean and shiny. It looked beautiful brushing his shoulders next to a crisp blue T-shirt. I stared at him squirming in his seat, envying his clear skin and the confusion on his face. I wanted to rip my jabot from my throat and run to him, scooping him up and taking him out for ice-cream. *I don't belong here either!* I'd shout, bursting through the double doors and out to the beach. The woman with him couldn't have been much older than forty and was extremely overweight, with beautiful dark features and perfectly ironed clothes. She held her hands in her lap, the tip of a hanky poking out from where her fingers tightly clasped together. The room was quiet enough for me to hear her sniffle.

'Is his Honour ready?' the prosecutor asked me quietly, breaking my curious trance.

'Yes, I think so.' I looked down, back to my work, quickly preparing the papers on my desk in order to accept documents and dictate Judge's sentence. Reester would be going to gaol, and it was already past 4 p.m.—that meant urgent processing and a cranky registrar. Everything had to be perfect or we'd miss the transfer bus.

'Daddy!' The shout rang through the room like a bullet. I looked up in time to see the boy run toward Reester, intercepted at the last minute by the woman who was surely his mother. *No . . .* My face contorted but I couldn't look away. I glanced to both counsel, noticing their shoulders sag as they turned to their papers with tired faces. As Reester got back in the dock the boy climbed onto his chair and reached his arm up as high as he could and placed his palm flat on the glass that separated him from his father. Reester looked down, smiling lovingly, and mirrored the boy's act, Reester's large wrinkled hand pressed against his son's tiny one. It was over-whelming. There were too many heartbreaking things happening at once. I didn't know how to process the new information. It was all so much easier to deal with when you couldn't see that bit. The love part.

I could not bring myself to end that moment. I would not separate their hands or interrupt that boy telling his smiling father what he'd learned at school that day. His mother was crying and trying to pull the child back into his seat, but his little body wriggled away, escaping her. I pretended I needed more time to prepare my own work and waited until the boy finished talking and his mother sat him down. Then I rose and went to get Judge from his chambers.

I stood in his doorway. 'It seems that Reester's new partner is here,' I said, 'with their young son.'

'In the courtroom?' Judge asked, one eyebrow slightly raised.

'Yes.' We paused and I sensed he was waiting for my comment, but I just shrugged. Most of the time I didn't know what Judge expected I'd say, or what he wanted me to say. If he'd asked me what I was thinking I would have told him: *I was just wondering if Reester only rapes female children.*

'Everyone is ready for you,' I said instead.

⌒

When people are sentenced, the language around them changes. In the eyes of the law, since Reester had been convicted, the allegations against him became truths. Allegations crystallised to facts. Judge didn't tell Reester he was being sentenced because someone *said* he was a rapist; Judge told Reester he was going to gaol because he *was* a rapist. Judge began a brief summary of the facts that the prosecution had proved, that Reester would be sentenced on, then paused halfway, realising the child was still sitting next to his mother, listening.

'This is quite serious content,' Judge said, looking at counsel. 'I wonder if it might be wise to take the child out of the courtroom?'

The boy left but the mother stayed. What had Reester told her? Did she know about the joinder application and that all three sisters had similar complaints? Did she think Clare and both of Clare's sisters were insane liars making false accusations? Had Reester ever touched the boy?

On Saturday night the four of us went to Mon Repos to see turtles hatching. The moon was so full and bright I got a shock every time I looked up at it. Thin strips of clouds with strong silver linings streaked across the sky as we waited our turn to be led out to the ocean.

'Are you enjoying being on circuit?' Judge's wife asked me. She was a lovely woman, kind and intelligent.

'Um,' I paused, thinking of Reester, 'the food is good?' I said, unconvincingly.

Shortly afterwards my mother pinched my arm. 'Try to be a little more positive about it,' she hissed. 'A lot of people wanted your job.'

It was true, I was being ungrateful, but later I wept as the turtles hatched. They broke through their shells and struggled up out of the buried nests, fumbling through the sand toward the ocean, toward the big white moon, to begin a journey that only one of a thousand of them would survive. People around me were gasping and cooing, but a child made a quiet squeal, 'Daddy!' and I broke again.

I was grateful we were in the dark where I could cry freely despite being surrounded by strangers and my mother and Judge. The ugly parts of my life kept crashing into the beautiful ones. Under one of the most spectacular night skies I'd ever seen, in a tropical paradise, I was witnessing a miracle of new life, and all I could think about was how many children were being brutalised at that very moment.

The park ranger came up to me, holding one of the hatchlings out for me to touch. It was smaller than the palm of my hand. Its tiny flippers swung madly in the air, programmed to push through sand and water for the next several days until it reached deeper oceans. I looked into its shiny little eyes and saw the moon glinting back.

'Isn't she beautiful?' the ranger whispered. I murmured assent. *And statistically speaking, she will be dead within twenty-four hours.*

I looked down toward the water at all the hatchlings racing to the shoreline, then back up the hill to all the children in the sand, and opened my palms to the moon, helpless.

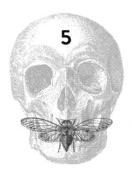

5

BRISBANE WAS TURNING NIPPY SO I got my thick stockings out of storage for the early morning walks to work. They cut into my stomach—a painful reminder of my size—and so despite the cold I lost a couple of kilos. Two people complimented me on my slimmer figure.

The problem was that the nylon and mesh stockings rubbed against the small cuts on my upper thigh so the neat red lines couldn't dry or heal properly. Bandaids didn't fit over the criss-crossing lengths either. One afternoon I made it home from work, dropped my bag, kicked my heels off and tugged at my stockings to pull them down from under my skirt, and an itchy pain exploded where my cuts were. I fell back onto the bed and hiked my skirt up to find a mess. The stockings were patterned, a lace-like effect, and as the tiny fibres had picked up on the edges of my scabs throughout the day, the slices had re-opened and then the blood had dried into the stockings, and I had just ripped the whole mess open. Stains covered the inside of my woollen skirt and the stockings were crispy, flecking dried blood onto my white sheets as I rolled them off. I checked my phone and swore; Vincent would arrive within the hour.

I'd seen him twice since my Jameson-fuelled self-harm, but we'd been out and about so there had been no risk of awkward questions. There was no getting around it this time. I also had no intention of actively trying to hide the scabs. I wanted him to see how much I was struggling so that I didn't have to find the words to start the conversation. If I was honest, it was a challenge. *Leave me!* they said, red and rippling like a cape to a bull.

In high school there was a girl, Katie, who put neat cuts onto her wrist, and we all saw but didn't say anything because they ran horizontally instead of vertically, so we knew she was 'posing'. The phrase 'cry for help' was tossed around.

My mother heard me say something about it one afternoon and admonished me. 'It's still very sad and she obviously doesn't feel like she has the right people to talk to about it,' Mum said while I downed a Milo.

It was in Grade Eleven and I'd started cutting my thighs sporadically the year before. The following week I heard an announcement over the school speakers: 'Would Mr and Mrs McIntyre please report to the school reception', and I was flooded with a strong mix of envy and pride that I immediately hid, and then I saw them—Katie's mother and father—walk straight past me. We'd met several times in the past few years, but their eyes weren't taking in any faces or details. They took long, fast strides. I wanted my parents to rush to the school and ask me why I was sad every day.

The friends I was with discussed the matter.

'She just wants attention,' someone said.

'You'd only cut on the wrist if you *wanted* someone to see it,' I added, and everyone nodded. It would be another five years before I had something even resembling a boyfriend, and I always wore board shorts to the beach. Easy secret.

But then there I sat, on the edge of my bed after work, at twenty-three, a woman with a job, 'pulling a McIntyre'.

I went to the bathroom and washed myself, dabbing iodine onto the lines with a cotton bud, and shaping a custom bandaid with nail scissors to cover the worst bits. It felt a bit nice to be caring for myself like that, playing nurse to the determined version of me. I hunched over myself, dressing the little wound, and whispered to the soldier, nodding, *do better, be better*, and felt proud.

Two years earlier Vincent and I had been in bed, cuddling and watching movies, when he'd noticed the scars—at that stage dormant and fading—on my thigh for the first time.

'What are these from?' he asked, running a finger over the pale ridges, and I froze.

He held me for about twenty minutes of silence, and then he said 'fine' and got up to go, and I blurted it out. I told him, trying to joke about it, that I was 'just an angsty teen', and he came back to bed and hugged me for a long time, kissing me.

He didn't know I still did it, and in truth neither did I. It had been years. I couldn't remember the last time, but when I'd done it again the rush was the same and I realised immediately that it was also the same feeling I had when I purged. I would talk to myself angrily, making lists of faults and wrongs, then begin the act, the small ritual masochism, making promises to do better, to be better. I only ever cut at night-time right before bed, the same with purging. A desperate attempt to demarcate a 'before' and 'after' Bri, so that I could leave the 'before' Bri in the dirt, and commit to a new self in the morning. I neatly traced new cuts over old scars. My panicked need for self-improvement could only ever come from self-loathing. Diary pages from those nights are full of the most horrible things, all written to myself in third person. Looking at them in calm daylight is like seeing myself in an upside-down spoon. That girl is nearly, but not quite, me.

When Vincent and I went to bed and he saw the bandaids, he became sad and confused. I told him I was struggling with work, and I sort of thought that I was, but I genuinely didn't have the words to explain the other half of it. He was good to me, of course, and held me again, but in the wee hours he had to shake me awake from screaming nightmares. I wondered how much more 'crazy' he could take. I was unravelling as I tried to reckon with my past, but I felt as if I had to get my shit together and be a good, chill girlfriend before I told him everything in case he thought it was all too much. I imagined things he could say: 'I didn't sign up for this shit.' 'We're so young, I don't want to get stuck dealing with you and all this.' 'This isn't fun anymore.' 'I don't feel the same way about you now.'

At times it felt so strong, the problem with me, the wrongness, that it was corporeal. If I was thinner, more beautiful, then maybe he'd be less likely to leave when I told him about being molested. If I fixed up the other parts of my life, fixed my body, then perhaps I wouldn't be such a crap package. I thought if I was hot enough he'd be attracted to me regardless of the damage.

⌒

The next morning I woke up, put my stockings on, left Vincent sleeping soundly, and went to work a little early. I figured it was time to talk to someone. Although I'd been miserable for months, it was a high-functioning miserable. But while the vomiting was an easy secret, Vincent would now be watching for new scars. In our associate's training session, one of the HR managers had mentioned that free counselling had been made available to all Department of Justice and Attorney-General (DJAG) employees, so when I got to work I found the phone number. I glanced at the clock—making sure there was still a good half-hour before Judge would arrive—shut my office door, and dialled.

A woman answered. I told her I was a DJAG employee looking to access the 'complimentary and confidential' counselling, and she said she would ask a few preliminary questions.

'Do you think the reason you are calling is affecting your ability to do your job?' she began.

'What do you mean?' I replied.

She paused as though she'd never had to clarify the meaning of the question.

'This job is the thing that's making me sad,' I said.

'I see,' she said, but as though she didn't.

'But I'm still doing it.'

'Yes.'

'And that's why I'm sad.' I waited for her to say something but she didn't. 'So I'd say "no"?' I said, still confused.

'Okay,' she replied.

It came time for her to schedule me in, and she asked what location I'd prefer. I told her I worked in the city so anywhere central would be good and she confirmed they had an office in the CBD.

'And do you have a preference for a man or a woman?' she asked.

'A woman, definitely, please.'

'Of course, and when would you like to speak to someone?'

'As soon as possible?'

'Well, I have one of our female counsellors free most of Friday next week.'

'Oh.' I was disappointed. More than another week alone seemed impossible. 'If that's the soonest, then sure, thank you.'

'So what time would suit you?'

'Any time after work, I suppose. If the office is in the city I can get there by five-thirty.'

'The facility is only open during business hours.'

'Sorry?'

'There are no counsellors in the city available for out-of-hours consultations,' she repeated.

'But I work full-time. That's why I have this number, because I'm an employee of the department.'

'We can email you an appointment slip that you can take to your supervisor.'

'But I thought this service was confidential if I wanted it to be?' I asked her.

'Yes, that's right,' she replied.

I fought the urge to hang up. I couldn't imagine asking Judge to adjourn a trial so that I could go talk to someone about my feelings.

'Does anyone go in early?' I asked. 'Is there a before-work time available?'

'Ah, if you make a special request and really need it, I could ask someone to come in early for you.'

'Is that possible? Yes please.'

'Sure, so sometime next week at eight-thirty?'

'Oh, well, I need to be at work at nine, like, *by* nine, actually, so that wouldn't work.' I scrunched my eyes shut, pressing the receiver hard into my face.

'There's someone who can do eight-fifteen starts, but he's a man. The out-of-office-hours slots are booked weeks in advance and I don't think we have any women who offer them in the city. Unless you're happy to go out to Capalaba?'

'Well okay, great, what time at Capalaba?'

'The session would be from 5 p.m. to 6 p.m. because they close at six.'

'But I don't finish work until at least five and I work in the city.'

It was like a shitty Monty Python sketch. All the absurdity but nobody laughing. In the end I booked an eight-fifteen session, over a week away, with a male counsellor. I hung up the phone and wept. I had thought that working up the courage to ask for help was supposed to be the hard bit. I began worrying that the office phone would register the number I had dialled and send a message to HR, flagging me. Had I given them my payroll ID? I couldn't even remember what else the woman had asked. What if Judge found out somehow? It was only 8 a.m.—how would I last the day? What about the rest of the week?

I closed my eyes and imagined writing my worries on slips of paper and putting them in a box. *I am fat.* I folded the paper and put it in the box. *I am not good enough for my boyfriend and he might leave me.* In the box. *I am not smart enough for this work.* In the box. *I don't know how to start dealing with what happened to me.* In the box. I imagined closing the lid of the box and putting it up on a shelf, and I took a deep breath in and a deep breath out. I would take the box down later, at home, in the shower, after dinner; and in the meantime, I would work.

⟿

By some administrative error-miracle we were listed for a single sentence that day. Normally a sentence only takes a couple of hours, and I thought I'd have the afternoon free to catch up with a lot of my Practical Legal Training (PLT) assessment. Like most of the associates, I was doing extra studies after work and on weekends to meet the requirements for admission to the legal profession. The law degree doesn't make you a lawyer—there's an extra six-to-twelve months (and $10k) or so of academic hoops, then another thousand bucks and a month's worth of paperwork and filing to do. Both Judge and my dad regularly checked in on my PLT progress.

I got to Judge's pigeonhole where our files normally sat waiting, but it was empty. I phoned the basement, and the young man who answered my call seemed excited. 'Oh yeah! This indictment is from 1983, it's all old, and it's in special plastic, we didn't wanna leave it out.'

'Holy shit, 1983!?' I replied.

'Yeah!'

'Be right there.'

I knew Judge had worked on the Fitzgerald Inquiry and even that didn't start until 1987. I was so excited to show him. I made it down to the basement where the file-room clerk handed the indictment to me gingerly. It was three sheets of old brown paper, bigger than A4, and a rusty staple held it together. Looped handwriting crisscrossed all over it, impossible to read; the defendant's name was in proper calligraphy, and the dates had been entered by a typewriter. Stamps and seals were plastered across different spots.

'What's it for?' the clerk asked me, and I realised that in my excitement about the oddity I'd forgotten the paper represented a criminal matter.

I turned the sheet over. 'One count of indecent treatment,' I replied, and we both shrugged. 'Some things don't change, hey?'

Back up in chambers I showed Judge. 'Look at this,' I said, pointing, 'just the one count, and he failed to appear on his court date, so there was a warrant out for his arrest, and now here we are! Twenty-five years later!'

Judge wasn't very excited. 'I wonder what a single count of indecent treatment got in 1983?' he asked, and I responded with a blank expression. 'We have to sentence him according to what he would have received at the time he committed the offence,' Judge clarified. My jaw hung open, and he started teasing. 'You knew that, didn't you!?'

'So that's why we don't have any other sentences today.' I groaned. 'Time for some research.'

As it turned out, comparable sentences for a grown man molesting a girl under sixteen, in the Year of Our Lord 1983, were good behaviour bonds, fines, or a touch of probation. Whipping was an 'optional' additional penalty for the odd case. I raised it with Judge and was quickly informed that the point-in-time rule didn't apply to any types of capital punishment.

'Bummer,' I said with a grin.

'Well, he's been in custody for the past three weeks awaiting sentence now, when he would never have received any actual imprisonment,' Judge said, seeming to suggest I should temper my attitude.

'I guess people shouldn't skip town when they're charged with sex offences,' I said, my hands on my hips, and after a beat we smiled at each other.

⟳

In court things went smoothly. Both prosecution and defence came prepared to deal with the unusualness of the matter. Defence made submissions that in '83 even lineal descendent and stepfather sexual-assaulters normally only had to sign a good behaviour bond. I was livid.

'The defendant has led an otherwise blameless and unremarkable life,' the defence barrister submitted. 'He has five children and he's been working for the state rail company for twenty-five years.'

What is an unremarkable life? I saw the corrective services officer and the solicitor, both women, being pleasant to him before court began, and he did just look like an average dude, but I was still mad. How many of these men looked like average dudes? How many men walking around in any one Australian state had outstanding sexual assault complaints against them in other states? Did his wife know? Did she have a right to know, before she married him, that he was a sex offender?

⟳

Judge began his official sentencing remarks by saying, 'I must put aside what the current attitudes toward sentencing this kind of offending are.' And the man was, of course, released immediately. I processed the paperwork as 'urgent' and went back upstairs to chambers.

Judge came to my office with a small task but then lingered. 'Should I check the orders you dictated? You didn't put "whipping" down on his order sheet, did you?' he asked, grinning.

'I just can't believe men could rape their daughters and step-daughters and get good behaviour bonds?' I spoke it as a question he might have the answer to. 'It's not that long ago! It's not long enough ago for that to have happened.' I slumped back in my chair.

'The past is a different country,' he said to me.

'Yeah, well, it sounds like a shithole,' I replied, and he gave me that sad smile.

I got up to walk to the elevator and noticed Megan was in my spot—not so much a physical location, but she was staring out the huge glass panes onto the city below, alone—and asked her what was up.

'Yesterday we had to watch CCTV footage of an Aboriginal woman getting raped.'

'Holy shit—'

'—right there.' She pointed down to the Roma Street Parkland.

'Fuck.'

'And it looks like today we'll have to watch it again.'

'What?'

'There might be a plea deal. He's been charged with two counts, and my judge reckons they might drop one of them if he pleads to the other, but counsel have to watch the footage again to see how valid it is that he's been charged with two separate counts.'

'And it's all there? On tape?'

'Yep.'

'And he's still fighting it?'

'Yep. And this woman's life is wrecked. Her community didn't support her going to the police, because of course they don't trust the police, which I get. They wanted to deal with it internally, with their elders. He's some kind of community figure, and he's huge. She passed out, completely unconscious, and he just climbed on top of her. You could see her body being shoved along the ground, like *uh-uh-uh*, as he did it.'

'That poor woman.' I shook my head.

'I know. Can you imagine how hard it would be to have to turn against your whole family to take your rapist to court?'

We both fell silent.

'Are you okay?' I asked her.

'Oh, yeah, I mean, as good as you can be, right?'

'Right.'

'What about you?'

I told her about my morning. 'How many other files have been sitting down there for decades?' I wondered out loud.

'Yeah, it's way too easy to just drive across state lines and disappear,' she said.

'Can that still even happen? Does that really happen?' I asked her, but I would get my own answer the following week.

⌐

The Friday of my counselling appointment rolled around, and I got to the office in the middle of the city at ten past eight. There were three other people in the waiting room and I had just sat down when a loud voice called out my full name. *So much for anonymous.* My counsellor's name was David, and he wore a short-sleeved business shirt and synthetic trousers that made a *schh* sound when he moved. He stood smiling, his stance wide and strong, holding the door to his small office open for me.

'Good morning,' I said, shuffling sideways under his arm and into the room.

'Have a seat,' he said, gesturing to a low couch, and as I sank into the cushions he clicked the door closed and took a seat in his wheeled office chair opposite me. He placed each of his black leather shoes on separate prongs in the foot of the chair so that his crotch was wide open and closer to my eye level than his eyes were. I tugged at my pencil skirt, as it now sat up on my mid-thighs, and tried to cross my legs in a way that allowed me to sit up straight, but the couch had swallowed my arse. I had to bend my neck to look up at him.

'So, why are you here today?' he asked cheerfully, before glancing at some notes and answering his own question. 'You're a bit stressed about work?'

In that instant I knew I couldn't tell him the real reason for my visit. It would be an exposure; it felt too risky somehow, as if I was a hypochondriac for even making the appointment. I wouldn't be able to articulate my complaints clearly enough to convince David of something. Samuel's name wouldn't come out of my mouth. I didn't want to be dramatic. I knew I wouldn't have time to fix my makeup before work if I cried, and there was no way I could even start talking about my problem—the real problem—without crying. The whole thing was a waste of time. I'd been holding myself together for so long, waiting for the appointment, and the horizon of deliverance had been a mirage.

Instead, I told David a partial truth: that I was worried the job was making me hate men. That I couldn't walk around Brisbane without seeing places where crimes had been committed. That what I saw in court was bleeding out around the edges, seeping into the rest of my life and spoiling everything. He listened for a few minutes until I trailed off and shrugged, then he started telling me a story about one of the jobs he had before becoming a counsellor. He was a support worker at a halfway house for men who had domestic violence orders against them.

'You know,' he said, 'I'd sit in that room with them, and we'd try to get to the heart of the problems. Some of them were able to acknowledge what they'd done and they would try to work through that part of their history and work through that guilt, but some,' he paused as though trying for maximum impact, exhaling and shaking his head, 'just never admitted they'd made a mistake. And these were really bad men. I mean, *really* bad.'

I stared up at David's face, trying to hide my disbelief. It had taken me so long to feel as though I wanted to open up and tell someone what I was going through, and there I was listening to a dude's crotch as he competed with me for who had the job with the most fucked-up men in it.

I watched him push his weight around on his wheelie chair, his face friendly and animated as he recalled how hard he'd found it to truly see into one particular man's soul. This one guy had beaten his wife to a pulp and insisted it was her fault, but David kept working with him and didn't give up because David believed everyone had some good in them and a chance for redemption.

I told David I didn't know who to talk to because I didn't want to unload on Vincent, and he commended me for being such a good girlfriend.

Next he drew diagrams on the whiteboard. I left his office with a triangle-shaped exercise to do when I felt 'emotional and over-whelmed'. I was to try to separate the thoughts from the feelings from the actions. The triangle was supposed to keep 'think', 'feel' and 'do' separate from each other. I found one recently that I had scribbled on while in court. On 'think' I have: *It's not fair that this man gets to go around ruining women's lives for his own gratification. Taking what he wants and leaving abused children behind. I am so powerless to stop them or protect myself. What if he's not found guilty and he goes out and does it again? I don't know who to trust.* On 'feel' I have: *Angry. Scared.* On 'do' I have: *Not allowed to cry in court.* I don't know which trial those notes are from—they fit too many.

Walking back to work after the appointment finished a merciful five minutes early, I stopped for a cigarette and felt a bit bad that I hadn't been clearer with David.

'Do you feel like we're off to a good start—that we achieved something today?' he'd asked me earnestly.

'Absolutely!' I replied, smiling, picking up my handbag and moving to the door.

One of my best friends, Anna, lived in Melbourne, and the last time we'd spoken on the phone she'd told me that sometimes when she slept with a guy who was a dud in the sack she would try to teach him lessons in foreplay and intimacy, as a favour to all women who might see him in the future. I thought about David's crotch in my face and how maybe no woman had ever told him that he was a shit counsellor.

The only thing he'd said to me of any value was, 'When you are lumping all men together, try to remember the good men in your life. Think of their faces and what you admire about them.' As I walked to work I thought about my dad, and what he would think if I told him I didn't want to be a lawyer. I walked to work and thought about Vincent and felt anxious that his love was retractable because I couldn't be a clean, beautiful thing for him. I walked to work and thought about Judge, and that I couldn't get through a single year without crumbling. I *was* surrounded by good men: three of them, giving me all the good things a young woman could need from the men around her. Giving me a strong father figure and a generous lover and an admirable mentor. It seemed like I was the problem.

I arrived at the courts building and saw Evelyn walking in, holding a coffee, her head of shiny hair tipped back in laughter as she spoke with some Supremes. All those men who gave me all those things, and all I wanted to give them was Evelyn. I fantasised about stepping back and her stepping forward, taking my place, relieving me of the pressure to be daughter, girlfriend, associate. She could do it all, be them all, better than I could manage even one role. It was comforting to imagine my parents taking Evelyn as their changeling. She and Vincent would make a finer pair of lovers than he and I. And I would just disappear. Float up, fly away to nowhere and sleep forever.

The bells of the Brisbane clock tower chimed, pulling me back to the beginning of the day, telling me I was late. I stubbed my cigarette out, crunched down on some mints, slapped my cheeks a little, and went to work.

That weekend I went out to a cafe with my mum on Sunday morning before she and Dad went away for a few days. I'd barely seen her or Dad on the weekends since I'd started working—they spent them out on a block of land they'd bought to retire on.

'We had a lovely time at Maleny yesterday,' she told me as our coffees arrived.

'Oh cool, why did you go?' I asked. 'For that famous gelati place?'

'No, we visited Samuel's parents' new house,' she went on, licking foamed milk from her spoon as my body started its familiar shut-down ritual. 'It's architecturally designed and so lovely. I said to your father, "This is the kind of house I really wanted."'

'Mm?' I picked up my cup and pretended to blow on it to cool it down but I just held it in front of my face as it flushed red. My eyes were going blurry at the edges, as she went on talking and stirring sugar into her flat white.

'And it's so nice and *green* up there! I said to your dad, "Why don't we just sell and move up here? Everything would be so much easier to grow!"'

'And why were you there?' I asked, struggling to sound casual. 'Did they just call you out of the blue? Or did he invite you? Was he there?'

'Well, Samuel invited us and I think he thought your brother would be there because he's got some new investment idea and—'

'He's such a fuckwit.'

'Yes, well, we just told Samuel on the phone that we weren't in a position to invest, and then he called on the morning of our visit and cancelled. But we still had a lovely day with Samuel's parents. Did I tell you it's a kind of hexagon?'

'What?'

'Their house, it's architecturally designed. A hexagon shape. And they have the most amazing kitchen. A brand-new kitchen. Leslie—his mother—told me it cost them over fifty thousand dollars.'

'That's a lot.' My pulse was rising, the pressure behind my eyes building. Every time she'd said his name, the feelings had got worse. 'What the hell does he want Arron's money for now?'

'Oh we didn't ask. Your brother's old enough to deal with that himself now. And I didn't want to spoil the mood.'

I wanted to tell her about Samuel right then and there in that cafe, but it was stuck up in my throat. If she'd just asked me, 'Why do you hate him so much?' I might have spilled it all out, but I was too afraid. I told myself it wasn't the right time and made an excuse to use the bathroom. But when I got home later, I realised there would never be a right time and immediately felt as if I missed Mum. I hadn't really listened to anything she'd said; she could surely tell I was distracted or that I didn't want to be there. She probably thought I didn't want to see her so much—and that was true, but only because whenever I saw her I spent the entire time trying to tell her what had happened to me and fighting through The Freeze again.

⌒

That night, home alone, the guilt became too much. The only meals I'd eaten in the few days beforehand were dinners that I had vomited straight back up, and I reflected on that achievement being my single source of personal pride. But it also meant that my body wasn't behaving normally. I sat outside with my cigarettes, a glass of ice, and a bottle of Jameson, looking up at the stars. I already felt an unbearable surge of regret for how rude I'd been to the mother who just wanted to spend time with me, and when the alcohol and nicotine hit together I slid down in my chair, my head lolling to the side.

'Do you want me to pay for coffee?' I'd offered, trying to use my new money to say what I couldn't, and the look on her face pained me. But I also felt so mad at her. How little she must think of me, to presume that I simply couldn't be bothered to be kind. Why couldn't she tell what was wrong?

A mosquito landed on my forearm and I watched it twitch, trying to tell if I could feel it there, but I couldn't, and it sat there drinking until I used the arm to lift the bottle to my lips again. I drank two more huge mouthfuls in quick succession, dribbling onto my shirt after the second, and knocked the bottle against my forehead. Was all of the wretchedness trapped up in there? I smacked my head with my other hand, then hit my fist hard against my chest. Was the ugliness in my heart? *How do I give them what they want? I don't know how to be this girl.* Only skinny enough when starving, only successful enough when exhausted. My legs were itchy from mosquito bites and I scratched up and down them, scraping faster and harder, breathing in quickly with my head between my legs, and then I took another drink, stood up quickly, and caught my reflection in a window. *So big. So ugly. So fucking stupid. Such a shit daughter.*

Something was coming, a feeling was on the way. I took the bottle inside and found my phone, scrolling messily through the numbers. I couldn't let my parents know I wasn't grateful for my life. I didn't want Vincent to think I was some melodramatic chick. And if I really wanted to die why would I call either of my best mates? I didn't want to talk to them. I didn't want anyone to make me want to be alive again. I just wanted to rest. To know that nobody would ever look at me again. To not have to be so embarrassed of myself in front of everyone all the time.

I thumped through the house and pushed open the door to my dark bedroom and looked up at where I knew the ceiling fan was, waiting for my eyes to adjust. Would I do it with the lights on or off? Off, surely, so that I didn't accidentally see my reflection again. I wiped my mouth with the back of my hand, put the bottle on my desk and went to my cupboards, looking for something to use, and became frightened. It had to be done, but I was scared. The thought of waking up the next day wasn't an option. Having to get out of bed and talk to people, inevitably disappointing them, my pimply face and fat body, my idiocy and crude behaviour like a flashing billboard. It was all unbearable. The pity in their eyes, the hurt in my mother's—I couldn't do that. But what if it hurt? What if I got it wrong, and I didn't die, and it made everything worse because then I'd be even more of a disappointment? Take up more of their time and cost them lots of money? Be so lame and stupid that I couldn't even get this thing right?

I scrambled back to the bedside table, found an old pair of nail scissors, and took a deep breath out before peeling back the bandaids and taking to my thigh again. The blood rose to the surface, the lines laid out like a red tally, but the release didn't come. The panic was still inside me. I looked up at the ceiling fan, my eyes having adjusted so I could see it swirling slowly on its lowest setting, as though waving to me.

I pushed off the bed. 'What do I do!?' I cried out into the wardrobe, grabbing coats and dresses, screaming into the fabrics. 'I'm so scared!'

My hand closed on a thin piece of leather—a belt—and the shock of it hit me and I fell to the floor. *Please, no.* I thought to myself, and I imagined my body hanging from the fan for several days, what it might look like by the time my mum came looking for me. I thought of her seeing it there, and I heard how she would scream, I knew how she would hug the corpse even if it was decomposing, how my dad would have to pull her away. And then there, on the floor, I wailed. I couldn't do that to them. I couldn't just tap out.

It was going to be so much harder to tell them all, to start dealing with it, but I had to, and I was so tired just thinking of it that I laid my head on some clothes I'd knocked down and cried.

I woke up there, on the floor, the next morning. My daily 7 a.m. phone alarm was going off where I'd left it out near the kitchen. I looked down at the belt on the ground and felt disappointed. There was dried blood all over my hands. The room was a mess, but the ceiling fan still turned and I was still there. Hungover, and late for work, but alive.

6

WHEN A WOMAN COMPLAINS OF mistreatment by a man, it's pretty
common to hear her referred to as a 'crazy bitch'. The label is often
articulated explicitly by the accused and his supporters, but more
insidiously it's the subtext of news stories and plot lines. Loose
cannons with daddy issues, nymphos who just need a good fuck,
narcissists and attention-seekers, all out to wreak havoc in cheap
pumps. When I hear the stories and see the tropes, I now have a
name—Jessica—and a face and a voice for her. The case was *R v
Phillips*, a rape trial that began like most others but rapidly revealed
itself to represent everything wrong with the wretched system.

I got suspicious when I flipped through the file on my way to
chambers and realised that this was to be the second time the trial
would be run in full. On the first occasion, over six months prior,
the jury couldn't reach a verdict. I turned to the depositions. There
had been a pre-trial hearing where defence fought to keep something
out of court but failed. What was that something? I searched again.
*A confession! And some discussion about Phillips's departure from
Queensland!* My heart leapt but was then caught. What could
possibly have happened in that courtroom, that a man who'd fled
interstate and then confessed wasn't found guilty?

Phillips had a really square head and pale hair that was shorn
back into a barely visible buzz cut. He was tall, with the strong

shoulders of a labourer, and wore a pale blue business shirt already rolled up at the sleeves. I thought I noticed horizontal creases across it—sometimes the male defendants wore shirts straight out of packets. As I set up court in the morning I saw the defence solicitor, a woman, smiling at him and having a light conversation. She was a beautiful woman in her thirties, and I noticed her long, manicured nails as she poured a glass of water and handed it to him. The barrister, a man, caught me looking and I smiled, wiping the cynicism off my face. Everyone deserves the right to a fair trial, sure, but I knew I couldn't exchange pleasantries with a man who refused to plead guilty for a rape he'd previously confessed to committing. Phillips had been out on bail since the last mistrial. I imagined all the people he'd met in the preceding six months—between the old trial and this one—and wondered if he'd slept with anyone. How many coffees had he ordered? Did he live in my suburb or get the same train as me like Mr Baker?

I sat down at my computer in court and tried to find statistics for how many people were on bail at any given time in Australia. Then I stumbled onto other research about public misconceptions of recidivism in sex offenders. Contrary to the ghoulish portraits we're painted, the majority of rapists aren't actually repeat offenders; they're not afflicted with an uncontrollable lust. Mostly they're regular men, with otherwise regular sexual preferences, who see an opportunity and take it. I stood up from my desk, feeling uneasy.

Prosecution had arrived during my internal monologue and I recognised Eric's face from Gladstone. He looked tired, and I smiled at him realising he was probably thinking the same thing about me.

'Everyone ready for his Honour?' I asked aloud to the courtroom, and everyone replied 'yes', nodding respectfully. I turned on my heel to go get Judge, my robes billowing behind me.

On the elevator up to chambers I thought about how Tinder and other dating apps had only been developed after Vincent and

I got together seriously. I'd never been on a date with someone I didn't have at least two dozen mutual friends with. If I was single and working in the District Court, would I be too afraid to enjoy casual sex? I thought about going back to a man's room, and in my mind I saw all the crime-scene photos from the year so far: the lounge rooms and the bedrooms with mismatched sheets, couch pillows strewn around carpets overdue for a vacuum. Dirty dishes on bedside tables. Nobody starts a date night presuming that their home will appear in crime scene photos.

Bing! The elevator doors opened, interrupting my thoughts, and Judge was standing there waiting for me. 'That looks like some serious thinking,' he said, stepping in.

'Nah, not me,' I said, putting on another smile, 'not serious and certainly never thinking.'

He laughed and then we got to work. I pulled twelve names out of the barrel. One woman excused herself: same reason as always. I pulled out another name. Judge welcomed the jury, and I finished my preliminary trial paperwork. It was all standard fare until Eric got up to deliver the prosecution's opening remarks.

'Ladies and gentlemen, you will see for yourselves shortly, that the complainant in this matter, Jessica, has a somewhat nervous disposition,' he began, and I felt the room collectively raise their eyebrows. Eric said that defence would try to argue that Jessica's temperament made her an unreliable witness. That she would be changing her story and changing her mind. 'But the prosecution case is quite clear,' he said firmly. 'Jessica went to sleep, and when she woke up the defendant's penis was inside her vagina. She was confused for a minute or two, as she woke up, and then she immediately raised the alarm. The defendant, Mr Phillips, left in a hurry—and he didn't just leave the building, he left the state.'

It was in New South Wales a few weeks later that Phillips said to a counsellor—whom he thought would be held to laws of confidentiality, but was not—that he had raped a woman in South Brisbane.

'The prosecution's case is that there is enough evidence here that you can be convinced, beyond reasonable doubt, that the defendant knew Jessica didn't consent to intercourse, and that far from Jessica's personality casting doubt on this, the defendant saw her as an easy target and took an opportunity to offend against such a woman.'

Eric's opening address went for nearly two hours and there was a merciful morning tea-break afterwards. Judge and I went back up in the elevator together.

'She must be pretty bad,' I said to him sadly, 'for a jury to have doubted her evidence so much that it overcame a confession.'

'Mm,' he took his glasses off, rubbed the bridge of his nose, and put them back on, 'we'll find out soon enough.'

⌒

Back up on level thirteen in the short break, I walked past a group of associates chatting about their jobs and plans for the following year. Who was going to which big firm, who was going to the DPP, who was moving overseas for a coveted secondment. I pretended to be too busy to join them then sat in my office doing more searching online. *Why don't people believe women? Why do people think women are liars?*

The most convincing research came from medicine, where a woman's self-reported pain was routinely questioned where a man's was not. Women received significantly lower dosages of painkillers to men, even after accounting for variance in body mass. Endometriosis affects the same number of people as diabetes but gets about a tenth of the funding. The disease is woefully misunderstood because it relies on women complaining of extreme period pain, and for the vast majority of Western medicine's history, doctors and researchers either didn't believe women or just didn't give a shit about them.

The Queensland benchbook has a section on 'lies'. It says, 'Bear in mind this warning: The mere fact that the defendant tells a lie is not in itself evidence of guilt.' I wondered if we had better evidence of the epidemic of disbelief in women, the jury could be warned of it: 'Bear in mind this warning: There is a strong statistical probability that you will presume this woman is a liar. Be aware of the subconscious bias, and do not let it affect the duty you have to weigh evidence evenly.' False accusations of sexual assault are notoriously difficult to define and gather for statistical significance, but anecdotally they're witch hunts. There are so many gatekeepers and decision-makers for matters being dropped or proceeding, but the percentage of false rape accusations is pretty widely agreed upon within the profession as sitting in the low single digits—the same rate that people are falsely accused of other serious crimes.

The benchbook also has a section called 'distressed condition' that tells judges what to say to juries when they hear evidence of a complainant being distressed after a sexual assault or rape:

> It is a matter for you as the sole judges of the facts whether you accept the evidence relating to the complainant's distressed condition. If you do, then you have to ask yourself: was the distressed condition genuine or was the complainant pretending? Was he or she putting on the condition of distress? Was there any other explanation for the distressed condition at the time? It is customary for judges to warn juries that you ought to attach little weight to distressed condition because it can be easily pretended.

Judges tell juries: if a defendant lies, it doesn't necessarily mean he's guilty, but if a woman is crying as she dials triple zero after being raped, she might just be putting on a show.

Jessica spoke in staccatos, stuttering and pausing even as she repeated after the bailiff, swearing to tell the truth. 'The three of us. Rolled some. Ah. Cigarettes. You know. Together,' she said, her eyes darting to each side as the prosecutor slowly stepped her through the events of the evening. Jessica had long, dark, wavy hair that frizzed out at the ends, and a purple lace blouse with sleeves that went past her tiny wrists. She had been in the witness stand for about five minutes before she started tugging on them and fidgeting.

'If you need a break, or want to slow things down, please just let me know,' Eric said to her as we all noticed her nerves.

'Nah. Yeah. It's alright. Sorry. This is just, like, the most public speaking I've ever had to do. In front of all you.'

It was a punch in the gut. My mother had enrolled me in speech and drama classes from primary school, and I was a debater for seven years. At university I performed comedy acts for thousands and I sometimes got invited to talk at events. Most of the people I grew up with wouldn't even consider giving testimony in court 'public speaking', we were so used to tabling our thoughts and having our opinions listened to. But here was Jessica receiving the most attention she'd ever had, in her whole life, all eyes on her, as she told people how she was raped.

'I remember he was above me. And. Because. He was supporting all his weight on his arms. Like, above me. So that he wasn't touching me or bumping me, you know. Apart from down there.'

The events of the evening took place in Jessica's ex-boyfriend's unit, just across the hall from her own. Her ex-boyfriend and Phillips had met that week on a job site, and Jessica had been invited over to join them for a drink. Jessica said that when she first woke up she didn't scream right away because she thought the man on top of her, inside her, was her ex-boyfriend, but that as she fully came around she realised that his figure was different, the silhouette of his hair didn't match her ex-boyfriend's, and that it was in fact Phillips. The prosecutor had to paint her early minutes of confusion as reasonable—that as she was coming round she might have thought he was just her ex-boyfriend—but I wanted to get up and point out that commencing intercourse with a sleeping woman is rape regardless of the pair's history. Yet another level of heartbreak: Jessica would not have been surprised, would not have raised an alarm, if her ex-boyfriend had entered her while she was unconscious.

Jessica was so difficult to get information out of that her evidence-in-chief carried over until the late afternoon. Eric had to loop back over things twice, three times. She said that after she woke and pushed Phillips off her, yelling out, she ran to the bathroom and locked herself in there. That was when she remembered that she had her period, and needed to get her tampon out from where it had been shoved right up inside her.

'And you flushed the tampon down the toilet?' Eric asked her.

'Well yeah, I mean, I wasn't really thinking straight,' she said defensively. I winced at the wasted opportunity for DNA testing before remembering that even if a tampon full of semen could have helped her prove intercourse, it wouldn't have helped her prove a lack of consent. Nothing could help her 'prove' that, not really.

Jessica refused to answer questions about her alcohol intake that evening, and this became an issue. She was unable to be clear about the different statements she'd made at different points in the investigation: sometimes she'd said 'I never drink' and sometimes she'd said 'I didn't drink on that night' and sometimes she'd said that she had 'one or two UDLs' but that she 'didn't normally drink'. It interfered with her medication.

'What difference does it make!?' she would say back to Eric when he asked her to clarify her answer, again. 'I could have had ten drinks and still never said "yes" to that creep.' Unfortunately

Jessica seemed only able to string entire sentences together when she was angry.

Sensing that tensions were high, or maybe just exhausted himself, Judge adjourned for the day once Eric announced that evidence-in-chief was finished. 'We'll begin cross-examination tomorrow morning, thank you.'

The cross-examination started in the morning and went for hours, all the way through to the afternoon. Jessica's evidence-in-chief with the prosecutor had been difficult, and she arrived in the morning already anxious and aggressive, as though she'd been on the stand in her nightmares throughout the previous evening. She was like a cat stuck in a storm drain: panicked, lashing out, too terrified to differentiate between those trying to help or harm.

Defence started at the top of the night and combed through every inconsistency from across her previous statements. There were many, and the alcohol intake was a pain point. The defence barrister asked her many times how many drinks she'd had, and she refused to give a straight answer, until they got angry at each other. She insisted it wasn't relevant information, and that regardless of how many drinks she'd had, it hadn't been enough to impair her judgement. Defence replied, correctly, that she was in the stand and needed to answer the question.

They got so heated that Judge interrupted them. 'I don't think that line of questioning is getting us anywhere,' he said.

'Yes, your Honour,' the defence barrister replied.

As though testing Jessica's memory of the evening, he asked her what she had been wearing, saying he wanted to check it against the police records of that night.

'But the skirt you were wearing was a *short* skirt, correct?' he said.

'Why are you asking me about my skirt?'

'Answer the question.'

'Whatever! Fine!'

'So you admit you were wearing a short skirt? A miniskirt?'

'Fine.'

When the barrister got toward the climax of his interrogation, he suggested that she'd simply regretted her choice in sexual partner then changed her mind the next morning. The story seemed to be that Phillips wasn't even that 'into' her.

In response, Jessica called the defendant 'ugly' and said that tradies weren't 'her type'. I flinched and looked through the juror cards: four of the men had a trade listed as their form of employment.

'I put it to you that you initiated sexual intercourse with Mr Phillips, and—'

'No.'

'I put it to you that—'

'No.'

'Please let me finish.'

'Finish what!? Stop making these statements at me! Are they questions? Why are you just telling me what you think happened!?'

Judge adjourned for us all to have a lunchbreak, but within ten minutes of resuming the tensions were even higher and Jessica seemed worn right through. One of the final questions asked her to name all the medications she was taking.

⌒

There was something about the process of cross-examining a rape complainant that made me want to slap even the gentlest defence counsel. The logical part of me knew that defence was all a part of the legal process and that if someone made an allegation, of course the onus of proof lay with them, and their version of events could be challenged. But when women and girls were crying and saying they'd been raped, surely it was unnecessary to badger them about why they flattered themselves to have caught the defendant's eye in the first place. Suggesting a woman was presumptuous to say the defendant would even want to have sex with her was just cruel.

How do we reconcile these competing interests? These horrors? It's impossible to have every inch of public space covered by CCTV, and even if we did, sex offences mostly happen in private. The acts are committed against vulnerable people by the ones they trust. There is no physical evidence. Even where semen is recovered, it can only be proof of intercourse, not consent. The women who have both levels to prove are fighting to convince jurors that they are both desirable *and* unwilling.

Studies show that we actively dehumanise overweight people and people who we believe look different to us—how is an overweight woman of colour, for example, supposed to convince an all-white jury that she was raped, if a fit, white defendant says he wouldn't want to have sex with her? Jessica had a nervous disposition, struggled to enunciate her words, had a temper and was medicated for anxiety and depression. She was at such a monumental disadvantage for not appearing as what average jurors might consider irresistible. It's the ultimate terror—perhaps the worst form of gaslighting—for a woman who complains of being raped to be told she isn't desirable enough for that to be true.

⌒

The next witness was the counsellor who'd heard Phillips's confession. Her testimony started simply. Phillips was at a clinic in New South Wales a few weeks after the incident, and he thought the counsellor was prevented by doctor–patient privilege from sharing what he said to her; in fact, she was obliged by her professional code and workplace to report threats or admissions of criminal conduct. Defence spent a while trying to tell the doctor that she was mistaken, that Phillips had told her that he *had been accused of* raping a woman, or that he *may have* raped a woman because *that woman* had said so.

'No, that's not what he said,' the counsellor responded. 'I made notes at the time. He said he did it.' She was clear and succinct. This felt good to me, as if things were back on track in time to wrap up, so I started doing some paperwork. But then defence asked the doctor about her sister having been attacked. I swivelled my chair around, my eyes wide.

'What does that have to do with this?' she asked the barrister.

'Just answer the question.'

'What was the question?'

'Are you sure your judgement in this matter isn't impaired because your sister was sexually assaulted by a man relatively recently?'

'No, it is not.'

Defence badgered her until she admitted that, on some level, these 'themes' might make her 'upset'. Strange, though, that someone being emotional about a horrific crime makes them *less* believable.

I didn't have time to wonder how he knew about the woman's sister before I was doing the paperwork for the next witness—the doctor who'd inspected Jessica in the wee hours of the morning after she called the police. Unfortunately for Jessica there was no physical harm. No real bruising, no wounds—not even small ones—and her vagina hadn't shown signs of trauma. The doctor explained that this lack of injury did not necessarily mean Jessica wasn't raped. I thought back to her evidence of how careful Phillips was as he tried not to wake her. Of course there wouldn't be grazes and bruises. He fled as soon as she called out; struggle and violence wasn't a part of this narrative.

As though I needed a final reason to loathe the defence barrister, he asked Jessica's doctor about the medications she was on, and the doctor answered with a variety of specific prescriptions.

'What about anything else? Any contraceptives?' the barrister inquired, pretending to be casual about it. He had put on a now-the-grown-ups-are-talking attitude with this doctor, the first man in the witness box.

'Yes, the contraceptive pill,' the doctor replied.

It was lucky we took a break after the doctor's evidence. I was fuming. I'd had Implanon—a semipermanent contraceptive implant—injected into my arm just weeks before. If I were raped on the way home from work that night, a barrister like this one might use my Implanon as a sly suggestion of promiscuity. What else could it be? There was no other reason for defence to inform the jury of Jessica's being on a contraceptive but to suggest she was the kind of woman inclined to engage in casual sex. It was slut-shaming at its finest, proudest pinnacle. The jury had been listening, some taking notes, some sipping water. Did they buy it? Were this barrister's bullshit antics only apparent to me?

We heard from the ex-boyfriend that afternoon too. I was optimistic before his testimony because it's rare to have someone be so near to an assault of this nature. It could be incredibly valuable to have someone—especially a man—describe the complainant's and the defendant's actions immediately after the event.

His evidence was that he woke up in his bedroom to hear Jessica screaming that she'd been raped, and he heard Phillips leave, then he went back to sleep. When the prosecutor questioned his behaviour, he explained that he was just tired of Jessica bringing so much drama into his life.

'Maybe *he* should be on trial for being a top-notch loser,' I said to Megan at lunch.

The verdict wasn't up to us: it was up to twelve random people. Supposedly a cross-section of society, but really they were mostly

men—because defence had vetoed eight women and one had with-
drawn—four of them tradesmen, and nobody under or even close
to thirty. When they entered the courtroom I tried to image how
old they were when the pill went mainstream, and what they all
thought about the 'kind of women' who took the pill.

⌒

I kept my sunglasses on for the walk home that afternoon, considering the chasm between morality and the law. Everyone in the room
looked at Jessica as if their shoulders were shrugged and their hands
in the air, palms up. *Nothing we can do about it, sorry love!* And I
imagined myself in the courtroom, in the witness box, telling my
story to a room of men with their shoulders shrugged and their hands
in the air and the corners of their mouths turned upward in pity.

Later that night I drove to the shops to get something for dinner,
but one block away from home I came across a possum that had
been hit by a car. It was dragging one paw along the ground but
there was blood coming from its mouth and anus, and I knew—from
a childhood in a possum-filled area—that the RSPCA would say
what they always did: if possible, and if the poor bugger is this far
gone, put it out of its misery. I checked that the street in front and
behind was empty, shifted gears and hit the accelerator, *thump*, then
stopped the car again. The noise made my arm hair stand up and I
stretched my neck around, the natural human response for disgust
or shame. I checked the back mirror to make sure no cars were
around, then I saw the possum was still twitching. *No! It couldn't!?*
How cruel could I be? Had I only hit a leg? Had I made it worse?
I couldn't leave it there now. I reversed over it and the *thump* wasn't
as loud—I couldn't go as fast in reverse. The car rolled back far
enough to reveal the animal from under the bonnet.

'No!' I screamed out, part in horror, part in anger. Its entire
lower half was a squashed and wretched mess, but it was still

twitching. I cried as I shifted gears into drive once more, checking again that nobody was around, and changed the angle of the tyres so I would run over the head. This time, after a fast, third *thump*, I didn't look back.

'Oh, the nerves still twitch sometimes after they're long dead,' my dad said, giving me a rough hug when I turned up to the front door crying. 'They look like they're alive but they're not.'

'You did the right thing,' Mum added.

When I was falling asleep I wondered why we draw so many distinctions between animals and humans. We will put a possum or dog 'out of its misery' but euthanasia is mostly still illegal for humans. And why do we think there's so much difference between physical and emotional pain—chronic, debilitating emotional pain? It's a sliding scale. A possum run over is okay. A person choosing to end their physical pain is almost, kind of, sometimes okay. A person like me choosing to end an internal type of suffering is definitely not okay. I fell asleep with a box cutter in my hand. *Definitely not okay.*

In his closing address the next day, the prosecutor showed the jury a photo of the mattress on the floor where the rape allegedly occurred. It had a sheet quite neatly placed over it, with an assortment of personal belongings and household items sitting on top. It looked awkward.

'Does this image seem like it fits the rest of the apartment?' the prosecutor asked the jury quite casually. 'The apartment is very messy, and Jessica remembers that when she woke up with the defendant on top of her, with his penis inside her, they were lying on the bare, dirty mattress.'

I shuddered.

'And this mattress has a sheet placed on top, and lots of little things placed on top of it . . .' He trailed off, allowing the jurors to consider the image, also allowing it to seep into their minds to make the picture they were all painting more real. 'The prosecution submits that the sheet and the belongings on this mattress were placed there by the defendant before he fled the scene, in an effort to make the bed look like it hadn't been used at all, while Jessica was in her room across the hall, calling the police.'

The Phillips case was the first time I saw a highly paid defence barrister explain the differences between consent and mistake of fact. In Queensland it's not enough to prove that there was no consent: the defendant is allowed to argue that they had an 'honest and reasonable belief' that the complainant consented. Everyone may know and agree that she did not want to have sex, but if defence can prove 'mistake of fact' the defendant will not be convicted. That's what Phillips's defence was contending, that Jessica was extremely drunk and not only consented but also initiated the sex, and that either (a) she was awake the whole time then changed her mind and 'went nuts', or (b) she passed out and he kept going, mistakenly believing she was still conscious.

'He can't know that she was thinking it was her boyfriend,' the defence barrister said in his closing address.

But that didn't seem to me to be the point. Jessica had taken about a minute to fully come around to consciousness and realise she didn't recognise the shape above her. It was disturbing to me that a sleeping woman could wake to a man inside her and think: *Oh, it's okay, I know him.* Did this woman not know what consent meant, or did she not care? Had their relationship been respectful? The mistake of fact defence wouldn't be so openly available nor so flexible in fitting so many defendants' situations if there were more women making laws, more women enforcing laws, and more women on first-response teams. I don't like mistake of fact because it gives juries an easy reason to acquit. They can say, 'Sorry love, you didn't ask for this', but simultaneously, 'He's not responsible for his actions.' Without mistake of fact, at least jurors would have to admit they were calling women liars. I like to think that might make a difference.

'She wouldn't be the first or last man or woman to regret what was done under the grip of intoxication,' the defence barrister said. But Jessica didn't just wake up the next day with a hangover and a bad feeling. She woke up with a stranger inside her and yelled out and screamed as soon as she had the physical consciousness and capability to do so. Would it be enough?

⌒

Later in chambers, while we waited for a verdict, Judge and I talked about juries and what they wanted. Judge told me that women jurors were often tougher than male jurors on women complainants. I thought that must be a generational thing too. I wore miniskirts and had a contraceptive implant; so did many—if not most—women my age. Judge said that statistically and anecdotally, juries prefer big-eyed child victims, along with defendants who are scary and jump out of bushes.

Hours went by and no note came. After six hours, Judge recalled everyone and asked how they were doing, and they didn't have an answer, so he sent them out to try again, and we waited. I always had a panicked feeling while I waited for a verdict. A claustrophobic feeling, that I was strapped for time, that a monumentally crappy thing would happen at any moment. That the worst day of either the complainant's or the defendant's life was about to happen. Each verdict I waited for reminded me that one day it could be *my* verdict. The old dizzy feeling would return. The blurry vision at the edges. The pressure building behind my eyes and the tightness of my chest. My ears would fill with a static fuzz. White noise.

⌒

When I finally stood to take the verdict, it occurred to me that I was the only woman to speak for the court. Judge, the prosecutor, and the defence barrister were all men. One witness had been a woman—the counsellor who'd heard Phillips's confession—and the defence barrister had implicitly accused her of being motivated to somehow avenge her sister, who had been attacked by a man.

Phillips was not found guilty, but he also wasn't discharged. The jury could not reach a unanimous verdict. It was to be documented as another mistrial.

'He may as well have been acquitted, though,' I said to Judge. 'I don't think they could put Jessica through that process again.' The only thing worse, perhaps, would be the likely outcome of the DPP refusing to re-run the trial. She was too strange, too emotional. Her hair too frizzy and her skirt too short. She wasn't a good little innocent girl. She wasn't a good enough victim to get a conviction against a man who confessed and fled.

My notebook for the Phillips trial finished with: *I AM ANGRY. I AM ANGRY. I AM ANGRY. Can I please scratch his face? Can I please punch him so hard that his glasses crunch into his eyes?* That last note is curious to me now because the defendant didn't have glasses. I think I must have been writing about the defence barrister.

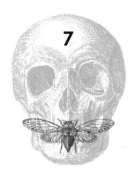

7

IT WAS SUNDAY AFTERNOON AT the Qantas Lounge and I was sipping a black coffee but gazing longingly at FIFO workers with free schooners. On the flight I read a magazine I'd nicked and drifted in and out of embarrassed sleep. We landed and wrangled the thirty-kilogram suitcase full of briefs into the hire car, and I drove us extremely cautiously to the shitty motel where we dropped our luggage off and went to find the IGA before it closed. I was getting the hang of circuit.

'Do you want to take a look at the courthouse?' Judge asked me on our way back to the motel. 'It's a beautiful old building.'

'Sure.'

'Turn right at these lights.'

We cruised along the wide, quiet roads, and I looked out across the scores of single-storey, brick-facade homes. I thought about how the IGA had a disproportionately high number of shelves dedicated to pre-packaged and junk food, and how the high prices of the fresh produce had thrown me. In Roma, weren't we closer to the farmers?

As promised, the courthouse was beautiful. Judge's chambers had an old fireplace behind his desk, and my associate's desk area in the courtroom was on a slightly raised platform. The building was completed in 1901, but a few decades before that, in 1872, there had been a famous trial of a man named Harry Readford for stealing a thousand head of cattle and driving them from Longreach in Queensland right down to South Australia. Burke and Wills had died on that same stretch less than a decade earlier. When Readford went to trial the jurors refused to convict him because they knew him as 'Captain Starlight', and his feat was so impressive that they considered him some kind of bushranger hero. When Judge told me the story I laughed, but at the end of that fortnight—when I'd taken verdicts for two trials, one against a white man and one against an Aboriginal man—I wondered if Roma's jurors had changed much since 1872.

The next morning we turned up and set the tone. Judge asked why certain matters were still on the list despite him having made orders about them when he was last there twelve months ago. We crammed our schedules full of sentences and solidified plans for two trials: one to start that morning and the other the following week.

I started struggling with the bailiff immediately. He was a very old, very slow man. We scheduled appearances via videolink and he didn't mention that he had no idea how to operate the controls. He fell asleep regularly, and was half deaf but refused to wear his hearing aids, so could not be relied upon to respond unless you were physically in front of him. The registrar apologised to me on the bailiff's behalf multiple times throughout the week, and even Judge seemed to be turning a blind eye to his incompetence. The bailiff kept asking me whether or not he could go home early, and when the latest was that he could arrive in the morning.

'Well, we have a videolink scheduled for 9.30 a.m. so however long you need to set the courtroom up to be ready for that,'

I replied to him once, quite curtly, and he didn't look embarrassed or perturbed in the slightest. He'd been cruising through that job with a bare-minimum output for longer than I'd been alive.

'I can't always do his job *and* mine,' I said to Judge at the end of the first week, exasperated, trying to get a response to validate my frustration.

'Yes, I wonder about some of these bailiffs sometimes,' he said. 'I think some of them may be veterans.'

'From what war?' I asked, confused. There was no way this incompetent dude had been anywhere near the Arab–Israeli conflict.

'Vietnam?' Judge wondered.

I didn't criticise the bailiff after that. It felt like some kind of Aussie blasphemy. Diggers, veterans, bushrangers—all beyond reproach.

⌒

The trial that first Monday was estimated to go for two to three days, and the estimate held true. As with most rapes, there weren't any third party witnesses or much in the way of expert testimonies, but the battle was about to get harder for the Crown. Brendan Strow stood in the dock and as the prosecution opened their address and outlined the charge, I could see the confusion on the faces of the jurors. Even the local journalist in the back row of the public seats crossed something off her pad, furrowed her brow, and started a sentence again. The rape was 'digital' not 'penile'. If convicted, Strow would have a rape on his record, but it seemed to be on the tips of their tongues, that it wasn't a 'real' or a 'serious' rape.

Strow didn't give evidence, but certain parts of the night weren't disputed. It wasn't disputed that Strow's wife had dropped him off into town for a weekend night of drinking, and that at some point that night he met a young woman, an American backpacker, who was working in the pub to pay for her stay in town. There was

CCTV footage of Strow buying some things for her at a convenience store after hours of drinking together, time-stamping them being in each other's company at the right time. And through the grainy footage, much to defence's frustration, it could be seen that Strow had taken off his wedding ring for the night.

Thirty minutes passed and Strow, the young backpacker, and two friends were back at the pub, this time on the second storey, on a balcony outside the shared living quarters of the transient staff. There is video footage from this balcony showing them all having one last beer together before people peel off. The complainant goes to her bedroom and turns the light out. Strow waits for a moment and then goes into her bedroom, is there for less than ten minutes, then leaves the bedroom, walks out on the balcony and away into the night. Moments later the complainant emerges, upset, and the police are called.

She alleged that she'd awoken to find Strow sitting on the side of the bed with his fingers inside her. About two years had passed since the alleged act, and the complainant had flown back to Australia to give evidence at the trial. Strow had probably been banking on the whole thing fading off into the distance.

After the opening addresses we adjourned for the day and sent the jury home. None of them excused themselves for knowing Strow, but I doubted that none of them hadn't at least heard of him, or heard about the trial, or spoken about it at the main pub in town, the same one where it had all gone down.

⌒

I wondered all the usual things: How much had he told his wife? Did he still have the same job? Was this the first time he'd done something really, truly bad? Had he spent the night drinking with that young woman expecting to have sex with her, presumably cheating on his wife in the process? Perhaps I was a moral absolutist after all, focusing on this aspect of his psyche somehow making things worse. Why had he taken off his wedding ring if not to do *something* wrong? All rapists are guaranteed dickheads but not all dickheads are rapists. Was his wife at home that night, waiting for him to call asking for a lift? Did she think he'd just be with the boys? What specific kind of surprise did she feel when the story emerged? What was her life like, from that night onwards, in that tiny, suffocating town?

Judge and I had dinner together at the small restaurant attached to the accommodation. We agreed that it would be difficult for the residents of Roma to feel comfortable convicting a man of a rape when it was digital.

We also spoke briefly about jobs in the industry, and I assured him my PLT studies were on track. But as I popped some roast potato in my mouth, I chewed over the idea that I wasn't cut out for his line of work.

At the end of dessert I went back to my room, grabbed a cigarette, and snuck outside around the back of the building to smoke. I felt sick from eating too much and christened the third circuit bathroom of the year by crying and vomiting in the bottom of the shower. I thought of Strow's fingers as I stuck my own down my throat. In my exhausted packing I'd forgotten pyjamas and when I got into bed the feeling of the sheets on my bare skin irked me. Roma was all over me, around me, inside me. I couldn't sleep.

⌁

The morning was a little crisp and I liked seeing my breath puff up and out into the air, but I hated seeing my lumpy body in my old running gear. Binge, smoke, vomit, run. I knew it wasn't sustainable, but I couldn't see ahead with any clarity to a point where I felt good about myself but wasn't starving. I couldn't break the cycle. Every few weeks I would drop a couple of kilos, start feeling confident, relax, enjoy life, and put on weight again. Self-confidence was perpetually out of reach.

Hitting the button on my Fitbit, I started jogging out of the motel complex, to the side of the road, and tried to find a steady pace. The bush on either side of me felt familiar but also frightening. It was tough to come to all these towns and only learn the names and faces of the rapists. We never met the self-sacrificing teachers, or the community-minded cafe owners, or the local Scout leaders.

A couple of minutes of puffing later, I reached the low-density town centre. Cement footpaths in generous grids reached out all around and I stared through huge glass shopwindows, admiring the lettering on the old signs and smiling to think that every one of these towns had a generic-Asian-food-restaurant that sold Chinese fried rice beside pad thai and Vietnamese noodle soup. Lace covered every surface of a haberdashery shopfront. The local hippy ran a trinket store full of imported incense and crystals.

A few more minutes in and the density of utes driving past increased, and I felt eyes on me. A man in hi-vis necked a bottle of Ice Break while watching me from across the road, and I saw him lower the bottle and wipe the brown milk from the top of his lip onto his sleeve. I felt immediately self-conscious of how my shorts were bunching up between my thighs. He might have known most of the people around Roma and just been trying to figure out if he'd seen me around or if I was new. After all, I never saw anyone else jogging in the morning in Roma. Maybe he was gazing off into the distance and I simply passed his line of sight. These are the things we tell ourselves in the middle of confronting situations before the clarity of hindsight illuminates, yet again, how we should have trusted our gut. I saw more men that morning, most with utes, and sure as shit they saw me. They stared. Two others that morning alone were also drinking Ice Break and they laughed with each other a moment after I passed them. Who the fuck even drinks Ice Break past the age of fifteen? It's a litre of sugary milk with some coffee flavouring. Was I being classist?

I was deep in revenge fantasies when I misjudged a crumbling part of the tarmac, faltered mid-stride, and watched in slow motion as my heel slipped into a pothole and my body was flung away from where my mind willed it to travel. My left knee came down hard on the cement kerb and my left arm slid along the ground, sacrificing a few layers of skin to narrowly preserve my face and teeth. The shock of the fall lasted for just a second before I was winded with pain. The cold town was still quiet as I used my good leg to push myself along the ground, off the road, stuffing my sweaty singlet into my mouth and biting down. Blood came out of a few places, hot and fast, smearing across my clothes. I felt along the bones in my leg, pushed and prodded, decided nothing was broken, but the knee wouldn't bend. A huge truck came rocketing down the road and kicked dust onto me, and as I gazed up at it I saw dozens of terrified cows in the back, and after the truck passed its stench followed. Cattle piss and shit filled my nose and mouth, and the muck and gravel it had flung at me had settled from the air into my open wounds. I looked up and around but all the strapping Ice Break-guzzlers had disappeared. I was still on my arse as the sun rose, then I finally started hobbling home. I got back in the shower and scrubbed the cuts, thinking how absurd it seemed that I would sometimes cut myself deliberately, and yet be so upset and perturbed when I did it accidentally.

The feeling of those men's eyes on me before I'd fallen reminded me of one morning in my first year of university. I had been running along the Brisbane River, and I was self-conscious about not having jogged for a while, but I'd pulled my shoes on and left the house, feeling proud of myself. I got a fraction of the way I'd previously been able to run non-stop, but pushing my lungs and stretching my legs felt good and I thought to myself that the spring was full of promise. My face was bright red but it was a beautiful day, and I dropped down to a walk for the final stretch home.

'Hey!' a man yelled from a car. 'Why aren't you running!?' It was Samuel calling from far across the road, leaning out the side of his bright blue Toyota Hilux. 'Come on!'

'I just finished running,' I called back.

'Yeah, yeah,' he said, driving off, and when I got home I cried in the shower.

⌒

The bailiff made a condescending remark when he saw me limping, and we settled into our new routine of mutual avoidance. The Strow trial continued and things got messy.

The police had recovered transfer DNA from the complainant's underpants that belonged to a man who wasn't the defendant; they were trying to pre-empt the shitshow that we all knew would take place as soon as cross-examination began. Photos of the shared bedroom were tendered by the Crown that depicted clothing strewn all over the floor, and showed that the room was shared between men and women. It was suggested that the DNA could have simply been transferred from the floor to the complainant's underwear before she put them on; it was suggested that they hadn't been cleaned thoroughly since a previous sexual interaction; it was suggested that they weren't even hers but that in her intoxicated state she'd put them on that night before going to sleep unawares. A forensic specialist said that if the allegations were true, the defendant's DNA wouldn't necessarily have transferred onto her underpants, so the lack of his DNA didn't indicate anything in particular either.

We broke for morning tea and when the jurors finished their Monte Carlos, defence dug in. 'Why didn't you scream or cry out?' 'How do you know it was him if you were so drunk?' 'Are you sure you didn't invite him into your room?'

I emailed Megan when defence got to the underpants part. It was all too exhausting. What the wedding ring was to me, the underpants were to the jury. I judged the defendant's credibility because his conduct indicated he was deceitful; those jurors probably doubted the woman's complaint because she was careless with laundry. I felt alone sitting there, unable to call out the slut-shaming inherent in the barrister's cross-examination. Megan replied to my email with sympathy and understanding, but she was in Kingaroy where things were even worse. I'd heard about Kingaroy, all the associates had.

I limped down the road for a coffee while the jurors deliberated. I'd asked the bailiff loudly and clearly to call me if there was a note.

'Of course!' he said, as though he knew what his job actually was.

I stirred my long black, waiting for it to cool, keeping my sunglasses on, mulling over the case. They had the most CCTV footage any woman could hope for: there Strow was entering and leaving her room, and she made a complaint just moments after he left, and she never changed her story. I thought it went to her credit that she was alleging one count of digital penetration—there was no witchy conspiracy. She wasn't out for some vendetta or man-hating revenge. I felt she was telling the truth, completely, and she'd flown all the way back to that wretched place to do so. There seemed to be nothing else she could have done.

But later that afternoon when I took the jury's not guilty verdict, I wasn't surprised. I couldn't be. She should have been a virgin. She should have been a born-and-raised Roma resident of many generations, like he was. She should have displayed cleanliness next to godliness. Then maybe people would have believed her.

⌢

My leg improved over the middle weekend back in Brisbane, but I felt panicked not knowing how long I wouldn't be able to exercise for while it healed. I spent some time with Vincent but struggled to feel as though I was really there with him. In the four months since starting work at the end of January it had been a-few-weeks-home, two-weeks-away, and my disgust at my body didn't help. When we went more than a week without sex, some alignment—like a level or compass in my brain—slipped a little, and I became unsure of him as well as me. I grew convinced that he didn't want to see me naked. My head was in a kind of hurricane. In my nightmares I carried suitcases full of heavy briefs until they broke my knee, the rapes toppling out everywhere onto the ground, then growing up around me, manifesting.

'Do you not want to have sex with me now that I'm fat?' I asked him eventually on the Saturday night, so quietly that he asked me to repeat myself. 'Is that why we don't have sex anymore? Because I'm big now?' We were facing each other, just resting on the bed, and I buried my head in his chest, crying before he had the chance to answer. He protested as much as any good boyfriend ought to have, and in my exhaustion I decided to just believe him for the night.

Going from Vincent's bed back to Brisbane Airport on Sunday afternoon was gruelling. Managing suitcases with a bung knee was one thing, but the real struggle was emotional. I felt as though I were a lightweight amateur among heavyweight pros. The courtroom— that ring—was work to Judge, but each blow was flooring me. So early in the year and already stumbling. How long before the black lights? I knew they were coming for me, it was just a question of when I wouldn't be able to get back up before the bell.

⌐⌐

The second trial in Roma was the ugly, embarrassing part of our time there. Embarrassing for everyone—for what it said about regional Australia, White Australia, and all of us as a society. The defendant was a young Aboriginal man. He stood tall and fit while I arraigned him for the attempted rape of a younger girl.

Three kids—the young complainant and two boys of the same age—had been playing by a riverbank when the older defendant and one of his friends joined them. It was agreed by all of them that the older boys' arrival meant they moved from playing by the river to hanging out up around a bridge.

The complainant's evidence was a tape recording, and was almost useless. She said the defendant 'hit her over the head' with a big stick and dragged her off, and for a few hours everyone in the courtroom was extremely confused, because those weren't the facts the prosecution was alleging. Then the second tape played, and we heard about how the girl watched R-rated films at home, and how she thought the defendant had taken her on a motorbike to rape her, or maybe not, and that she was passed out but not really. When the tapes ended, everyone sort of looked at each other for a little while, not knowing what to make of it all, and the prosecutor sighed audibly and made a submission that things would 'become clearer' once we'd heard the combination of the other witnesses' testimonies.

After the tea-break, the prosecutor's words came good. The three others gave similar and more realistic accounts of the events. The defendant had pressured the group to leave the water and hang out by the bridge up near the bush, and there he'd taken the complainant away from the group, laid down a towel, and tried to initiate intercourse. It seemed that none of the others were willing to be the first to call bullshit on the defendant's actions, and that it wasn't until the girl started screaming and crying out that someone stepped in.

The two young boys had guilt all over them, and reading between the lines it became clear that they had been acting sexually with the complainant before the older boys arrived. They had a language for deeds, quite casually calling oral sex 'giving a gobbie', and they carried an arrogance toward certain acts and genuine confusion toward others. This guilty feeling they shared seemed to affect their inability to just say 'no' to the defendant. The older one, the defendant's friend, wasn't much help in this either. He couldn't give a straight answer to whether or not he understood or suspected why the defendant had left with the complainant.

The trial lasted three days. There were so many tapes of the different witnesses, and they were frustrating in their evasive responses. Perhaps I was being impatient with them and it was just their youth that made the process tricky, but by that stage of the year I'd seen almost twenty trials, and that meant seeing plenty of children give evidence on tape. There seemed to me to be a difference between a child needing time to understand and try to answer a question, and what those boys were doing: giving the adults the answers they wanted without implicating themselves. Later that night, though, when I couldn't sleep, I wondered if I was losing my mind. Was I so quick to see guilt, so quick to convict, that I was projecting a maniacal misandry onto innocent kids?

The next morning Judge and I shared our thoughts on the question of the two young boys' statements.

'It seems that perhaps they were just doing some young experimentation by the water,' Judge said.

'They're too old for "experimentation"!' I objected quickly.

'That's what I mean,' he replied. 'Things clearly got out of hand when the older ones arrived.'

'Oh, right.' I nodded.

The defendant didn't give evidence and so the jury started deliberating on that third day. I looked out across the dry grass at the front of the courthouse, wondering what the area looked like before colonisation. It didn't help the defendant that the complainant was white, and with hair so blonde as to almost be light gold. Would we be in an attempted rape trial if the complainant was a little Aboriginal girl? The rape case that Megan had dealt with from Roma Street suggested not. I saw the defendant kicking dust around outside the courthouse and watched his movements, but there was nothing to read.

⌒

The jury took a few hours to do their job, and when court resumed some people were in the public seats on the defendant's side of the room. The jury had chosen an older man for their speaker—a trend I'd placed in the 'duh, men' pile of things—and he stood up straight, spoke clearly, and nodded.

'Guilty.'

Judge dismissed them, and we moved straight to sentence. A few jurors re-entered the courtroom at the back to listen, but most left. Did they leave because they didn't care, or because they were like me and cared too much?

We heard from the prosecutor that in various pre-trial interviews the defendant had completely denied he'd done anything wrong. It had implications for his sentence because his refusal to take responsibility for his actions was a strong indication that he didn't feel remorse, and therefore didn't have empathy for the victim. A psychologist asked him how he would feel if one of his mates did something like that, and he replied that he'd feel 'sick, filthy, and dirty'—but this was around the same time that he denied the acts, so the court was told that at least some parts of his responses were performative.

The prosecutor said the families of the complainant and defendant often saw each other around town, and that a feud had started when the defendant had denied the offending. It had escalated to the point where someone was nearly run over. The complainant refused to leave the house anymore because she saw him outside sometimes, and she was wetting the bed and not leaving her bedroom.

⌒

The most heartbreaking part of the sentence, though, was the defence barrister's submissions on mitigating circumstances. The court was told of the defendant's 'low intelligence' and that he had no education, let alone a sex education. I took a chance to really look into his eyes, and I wasn't sure if what was there was a dullness or just sadness, but there was a noticeable lag in his responses. When he was looking off into the distance and his name was called, it took him a moment to register the sound, glance up and find where the noise came from. His mother had been an alcoholic when he was in the womb. He wasn't working and didn't attend school, and an Aunty supported him.

In the 'careers' section of his rehabilitation potential, Judge addressed him directly. 'What do you want to do with your life?'

'I wanna play football,' he replied.

'He's looking for work but there's not a great deal of work around,' the defence barrister added.

In the end, the defendant couldn't be sentenced. Reports were required to inquire as to his mental capacity.

⌐⌐

I chatted with the registrar afterwards while I showed him the paperwork. He was a nice man. Round belly and soft face.

'Got a ticket for the lotto?' he asked me when we were just about done.

'Huh?' I thought I'd misheard him.

'It's a big one, the Powerball.'

'Oh, haha.' I started backing out of the room slowly without turning away from him. 'Nah, not much of a gambler.'

He shrugged.

'But good luck!' I smiled at him, remembering at the last moment to try to be nice.

'You know,' he added, as though it was just an afterthought, 'I think this is only about the third guilty verdict we've had in over ten years.'

I stopped in the doorway. 'Third?'

'Yep.'

'In over ten years?'

'Well, that's how long I've been here, and I'm pretty sure this is only number three,' he said matter-of-factly. 'They happen so rarely, I remember 'em.'

I rushed across the building to tell Judge, but he didn't seem to share my outrage.

'What a coincidence, that the third guilty verdict in over a decade is for an Aboriginal man!' I said.

'Mm,' he replied noncommittally.

'And that man from last week, Strow—now I look back and feel like, what was even the point of taking it to trial!? They were never going to convict him!'

'Well, it's always worth taking things to trial,' Judge replied, speaking reason.

But I didn't want reasonable: I wanted angry, I wanted affected, I wanted someone to reassure me that I wasn't just being hyper-sensitive or imagining the patterns that were emerging.

We cleared the list in Roma then flew home. I looked out over the town from the aeroplane window, the blazing sunset casting long shadows from car yards and cattle. Were the constellations truly more shocking out in such places, or did the bad deeds burn brighter simply because I couldn't see anything else in between them? Travelling up north or out west felt more like travelling back in time, but if that were true then I would have looked forward to returning to the city.

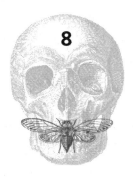

8

JEREMY PULLMAN WAS A TALL and slim man with pale grey eyes and a number three buzz cut along the sides of his skull. His dark hair was pulled into a ponytail and tied together at the base of his neck, and then plaited down until it reached his waist. The way it thinned on top made it look a little greasy, and I wondered if his solicitor had advised him to cut it off before getting in front of a jury. When he cocked his head to the right I caught a glimpse of a smudgy neck tattoo, but I couldn't make it out because his skin was that permanent red-brown indicating years of accumulated sunburns. A literal redneck. He was on trial for violent, sexual acts against his twelve-year-old stepdaughter that I wish I hadn't read so much detail about that morning. When he turned his head again and looked straight down the middle of the courtroom, right at me, I felt myself sweat. He didn't blink his pale eyes and I couldn't hold them for more than a moment; I flushed in panic and glanced away.

The twelve jurors were excitable when they came in and took their seats, but once the prosecutor finally finished his opening address a sombre reverence replaced everything else. They stopped looking around the room at the funny wigs. They stopped flipping through their complimentary notebooks and sipping their chilled glasses of water. They were still and silent.

Sophie, Pullman's stepdaughter, was young enough to be automatically allowed to give evidence via videolink. The screens around the courtroom flickered on and we saw her in a bare room, her head and shoulders just visible over the top of the adult-sized desk in front of her. I noticed Pullman's barrister becoming uncomfortable as her chair and the angle of the camera were adjusted, and she was asked to 'sit up as tall as she could!' I knew why he didn't like the fuss. We were all looking at this little girl with her blue T-shirt and her messy pigtails, a girl too small for regular furniture, wondering what kind of monster could violate her. It felt wrong that she had to defend herself in our adult world of arguments and loopholes. Pullman was looking down in his lap, seemingly calm and respectful.

The prosecutor probably appreciated the opportunity to run a trial with such a perfect complainant. I knew by then that if Sophie had been fifteen instead of twelve, they would have taken a different approach. They would have had to. It was a relief to see a jury not immediately suspicious of a complainant's testimony. Defence couldn't ask this little girl about what contraception she was on, then draw inferences to her promiscuity by reminding her that she also didn't have a boyfriend. They asked her what she was wearing to actually test her memory, not to suggest a shorter skirt had been selected to indicate willingness. She could, in no way whatsoever, have 'known what she was getting into' or 'asked for it' or 'made a drunken mistake that she regretted the next morning'.

⸝⸏

I doodled cracking skulls in my notebook while the prosecutor stepped Sophie through several separate, heinous occasions. The term 'eggshell skull' refers to the legal principle that a victim must be accepted for who they are individually, regardless of where their strengths and weaknesses place them on a spectrum of human normality. If you strike a person whose skull happens to be as thin as an eggshell, and they break their head open and die, you can't claim that they were not a 'regular' person. Full criminal liability— and responsibility—cannot be avoided because a victim is 'weak'. I had slowly grown obsessed with the concept.

In Pullman's case, he was at a disadvantage because his step-daughter was young enough to be judged as a child instead of a woman. She had been an easy target for Pullman, but in a sick way her weakness had now become her strength. The Crown would make the most of what they had by highlighting Sophie's innocence, and she was bloody adorable so it wasn't that hard. When she began crying during the third hour of the video, I looked across to the jury and saw their brows were furrowed. They were feeling sympathy, perhaps even sorrow. Women like Jessica get 'emotional' but children are allowed to cry.

When Sophie had finally finished giving evidence and Judge adjourned for the day, the jury looked exhausted.

Back in court the next morning we heard Sophie's mother— Pullman's former partner—give evidence. She was the first witness to be physically in court in front of us, and if you had just walked in you'd have been forgiven for thinking she was on trial. I saw the questions practically burning behind the eyes of the jurors. How could she let this man anywhere near her child? It emerged that she and Pullman were on ice during the relationship and that he'd supplied it to her. He was frequently physically violent to her, but she loved him and stayed.

At lunch I met up with Dad at a cafe between our two buildings.

'They just choose not to notice things if it means they're getting their drugs,' he said to me calmly with a shrug.

'What about him, though?' I struggled not to raise my voice. 'Isn't it possible that he has cultivated an abusive, drug-dependent relationship with the mother so that he can enjoy unrestricted and unquestioned access to the child?'

Dad took a sip of his flat white and smiled at me. 'That too, my dear, is very possible.'

I couldn't understand how he could seem so detached. Even if I worked in that shithole for fifty years I hoped that I would still be affected by the horror. I wanted to feel—more than that, I knew it was important to keep feeling. It would be infinitely easier to sacrifice empathy for the ability to sleep at night, but I didn't like those kinds of humans. Did that mean I didn't like my father? I was angry at how calm he seemed. I wanted to yell at him, pushing his flat white into his face, 'What if this girl was your child!?' But a question like that would be the beginning of a conversation I wasn't ready to have.

As I walked back into the huge chrome building and my eyes adjusted from the bright Queensland midday sunshine to the shady interior, I felt a tension headache forming. I had been frowning the whole day, probably also grinding my teeth. How many years had it taken my dad, or Judge, or any of the people in this building to leave work at work? What did that make them, and what did that make me?

━

Back in court Pullman's counsel announced that he was going to give evidence. I thought I'd misheard. It would be the first time I'd heard a defendant speak in his own defence since that first trial in Gladstone.

Pullman swore on the Bible to tell the whole truth and nothing but the truth. Then he told his version of events, which included a story about there being a rat under Sophie's bed, and that he'd been trying to chase and catch it in the dark with his bare hands. This was so preposterous, I found it offensive that he could think we would believe him. He offered this rat as an explanation as to why he was found in Sophie's room one night after everyone else had gone to bed. None of the other witnesses said they'd seen a rat in the house, let alone upstairs near the bedrooms, and certainly not that night.

When discussing another occasion—a car trip ostensibly to get food for the family—witnesses disagreed with Pullman about the food being cold by the time he and Sophie finally returned. He said they'd been gone only as long as it took to get dinner. 'She was always pestering me, wanting to be with me all the time and go with me everywhere, you know?' he said, shaking his head with an expression that communicated a tsk-tsk. He'd been asked why he had chosen to take only Sophie with him for the drive, and not any of the other children or his partner.

His relaxed demeanour infuriated me. He denied everything, he was saddened by the accusations, he thought it had something to do with Sophie's mother being jealous and resentful of his new relationship with a younger, more beautiful woman. He felt sorry for Sophie's mother and said he thought this trial had something to do with her, said she was 'unwell'. The subtext was clear: *Chicks, huh?*

When Pullman finished testifying the defence case was over, and we sent the jury out to their little room with tea and biscuits. I sat in my office, mindlessly pushing papers around my desk, thinking about Sophie's mother. Did Sophie resent her mother? Could any of us ever come to understand the complexity of an emotionally and physically abusive relationship? Did the drugs make things less or more understandable?

It's easy to question how a mother could ignore or not notice this type of offending, but human coping mechanisms are amazing. We find ways to keep going, our minds coursing *around* things we might not have the ability to fully comprehend or acknowledge, so that life can keep propelling us forward through time. I was able to keep my memories in a walled-up space in my brain. Sometimes they would leak out, sure, but I understood the need to shove something into the corner of the mind and board it up in order to just survive. I existed in a perpetual state of double-think, behaving as though one set of facts was true when I knew it to be false. I acted as though I couldn't feel my past rushing up behind me. I pretended I didn't have my foot on the accelerator and that the brick-wall breakdown was still far away in the distance.

⌒

The jury deliberated overnight and I liked the idea that Pullman might be sleeping badly, waking into a nightmare. I pictured his greasy head resting on a state-issued pillow, his legs tucked up against the cold and his filthy ponytail dangling off the edge of the bed. Was he one of the men who had managed to convince himself he hadn't done it, or was he reflecting on his actions? Did he realise he belonged down there? When I got in the elevator and went all the way up to the thirteenth floor, into the sky, he got in and went way, way down, underground.

There was one part of Sophie's evidence in particular that I couldn't shake from my mind. She said that when Pullman had driven her to an abandoned area and started doing the awful things, that a police car had come past. She must have felt such a flicker of hope that she was being saved, right before Pullman punched her again and forced her head and mouth down over his penis, saying he'd kill her if she made a sound. She said Pullman pretended to be on the phone and the cops drove on. Of all the disgusting things Sophie had endured, that flicker of hope being so violently extinguished saddened me the most.

My dad must have dealt with so much of this stuff, but how much had he also, unknowingly, driven straight past?

Later that afternoon, right on dusk, I was driving home from Vincent's place, and the stretches of road between Indooroopilly and Yeronga were leafy and proudly suburban. When the Brisbane River appeared before me, it reflected a bright orange and pink sky. It was odd that everything seemed as though it should be beautiful but I couldn't just say, 'This is beautiful.' As I passed an AFL oval on my right and glanced over at the children's lively bodies as they trained, I wondered how many of them had terrible secrets that they were pushing to the backs of their minds.

Then I looked back to the road and saw her, and slammed on my brakes.

The woman was screaming at something further ahead. I followed her terrified gaze and saw a huge pit bull charging toward her from the other side of the road. The woman had two dogs of her own, small white poodles, and they were yelping and tangling their leashes around her ankles. She fumbled, trying to pick them up and move, but they were pulling against their collars, choking themselves with their necks at sharp angles, trying to escape. She was only metres from me, just on the footpath, but as the pit bull grew larger and closer to their tangled panic, I froze.

The pit bull darted across the road in front of me and I saw its huge jaw open, heard a loud bark emerge through its giant teeth, and I thought I should hit it with my car. *Put your foot down!* I screamed at myself, but I was frozen.

The pit bull passed in front of my car, leaping powerfully up onto the footpath. As it closed in on the fluffy poodles and their choking diamante collars, the pit bull screeched to a halt and bowed its head, and its stubby tail began wagging furiously. The woman was reeling, yanking the leashes away from this huge thing that was now nuzzling her pristine poodles. The pit bull was so excited it let out another bark and rolled onto its back and wiggled toward the poodles again.

Another woman rushed onto the scene, apologising profusely, and in one motion she leaned down and swept the pit bull into her arms, cradling it like a baby with its belly up, and as its tail kept wagging it licked her face. 'Sorry! He's still—' the pit bull's owner was interrupted by a huge lick to her face '—a puppy!'

I drove on for a few minutes before the adrenalin subsided, then I pulled over and started crying. My face burned with the shame. After all those years I had just frozen, again. And I cried out again, thinking that if I hadn't frozen I would have hit and killed that puppy because of its breed. Because someone else was afraid of it and because I had heard stories about 'those kinds of dogs'.

I couldn't see beautiful things anymore. I couldn't do anything right. I wanted to call Vincent but I'd only just left his house and I didn't want him to think I was too much hassle. I fell asleep in the car on the side of the road and drove home in the dark when I woke up.

The twelve random adults who were responsible for deciding Pullman's fate regrouped at 9 a.m. and there was a note at 10.30 a.m. The bailiff called me and read it out: *We have reached a verdict.* I hung up the receiver and decided to put in a little prayer. Couldn't hurt. I'd gone to a Catholic high school but I couldn't remember if I was supposed to address God or Jesus when I made requests. Were they kind of the same thing? *Hey Jesus, if you're there, make sure this guy goes to gaol.* I pulled my robes on again, and thought back to Pullman's neck tattoo, realising he was probably praying to Jesus as well. We're all fools when we're desperate.

I stood in front of the silent, tense courtroom and read out the questions to take all the verdicts. *Guilty, guilty, guilty,* they said to each question, to all counts, and my hands shook as I sat back down and madly started preparing documents for the sentence.

When the jurors filed out and I'd prepared for what normally came next, I looked up and stifled a gasp, my hand flying to conceal my mouth. Pullman had changed. His whole face and his whole body looked different. Somehow his pale eyes were dead now. His fists were clenched on his thighs, the veins in his neck bulging. He had dropped his chin and he stared up at Judge from under his eyebrows, snarling. I tried not to look away from him but my body betrayed me, a surge of adrenalin making me sweat and panic again.

Pullman had spent the past three days looking like a relatively normal man but suddenly it was blindingly obvious. Of course this was a man who drove his tiny stepdaughter around to abandoned industrial areas to beat and rape her. Perhaps he now thought he no longer had anything to gain from maintaining a semblance of decency. But how had he hidden it before? How had he hidden this thing under his skin? It must have been rippling along just underneath. I fought the urge to run from him and from that whole building that was full of people like him. I needed fresh air. The robes weighed my arms down and the jabot was so tight at my neck. Both counsel had come prepared to move straight to sentencing, though, and so we did.

The first thing handed up was the defendant's criminal history. First entry: the violent rape of a woman in a public bathroom, committed when Pullman was just seventeen. The facts of the offending were precisely the scenario that runs through every woman's head when it's late at night and she needs to use a public bathroom. I looked back up at Pullman and sighed, realising I would recall the face of this monster any time I needed to pee while out at night for the rest of my life.

Some jurors had stayed for the sentence and sat just beside the dock, and I watched their faces as the prosecutor read out Pullman's previous convictions. They exchanged glances and nods, and I saw one visibly relax. *We got it right*, they were thinking.

I understand our legal system is based on the premise that you accept your punishment, serve your time, then move on with your life. I understand that the state doesn't want to institutionalise people and that we simply can't afford to lock up criminals for their whole lives. I also believe the primary function of sentencing should be deterrence, rather than punishment. But I have never believed that between Pullman's first offence at seventeen and his offending against Sophie some thirty years later, he lived an innocent life. I do not believe that he didn't commit a single other sex offence—either against the woman he was violent toward for years or another stranger. I do not believe that he won't reoffend when he is released from prison at approximately fifty-five years of age.

At the time of his trial, though, it wasn't my job to think or feel. I recorded the time stamp of his sentence beginning, and put stickers on sheets of information for the file. What I believed didn't have an effect on anyone but me; I could only absorb and react, never fix or solve or complete.

When Judge finished the sentence and the prison officers approached Pullman, I flinched when they reached out to touch him. How many people had I ever shaken hands with who were actually awful sex offenders? Then, just as he was disappearing out the courtroom door to be taken to gaol, there was a loud shuffling of feet and a flurry of action. A young woman let out a loud wail.

Pullman turned to look back at her. 'I will appeal this!' he yelled, being dragged out. 'I will be back out with you again soon, baby!'

She cried out, 'I love you!'

The door shut loudly behind him and the rest of the courtroom fell silent, all of us looking at the woman. The jurors sitting nearby stared at her with a mixture of pity and horror, their eyes wide. She hadn't been in court for the trial—I would have noticed—but she must have sat through the whole sentence. She must have heard about Pullman's previous convictions and been there when Judge summarised all the ways Pullman raped his stepdaughter, using different parts of his body in different places with varying levels of physical violence. But this woman believed he was wrongly convicted and I watched her weep in her seat, alone.

⌇

'Did you see the new girlfriend?' I asked Judge later in the elevator.

'Yes I did.'

'Yikes.'

'It's a comforting thought, isn't it, that no matter what horrible things us men do, there will always be women out there willing to love us.'

The elevator doors opened and we walked out. When he saw how low my jaw hung open, he grinned.

'No comment,' I replied. 'But I will never forget that image, of that woman having just heard not only what he did this time, but also his criminal history, and then blowing him a kiss.'

'She blew him a kiss?'

'Yeah, and then she held her hand to her heart.'

'True love, I suppose.' He smiled again, but in a sad way.

Who was I to judge true love? Is that what we mean by 'unconditional'?

I turned into my office, dumped the files on my desk and shook the mouse to wake up the computer. While I waited in front of the buzzing screen I wondered if Vincent loved me unconditionally. Not yet, but I thought we were probably pretty close. It's one of those concepts you never want to have to test. Would he love me if I had something swimming under my skin that was itchy and deadly and constantly wanting to be let out to do a horrific thing—if in a moment I could change my eyes to be dead and cold like Pullman's? What if I found out Vincent had a something under his skin? Would I still love him? Women in relationships with men all like to think that we'd leave them if they struck us, but mainly we hope we never have to test our resolve.

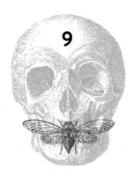

9

I DROPPED MY BAGS AND pressed the buzzer in front of the large steel gate through which I could see fancy landscaping and a lap pool. I was meeting Judge at his apartment before we headed off to Southport for circuit.

'Hello, Brianna.' Judge's voice rang out from the speaker box.

'Hi, Judge!' I said back. 'Ready for an adventure?' I imagined him smiling on the other end of the line while he described how to get to his front door.

The gate buzzed open and I grabbed my stuff and stepped over the threshold. It was an inner-city apartment complex but reminded me of a fancy hotel more than a permanent residence.

The Brisbane River is a developer's delight, twisting and turning a hundred times, offering up kilometres of riverfront homes. Until it floods. Judge's apartment was on the ground floor. Would it be rude, I wondered, to ask him if his home flooded in 2011? Was that one of the things I could reasonably ask him or was it too close to home?

'So did this place flood?' I asked. I sipped a glass of water and gazed out over the river.

'The carpark underneath the building almost did, but we're up high enough,' his wife replied.

'Even though you're the closest to the ground? Wow. I suppose the developers wouldn't bother building an apartment without a river view.'

We weren't in a rush and so the three of us stood on the balcony chatting about delightful and inane things. I liked seeing Judge's home. It was minimalist but comfortable and their love of art was clear—on display but not to be showy, only to do it justice. I asked Judge about one of the pieces and his answer turned into a small tour.

I admired Judge so much. I had met him almost at the end of his career, and I wanted to know how he'd got there. I wanted him to narrate his life to me. The snippets I knew of him seemed incongruous sometimes, and I yearned to understand how he had slowly amassed so much wisdom and calm. This was a man whom most people only ever saw sitting at the tall end of the courtroom, wearing a wig and robes, making monumental decisions about people's liberties. But I got to know the man underneath all that.

Judge was an only child born in Yeppoon, which he called 'pineapple country'. I knew he fell asleep on the train sometimes when he was young and that this was okay because he and his wife lived in a cheap, tiny house at the end of the rail line. I knew he'd worked in both prosecution and defence, and never tried any other career paths.

The looming question that could never be asked, of course, was why he and his wife didn't have children. Sometimes when he and I were exchanging life stories and getting to know each other, I felt perhaps it was an elephant in the room, but more likely I was emphasising something I was insecure about. His wife was friendly and easy to be around, and as we said goodbye to her that day and went to the car I entertained the idea of Vincent and I growing older together with just the two of us. Would he be fulfilled? One of those vases was probably the price of high school fees for one kid. I'd take the vase.

⌒

Judge and I pulled into the hotel a couple of hours later and we joked about how it was named Xanadu. I pushed the door open to my room and grinned. There was a lounge area and a dining table, a full kitchen, and a verandah facing a spectacular shoreline vista. A hallway led to a master bedroom with attached ensuite and walk-in wardrobe, and a huge king-size bed sat heart-thumpingly close to the floor-to-ceiling windows. I flopped onto my back on the bed, scooted up so my head sank into the fluffy pillows, and took off my jeans, feeling the cool white sheets against my thighs.

I found my phone and called Vincent. 'Hey, handsome boyfriend.'

'Hey, pretty lady.'

'I'm looking straight out to the ocean at sunset, lying on a big white bed, with no pants on. When do you get here?'

'Wow, yeah? The apartment is nice?'

I had only just left him back in Brisbane but I missed him already. I told him so and he told me the same back, and when we hung up I tried to be grateful for the love I'd found instead of terrified by how much power it had over me. It would be our three-year anniversary in September. I remembered how nervous I'd been to impress him when I dropped him home on our one-year anniversary. How much I'd cared. How I'd ached for constant confirmation that he loved me, but refused to ask.

'I had such a great day,' I'd said to him.

'The only thing that could top this will be our second anniversary,' he said as he kissed me goodbye, and my heart exploded.

I fell for him at first because he was more handsome than me, and I fell in love with him after about six months because he was much smarter than me. I considered him my better in every way, and every day he stayed with me was an incredible reaffirming of my worth. But any moment of doubt between us would cripple me. He could be cruelly unresponsive to text messages, often accidentally, and I would withdraw. He would cancel our plans if he was too hungover and I tried as hard as I could to give him the cold shoulder, but I found it very difficult to determine my worth independent of him. Since puberty I had accepted, as a fact of my existence, that I wasn't worth anything; that the ugly thing was ever-present inside me. That it was the dark truth, a rotten core, and that the smiling daytime Bri was the facade. It wasn't until years later that I learned that so many of the feelings I struggled with are perfectly normal for abuse and trauma survivors.

Lots of people like to go around saying that 'nobody else will love you until you love yourself', but I didn't love myself when I met Vincent, and through his love I became stronger within myself. To share your life with someone is to see the world through their eyes, and when someone loves you wholly it is almost impossible to keep hating yourself as much as I did back then.

In my office at Southport that week, I wondered if I should try to contact the magistrate I'd done some work experience with in Magistrates Court during my law degree. He'd always been approachable and generous with his time. 'Work experience' was a great look on my CV, but really I was just sitting quietly in court and then I'd get to ask him a few questions at the end of the day. I remember a thirteen-year-old defendant, appearing via videolink from a correctional facility, who knew more legal terminology than I did.

The magistrate had once had to put someone in gaol for a little while, which isn't that common in Magistrates Court, and he adjourned to consider his sentence.

'I always take a break before handing down a sentence where someone is locked away,' he said to me in his chambers later. 'It's a serious thing to remove someone's liberty, and nothing is lost by taking a tea-break for fresh air and consideration.' It's good advice— nobody ever regrets cooling their jets before making a call.

Now he was running the brand-new trial of the specialist domestic and family violence courts. This trial was one of the recommendations of Quentin Bryce's *Not Now, Not Ever: Putting an end to domestic and family violence in Queensland* report, released early in the year, and the system was supposed to have a lot of extra-specially trained support staff and service infrastructure. In urgent cases the magistrate could make same-day protection orders, and legal aid people were there for both men and women all the time. I read more about it while I was working up the courage to pick up the phone. It wasn't coincidence that the trial was taking place in Southport. Judge had told me the area was experiencing real trouble, and when I looked it up the stats showed this. The *Gold Coast Bulletin* said that drugs, alcohol, and porn were 'driving' the domestic violence crisis, and this claim angered me. Papers always point to external factors, to things that exacerbate the pre-existing problems rooted in culture and society.

'It's always seemed to me to be about control,' Judge said to me once, when we were dealing with a nasty rape case between ex-partners. 'He wants to control her and if there are children, he thinks they are his too.'

'I hate how people blame alcohol,' I said, and we agreed. It's an easy way to demonise something external to the self, instead of acknowledging that the demon of disrespect lies within the man.

I should have used the opportunity of being in Southport to hear first-hand from the magistrate about how the trial was going—if he thought the specialist courts were working, and why some areas are worse for DV than others. But I didn't. I put my hand on the receiver of the phone in my office and felt fatigued. I didn't really want to hear what he had to say. I didn't want to hear about why so many women and children were at risk in this casino-filled, palm-lined paradise. What if he said that the courts were really effective and we needed them all over Queensland? It would be productive, but also super fucking depressing. My misery quota had been overflowing maximum capacity since my first day of work: the first mention of a Hills hoist.

The work in Southport was stilted. The lawyers didn't seem to have their shit together and weren't used to a judge not letting them adjourn whenever they wanted to. It seemed to me that matters were dragging on for far too long considering that permanent judges were sitting there as well. We tried to list trials but they all fell through, so we ended up with a load of sentences.

One was particularly awful. When court commenced I saw a woman with a pram in the back of the court and immediately suspected the worst—that she was there as the new partner of a sex offender we were sentencing. She sat silently, rocking the pram occasionally to calm the quiet newborn, barely looking up. I imagined she was trying to focus on the love, on the baby, on the good.

Her partner's matter was called. Mr Lucas had pleaded guilty for dangerous operation of a motor vehicle causing grievous bodily harm, and the prosecutor launched straight into a summary of the events. Lucas had been driving for several hours straight on sparse country roads, trying to get to a different state, when he didn't notice plenty of roadworks signage. Cars in front of him were slowing down, and he slammed straight into the back of one at over a hundred kilometres per hour. The man driving the car Lucas hit was a tradesman on his way home from work. A father of three who had to have multiple surgeries on his head and brain, who now felt 'worthless' and a 'burden on his family', who would spend the rest of his life with a steel cap over his skull that brought with it some sporadic pain, a threat of infection, and many other possible complications.

Tests had found evidence of unusual levels of prescription drugs in Lucas's system at the time of the crash.

Then defence began submissions and the moral tennis really commenced.

'Your Honour, on the afternoon of the incident Mr Lucas received a phone call in which he received information indicating the name and the address of the man who had abused him, quite severely, as a child.' Lucas sat still, staring at his hands together in his lap. 'What followed,' defence continued, 'seems to indicate some kind of psychological breakdown, followed by an irresponsible intake of prescription medication, and the defendant set off on an impossibly long trip to attempt to locate his abuser with the intention of seeking some kind of revenge.'

Defence listed examples of comparable sentences that didn't include immediate imprisonment. We heard about Mr Lucas's partner and his baby, about how he was a good father and a responsible citizen, and that Judge need not consider a severe penalty for personal deterrence, because Lucas was no risk of reoffending. It's the job of a defence lawyer to make sentencing submissions that paint their client as the exception to the rule, but it felt as if Lucas truly was.

Judge adjourned for some minutes to consider his ruling while the rest of us waited quietly in court. The range for sentencing was wide, and there were a lot of competing interests. Lucas didn't seem like he needed to be punished, but I could practically hear Judge's voice in my head while he drafted, that 'consideration has to be given to the victim' who would never be the same. This grievous bodily harm was about as severe as it could possibly be, save for paraplegia or quadriplegia, and the father of three could no longer live the same way. He couldn't work to provide for his family, he couldn't enjoy sexual intercourse with his wife, and he couldn't play with his children. He used to pick them up and throw them into the pool, just like my father did with me. Post-accident this man had been showing signs of depression. When I used to volunteer with a food van for homeless people, some of them described freak accidents like this as the beginning of the end of their former lives—a slippery slope to losing everything.

Ten minutes ticked by so slowly. The two fathers' lives, and therefore the lives of their loved ones, were diametric forces. I drew concentric circles on my page like ripples, considering that the steel cap on the man's skull was, in a way, on the third ripple out, the fault of Lucas's abuser.

I thought about the ramifications of abuse and the ongoing effects of trauma. How long a secret can lie dormant before it bursts up and out, unable to be contained. A photo was circulating online, originally from ABC News, showing a class photo in which over half the children's faces were blacked out, indicating that they had died from substance abuse or suicided. They had all been 'cared for' by the same Catholic priest. I got the photo up on the court computer, and then I watched Lucas again, trying to see which parts of the two of us were similar. Scanning him for signs or scars. Markers. After the abuse, Lucas had built a beautiful life, but without the foundation of closure and justice it had all come crashing down in one afternoon.

Was dealing with my abuse really inevitable? Was there any way I could control how it came out? It didn't feel like it. Some days I fantasised about high-impact car crashes. Lucas was the first defendant I truly felt for.

'I have decided that today there will be no actual imprisonment,' Judge announced, but I don't remember what he said next because the woman with the pram started crying. She held her baby to her chest and rocked back and forth, her tears splashing onto its downy little head. Lucas turned and saw her, and when he looked back up front, over my head at Judge, I saw he was crying too. He squeezed his eyes shut, trying to stem the flow, and clasped his hands together so tight in front of him his knuckles went white. Judge addressed him on the severity of his offence, and how he was on a suspended sentence and so couldn't be arrested without going straight to gaol.

'Yes, your Honour,' Lucas said, again and again, nodding his head. 'Yes, your Honour,' his voice breaking.

When the bailiff signalled court was adjourned, I didn't follow Judge out immediately the way I was supposed to. I couldn't look away. I watched Lucas turn from the dock and stride toward his family and take them in his arms, and they all cried together. Relieved but unable to celebrate. Reunited, against the odds, but stifled by the overwhelming unhappiness of everything around them. All that awful context.

The prosecutors and duty lawyers gave them a wide berth and exited the room quickly, and I became aware of my own voyeurism. I gathered my pile of files and left the family to just be together, when it could have gone the other way. My final image of Lucas's family was them holding each other, but I couldn't picture the victim's family. How would they feel when they heard the news? It probably wouldn't be enough for them, but it never could be. At the end of our first week in Southport, the pile still heavy in my arms, I thought to myself, *This is the world you live in now: a world of awful context.*

The walk from that courtroom back to chambers took me across a kind of bridge that allowed me to look down several storeys to the courthouse foyer. I stopped to people-watch. The bridge was a telling architectural feature—nobody down below would ever have reason to look up at this particular spot, and yet I could watch them all from up high.

On the other side was a glass window, and sitting on a beam outside it was a bird's nest with two eggs inside. I looked at the eggs in awe, incredulous at how odd they seemed, so out of context next to the hard steel and glass, like a baby in a courtroom.

⌒

When Vincent arrived at the hotel on Friday evening, I got giddy and ran up to him yelling it was going to be the best weekend ever.

'Wow,' he said, dropping his bag and looking around the apartment.

'I know,' I replied, gazing out to the beach, 'but this is definitely the nicest so far.' I snorted. 'I didn't invite you to the Roma Motor Inn. Circuit isn't always paradise.'

He turned to me, taking me in his arms. 'Anywhere is paradise when I'm with you,' he said in a faux-sexy voice, and I groaned and we laughed, and he kept his arms around me, kissing my neck.

'Hey, I just have to give you a tour of the place,' I said, pulling him toward the bedroom.

'Oh yeah, what, ah, what kind of room is down here?'

We stayed hugging and waddled down the corridor together.

'I, ah, mentioned this to you on the telephone,' I said, pretending to be casual.

'Hmm, really? I don't recall.'

We bumped into the doorframe.

'Oh,' I said, dropping my arms, 'I suppose it doesn't matter then,' and went to turn around, but he grabbed me from behind and I let out a tiny squeal. He knew I loved to be chased, needed to be affirmed.

The next evening we went to see *Mad Max: Fury Road* at the cinema, and I lamented that more feminist films didn't have explosions or, rather, that more films with explosions weren't very feminist. We stopped to have beers at a German restaurant where a live band was playing what I could only guess was traditional German music, and we watched on, laughing, as drunk men got up and moved awkwardly with the professional dancer. Everyone was clapping along loudly and shouting encouragement. One guy started doing handstands on a chair in between pints, and Vincent and I cringed, the lawyers in us kicking in; we jested estimates of how much a settlement would be if he broke his neck.

It was a crisp but beautiful Saturday night, and we held hands walking along the fancy strip of shops and restaurants. I asked if Vincent wanted an ice-cream and he said 'no' so I didn't get one.

'You want an ice-cream, get an ice-cream!' he said, standing outside the shop. I hadn't told him I'd vomited up my dinners at least three times that week.

'No, I'm trying to be good.'

He gave me a look and kissed my forehead, and we walked home.

In court the next week, in one otherwise boring sentence, a man convicted of punching another man presented a certificate of appreciation for being a foster-dog carer while in prison. I was so desperate for a good news story, so genuinely surprised by the loveliness of the thought, that I was squirming in my chair with excitement and happiness. That huge, tattooed, thick-necked man in front of me had cared for a pound puppy. I madly googled the name of the program on my court computer and found a story about it in the paper where the reporter said, 'When you're walking a dog out on the oval, you could be anywhere in the would—at least for a couple of minutes.' The story was about how those tough, oftentimes brutal men used the dogs as an excuse to be gentle. The animals were a conduit for a special love and affection they weren't otherwise able to express in prison.

I finished the paperwork for the sentence and thought about prison. Dad had told me that child sex offenders got raped and beaten in prisons and often had to be sent to high-security facilities for their own protection, but that the same wasn't true for rapists of adult women or men who beat women and girls. I wondered where all those men in gaol, collectively, drew the line. How old did a woman need to be before it was okay to forcefully penetrate her? After she had 'become' a woman because she got her period—that age-old absurd marker for growth, simultaneously signifying impurity and fertility? It couldn't be. Some girls are only ten or twelve when they get their periods, and of all the offenders I'd seen so far, I couldn't imagine any of them checking if their targets had met Aunt Flo yet. No, it must be situational and societal. Maybe cultural. Definitely learned. People learn how to treat others from what they experience in their home (or lack thereof) and their schooling (or lack thereof) and society (often lacking).

I didn't think I wanted a rapist in prison to be allowed a puppy, but I also knew that rehabilitation had to come first. Repeat offending doesn't help anyone.

⌒

In another sentence, Judge and I learned about a man who'd taken a steak knife to a petrol station then a Domino's, threatening staff and demanding money—but then he used the money to buy sandwiches, lollies and a taxi home.

We heard evidence that he would have stolen barely enough money to cover the cab. It seemed he wanted to go back into custody—he'd even turned himself in—and the prosecutor said he would have been dealt with by the mental health court if he hadn't also been drunk at the time of the offending. He desperately needed support services and couldn't get them out in the real world.

'Don't worry, I'm nervous too,' he'd said to the shaking cashier.

Did that man deserve to be locked up with the rapists? Did he deserve a puppy? Was there even such a thing as 'deserving' or was that just another word we allocated to a concept to make the system seem less idiosyncratic?

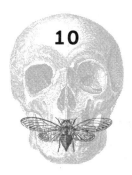

10

AFTER SOUTHPORT I MOVED OUT of home and into a Paddington share house that was about a twenty-minute walk from the Brisbane courts building. Mum kept asking me why, and the only answer I had for her was 'it's time'. I lost two kilos within a fortnight of new 'good habits' that involved walking to work, getting a long black, then not eating until dinner, and if Vincent wasn't around, vomiting that dinner back up in the bottom of the filthy share-house shower.

I didn't have any proper markers of success to cling to, and as the year crept onward—and I grew unhappier with the prospect of being a lawyer forever—I despaired at the thought of having to tell Judge what a disappointment I was. And as I thought more about telling people about my abuse, I was terrified I would never again be desirable to Vincent. I would sit on the back deck smoking a cigarette after work, and think: *At least I'm thin.*

We began a new trial that had been on the books for a little while because it required a Mandarin interpreter. It was a rape case, and when I flipped through the depositions I realised that it would be messy. Neither the complainant, nor any of the witnesses, would be testifying in English. What would normally be a three-day trial would easily blow out to double that length. The jury would grow frustrated. It would be harder than necessary for the complainant. In court when the Crown kicked things off, I knew it'd only get worse. There was a bisexual love triangle. There was alcohol involved and a question of the consciousness of the complainant. There were gossipy phone calls made and texts sent between witnesses both before and after they gave police statements on the night.

I pulled the names out of the barrel and almost snorted at one of them. The name was something like Christopher James Williams, and he was a fitter and turner from Capalaba in his fifties or sixties, white, with a beard, a slight belly, and wire-framed reading glasses. It was as though I'd drawn out the prototype juror: the 'average Australian' who supposedly most represented a 'fair cross-section' of society. He seemed calm but authoritative and I felt vindicated for my snap judgement when he emerged as the speaker for the jury a few hours later. I looked across to the rest of the jurors and examined their mostly white, mostly older faces. It would be an uphill battle. I couldn't tell just by looking at their faces which among them feared the 'Asian Invasion' enough to vote for Pauline Hanson.

Judge, in his ever-patient manner, pre-emptively warned the jury of the stilted translation they would be hearing, apologising in advance that their task was perhaps trickier than normal. He made light jokes with them and put them at ease in a way that I think gave them trust in him, and in the system.

In cases where consent was a question, Judge would often give the jury a warning that it's not a he-said versus she-said question: there is a level to which any jury needs to be convinced of the complainant's account, and that is 'beyond reasonable doubt'. But mostly, I think, Judge's warning fell on deaf ears. The jurors had seen it all on TV and at the movies; they knew the courtroom was a battleground. They wanted to hear the clashing accounts like crossing swords.

The following year I would watch Pauline Hanson get re-elected to the Senate and commiserate with my Asian and Muslim friends. We longed to know who among us—on the train, at the supermarket, in our workplaces—had cast that ugly vote.

I looked at the jurors' faces, lodging a small and silent prayer to something, I didn't know what. *Please let these twelve people not be racist or sexist.* But I looked out the window at the palm trees in Roma Street Parkland, and the constellations beyond, and was filled with dread.

That afternoon Judge sent the jury home after opening addresses and we finished a little early. A few of the associates were congregated outside the elevators, bubbling with whispered chatter. I sidled in beside Jonathon, an associate normally in Beenleigh who was smart and gentle.

'What's up?' I asked everyone.

'We're waiting for Alice's verdict to come back,' Hugh, a strapping young R.M. Williams walking billboard replied. Alice was normally in Ipswich with her judge.

'Apparently it'll be any minute now,' someone else chimed in.

I turned to Jonathon. 'What have I missed? Why do we all care about this?'

Jonathon explained to me, in a sombre tone absent from the others' excited replies, that the defendant in the rape trial was from an elite inner-city private boys' school. Vincent had gone to that same school, and he and I had gotten into disagreements previously when I mentioned the bad reputation the boys at that school have.

'Well, he's at uni now, they both are, but I think it happened in their final year of school,' Jonathon clarified.

'Holy shit,' I said.

I asked him to wait for me while I dropped my files back in my office and de-robed, feeling strangely panicked. 'What was the situation?' I asked Jonathon as we travelled down together in the elevator.

'Alcohol involved. In a bedroom. They'd been dating previously, I think, then she texted him to come over, but she said she didn't want the intercourse. Didn't realise until she went to a sex education and consent information course at uni that what had happened was rape. He gave evidence.'

'Woah!' I gasped—they never did.

'I know, and apparently he was hugely arrogant. Someone told me he was saying stuff like, "Oh I broke up with her and didn't even want her back but she kept begging me and so I went over and she totally wanted it."'

My stomach sank at the gaslighting. The arrogance of this tone tweaked a memory of a case I'd come across in research where a young man said 'we had sex', but the oral sex was only performed on him until he ejaculated, and was completely unreciprocated.

The elevator doors opened and we all fell silent, and as we filed into the courtroom I realised I was sitting diagonally in front of the complainant. It couldn't have been anyone else. She was about my age and flanked by people who could only have been her mother and father. I saw the mother holding her daughter's hand, stroking it with her thumb, like my mum did for me whenever I was sick in bed or sweating through a migraine. The father looked stony. The world told him it was his duty to protect his daughter, and yet she had been violated and was now violated again, publicly; told she was a liar. I wondered how my father would look, sitting in the back of one of the courts in this building, maybe even this one, if Samuel made me go to trial. This father shared the same jeans and buttoned shirt as mine wore, right down to the careless brown belt with black shoes. My heart ached for him and I felt a little panic, remembering that coming forward would have ramifications for the people I loved. Perhaps I couldn't put Dad through this.

'That's the defendant's family,' Jonathon whispered to me, barely audible, and gave a tiny point with his finger in his lap toward a row diagonally in front of us to the right, on the other side.

It was a row of several young men, all tall and square-shouldered, that ended with an older man and woman. The boys sat fidgeting, restless, jiggling with their legs spread wide over the sides of their chairs. The defendant was brought back in and looked over to them and nodded, firm, defiant, and the row nodded back at him. Those boys were the same, just like she and I were the same. Those boys feared being accused. Most of us have had sex while drunk; *who's to say*, I could imagine them thinking, *a girl doesn't just change her mind the next morning when she feels guilty? This one did, but she waited over a year!*

I didn't hate them, but I loved her. I loved her for the same reason Australians love underdogs. I loved her because after growing up in Brisbane—with all the bullshit we hear and see and experience every single fucking day—to accuse a boy like this of rape was a gargantuan act of bravery.

A memory came back to me at that moment, while we were all sitting quietly waiting for the judge to arrive. I saw it with absolute clarity. I remembered being at a high school dance, and passing a girl and boy dancing close, and noticing she was crying. Kathy was a popular girl, and I wasn't popular, and the boy was a football player I sort of recognised. I told the friends I had been with that I would meet them outside in a minute.

I found the crying girl's group of popular friends and walked over to them, nervous. They looked like models with their straight hair, perfect skin and expensive jeans, and I was frightened of them. One saw me approaching and eyed me, sceptical as to why I might be crossing this normally sacred social divide.

'Hey, I just saw Kathy dancing with a boy, crying,' I said to none of them in particular, 'maybe someone should go check on her?'

I thought that this would be all I needed to do, but as I turned away the dynamic of the group shifted. Nobody answered and nobody looked at me. I stayed, turning back, uneasy.

'Do you know she's crying?' I asked again, confused. Again, no reply.

'Al is being a dickhead,' Lillie finally replied.

'Okay, but she's alright, though?'

A pause around the group again. I looked to Lillie and just stared at her, waiting.

'We think maybe he's doing stuff she doesn't wanna do,' Lillie said, quieter this time.

'Shit,' I said. 'Is someone gonna go get her?'

Lillie looked to Caroline, who looked to Mel, but nobody answered my question, nobody volunteered.

I was still confused. 'Do you want me to go get her?' I offered lightly, confused, and they leapt on me.

'Yes!' they all replied, one even touching my arm as if to thank me, and many started talking at once about how 'gross' the boy was.

I went back into the crowded dancefloor where Al had taken Kathy, where you couldn't see for the wall of sweaty bodies, and I tapped on his shoulder. My interruption was met with a mixture of surprise and disdain.

I shouted over the music, 'I need to talk to Kathy for a minute,' and in the moment of confusion I grabbed her hand from his shoulder and led her away. She followed, obediently and without question, and only now do I recognise her glassy eyes as The Freeze. I deposited her back with her friends and she still seemed in shock.

'No worries,' I said, shrugging off their thanks, and left, not wanting people to think I had been trying to hang out with them.

Later, at the end of the night when we were all waiting for our mums and dads to pick us up, Lillie came and found me. 'Thank you,' she said. 'What you did was really brave.'

⌒

'And do you find the defendant guilty or not guilty of rape?' the associate's—Alice's—voice boomed out into the still air.

'Not guilty,' the speaker replied.

Behind me the girl let out a guttural noise. An injured cry that came from somewhere deep inside her. In front of me the young men clapped and shouted; one triumphantly punched a fist into the air. It was a confusing, contradictory surround-sound experience. The defendant turned and flashed his supporters a huge, sparkling smile. He didn't see the young woman fall as she stepped from her chair, wailing. He didn't see the father carry his daughter from the room, her mother holding the door open for them, watching her child crushed, the despair gushing from them all in clumsy waves before the doors shut behind them. I took it as a warning sign. Perhaps bravery wasn't enough.

⌒

As I rode with the associates back in the elevator to our level, their chatter followed a predictable narrative. He certainly seemed like a dickhead, but being a dickhead doesn't make you a rapist, but she couldn't prove it anyway, and she waited too long, and besides, who feels drunk after two beers?

I listened. If the complainant's story was true, I didn't know how she could have possibly proved it; there weren't cameras in her home. And if it was true, the same thing that made him feel entitled to her body, that same invisible pressure, is what stopped her from coming forward earlier. The odds were stacked against her from the beginning.

'Imagine if that consent class had been taught earlier, while they were in high school, before this happened,' I mused aloud. 'Maybe it wouldn't have happened?'

But most of the associates were peeling off, already chatting about weekend plans.

'I think I get too worked up about this stuff,' I turned and said to Jonathon, once all the others had gone. His temporary office in Brisbane was near mine.

'Oh yeah?'

'I dunno. I get too into it. I care. I think about things being unfair.'

'Ah, but it's not about fairness.' He gave a sympathetic smile.

'I know, I know. It just pisses me off, you know? Seeing the same bullshit everyday, all the worst stuff.'

'You get a lot of the sex crime?'

'Yeah, and the kid stuff. Don't you? Or does your judge do civil?'

'Nah, we do a mix,' he shrugged lightly, 'but I've only been in a couple of nasty ones this year.' He paused before adding, 'But it also doesn't get to me, not like what you're saying. It's the law. I feel like we're helping people deal with that bad stuff. I'd care if I saw people misusing the law, or something, in a way that was unfair, but it's what we do. We provide the legal system.'

'But what if the legal system *is* unfair?' I looked into his eyes, searching through the thick lenses of his glasses to see if he understood. That he might hear my question was a plead. But I felt silly, as though my frizzy red hair was a tinfoil hat. 'Argh, I guess that's above our pay grade,' I smiled and shrugged, 'see you tomorrow.'

⌒

The next morning I ran into Megan at the coffee cart, and a touch of happiness returned to me. I'd had too many cigarettes then horrific nightmares the evening before, unable to shake the image of that girl's father carrying her from the courtroom. My stomach churned with a pre-emptive guilt as I looked up at the courts building, thinking of how selfish I'd have to be, to drag my parents through it all. But Megan made me happy. She was a jet of air-conditioning on a muggy Queensland afternoon. We shared outrage and disgust, but most of all we often shared confusion. Some things we saw, some of the horrific things people did, we would never be able to understand. Sometimes it's important to hear your friend say that: *I don't understand.* And sometimes it's important to hear your friend say fun stuff. I wolf-whistled as I approached the coffee cart, Megan's back to me. She whipped around and I gave her a dramatic wink, and she responded by overzealously flipping her hair.

'Ready for another day in paradise?' I said confidently.

'Oh, can't get enough of it!' she shot back. I placed my coffee order and stepped away from the cart to stand with her, the two of us teetering on our heels between the pavers.

'Your trial finished?' I asked. Most sex trials took three days, so a Thursday often meant a jury was out, or there was a new list of work to be done.

'Yeah, he got guilty but I think he'll appeal,' she replied, annoyed, 'and now we've got a big child exploitation material sentence this morning.'

'Jesus, you guys just can't catch a break, can you?'

She rolled her eyes.

'So you've got Commonwealth DPP rocking up?' I asked. Child exploitation material (CEM) was dealt with under federal laws, not by the normal state prosecutors.

'Yep.'

'And the envelope shit?' I asked.

'Yep.'

'I fucking hate those envelopes, hey.'

'Yep.'

'Have you ever seen the stuff?' I asked, genuinely curious. At every CEM sentence the prosecution would tender an example of the defendant's cache. The images were classified on different levels of heinousness—bondage and bestiality being some of the worst—and also for the levels of penetration and violence.

'No, my judge barely even looks at it, and then he puts it in the envelope and seals it before handing it to me,' she replied.

'Yeah same,' I said. 'It's always a relief.'

'Yeah, and my judge has kids that age, you know?' Her voice getting sharp, defensive. 'I can't imagine how he feels, seeing that stuff then going home to them. Anyways, let's talk about something else. Did you hear what happened to Lizzie yesterday?' Megan asked this after checking nobody was in earshot while we waited at the lights near Roma Street Parkland.

'No?' This was gonna be some good gossip.

'Lizzie wore a skirt to work that came just above her knees, like, totally a normal and okay length, and her judge said she was unprofessional, and made Lizzie go to the city to buy stockings or a new pair of pants.'

'Oh my god!' I mouthed, my jaw wide open in outrage.

'Yeah, then her judge was gone by the time she got back from the city anyway.'

I groaned. 'How's Lizzie holding up?'

'Not good. She was in my office crying again yesterday after I got back from court.'

'Ugh, you have more patience than I do.' I shook my head. The green man flashed and we crossed the road. 'This job is so shitty sometimes. I can't imagine how awful it'd be if I felt like I couldn't talk to Judge, or that we didn't really get along.'

'I know, let alone if he bullied me,' Megan added, 'and Lizzie tried to go to HR but they said there's nothing they can do. She either stays or quits.'

'Fuck!' I said, too loudly, as we swiped our security passes and approached the elevators. 'But if she quits it'll ruin her career.' I was whispering now, people all around us. Megan nodded and we rode up the elevator in silence, with other staff and the public around us. Right before we split, me to level thirteen and her to level fourteen, Megan added, 'At least her judge is barely ever here,' and we exchanged cynical smiles and parted.

⌁

True to Judge's pre-emptive apology, the trial in Mandarin was slow agony. All the women had different gripes with each other, and it seemed as though they'd all dated each other at some point. Photos from the crime scene showed blood all over the defendant's penis, and quite a lot of blood around the bathroom, but defence brought in an expert doctor to say that an erect penis can bleed out quite a lot from a tiny, otherwise insignificant cut. Defence was full of objections to the jury seeing too much of the blood, or being directed to consider it important.

The translator, to her credit, was phenomenal. She was fast and specific, and rarely needed the breaks Judge offered her. It was Thursday afternoon when all the evidence finished, and the jury began deliberating on the Friday.

'I wonder what difference it makes,' I asked Judge back in chambers that day, 'if they go deliberating over the weekend?'

'Oh, not much, I think. People have other things to do. I suspect they just get on with their lives like we all do.'

I wasn't sure I agreed. Those jurors would walk to the train station and see schoolgirls yelled at on the street. They'd return to homes where women did most of the cooking and cleaning. Maybe their kids complained about Asians at school 'getting all the good grades'. Their teenage sons were called 'fags' if they couldn't 'pull'. Maybe the male jurors got massages by Filipino women, and their mates made loud jokes about 'happy endings'. They'd see barely any women in parliament, and Pauline Hanson running for re-election as one of the most visible women in politics. Many of the jurors would have seen or heard their mothers slapped or hit by their fathers. In Australia it was impossible for a man to rape his wife right up until the 1980s—until then he was perpetually entitled to her body. What a world of information the jurors have absorbed! Anything could happen in forty-eight hours.

But Judge was right, and I went on with my life over the weekend too. I had drinks on Friday night, I spent the weekend with Vincent and we had a beautiful lunch with his family, I bought some new clothes, I was happy. It wasn't until Sunday evening, when I prepared my outfit for work, that I remembered I'd be returning to take that verdict. I went outside to have a cigarette and looked out over the rooftops of Paddington, feeling guilty for not caring enough. Worrying that I was hardening like I'd sworn I wouldn't.

Monday morning began like it always did: Judge and I worked on things in our respective rooms, waiting for the phone call to say the jury had reached a verdict. It came after less than two hours, and we pulled on our robes and went down in the elevator together. I stood to take the verdict—not guilty—then tried not to think about the complainant, but as always I pictured her receiving the news. I wanted to try to feel that disappointment, to test if I was ready for it myself.

I finished up the paperwork and returned the file to the registry. The listings staff were glad to know we were available to start another trial the very next day, so I spent a few hours madly rushing around, gathering the depositions for Judge to read and prepare for. There was just such a backlog; always more trials waiting to go. A never-ending tide of them, wave after wave, and only a tiny fraction of women ever complained, and only a tiny fraction of them ever even got a court date listed.

The new case was another sexual assault, but this time with the added element of deprivation of liberty. I had to go down to the filing room underground to pick it up straight from the source, whereas normally it would have been deposited into Judge's pigeonhole for us. While I waited for the single folder I needed to be retrieved, I looked around at the rows and rows of filing shelves. People had to be trained to know how to store and find them because there were so many. The room was clean and cold, over-lit by fluorescent tubes, like a strangely silent hospital. I looked down at the carpet and imagined who might be in the cell right under my feet, remembering the tour I'd taken earlier in the year. If I'd been alone I might have got down onto my hands and knees and pressed my ear against the ground. Would I have heard a cough? A call of anger, or a call for help? Would it be a woman or a man? And how was this human different from me? How would my file look different from any of these thousands of files? It wouldn't.

'Here you go!' the young clerk said to me, passing me the folder I was waiting for. 'Sorry it took a while, there are a lot of people with that same last name.'

⌒

I never found out what the deprivation of liberty charge was all about. When I was preparing court the following morning, the prosecutor rushed up to me—it was Eric from Gladstone, saying they'd hit a snag.

'It seems like we don't have our main witness,' he told me, and I waited for defence to mosey over before I said anything.

'Do you mean late or not at all?' I asked.

'That's what we're trying to figure out at the moment,' he replied. 'We definitely can't start at ten, but it's a medical situation, so we're trying to get in touch with her now and find out if this whole week is out or what.'

'I'll go tell his Honour, but I suspect he might want to come down at ten and have it on the record, what's going on.' I gave both men a nod and went upstairs to relay the news. Judge was frustrated. We'd both been back late the day before to prepare for something that might not eventuate.

'So what's going on, gentlemen?' Judge asked once the session in court began. Both counsel were on their feet and I enjoyed how frank the atmosphere was when only the professionals were in the room. It was less guarded, less pedantic, more conversational, and made me want to belong to the profession—to a group of important people with important jobs who respected each other.

Eric explained. 'My instructor has just been on the phone to our key witness, your Honour, the sister of the complainant, and it appears that she has been extremely carsick on the drive here from Sandgate.'

'Carsick?' Judge queried. It wasn't a strong excuse. To be called as a witness was a serious request: the woman could be in contempt of court if it was found she didn't do everything within her power to testify.

'It seems that the young woman has only, just this morning, discovered that she is pregnant,' Eric paused, looking at some notes, 'and that the carsickness is exacerbated by morning sickness. She is unable to travel more than ten minutes without needing to stop and, ah, be sick, and it's over an hour and a half to drive from where she resides.'

'And the Crown cannot proceed without this witness today?' Judge asked. 'We can't just start today and get her in tomorrow? We have a group of sixty people waiting to know if they're jurors or not.'

'I understand, your Honour,' Eric replied. 'But there is a chance she won't be able to make the drive even tomorrow.'

'Well, what does "a chance" mean? And is this information coming from a doctor or is it self-reported? People need medical papers to be excused from court.'

'Yes, sorry your Honour, perhaps if I could request a short adjournment and make some more calls, I might be in a better position to advise.'

'Very well, we will wait outside,' Judge said curtly and we all stood.

In the antechamber—small, glass areas between the courtrooms and judges' elevators—Judge took a seat and gazed out at the view of the city and river.

'Gosh, that witness is only nineteen,' I squeezed my hands together in front of me, 'and she has just found out, by surprise, that she's pregnant. I'm twenty-three, and I can't imagine what it would feel like to be surprised with a pregnancy. And then to have people calling you trying to make you travel to sit in a rape trial.'

I paused, but there was no reply. I could only hope he understood my subtext: that three men were trying to decide the validity of a very young, newly pregnant woman's experience.

When court resumed, the prosecutor brought his anxious irritation back in with him, but I thought I detected a shift in Judge. Perhaps a tiny softening. The trial was adjourned for several weeks, the jurors dismissed. The Crown was instructed to liaise with the witness, and to bring the matter back when she was feeling well enough.

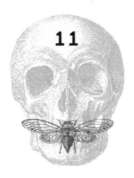

11

THE DRIVE FROM BRISBANE TO Warwick takes about two hours and can be quite beautiful if you don't spend the entire journey panicking that you are going to crash an important man's expensive car. As you leave Aratula and come over one particular rise, a huge valley of farmland opens up to make a beautiful landscape bordered by the mountains that form Cunninghams Gap. Some patches of land are grey and brown, scrubby and dry from cattle grazing. Others are rich green crops constantly being watered by huge paddock-spanning sprinklers, while other patches still are bright green and seem impossibly smooth. Fluffy white sheep make spots and streaks across the fields like a reflection of the clouds against the bright blue sky. I noticed a small sign nailed to a tree on the side of the road that said something about Jesus Christ saving us all because the end was near. I wanted to point it out to Judge and laugh about it together, but soon enough we got to the entrance to Warwick and saw a massive billboard with a Bible quote on it. *Proverbs 13:10 Pride only breeds quarrels but wisdom is found in those who take advice.*

'Woah,' I said, but Judge seemed unperturbed. He'd been to Warwick on circuit the year before; nothing that happened there would be new or shocking for him.

When we finally reached our motel and stepped out of the car, a storm was brewing overhead. There was a mixture of moisture, electricity, cicadas and manure on the air, and it would have been exciting if I wasn't so exhausted and cold. I had a piece of assessment for PLT scheduled for that night—it had to be done via video conference so I could pretend to take someone's instructions for a will—and as I finally brushed my teeth before bed at midnight, the water was so cold it hurt my teeth and gums.

'Aren't some of your folks from Warwick?' Judge asked me on the way to the courthouse the next morning as we joked about the rest of the town. I'd told him some time ago that an uncle of mine used to run a sheep station out that way.

'Yeah,' I said, not bothering to indicate as I exited a roundabout, 'but my mum and dad aren't cousins, so it doesn't feel like home, you know?'

'That's a bit harsh!' he replied, but laughing.

There was something really special about the courtroom in Warwick. It was the only room in the courthouse building with heating and as it hadn't been open to fresh air for such a long time, its smell of leather and books was overwhelming. Stepping inside from a morning too cold for me to smell anything, a cold that stung the inside of my nose, into that quiet, reverent place, and setting up for the day's work ahead, felt nice. Wigs sat on each end of the bar table like sleeping pets, waiting patiently for their masters' return. Light refracted through the glass of the dock box, turning it into a thing of beauty rather than a cage for beasts. Some buildings and rooms feel empty without people inside them, but an old courtroom is different. Being there is like holding an ancient coin. Too many things have been absorbed over time—too much human contact for it to just disappear when the people leave.

By nine-thirty we were elbows-deep in files and I was feeling significantly less philosophical. There was a double-header sentence for a mother and stepfather being cruel to their daughter. The girl had dermatitis so her hands were dry and split, and the two adults had rubbed chillies all over them. They'd also made her eat the chillies, shoved them up her nose, then made her eat even more, threatening that they'd 'shove it down her throat' if she didn't. The mother and stepfather would stand in front of her taking turns to hit her hands with a wooden spoon, and sometimes they would make her brother hit her because they were too tired to do it themselves. Her mother had stabbed her once—a small wound that didn't require stitches—and her stepdad had pinned her to the ground and hit her, whacked her with a wooden rod, and put pressure on her throat so she couldn't breathe and covered her mouth. I looked over at his very large body and imagined his weight on top of me and those hands on my mouth.

The worst thing about sentences was always when the prosecutor went through three or four cases of similar offences, in order to make recommendations for comparable terms. Not only did I have to sit through hearing about four other times people had done horrible things, but it was also a reminder that people did that shit all the time, and that the people in front of me weren't unique. They didn't exist in unfortunate isolation; they weren't special, just results of our system and our society.

The mother and stepfather's acts were categorised as 'excessive measures in discipline', and this infuriated me. It was impossible for me to understand how the court didn't treat their actions as serious assaults. The stepfather pinning her down and smothering her, in particular, was deeply troubling. Quentin Bryce's report *Not Now, Not Ever: Putting an end to domestic and family violence in Queensland* had made 140 recommendations for how to address the ongoing crisis. One of those proposals was for strangulation to be a specific offence because research shows that as acts of intimate partner violence escalate, strangulation is often the penultimate violent act before homicide. As it is impossible to prove intent to kill by strangulation, defendants couldn't be charged with attempted murder, and as there was often no lasting damage, the action couldn't even be classified as grievous bodily harm; the result was that a man could strangle a woman in her own home, release his grip after she lost consciousness, right before he killed her, and get charged with common assault, if anything. If this stepfather and I walked outside and he did the same thing to me, his sentence would be significantly more serious, but because the child was under their care—their 'dominion'—the offending was categorised differently. It's odd that our standards for a parent caring for a child are so much lower than our expectations for gentleness and respect from a stranger. One would think it should be the opposite, that to have and raise a child comes with obligations to care for that child.

Was there anything sexual about this stepfather's abuse? Perhaps the girl was too embarrassed or ashamed to talk about it, and hoped that by reporting the physical violence the sexual violence would stop as well.

'The sentencing range seems to be very broad indeed,' Judge said. There were court of appeal decisions where the primary judge only imposed community service. Surely such decisions were based on lingering attitudes from when society thought the law had no place interfering with how a man controlled his household?

The Department of Communities wasn't doing anything further about the family because the other six children were reportedly fine. Defence counsel said it was just that one daughter who was 'in need of discipline' and that the other siblings were supporting their mother and stepfather in court.

The mother cried while Judge addressed her in his sentence, but they walked out of court with no real gaol time. Not even close to real gaol time. They'd all go back to the same house. Would anything change? It felt absurd.

⌒

My dad arrived in Warwick to visit his mum, my nanna, with me on the Thursday of that first week. She had moved from her big old house into the local nursing home the year before. I organised for Judge, Dad and me to go to the Horse & Jockey for a steak together afterwards.

Nanna seemed overly pleased to have 'another lawyer in the family' and asked me to explain each piece of jewellery I was wearing. The last time I had been at her house, she'd said to me as I went in to kiss her goodnight, 'You know, dear, you are *almost* as pretty when you don't wear any makeup.' While I spoke to her that afternoon in the nursing home, she seemed to float in and out of herself. The dementia was gradual. She didn't get alarmed or confused while we were chatting, but it was sometimes as if her eyes, as a lens to her mind, were struggling to maintain focus. Specific memories would be sharp, but then whole passages of time would be fuzzy.

'She seems to be doing okay!' I said to Dad as we drove from the nursing home over to dinner.

'She has good days and bad days,' he replied.

'Does she like it there?'

'Last week she phoned me and complained that the young nurse allocated to her was being extremely rude considering she *owned the place.*'

'What!?'

'I said to her, "Louise, you do not own that place and you are not the boss of those people, and you'd better start being nicer to them all,"' I laughed and Dad continued, 'and she said *oh!* as though she was so surprised.'

'Classic Nanna.'

That afternoon would be the last time I ever had a conversation with her. I thought about her for a while after that visit, in a mostly self-centred way, wondering what would constitute my life's meaning and identity if I grew old and didn't have children. Nanna had lost the ability to define her days by the capabilities of her mind, but she had four sons, each with multiple grandchildren, who had her to credit for their existence.

I still longed to ask Judge about why he didn't have children, but I knew I never could. He had spent his life devoted to his career and had a brilliant mind and temperament as a result. I wanted to hear what he thought about ageing without having had children. I needed a role model for it.

Dad and I pulled into the carpark for the Horse & Jockey. It wasn't a pub but it definitely wasn't really a restaurant; it was something in between with tons of Keno forms and a drive-through bottle-o attached.

I was nervous for the two men to get along and I was nervous for myself. My real dad was meeting my work dad, or something like that. My dad had only ever really dealt with magistrates, not judges, and I didn't want him to feel as if somehow his and Judge's careers were being compared. I felt protective of Dad, but I also didn't want him to share some of his more far-reaching ideas for how he thought the justice system could improve.

It all turned out fine, though, because I broke the ice by spilling an entire gravy boat of diane sauce on myself. Even as the event unfolded in slow motion and I saw my beautiful blue velvet dress being ruined, I was mostly just relieved it didn't spill anywhere near Judge. I remembered in my training for the job my prede-cessor, Rebecca, telling me she'd 'take a bullet' for Judge. I laughed

internally, thinking I'd tell my replacement quite sincerely that I'd
'take a gravy boat' for him.

When dinner finished I was sad to see Dad get in his ute to go
back to Brisbane, and I felt an ache of homesickness. I waved goodbye,
watching his lights fade down the road and around the corner.

⌐⌐

We started the trial against Mr Delaware on the Monday. I hadn't
noted anything remarkable about it at the callovers we'd held in
preparation: it was another historical child sex offence case and
the defendant had been 'Mum's new boyfriend'. The most unusual
thing about it seemed to be that it had a one- to two-day estimate,
rather than the normal two- to three-day estimate.

'There will be no witnesses called, other than the complainant,'
the prosecutor told Judge.

I paused and looked back through the depositions, and realised
that it was true. It was also then that I noticed the complainant's
name—George. How had I missed that? For the first time all year,
I'd see a sex offence trial with a male complainant. I looked over
to the defendant sitting in the dock. He was old, with a greyish
beard and a walking stick.

'Mr Delaware absolutely denies the offending,' his barrister said.
Of course he does.

The prosecutor's opening address was straightforward. Aside
from George being a fifteen-year-old at the time of the offending,
everything else was standard. George's mother's new boyfriend,
Delaware, had started with small, inappropriate moves and touches
toward George. Fleeting interactions that could be brushed off
gradually developed into more bold and invasive acts over a series
of months. George tried to tell his mother, but his complaint didn't
come out right, and it was dismissed. Delaware's assaults grew more

intense until one truly awful night, and then George ran away from home at sixteen.

Delaware wasn't the most composed defendant. He huffed and shook his head as the prosecutor stepped through each allegation. Once I even thought I saw him stamp his cane.

George was in his forties. He wore a flannel shirt, thick blue farmer's jeans, and polished brown boots. His hair was combed and held in place with just a touch of gel, and he was clean-shaven. The image he presented was one of a perfectly standard, white Australian middle-aged man being told to dress 'smart-casual'. He seemed a touch nervous but was simple and clear when answering the prosecutor's questions. The story felt real. George spoke about shrugging off the first few incidents, but then after some time Delaware would insist on watching him shower or showering with him. He wrung his hands a little when relaying the fight he'd had with his mother about Delaware being in the house.

'And did you tell your mother about Delaware's behaviour?' the prosecutor asked.

'No.'

'And did Delaware leave the house?'

'No.'

'And the offending then continued?'

George pinched his nose and rubbed his eyes hard. 'Yes.'

George had tried to ask his mother to kick out Delaware without explaining why, just like I'd tried to complain about Samuel to my mother so many times in different ways. It was easy to feel angry at George's mum, but I suspected that employment prospects for a single mother in Warwick in the 1980s were slim, and no mention was made of George's biological father. Had Delaware, like Reester, offered financial stability? Had he been emotionally manipulative or physically abusive like Pullman? It didn't matter.

George's mum didn't act, didn't listen to her son enough to read between the lines, wasn't willing to open her eyes, to peel back the double-think.

'Would you like to take a break before cross-examination?' Judge asked George. He looked a bit ragged, his eyes a little red, his shoulders slumped.

'No thank you, your Honour, I'd like to get it done.'

'Very well,' Judge said, and nodded at the defence barrister, who then stood up.

The cross-examination was short but it also looked and felt completely different to the normal adversarial display. The barrister was, as usual, a man, but he had a more casual, respectful tone and approach to the questions than all the others I'd seen. My notes describe it as 'gentlemanly'. I thought perhaps that cross-examination was what the court process looked like when counsel were actually all trying to get to the truth, rather than to get their client acquitted.

'And why didn't you tell anyone about Delaware's alleged behaviour?' the barrister asked.

'Nobody talked about this stuff,' George said, 'especially not men. People didn't even talk about being gay, and what he was doing was gay, and I was afraid people would think I was gay, or that he would make me gay. I don't know. When you're fifteen you're not thinking straight. I just ran.'

'No further questions, your Honour,' the barrister announced shortly after, and then we heard that Delaware wouldn't be taking the stand to give or call evidence, and so that same afternoon we sent the jury out to deliberate.

'This will be our shortest ever,' I said to Judge back in chambers.

'Yes,' he replied, interested. 'What do you think?'

'Oh, you know me,' I said, waving a hand in front of my face, 'I think they're all guilty.'

After about three hours the bailiff found me, and we all went back in. I watched George in the seat at the back of the courtroom with his wife.

'And do you find the defendant guilty or not guilty?' I asked the speaker.

'Guilty.'

In my peripheral vision I saw George hang his head. His wife squeezed his hand then leaned over to kiss his cheek, looking upward to keep her mascara from running, dabbing a tissue under her eyes. He rested his head on her shoulder, and she put her chin against his forehead, holding his cheek with her other hand.

When I sat down, having taken all four verdicts for each offence, Judge announced that we'd move straight to sentence. The prosecutor advised the court that George had prepared a victim impact statement, and that he would read it aloud himself. I stopped what I was doing and looked up, confused. Victims were entitled to write and present statements to the sentencing judge. There were fuzzy rules about how victim impact statements weren't supposed to affect sentencing too severely, but the statements were widely agreed upon to be an important opportunity for the victim to feel that their voice and perspective were being heard in their otherwise powerless situation within the system. The thing was, complainants normally typed the statements up and tendered them as documents. We had always just paused during sentencing proceedings to allow Judge time to read a victim impact statement, and then counsel would continue with their submissions as to comparable sentences. So while I'd read a few, I'd never heard any out loud.

George returned to the witness box and held a single A4 page, folded in half, and I saw it shaking. He remained standing and started to read, slowly and clearly. He began with a little bit about how happy and normal his life had been, then spoke of how confused and sad he'd become when Delaware started molesting him, and the struggles he'd faced having moved away from home so young. It had been difficult for him to get a decent job so he'd moved from town to town, leaving friends and security behind, falling in with 'rough crowds'. As he aged and started relationships with women he struggled with intimacy and expressing his sexuality, second-guessing his feelings and pushing away people who cared about him.

When George said that he blamed Delaware for ruining his relationship with his mother, the piece of paper trembled more, and George's voice broke. 'I don't see her or talk to her anymore,' he said, wiping tears off his face, 'and I miss her.'

He took a deep breath and stepped his hands down the page for the final section: having to deal with what had happened. He accused Delaware of dragging out the court process and refusing to acknowledge or take responsibility for his actions.

'I'm just so grateful to be able to put this behind me now. I have a loving and supportive family, and now I have closure. I ran from this for years, but now I can finally move on from my past properly.' George folded the paper back in half, thanked Judge for his time, and walked toward his wife, and when he reached her he fell into her arms, crying, and they cried together, rocking a little, while the sentence proceeded.

I felt the shift immediately. The realisation was a physical sensation, at first an optimism and wonder, a pure hopefulness, like new breath in my chest, and then it quickly grew hard and firm into resolve, dropping into my stomach. I watched George cry—a manifestation of absolute relief—and I knew that was what I wanted. I longed for those tears, I was sure I would know how they felt, I could imagine them for myself. He had spoken about carrying the burden of his abuse for years unnecessarily, and how afraid and full of shame he had felt to tell people about it, but he'd said it was all 'worth it' now it was done. His wife was there with him, she didn't flinch or pull away from him; she moved toward him, held him, cried with him. They did it together. George had nothing but his own memories, and he had taken his abuser to court, and he had won justice. For thirty years he'd carried it around, and in one day, that single Monday, he'd finished it properly. It was over. He would walk out of court and into the rest of his life. He'd used the word 'lighter'. I wanted 'lighter'. I wanted to be able to let it go, to move on.

I stopped documenting the sentence and started scribbling in my personal notebook fast. I would tell Vincent about Samuel, and I would tell my parents about Samuel, and then I would tell the police about Samuel. I would take him to court if necessary. I would make a statement and I would risk a trial for the chance to feel what George was feeling right there in front of me. Finally I knew what the brightness at the end of the tunnel might look like, and I would do whatever it took to make it out the other side.

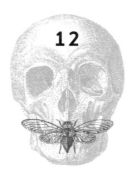

12

BACK IN BRISBANE THE FOLLOWING week, I rode the elevator down to the courtroom alone. I couldn't stop thinking about George and his 'lightness'. It wasn't a coincidence that the only trial I'd seen without a single bit of corroborating evidence, from over three decades ago, had a male complainant, and the defendant got a guilty verdict. By hours and minutes it was the shortest trial we would do all year. With hindsight, I genuinely believe that a woman saying the exact same words might not have been able to secure a conviction. The police and DPP might not have even proceeded with her allegations. After all, why would a man lie about something like that? What did he have to gain? But a woman, well, you never know what they're up to.

The elevator opened and I stepped out, and as I rounded the corner the waiting space outside the courtrooms opened up in front of me, crowded with people. Some were in robes, many were managing trolleys and boxes of folders. They were all chatting loudly in groups or yelling into mobile phones. My heels clipped the floor as I crossed the space, and one by one the figures turned toward me and fell silent. I spotted two silks holding their wigs in their hands who had been whispering but now stood still. I was easily the youngest present, but nobody kicks one of the Queen's corgis. I walked with the adopted weight and respect of my judge, and it felt good. I had significance. People listened when I spoke; I wasn't interrupted or doubted, because the words were his.

That morning I realised how much I would miss those robes. How I would spend the rest of my life fighting for the respect people showed me when I wore them. It was like a superpower—a rich old white man suit that gave me the superpower of privilege.

⟋⟍

I thought a lot about clothes in court, and about grooming and presentation, and how much we underestimate our own biases. It's about money and priorities and the way we were raised—all the kinds of things that get magnified in court. When people wake up and get dressed on their regular Tuesday mornings, they don't usually think they'll have to identify themselves repeatedly in CCTV footage years later, or justify their sartorial decisions to a room of strangers searching desperately for meaning. Solicitors try to dress their clients for court because they understand that juries look for shortcuts to categorise and judge both the complainant and defendant. A grey hoodie pulled over a buzz cut has meaning. Smart black slacks and comfortable old ballet flats have meaning. Tattoos and piercings have meaning.

Sometimes people get confused when they try to interpret the meaning of a woman in a minidress. Does a woman's attire mean something? Of course it does. Does it have anything to do with her right to go about her day presuming that she won't be the victim of a violent crime? Nope.

My associate's robes were easily my favourite outfit of all time. I bought them from my predecessor, Rebecca, who bought them from an associate before her, who bought them from someone else. They had a pedigree, had absorbed meaning from their previous owners. When I wore them I didn't get nervous about my weight because they hid my figure and I didn't need to show my figure when

I wore them anyway because they highlighted my best asset: my brain. I could be in a hurry and it just looked as if I had important places to be. I could stare off into the distance, out one of the big glass windows that overlooked the city, and be thinking about getting a kebab for lunch, and it looked as though I was having an internal monologue about justice and humanity. It was helpful to remember that when having to deal with barristers. Just because they were in a robe and wig didn't mean they were beyond reproach, or weren't just plain stupid.

⌒

I was pretty fed up with barristers by the time we got to The Chickpeas Case that morning. There was one regular barrister on either side of the bar table, plus one Senior Counsel and one Queen's Counsel, and they all had their different jabots on their necks. *The strutting cocks need their plumage*, my notes say. A total of seven instructing solicitors and assistants bustled around, and the rows of seats at the back of the room were full of journalists.

A businessman had tried to save money by skipping Australia's strict fumigation requirements for imports and been caught. Hundreds of thousands of dollars in potential fines were on the line for both him individually and the company. It didn't seem terribly important considering we'd heard Pullman's case on the same level of the building earlier in the year and not a single reporter showed up to hear about a child being repeatedly, violently raped. *But chickpeas!? Holy shit! Why didn't you tell me! Someone call* The Courier!

One of the silks approached my table and a silk from the other side noticed, and left a conversation to join us.

The first one addressed me. 'Good morning, Madame Associate. The situation at present is that if we could have a few more minutes before court starts, we might be able to save a lot of time overall.'

I looked at the other silk, who nodded.

Judge gave a bittersweet smile when I relayed their message to him up in chambers. He'd been prepping for this trial for days despite having a pretty keen suspicion it would settle. Everyone knew how expensive it would be to run the trial with all those counsel.

When we resumed court, I had to arraign the corporation and a legal representative of the corporation had to enter a plea. It was absurd and I was getting tetchy.

On my lunchbreak I met up with Dad. 'Why do the men at that table get paid so much more than the ones trying to put child rapists in gaol!?' I pleaded to him, trying to keep my voice down. 'Did I tell you it was about chickpeas?'

'Yes—'

'Chickpeas!'

'Yes,' he said slowly, smiling a little.

'Can you imagine how much money the government would have to pay to put silks on *all* the rape trials?'

Dad just nodded and we fell into silence for a moment before a terrifying thought occurred to me. *What if my matter went to trial and I got one of the shit prosecutors? What if Samuel hired a silk?* My thoughts were interrupted with a reminder text message about a psychologist appointment I'd booked for the next day, and when I looked back up to Dad's face I thought I might cry. I was planning to go to the appointment after work, then have dinner with my parents and tell them about Samuel.

I told Dad I had to get back to work and left early. Being there without telling him felt duplicitous.

Back up in chambers I asked Judge the same question I'd asked my dad, hoping to get a different answer. 'Why do chickpeas get silks when the twelve-year-old girl Pullman raped gets the greenest and cheapest from the DPP office?'

He smiled at me in a way I had slowly come to understand didn't carry any intentional condescension. 'Well, twelve-year-olds don't have much money, do they?'

'Judge, that's not the answer I want to hear!'

He laughed and I turned to walk back out of his room. 'Chickpeas!' I shouted out in the corridor, to nobody. It was all so shitty and everybody knew it. They smiled because they understood my outrage, but outrage in that industry seemed unsustainable. Shelves downstairs were full of trials waiting to be heard. When one matter was finished, or cancelled, or thrown out of court, two more flew in, and no money was to be made from justice for twelve-year-olds.

I knew it wouldn't be an option for me to hire an expensive counsel. Criminal offences are committed against an individual, but 'The Crown' prosecutes them. It was good that I didn't have to pay for anything, but it also disempowered me.

⌒

A few of the associates were having lunch together and I joined them, sliding into a chair at the end of the kitchenette.

'We're comparing the most ridiculous shit we've heard people say in their defence,' Nikki said to me.

'Wow,' I replied, nodding to indicate I wanted them to proceed.

'One dude I saw was charged with a rape, right?' Amanda said, and we all nodded, 'And he said on the police record, repeatedly, that he knew she wasn't consenting, but that he didn't "rape" her because he didn't cum inside her.' We all burst out into loud laughter, and I slapped the table. 'He couldn't get legal aid to represent him, so he ended up just pleading at a really late stage.'

'Holy shit,' I said, my mouth hanging open.

'I know,' Amanda said, shaking her head.

'I guess she was lucky that he was too stupid to actually deny it?'

'I guess,' she replied with a shrug.

After we adjourned the chickpeas sentence to the next day, Judge left to go to a meeting and I started psyching myself up to make the phone call to the police. I had to use the work landline because I couldn't risk any of the judges seeing me chatting on my mobile. I couldn't call from home because I lived in an old Queenslander and at least one of my housemates was perpetually within earshot. So my office was the only place I could do it, and I'd been waiting for an opportunity for about a week—a chance within normal office hours when Judge was out.

Sitting in front of my L-shaped desk, I spun slowly on my swivel chair, taking in a 360-degree panorama, soaking in the stacks of folders of sentencing remarks, the piles of depositions for future trials, the textbooks and loose-leafs filling the shelves behind me. I had been breathing it all in, every day—the reminder that my abuse was one tiny teardrop in a putrid ocean. I wondered if I would be further clogging the system by making a complaint. Was there another young woman, somewhere, waiting for a moment like this too? Definitely. I closed my eyes and imagined her, and I put my hands out onto my files and thought of the faces of all the women and children I'd seen in court. I'd seen them crying. I had felt their fear and their freeze when they relived their horrors in front of a cavernous room of angry adult strangers. I thought of all the things I wanted to tell them but couldn't from behind my desk where I sat mute and neutral. That I admired them so much. That they were strong. That monsters were real, and that these men were what they looked like, and that everyone has a right to justice, and so did I.

I punched the number into the phone and a woman's voice carried down the line.

'Hello, Dutton Park Police Station, Constable Tanner speaking,' she said clearly, if a little unenthusiastically.

'Good afternoon, I'm calling to report a crime thing that happened to me when I was a kid.'

'Okay, sure,' she said, and I could picture her straightening up on the end of the line, 'are you able to speak to me about this now?'

'Yes.'

'And the matter you're calling about, how long ago did it happen?'

'About fifteen years ago, when I was in primary school.'

'Okay, I'm going to transfer you to someone from the CIB, is that alright?'

'Sure.'

On hold, I waited and listened to audio encouraging people to use an anonymous firearms hotline. I couldn't think of a single trial or sentence involving firearms coming across my desk all year. Why not provide an anonymous domestic violence tip-off hotline?

'Hello, are you still there?' the constable asked.

'Yes.'

'Unfortunately there's nobody from CIB available at the moment. Are you happy for me to take some information from you and pass it on to an investigator there?'

'Yes, sure.'

She took my personal details before things got more specific.

'And can you tell me a little bit about what happened?' she asked.

'Yes, it was a one-time occurrence,' I started, fighting through The Freeze coming back, 'and it was my brother's friend, he is six years older than me, and I was wearing my primary school uniform, and we were playing out the back of my house on the trampoline, and then my brother went inside the house, and when me and him were alone he put me on my back on the trampoline and,' I stopped talking, 'ah . . .'

I was sweating, panicking, and my eyes wouldn't open. All my muscles were locked.

The woman on the phone waited, silently. I pushed through the rest of the details, listing them off like dot points; the blood was rushing back to the centre of my body, giving me pins and needles in my fingers, so I fumbled with the phone. She asked something I didn't understand. I was still and silent for a while. Somewhere else.

'Hello?' she asked louder.

'Oh, yes, yes, I'm here, sorry, what did you say?'

'Are you still in contact with this person?'

'Not really, no. He comes to family events sometimes. I had to invite him to my eighteenth birthday party. Sometimes he's there when I visit my brother. He comments on my Facebook.'

'Okay, but you don't feel at risk that he will do anything again?'

'Oh, no,' I said.

'And can you tell me his name and any details you know about him?'

'Yes. His name is Samuel Levins.' It felt dirty coming out of my mouth, but kind of good. Like vomiting.

⌣

I left the constable with my mobile number and hung up the phone, stinking—I had sweated through my shirt and then through my blazer. I stood up to go to the ladies' room and felt unsure on my legs, wobbling on my high heels.

I knew I had to tell Vincent the next time I saw him, and that I was going to see him after work that night. I could have coffee with my father and look him in the eye and keep things from him, but I couldn't with Vincent. With him things needed to be fully transparent. Truthful. Once before, years earlier, when the two of us were really drunk, I had alluded to something 'maybe' having happened to me when I was a child, but I couldn't remember how much I'd really said or how he'd responded. It was time to get it out.

I needed to be honest when I told him I'd been molested, and in turn I trusted he would be honest if he no longer felt attracted to me.

Resting my head on the bathroom mirror I let cool water run over my wrists and tried to regulate my breathing. Each small hurdle took me right back to The Freeze. It was too soon for me to know if things would get any easier. I didn't know if I would ever feel that relief George had spoken about in Warwick. In the meantime I had to be careful not to lose my job or my boyfriend. I looked in the mirror and tried to fix the mascara that had run, slapping my cheeks to bring a little colour back to my face. I could leave this job and find another, but I loved Vincent so much it made my chest ache. *Does that make me a shit feminist?*

It was 3.30 p.m. I had an hour and a half to decide how much to tell him. What to divulge and what to withhold. Where could I draw the line between honesty and safety? What was the minimum he needed to know to understand? What was the maximum he could hear and still think me desirable?

Back in the office I sat with a pen and paper and tried to draft how I might tell him. At which points I might pause and give him the opportunity to hold his hand up and say 'enough'. How long I would wait before finishing my story before asking him if it changed anything between us, knowing he might not say anything then and there, and that this disease could slowly rot his lust for me, spoiling our relationship over gruelling months.

If I was honest with myself, that was what I most feared.

I was sure everyone would believe me, but I didn't know if it would change things. I thought back to George, how he'd left the witness stand crying and fallen into his wife's arms like a broken child. He hadn't looked to see if she would catch him: he'd known she was there. They were strong. It would be harder for me to be strong if I was alone—if Vincent left me—but I already knew I had to take the risk. I could be alone for the rest of my life, but at least I'd be able to live with myself.

⌒

Vincent and I sat on the front deck of my tiny share house in Paddington. When I'd first arrived I'd thought there was no way I'd ever let my bare legs touch the couch that sat out there, exposed to the rain and afternoon sun, ripping at the corners to reveal decomposed stuffing, but with the benefit of a little perspective I slouched into it absent-mindedly. My head lulled back as I inhaled deeply and tried to form a sentence.

'I have to tell you something,' I'd said to him when we got in the door and dropped our bags and hugged. He tried to mask a tiny panic in his eyes and it made me laugh. 'I'm not pregnant!' Then we both laughed. 'But let's have a cigarette, hey?'

He waited quietly, knowing that sometimes it took me a while to put things right.

'You remember that thing I told you about my brother's friend?' I asked. 'Because we'd been talking about things we never told anyone else?'

'Yes.'

'I'm going to the police about it.'

'Okay.' He nodded and waited for me to say more. I tried to hide how frantically I was searching for indications of disgust. If he had crossed his legs away from me or even crossed his arms in that moment, my heart might have broken. 'I thought you said you didn't know if you dreamed it?'

'Nah,' I exhaled, 'that's just what I said to kind of, I dunno, try not to have to deal with it. But what happened, I mean, kids don't dream that shit.'

Another moment of silence passed.

'Do you want to talk about it?' he asked calmly.

'Not really. I mean, not right now. Things are probably gonna be a bit crappy for a while. I'll just keep you posted.'

'Well, I love you and I support you and I guess just let me know if there's anything I can do.'

I stubbed my cigarette out and leaned onto his chest, and he kissed my forehead and put his arm around me. The sun was setting over the houses and cyclists whizzed by.

I pointed to the plant I'd potted when I first moved in. 'I don't know why this wattle won't grow. The lime is fine and the rose is chill and the lavender is good. It can't be me. I don't know what it wants. It's such a diva.'

'Isn't wattle a native?'

'Yeah! So it should be super chill! That pot is like a luxurious European holiday for a wattle.'

He kissed my forehead again and asked what I felt like for dinner. His kiss told me: *I know you want to pretend everything is the same, that everything is going to be okay, so let's just do that.* While we discussed the merits of pizza versus curry it occurred to me that just two months ago I'd felt dread about how average and suburban Brisbane seemed. That the normalcy was stifling and that I yearned for bigger things, that I missed New York, that I wanted stimulation and adventure. How quickly everything turned around and all I wanted was to be hugged by my city. To take it for granted and let it house me and feed me while I dealt with things.

⌐⌐

The next morning Mr Chickpeas was sentenced to some high fines and a short amount of gaol time. His story appeared in the paper the following day, and the expensive crowds dispersed. Pullman would never be in the paper, though, and neither would Samuel.

I was glad we weren't dealing with anything too heavy, because I was on Struggle Street. I had a coffee in the morning but kept having to slap my face and crack my fingers to bring myself back to the present. All I could think about was getting to Headspace that afternoon. Keeping it together until a door clicked behind me and I sat down with a woman who might just let me speak for as long as I needed.

When counsel finished making their sentencing submissions, Judge advised he would take an hour adjournment to consider his position. I accompanied him to his chambers and made sure I wasn't needed for anything, then went to the bathroom, closed the toilet lid and sat down, leaning against the tiled wall. When I closed my eyes I saw myself in a horror movie, dragging myself along the ground because my legs didn't work anymore. I tried to open my eyes but the lights were too bright and on automatic sensors so I scrunched them shut, but I just saw the trampoline again. The pool in the backyard reflecting the afternoon light. And The Freeze. Tears flowed out and I scrunched a ball of toilet paper to my eyes, then I heard high-heeled footsteps approaching the door. *Did I lock it!?* I cleared my throat and heard the steps stop and turn back.

'Fuck,' I whispered, getting up and seeing my red eyes in the mirror.

⌒

'Do you mind if I head off a touch early today, Judge?' I said, standing at the edge of his desk. 'I have an appointment across town.'

'What!?' he said with mock outrage, smiling. 'I don't know about this.' He looked across to the clock that showed the time as 4.50 p.m. 'I suppose I'll manage here, working hard into the night by myself.'

'I won't tell anyone if you want to go home early too,' I said, faking slyness and turning on my heel. 'In fact, there don't seem to be many other people on our level still at work.' I stretched the boundaries of the sass I directed at other judges sometimes, but he never took the bait.

'No, no, that's fine, you go on. See you tomorrow.'

'Thanks, Judge, see you tomorrow.'

When I walked past all the other judges' chambers, I wondered who would be allocated to my matter if it went to trial. I couldn't imagine sitting in front of any of them, looking at their associate, being on the other side of proceedings. They'd probably list it for a judge from Southport or Ipswich—someone I'd definitely never worked with. Maybe Samuel's lawyer would try to allege foul play?

How many Department of Justice employees were also complainants in serious criminal trials, though? I would never know. We hid in bathrooms when we cried.

⌁

Much to my disappointment, I was not cured after my first session with a psychologist. I was crying—wailing really—within fifteen minutes of arriving, and we spent most of the session cataloguing what was wrong with me so that she could figure out a plan for how to treat me and what approaches to take.

'Well,' she said at the end, 'there's a lot here for us to work with.'

I responded by blowing my nose loudly and taking another tissue from the box in front of me.

'And you're sure you're going to tell your mum and dad tonight?' she asked. 'There's no rush. You've had a big day.'

I decided against telling her that The Chickpeas Case was the furthest thing from a 'big day' I'd seen all year.

'I need to get it done now that I've decided what I'm doing—I feel like a liar every minute I don't tell them,' I replied truthfully.

'Alright.' She handed me a pamphlet with the phone numbers of suicide helplines and emergency call centres, and I laughed. She didn't laugh.

⌁

I fixed my makeup and went straight from her office to Mum and Dad's for dinner. I was surprised to see my grandparents there. Mum's parents, Tuttu and Poppa, lived locally and we'd always been close; I didn't want to tell them, though, and so I had to pretend to be fine through dinner, dessert and coffee. At the end of the evening when we all walked out to the cars I pretended I had to duck back inside to the bathroom, and waited until I heard Poppa's old car engine disappear down the road.

'Can I talk to you for a tick before I head off?' I said to Mum and Dad, and their happy, full-bellied smiles dropped.

I couldn't look at their faces as I told them the story. Something like this was one of the worst things you could dump on a parent.

'Do you want to do something?' Dad asked me.

'I want to report it. I called the police. I want to do the right thing.' I started crying again. I sat on a chair and Mum came to hug me, then Dad came over and held us both for a long time.

'Shhhh,' my mother said, 'it's alright, it's alright, it's going to be alright,' patting my hair, stroking my shoulder. I'd thought I had got most of the crying over with already, but in my parents' arms I felt I could relinquish the sarcasm and stoicism.

After some more questions and after I insisted I was fine to drive home, I left them. In the car as I pulled out of the driveway, I looked at my parents lit up in the headlights, waving and blowing kisses, and wondered what they'd say to each other when they went back inside.

How could you do this to them?

I felt as if I might vomit at any moment—the rich dinner and dessert churning around, being spoiled by an overwhelming sense of guilt. When I got back home I walked through the front door, straight into the bathroom, and brought it all up and out.

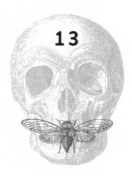

13

ONE AFTERNOON THE FOLLOWING WEEK I ran into Ellen, an associate from Southport, in the photocopy room, and we had a good chat. I found her, like Megan, to be a tonic to the wankery of some of the other associates. She was on circuit to Brisbane but had just been to Kingaroy recently. Kingaroy had one of the worst reputations—if not the worst—of all the circuits. Ellen said they had three child sex trials and that all the men were acquitted.

One of the trials was of a man and his stepdaughter in an incestuous relationship that the stepdaughter claimed began when she was eleven, but only had 'evidence' like texts and photos since turning seventeen. The jury acquitted because they weren't convinced the incest was happening before she was old enough to consent—and for incest charges, a loophole says that both individuals being adults and not blood relations is allowed.

'So they believed it for sure was happening when she was seventeen, and that he was basically her dad, but just absolutely couldn't conceive that he did it even when she was sixteen or fifteen?' I asked Ellen, knowing the answer.

She just nodded, the photocopier churning out papers behind us. The light travelled along under the glass of the machine and reflected in Ellen's glasses like an eerie indication of a passage of time as I stood there, silently considering how lucky we were by comparison.

At least I presumed Ellen had never been through something like that. She probably presumed I'd never been molested either. I looked in her eyes, searching for a signal, but I only saw the machine's lights passing over, left to right. I thought across the cohort of associates whom I'd just considered wankery and wondered how many I had incorrectly presumed were the 'lucky ones'. Statistically speaking there could be at least a dozen of us.

'The stepdad was gross, though, wasn't he?' I asked her.

'Oh yeah,' Ellen said, 'absolutely disgusting.'

Megan came into the copy room, dropping folders loudly on the desk in front of us.

'Oh my god, I can't believe this,' she started, 'we're in a trial, right? It's a rape case where this guy is at, like, a Christmas party and then takes his best mate's daughter upstairs and forces himself onto her, rapes her, then just comes downstairs and enjoys the rest of the party.'

'Yuck,' Ellen said, and I groaned.

'But get this!' Megan continued. 'Just now a juror handed us a note saying that while they were on lunchbreak they saw a security guard approaching the complainant's father to take him away some-where, and asked if maybe the jury shouldn't have seen it and asking the judge if the event had any significance. So we called in the security guard, and they said that one of the girls from a visiting school—they were sitting in, listening to the trial—had been walking out during an adjournment and felt someone feel her up, and that she turned around and saw the dad right behind her.'

'What the fuck!?' Ellie and I called out in chorus.

'You're telling me,' I said, 'the father of the rape complainant touched a schoolgirl on the arse as he was walking out of court?'

'Yep.'

The photocopier whirred on as the three of us fell silent.

'Well,' Megan clarified, 'allegedly.'

⌒

Later that week I arrived at level thirteen early enough for it to feel empty, so I found the right number online again and punched it into my office phone. While it rang I wedged the receiver between my shoulder and face, and started breaking all the nibs off my freshly sharpened pencils, pushing them into a slab of printouts I needed to edit, forcing the lead at a diagonal, feeling the wood give a little, focusing on the anticipation of the break. I was so full of anxious, angry energy. Ants were crawling into my skin through my pores and running along my vein lines. Why did I have to pick this phone up again? I pictured my brother when we were children as my hand smacked my face involuntarily: *Why do you keep hitting yourself?*

'Hello, Dutton Park Police Station, Constable Ian Grey speaking,' an unmistakably young man's voice came through the line, and I sat up straight and grabbed the phone again, dropping the impotent pencil.

'Good morning, Ian. I'm just calling to follow up with a complaint I made a little over a week ago. I left all my details and they said that someone would get right back to me, like, in a day or two, but nobody has.'

'Oh, I'm sorry to hear that, let's look it up. Your name and date of birth, please?'

I gave him my name and date of birth.

'I can't see anything here in the records,' he said with the slight distraction of someone scrolling down a screen.

'It is a complaint about a historical child sex offence,' I replied and told him the time and date of my phone call. He asked me if I had called Dutton Park, and I said it had been the same phone number I'd just dialled, and he asked the name of the person I'd spoken to, and I said I couldn't remember. We went back and forth for several minutes, then he put me on hold and went to see who'd been working the morning of my call, and I sat quietly in my office looking at the pencils and pockmarked paper.

The constable finally came back on the line and exhaled. 'I'm so sorry, there's no record of your complaint in the system.'

'What?'

'I know, I'm so sorry, I don't know what happened and I can't explain it. Are you in a position to go through it a little with me now? I just need the basics so I can pass it on to CIB, and someone will get in touch with you later today.'

'But that's what they said last time?' I must have sounded like a lost child.

'Yes, I'm sorry.'

'Wow,' I paused, 'okay, yeah, so, the basics,' and I started from the beginning, again.

The constable listened, asking the same questions as last time, taking my date of birth and contact details again. He told me someone would phone me within forty-eight hours.

I hung up and pushed my wheelie chair back from my desk and leaned forward to put my head between my knees. It stung somehow, a feeling like a rejection mixed in with the shame and embarrassment, but I also felt bewildered. It was crushing to think of how long it had taken me to build up the courage to pick up the phone and make that first call, to tell my story to a stranger and ask for help. The single worst moment of my life, the darkest point in my past that I'd nearly died reckoning with, was officially insignificant enough to slip through the cracks. This beast that so often made it difficult for me to breathe had fallen behind someone's desk unnoticed. I was shattered that something so important to me was of no importance to them—to the people who should care, who were paid to care.

Doubt tugged at my sleeve all day. What if my complaint was small and silly compared to all the more serious stuff the police had to deal with? After all, I should know better than most that I could very well be taking up too much police time with a one-off, historical matter. Was I wanting too much? Too greedy for attention and sympathy?

They'd asked if I was in ongoing danger and I'd said 'no', then they'd told me someone would call me as soon as they had time. *How many women less selfish than me wouldn't have followed up?* Those women's complaints wouldn't even be in the system and so wouldn't be statistics, couldn't be listed as attrition if they didn't proceed with the matter.

By the time my mobile phone rang later that afternoon, the self-doubt was being overtaken by the fire ants again. A policeman introduced himself as Sean Thompson, and we organised a time for me to go into the station after work the following week. I would make a statement and we would discuss the next steps.

When Judge left work that day I stood at the end of his chambers and looked over to the west side of Brisbane, the side where I grew up. The city fanned out under a bright pink sunset, that constellation of crimes, and I stood watching as mine joined the others. Its little warning light flickered on gently, taking its place on the map of human misery. The clouds streaked across the sky with highlights of yellow and orange at their tips and points as though the whole thing was on fire. Watching people go about their bustling lives was mesmerising. I counted the cars on the highway and calculated that if half the drivers were women and all drivers were over twenty-five then each of the red cars on the inner-city bypass that afternoon represented one victim of sexual violence.

I stepped onto the balcony and tipped my head over the railing. The panic hyped up my pulse and reminded me that I mustn't really have wanted to die, and so I just turned around and went home.

The working week went by normally. I had let almost twenty sentencing revisions pile up, and I struggled through them when I could. There was another textbook trial on Monday. The complainant was a beautiful young woman with dark hair and strong features, and she wore a gold cross around her neck. Her mother hadn't had any idea her partner was abusing her daughter. Prescription drugs were involved. I wondered when that girl had first called the police and what she would have done if she never heard back from them. During the graphic parts of her testimony I doodled on scrap papers. The defendant sat opposite me and I was grateful for being an unremarkable part of the system. I couldn't help but look at his hands when I heard her tell the court what he'd done to her with them. Fat, strong fingers with calluses. Every detail was too much.

The sentencing revisions panicked me, and it took me a long time to realise it was a pretty simple case of transferred trauma.

Reading had always been a huge part of my life: I loved books that transported me and writers who made me feel as if I was there in among the adventure on the page. A love for reading makes you a determined reader. Even with an average book I would always do my best to feel a part of the plot and become close to the characters. But I didn't know how to switch off that mechanism for other kinds of reading. Legal matters have settings and locations that need to be established, then you are introduced to the main characters, and there is dialogue and conflict. It's all there on the page and it was all being transferred across to my body, into my mind. I could tell you what happens in every Harry Potter book, in each Amy Tan novel and all of Malcolm Gladwell's essays. The court cases I read and edited collected in my mind like a sick library. All those women and girls were me. Every sentence referenced many other similar-fact comparable cases like an endless accumulation of completely unoriginal sins.

As Dad drove me to the police station the next week, we chatted about normal stuff. I watched him to see if he was nervous or sad but I couldn't read anything different from usual. It occurred to me that he no longer had the capacity to be unpleasantly surprised—that maybe he'd been a police officer for too long to think anything was sacred or untouchable. He pulled into the visitor's parking bay, and a childhood memory came back to me: Dad had pulled the car up in front of the house and I was talking to him about Arron's friends, saying something or other about them having girlfriends, and I went to open the car door but he didn't move.

'You tell me if any of them ever try anything like that with you, if they touch or kiss you,' he said sternly.

'Why?' I asked, immediately feeling some shame but not knowing why.

'Because that's against the law.'

'Why?'

'Because you're a child.'

I felt my cheeks burning at the memory. I loved those boys. They were the epitome of cool. I wanted their clothes and their toys and their attention, and the age gap between us was painfully awkward. I pretended to like their music even though I couldn't understand all those grungy haircuts and dissonant chord progressions.

Now, with hindsight, so many things I'd struggled with as a child became clearer and simpler to me. Intense tomboy behaviour through childhood, a struggle and isolation in Grade Seven—when I was just about to turn thirteen—and the boys from my class I'd previously spent every summer with no longer invited me to their birthday parties.

'Why didn't you invite me to your party?' I asked my friend Dylan that year, too confused to realise how pathetic I sounded.

He shrugged. 'It's a boys-only.'

The attention I craved from Arron's friends was confusing all of a sudden. I was a girl and that meant if I wanted attention from them it had something to do with the fact that they were boys and I was a girl, but when I was twelve I had no way of understanding what that meant to an eighteen-year-old. We were all young enough to be hanging out in the backyard together but as Samuel proved, the boys were old enough to render us different creatures playing at different games.

The shame I felt in the car with my father came from a fear of being branded girlish and attention-seeking, but all I truly ached for was to be cool like the boys. Their friendship seemed to have a depth and easiness to it that I envied and longed for. I didn't have the tools or the language to understand or describe any of that.

In Grade Six, when I had just begun to feel my male best friends slipping away from me, a teacher pulled me aside in class and told me that I was bad at maths because I was 'boy-crazy'. My face burned. I nearly cried for fear she was right. I did want their attention and it did make me feel pathetic, but I couldn't see what I was doing wrong. I didn't know a thing about sex, or if I did I certainly couldn't yet see how it related to me or my companions. My immature and short-sighted 'not like other girls' phase began shortly thereafter: a universally misplaced attempt to avoid the shame apparently inherent in girlhood.

It had taken years of conditioning to build the sense of insecurity required to make me freeze on that trampoline. Samuel knew it was there, he could sniff it—the desperate confusion part and parcel of a girl who doesn't realise she's on the cusp. How could I have 'just called out' to someone when the risk was being forever uncool? People were already looking at me and seeing a pathetic, boy-crazy creature; I couldn't afford to make things worse.

If I confront my memory fully, pulling it up and out of a deep, deep well, and if I hold it up to the light, wiping off the gunk, and if I'm honest, I remember walking away from Samuel that afternoon with a sense of happiness that he had paid some attention to me. Such were the depths of my self-doubt, already, and I hadn't even got my first period.

⌒

So there I was, walking with my ex-cop dad to the doors of the police station well over a decade after I'd been molested, having finally developed just enough disregard for potential social fallout. Finally feminist enough to realise I was all out of fucks to give. Still terrified of being called a liar or disregarded, but past the point of letting other people tell my story.

All that reckless resolve then whooshed back out the door that had only just swung closed behind us when the policewoman at the counter recognised Dad and I saw confusion then realisation flash across her face. He might have felt ashamed or embarrassed to be there. How might a firefighter feel if their child caused a house fire? What if a teacher's child needed an after-school tutor? My father had been a police officer and prosecutor for well over a decade and yet there we were, fronting at the desk with a historical sex abuse complaint. I looked up at his face, but again there was nothing. The nature of these things is that they are done by the people we trust, that offenders mostly fly under the radar as family or friends, and I knew that Dad knew that, but I also knew that shame and embarrassment weren't always logical. If he was suffering, though, he didn't show it. He could be absolutely relied upon as a man of his generation for that.

Sean came out of a side door and introduced himself to us. He was in office clothes and had a relaxed manner that verged on tired.

'Did you bring a book or something to do while you wait?' I asked Dad when Sean asked me to follow him upstairs to the interview rooms.

'No, no, I'll just wait,' Dad replied, taking a seat.

'But what will you do?'

'Patience, my dear,' he said and smiled in the same way as always, but I was full of regret as I turned from him. *I should have just done this by myself*, I thought as I climbed the stairs behind Sean.

When I stepped into the tiny interview room, with its fluorescent lights and icy, rattling air-conditioning, a second police officer came in and closed the door so it was just me and the two men.

'Ready to roll?' the second officer asked, and dropped a cardboard box of tissues onto the desk in front of me then sat down opposite.

I shouldn't have done any of this at all.

Considering the determination with which I'd tried to forget the incident for so many years, my recollection of it was ironically clear. Most of the time I put up an internal stop sign to the pathways that take me to the details of that afternoon, but closing my eyes and travelling down them is always as easy as it is miserable. The odd details about things Samuel said, and the way the offending progressed, was easily peculiar enough to defy the potential for fabrication by a child's mind.

'He said to me, "My sister likes it when I do this,"' I told the officers and began crying.

Sean raised his eyebrows and turned the corners of his mouth down, making notes. I was crying at how disgusting it all was, but also with relief. I'd spent so many years thinking I'd dreamed it up; for most of my youth I'd presumed the grotesque event was a fantasy I had created.

The other officer interrupted me at an awful point in the story. 'Do you remember if the fingers went inside your vagina or were they only on the outside?'

'There wasn't any penetration,' I replied, matter-of-fact, having anticipated the question.

'Oh, so not rape then, just sexual assault,' he said, shifting his weight back in his chair and crossing his legs. 'Well, not *just*, but you know what I mean,' and he waved his hand indicating I could continue telling my story. I was crying too much to say anything back to him. At the end of my account he said, 'Okay, so, based on what you said on the phone it sounded like a sexual assault case but this is actually more of an indecent treatment case if you were in primary school.'

'Yes,' I replied, too exhausted and upset to argue that I had not misspoken on the phone either of the times I called.

Sean explained that if I was ready, I could give my official statement that evening. Then the next step, if I wanted, was to make a pretext phone call. That would mean calling Samuel and trying to get him to admit to the offending while he didn't realise the call was being recorded. I'd only ever heard pretext phone calls on the other end, at work—when lawyers were fighting to make them inadmissible and keep them out of court. I was terrified of having to speak to Samuel but I knew I'd have to try. I thought that if I could just get him on tape admitting it all, I could take a short cut past the normally years-long process of pre-trial preparations. I needed that optimism for strength, but now I look back on it as naive idiocy.

⌒

I followed Sean up another flight of stairs and my thoughts returned to my dad sitting alone in the lobby. Over an hour had passed. I wanted to know what Dad was thinking but I couldn't bear to go down and ask. Perhaps he'd fallen asleep. He fell asleep the one time we went to the ballet, and countless times at the movies. Our family photo albums are full of funny pictures of him napping on couches after big meals.

Sean and I sat down at his desk, and he explained that we'd be preparing a written statement.

'I have to tell you everything again from the start?' I asked, confused.

'Yes, and I'll be writing it all down this time.'

It seemed absurd that I would have to repeat myself twice, but over the following hour I had to repeat myself *repeatedly*. Sean typed with his index fingers. I thought again about Dad waiting downstairs and guilt surged through me afresh. My inclination was to get the story out as fast as possible because it was so awful to linger on anything, especially some details, but Sean would hold his hand up to stop or slow me down. He interrupted to repeat words and names back to me, and I could see by the way he'd hit Enter then tapped the left arrow and then hit Backspace that he didn't understand the way the document was formatted and took unnecessary time to make each new paragraph look like the others. During a bad part of my story that made me cry, Sean looked up from the keyboard to the screen and realised he'd made a typo, then fumbled getting the cursor to return to the start of the line so that he could correct it.

By the end of another hour I felt the hot ants in my skin and I wanted to rip the keyboard out from under his two fingers and smack him across the face with it. I asked for a glass of water, and received it, and the process went on and on, with my dad still waiting downstairs. When Sean finally printed out a draft copy I looked through it and pointed out errors on every page. We sat together as he went through it all again. Was this the great, strong arm of justice? Was this my champion?

After I signed the statement, the other officer came into the room. I was freezing cold and exhausted, and he was frustrated that

I couldn't pinpoint the date of the offence. *I'm not stupid!* I wanted to say—I knew it was a problem.

'I know that I was wearing my primary school uniform, but I'd be lying if I said I could be much more specific,' I said.

'DPP normally don't even proceed with claims like this,' the second officer said, not even looking at me. 'You know, if you can't narrow down that timeframe, we could do all the investigating but then they might just decide not to proceed with it.'

I sat with my mouth open in horror.

'Well, often we find that once people start this process they start remembering more things,' Sean said. 'Let's give you a week or so, and you can give me a call at any time if you remember anything, then just pop in and make an addendum statement.'

'Can I do the pretext phone call tonight?' I asked Sean. I had been hoping to rip the bandaid off the whole ugly scab. I wanted it all done there and then.

'No,' Sean said, 'we have to schedule that, and you'll need some time to plan what approach you'll take.'

'What approach?'

'I'm not allowed to tell you what to ask or say on the phone with Samuel, but I recommend you have a good think about it—about what kind of person he is, what information you want to know and what kinds of questions you'll ask, how you'll start the conversation, that type of thing.'

The other officer was leaving the room and added, 'In the meantime, see if you can remember some more details about the date.'

'Also be prepared for the chance that he'll deny everything,' said Sean. 'And avoid all contact with him. We won't send any officers to knock on his door until after the call, otherwise he'll be suspicious. Think about what you'll say if he doesn't want to talk or gets angry.'

Sean stood up, and I followed. As we left, I saw the other officer at the end of a large room full of empty rows of desks. 'Thank you,'

I called out to him with a wave, but he didn't look up. He was swinging on the back legs of his chair, laughing, watching a video on his phone.

—

'All done for tonight,' I said to Dad with a nod and a small smile. 'Gotta come back in a week to do the pretext call.'

We shook hands, thanking Sean, and returned to the car.

'Sorry it took so long. You didn't get bored?' I asked Dad, fastening my seatbelt.

'No, no.'

'Did you have a nap?' I asked. I thought I saw something on his face then, finally.

'No,' he said firmly, disappointed.

I didn't recognise myself in the rear-vision mirror. Of course my father hadn't fallen asleep. Not every man was a monster.

I talked to him about the pretext call. 'I have to plan what I'm going to say to Samuel on the phone—that's my homework for the week.'

It was a rainy night and the city sped past, shiny and blurry through the car window. As Dad drove us home, an announcement about sexual harassment being rife in the Victorian Police Service came on the radio. My dad told me a little about the bad eggs in the police service. He'd caught one officer who had gone from one domestic partner to another to another, committing violence against each, and had been using his access to the records system to cover his tracks so that each time a woman complained it looked like the first time. Dad was rightly making the point that this officer was abusing his authority, but I also felt confused. Why was any single woman's complaint not taken seriously just because the defendant didn't have a record? There always has to be a first time—how many repeats were we missing because every first complaint was dismissed?

I thought about the impending pretext call almost non-stop, on each of the seven days that followed. Sometimes with ants in my skin, sometimes with my head on the pillow opposite Vincent's, sometimes on my hands and knees vomiting in the shower. I was on autopilot at work, but we were starting another trial and I already knew how it would go. A small child had (allegedly) been abused by a friend of the family.

When the jury asked to watch the video evidence of the child's testimony again, like they always did, I had four hours to draft the first lines I would say when Samuel answered the phone. Arron's thirtieth birthday was approaching. I would call to ask Samuel for tips for a present, and then I would say I just wanted to talk about one other random little thing before we saw each other again with people around. I went through a mental Rolodex of his possible responses. I didn't know what I'd do if he got angry.

As the days passed I became more anxious that he would deny it all and be offended at the heinousness of my accusations. I fell asleep with his voice in my mind telling me that it had been me imagining the events all along. Maybe he would yell, tell me he wouldn't touch me with a ten-foot pole, that I had been boy-crazy and was now ruining his life with a sick fabrication. A big stone of dread sat in the bottom of my belly, and it was there when I woke up, before I had even cleared my thoughts enough to remember why it was there. I couldn't vomit it out, god knows I tried.

Sometimes when I saw Vincent I would smile and be happy despite the dread. I went to his house. I asked him to come to mine. He muffled the scary voices, somehow; it was as if he extended a hand to me and, when I took it, I was carried to a peaceful place, and we sat on top of something, above things, and achieved a momentary clarity, and a respite. For a long time on either side of that week, but during that week especially, he felt like the only connection I had to an Earth where I wasn't a fully loathsome thing. Left alone I would incessantly write, still drafting and redrafting the phone call, working myself into a nervous state, convinced I could somehow prepare enough for what was to come. Vincent was the only thing that could cut through all that.

One afternoon I stubbed my toe on the corner of my bed. I gasped from the shock of the pain but then tears poured out of me and wouldn't stop.

'I'm so afraid,' I said as Vincent pressed me into his shoulder, holding me, 'I'm so, so afraid.'

He said I was brave, and he said that he was proud of me, and he said that he loved me, and I believed him.

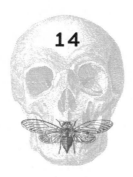

14

ON THE WEEKEND BETWEEN STATEMENT and pretext call I went out for dinner with an old friend. We'd made the plan months earlier and I felt I couldn't cancel, but I wasn't optimistic about having a good time. As it turned out we shared a bottle of wine and stayed long after the meal was done. We were at a nice restaurant in the city on an alfresco patio, a warm and clear spring evening, and we had plenty of hilarious stories to catch up on. At about 10 p.m. we parted and I began the walk home to my place in Paddington. The wine had softened my nerves and I was actually looking up and around me as I walked. I even stopped to get a scoop of chocolate gelato. I remember thinking to myself, *This is the first time you've been happy and relaxed in a while, make sure you don't get a tension-release migraine.*

Walking past the courts building, I waited to cross at the lights. A single car slowed on the amber light, stopping across from me. Its windows were down and the kind of rock music I love bled into the empty, quiet street. The driver hung his arm out on the side closest to me, and the one riding shotgun flicked a cigarette butt, and when the green man flashed up I began to cross the road and the driver wolf-whistled at me. I ignored it, stared straight ahead and kept walking, but when I was directly in front of the bonnet he yelled something out at me. Without looking I gave him the finger and turned to the left to reach the footpath on the other side of the road, when my peripheral vision tweaked and I saw the man in the passenger side lifting his whole torso partially out of the window. We were less than two metres apart.

'You fucking bitch!' he screamed out, so loudly that spittle nearly hit me.

I kept my head straight and tried to just walk leisurely, then I ducked behind a bus stop nearby and fumbled around in my bag for my phone. The car screeched as it took off in the opposite direction. I called Vincent and as the phone rang I looked up and out, my heart thumping, and spotted security cameras all around. Something tweaked in my mind about the angles of the cameras directed toward the Roma Street Parkland.

'Hey,' Vincent's voice came through the line.

'Hey, are you busy?'

'Not particularly, no.'

'I just . . .' I paused—was it silly of me to have called him? 'I just was walking home and these guys yelled at me from their car, but really angrily, like, they shouted at me, and I was so close to the car it scared the shit out of me. He called me a fucking bitch.'

'Have they gone?'

'Yeah, yeah, they drove on, I just, I'm just,' I sighed, 'I'm right beside the part of the Roma Street Parkland where a woman got repeatedly raped.'

'Shit.'

'It was Megan's trial earlier this year. Can you stay on the line for a bit? Chat to me until I get home?'

'Yeah sure,' he said. 'What do you wanna talk about?'

'Anything. Regular people stuff. Happy, boring stuff.'

I walked past the parklands to get to work the next morning and found Megan in her office to tell her about the incident.

'It was worse because I kept thinking about your trial.'

'I know what you mean. That's where the Korean woman was murdered a couple of years ago too, in a different part of the parklands, remember?'

'Yeah, true. The murder trial for that French girl found dead near Kurilpa Bridge is starting soon as well.'

'Oh yeah,' Megan said.

'She was raped too, the French girl. I didn't realise.'

'Hard to keep track of them all, hey.'

That day Judge had to sentence a defendant with a complex personal history. We were up in chambers afterwards and Judge complained to me again about defence making submissions that their clients were of 'below average intelligence'.

I sympathised. 'I also hate it when they say their clients have depression without going into it,' I added. 'Are they just unhappy? Have they been diagnosed? Is it related to trauma—is it a major depressive disorder?'

'Mm.' He nodded.

'If they're not specific then how do we know the defendants aren't just kind of sad? I mean, nobody is 110 per cent happy every single day.'

'Oh, I don't know about that, you seem to be!' Judge said with a big, genuine smile.

I just stood there with my mouth open.

I asked my mum to take me to the police station for the pretext call because I felt as if I needed to spread my inconvenience around as thinly on each person as possible. Mum would hold me if I cried, too, and I knew that I would cry the moment I was allowed to. The fear was illogical, like that of a dog in a thunderstorm trembling and whining under a bed. I had been snapping at people all week, inconsolable, unable to operate with the mental acuity required to think about the situation rationally and calm myself. I was terrified of something nobody else could see or understand. But I trusted Mum would love me the same no matter how that evening went. I didn't feel guilty making her wait—not because she'd brought a book so that I wouldn't feel bad, but because somewhere inside her I knew she understood I was trying to fight a great big powerlessness. If I was called a liar and a bitch that evening, she would still have my back. We rode together in her little white Daihatsu like we were driving a tank into battle.

A tape recorder was ready on Sean's desk. He said that for legal reasons the recorder couldn't touch or be attached to my phone, but that he was allowed to turn it on and then leave the room, and that if the call was on speaker phone it would be recorded. I hadn't realised I would be alone in the room, and that new information unbalanced me.

'Do you have Samuel's phone number?' Sean asked me.

'Yes,' I replied, and he turned the recording device on, gave the date and who we were, and then abandoned me.

I was sweating through my blouse from the nerves but shivering from the rattling aircon. I dialled the number Arron had given me, pushed the speaker-phone button, scrunched my eyes up tight, and waited for the grenade to go off.

It rang and rang and I willed the device to go straight to voice-mail so I could run away and hide somewhere.

'Hello?'

'Sam!' I said brightly. 'It's Bri here, how you doing?'

I was sitting on the edge of my chair, my legs crossed, my hands clasped on my lap under the table. I stared at a worn spot in the vinyl tabletop beside the phone and dipped into a certain mental state I've only ever accessed when particularly drunk or after running too hard for too long. It's a sense of being underwater, with audio goggles, shallow breaths and some dizziness.

Samuel and I exchanged the pleasantries I had spent so many hours painstakingly perfecting, then we stepped through fifteen minutes of birthday-present conversation. The plan was working. His answers fell into one of my flowcharts of predicted response patterns. I asked him where he was, what he was up to. As expected, he was eager to talk about himself and spent some time explaining he was in America for an exciting new investment scheme. It was a get-rich-quick idea, he was proud, and I felt ready to pounce on his unsuspecting ego. I said his name a lot so that he felt positive, because everyone's favourite word is their name. He was telling me how many millions of dollars he was about to make on a new deal, and with each stupid sentence that tumbled out of that pathetic dickhead's mouth, I grew angrier.

'So, um, the other thing I wanted to talk to you about quickly before we see each other again at the party with all the people around,' I said casually, the way I'd done it a hundred times in my drills.

'Yeah?' he replied, but it was a bit too slow and a bit too quiet. He delayed a fraction of a second before he said it and without enough of a questioning tone. He didn't wonder what I was going to ask next; he knew what I was calling about.

My heart was pounding and I heard it beating in my underwater ears, and I knew in that instant, somehow, that the question now was whether or not he suspected I was sitting in a police station beside a recording device and with a detective outside the door.

'It's about that thing that happened when we were kids,' I said.

'Ahh,' his voice had changed, 'when we were kids?'

'Yeah.'

'What do you mean?' He was an awful liar.

'The thing on the trampoline,' I replied. This was it. His reply could change my entire life. The way I trusted my own memories.

'Ah, yep, that thing,' he said.

Something split open inside me; my hands, flung to my mouth, were ice-cold. The same involuntary adrenalin responses from when he'd molested me set in. A clasp had popped open and a dark, ghoulish thing slipped out and into that tiny room. The gross creature responsible for the past decade of degenerate triggers was no longer within me; it didn't belong there inside me, it never had, it belonged to the man I was speaking to on the phone.

'I guess, I mean, I've just been thinking about it a bit lately and kind of wanted to clear the air, you know?'

'Yeah, right, sure,' he said. 'I'm just in a room full of people at the moment.'

He was suspicious, or perhaps nervous, and I could feel that he might hang up if I didn't keep things calm and casual.

I pushed it. 'Can you pop outside, just for a minute?' This was the most obvious time I had ever been responsible for making sure a situation with a man didn't escalate despite how terrified I was. I'd had twenty-four years of practice with losers at parties and inappropriate colleagues, though. I knew how to calm him, the words to make sure no egos were bruised, how to slip into channels of his mind where I could be underestimated. I hadn't even practised that part—I didn't need to—it's just a muscle women know how to flex. My voice lilted; I shrugged and put my chin in my hand even though he wasn't in the room. 'I'd like to just, you know, put it behind us or something.'

I communicated to him: *I'm sorry to bother you, please just indulge me this, and then this silly thing will be dealt with, and you will be fine.*

'Just give me a sec, let me just have a look and see if that's possible.'

'Cool, thanks, Sam.'

I always do my homework.

⌒

Phrases Samuel used on that phone call have been seared into my brain, and they'll sit there forever, his voice like a branding iron. He had always kept his sister at a distance because he was 'subconsciously' afraid he'd 'do something' to her. He had been abused when he was a boy, by an older male relative, and never told anyone.

'I'm not someone that becomes a victim,' he said quite firmly. 'I'm assertive.'

He had a few other reasons that he was glad he'd never told anyone about his abuse, and they touched my own insecurities in an uncanny way.

'If I bring this up my mum and dad are gonna get really fucking upset. So why would I do that? It's over. It doesn't affect my life anymore, but it would really harm my parents if it came out at all,' he said.

Also, he was sorry. He'd been caught doing inappropriate but not-really-serious things to girls in primary school—looking up their skirts and such—but nothing came of it. He said all the things he'd done were just opportunistic, that he was just experimenting somehow, or going around trying to prove he wasn't gay. He promised me he'd never 'pushed' anything non-consensual with a grown woman. He said that since reaching adulthood and having 'normal' relationships with women, he'd always treated them well.

The worst part came when he said, 'Yeah, I did it like two or three other times,' and I tapped out. I should have prodded him for specifics, tried to get more incriminating details out of him, dates in particular, but I couldn't. The words just didn't come; I'd used up all my bravery.

After that I wasn't even fuelling the conversation with questions—he just didn't stop talking. He asked me what I was doing with my life. I said that I was working as a judge's associate but also doing some writing. The final fifteen minutes of the police tape are just him giving me advice about entrepreneurialism and the publishing industry. He told me how he'd been thinking, lately, of how he'd be a good literary agent. He was already representing another girl he knew who wrote sci-fi books and they weren't that good but he'd get someone to buy at least one. He said I should write some kind of fantasy, nerd stuff, because that sells easily. I mumbled some single-word responses, wanting the ordeal to end, but he didn't stop. I was exhausted and still afraid that if I didn't play it cool he would jump through the phone and get me somehow.

His latest business scheme was apparently about to come good.

'Like, you know, I'm not really supposed to talk about what I'm doing because we're actually making a lot of money, but oh well, can I tell you a secret you can't tell anyone?' he asked me with a cheeky tone in his voice.

'Yeah, sure.'

'You've been pretty good at keeping a secret so far.'

'Oh.'

'Um, that was a bit below the belt, but oh look that's a pun too, ah, what I was going to say is that on Friday, by Friday, I should be about two million dollars richer.'

⌒

When he finally finished a sentence about how the publishing industry was changing and I should self-publish to save money, I could barely sit up straight, and I told him I had to go and that I'd see him at Arron's thirtieth. I said something about no hard feelings and he was pleasant saying goodbye, and I fumbled trying to hang up the phone.

Perhaps he felt a certain weight had been lifted off him since he'd had the opportunity to apologise. Perhaps he felt a bit good about himself.

I opened the door and Sean looked up at me expectantly. 'Finished?'

'Yep.'

'How'd you go?'

'He admitted it,' I said, and burst into tears. My knees went from under me and I fell backward into my chair.

Sean tried to ask about details but quickly realised I was in a state. 'Do you want to go back downstairs to your mum?'

'Yes!' I cried out to him, and he helped me down the hall, and I took the steps one at a time, and he held the door open for me as I fell through it and straight into my mother's arms. She rocked me like she'd done when I was a child, stroking my hair, pushing the side of her face against my forehead while I wailed until I tired myself out. I wet her blouse with tears and snot for a long time, and she kissed me until I quietened.

'How did it go?' she asked me gently. Sean had been waiting quietly in the doorway.

'The operation was a complete success,' I said, with a dead-eyed smile, wiping snot from my nose. 'He said he did it.'

Later that evening when Mum dropped me home, she said to me, 'I know this thing is horrible, but promise me you won't let it ruin your life. You have such a wonderful, incredible life. You're such a fantastic girl. I know it's sad and you're allowed to be sad, but promise me you won't let him win. If you let this get to you too much, he wins.'

I look back to that version of myself with some pity and admiration. I collapsed that night and stayed down—on some kind of emotional level—for weeks after, thinking that the worst was over, but I didn't realise it was only the beginning. Now I wonder if Samuel realised that on the phone, having just admitted to abusing me, he went on to mansplain my own career choice to me. Not for the first time I felt grateful for him being such a shit human—the longer you spent with Samuel the easier it was to hate him. Aside from everything else, all of it, the thing that got me through the next two years was his voice in my head:

'You weren't the only one.'

I replayed his words and the sound of his voice in my mind whenever I considered dropping my complaint. I inspected each phrase like a puzzle piece, pulling it out of my memory and turning it over, and when I put the picture together as best I could the truth was clear to me: I might have been the first woman to make that call, but there were other girls, multiple other girls, and he had been waiting for one of us to call. Either I got there first and he was ready, or he'd received a similar call previously and had time to polish his response.

⸺

Days later, once I'd relayed the contents of the conversation to Vincent, he questioned Samuel's honesty with a single word: 'Bullshit.'

I sighed. I'd spent hours wondering the same thing, sitting at a crossroads.

'I know what it feels like to be afraid that someone won't believe you if you say you've been abused,' I said, 'and I refuse to relinquish my own humanity by discrediting Samuel's claim to being abused himself.'

'Fair enough.' He nodded and left it alone.

It sounded like a grand, performative statement, because it was. I wanted to think Samuel was lying, but I couldn't do so without lowering myself to his level. I decided that I hoped I would forever be the kind of person to grant the benefit of the doubt to complainants. In the weeks and months and years that followed I would give up, completely, on his humanity, but I refused to give up on mine.

I did wonder, though, how Samuel could have said things that made *me* feel bad about making a police complaint when he didn't even know I had already decided to. It was true that I appeared to have been living a normal life without telling anyone about what he did—I finished high school, went to university, moved out of home, got a boyfriend—the regular, totally fine route. I felt defensive when he said 'I don't live my life as a victim', as though if I made a big deal out of it all I'd be playing the damsel in distress. It was also true that one of the main things that had stopped me from coming forward was how much it would upset my parents and brother.

The prospect that Samuel had been abused himself meant the waters were muddied. The bully was also the victim. I struggled with the feeling that my hands couldn't be clean if I proceeded with my complaint. If he was telling the truth then perhaps there was a shared pain between us—a crippling that I ought to understand and have sympathy for. I thought I had been tactful in communicating with him on the phone that night, but he had also played me. I came close to dropping my complaint because he had planted a seed in my mind: a possibility that he wasn't the bad guy, but that I could be the bad guy. By making a big deal out of a little opportunistic non-event, I would upset his life and his family and my life and my family. After the police complaint and phone call I kept getting up in the morning, kept stepping through my totally fine life with the outside world, but he had shattered me internally. For months, as I ruminated on what role I was playing, the good guy or the bad guy, over and over in my mind, trying to make a decision based on morality and logic. I flung far to both sides depending on my weight, on Vincent, on the weather, on anything. One minute I'd be proud of my bravery in shining a light on his insidious betrayal of my family's trust. The next I was a cruel banshee, out to upset everyone and get some attention.

Unfortunately for Samuel my line of work exposed me, every week, to men who used the same lines to girls and women they'd hurt, and none of them were original.

I was proofreading a sentence for Judge when a quote jumped out at me. A man addicted to ice convinced his prepubescent stepdaughter to keep his abuse quiet by making her feel guilty that she would just upset her mother if she spoke out. He used her siblings as leverage too. I finished proofreading the document and looked around at the building I was in—all those previous cases, all those briefs and files, representing only a fraction of abusers ever even brought before the courts. I wasn't special and neither was Samuel.

That afternoon was the first time I thought of *her*. She had a composite face of all the girls and women I'd seen in court throughout the year. She was out there, somewhere. Maybe she hadn't called Samuel yet, maybe she had but didn't do it at the copshop. She would be my ward.

I thought a lot about what would happen if Samuel's parents found out and he had to tell them about being abused himself. Was I responsible for the pain and suffering that would result? Probably, yes, in a way, but also, in another way, *too fucking bad, buddy*. He had wormed his way into my brain when I was just a child, and he was doing it again now I was a grown woman.

I said to Vincent, 'I think that it was his right not to do anything about the abuse that happened to him, but it's also my right to do something about the abuse that happened to me.'

'Absolutely,' he said matter-of-factly, as though the answer was self-evident and not muddied by layers of shame and guilt and confusion.

'I think the cycles continue when people don't speak out about it, right?' I said.

'Yep. It's people like you who break the cycle.'

'Or maybe I'll blow the whole fucking cycle out of the water.'

'That's my girl.' He smiled, patted my thigh, and kissed my cheek.

⌒

I knew Samuel didn't have prior sex offences on his record, because Sean—when scrolling through a record on a computer screen I couldn't see—had said something absent-mindedly about Samuel being a 'cleanskin'. I decided that I just wanted something on his record, and that I would do it for *her*, whoever or wherever she was, so that when she came forward, eventually, people would believe her. A mark against his name might warn potential girlfriends and would ensure he couldn't work with children or teenagers.

Making that pretext phone call was the bravest thing I'd ever done. I was sitting in a police station with a detective outside the door and my mother downstairs, my arse on a cushioned chair, in aircon with a glass of water, and it was still the most frightened I'd ever been. Bravery can only exist in opposition to fear. That may be trite but it's also true. The thing I had been most afraid of, for my whole life, was that the darkness within me was my own creation. That in my pathetic desperation for male attention I had fabricated a disgustingness that was incomprehensible to my conscious child mind. That I was manifestly unwanted and could only fantasise a world in which I could ever be desired. Not only all that, but also the possibility that in clamouring to create a narrative in which I was somehow appealing, I would unjustly incriminate an innocent man.

That phone call could have undone me. I don't know where I would have gone, if I really could have proceeded, if Samuel had denied the whole thing and done enough to act convincingly shocked and appalled. That was the fiery pit I saw burning, and I summoned my monster and ran toward it all on my own.

The relentless waves of similar trials and sentences I saw that year finally eroded the absurd idea that my situation was somehow different or unique. It was all the girls and women with fears like mine, and all the men with excuses like his. It was all the time alone in regional Australia, when solitude forced me to peel back my own memories, to put myself on trial, to cross-examine the inconsistencies in my own beliefs.

I went to work the day after the pretext call, like always, and Judge and I got on with dispensing justice from the District Court trenches, like always.

A few days later the anxiety left over from the phone call was starting to fade and I had ingredients to make myself a nice dinner and I watched some historical lady detective shows on television. When I washed my dishes I was thinking that perhaps I really was strong enough to get through the coming year, but then I looked out the window above the sink and saw the neighbours putting a brand-new trampoline together in the backyard, and I got ants in my skin again. The plate slipped from my hands and landed loudly on the counter, cracking, and the shock of the sound and breakage made me start crying. What an incredibly average trigger. I rolled my eyes at myself and sighed, letting my hands sit in the warm, soapy water. One day Vincent and I might have children and they would ask for a trampoline, as all children do, and I would say 'no'. We would pretend it was for their safety or that we couldn't afford it.

'If we ever own a house with a Hills hoist in the backyard I will hire a ute and tear it from the earth,' I said to Vincent once.

The kids wouldn't know why and the neighbours might not either, but I felt sure that Vincent would help me take it to the tip. That seemed a good example of what love is.

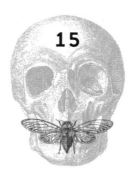

15

WHILE I WAS AWAY ON circuit in Gympie, Vincent stayed at my share house. He woke up in the middle of the night to a man outside screaming my name. Vincent presumed it was Samuel coming to get me, and with the bedroom window of the single-storey house open, Vincent lowered himself off the side of the bed and crawled to the kitchen to get a knife, crawled back to the bedroom, and waited. He stood absolutely still, staring into the dark night at nothing, listening for movement, poised for intrusion.

The man just kept yelling, though, and gradually a picture emerged out of the darkness. It seemed that I shared my name with the woman who lived next door, and that she had come home rather late at night to an aggressive partner. She'd tried not to wake him up when going through the front door but was clearly unsuccessful and, upon hearing his stirring and anger, ran and hid from him in the garden.

Vincent didn't relax until he eventually heard the woman answer to her name being called—until he was sure that nobody was looking for me—and then went back to bed. I only found out about the incident a fortnight later, after I returned home. A knife was lying forgotten just under the side of my bed.

'I didn't want to tell you,' Vincent said.

'Why?'

'I dunno, I don't want you thinking about it or worrying about it.'

I did think and worry about it, but not for me, for *her* next door. My housemates and I had exchanged stories about the way that man spoke to his children. He seemed impatient and unkind, yelling at them about why they couldn't follow simple directions and why they were so useless. I didn't like living next door to him, I didn't want to see him, to be reminded that for every case I saw in court, dozens never even made it into the system. Was he ever physically violent? Sometimes I wanted him to know that I was keeping an eye on him, but I was also afraid of him. No benches and bars separated us, I couldn't take my robes home to protect me, he didn't have to put on a state-issued jumpsuit, and when he washed his car in his driveway I reminded myself that there was no such thing as monsters. There were all kinds of people, all around me, a sliding scale. Reester, Baker, Phillips, they all had cars to wash. Everyone had trampolines and Hills hoists in their backyards.

⌐⌐

Once when I was young and asked my dad what he'd done at work during the day, he told me about a man who saw his girlfriend talking to another man in a car, and went out and punched that man. I thought this was a very romantic and dramatic thing to do.

I asked my dad, 'Doesn't that mean he loves her?'

'No, it means he is jealous and has a temper,' Dad replied.

But that was the apex of being cool for a girl in primary school: that two boys would fight over you. And I remember thinking that if a man was jealous and had a temper, it would just mean that he couldn't contain himself—he was so affected by love for you. Although I was young I knew what jealousy and passion felt like, and the thought that one day I might inspire those feelings in someone else was exhilarating.

I remember that afternoon, thinking about what my father had said as though it was silly, all I could hope for was a man who ran into battle for me.

⌇

Gympie was the nail in the coffin for any aspirations I had to work in the legal industry. On the drive out Judge and I spoke about his previous associate, Rebecca, and what her life looked like now. Rebecca and Judge had been in Gympie together on their final circuit for the year when she asked the local solicitor's office if they had any vacancies. Within six months she was an unsupervised duty lawyer—gaining experience and responsibility that wouldn't be available to her for years if she stayed in a major city. For a qualified young woman from Brisbane, moving to Gympie for a year or two was a significant lifestyle sacrifice. Rebecca drove back to Brisbane most weekends to see friends and family, and to go to the supermarket without having one of her clients approach her in the dairy aisle admitting to a new DUI.

'That's always an option,' Judge said to me casually, referring to Rebecca's move 'out bush'. I saw the countryside rushing past the car windows and wondered if I could be happy away from the city. I didn't mind the idea of having a small, anonymous house to write from, but even thinking about a future in which I made money representing defendants in court made me cranky. How could Rebecca have seen all the same shit I saw, for more than a year, and still have gone into defence? I lied to Judge—saying something about being a city slicker—and resented his kind, encouraging inquiry. I already had my own father to disappoint, a second was just excessive.

We were staying in large apartments that sat in a development area beside a deep-green golf course. Across the road from the big gates with their manicured landscaping, a scrappy old cemetery spread over some rolling hills. The grass was thin and dry, just gravelly dirt in patches, and old boughs from shedding grey gums lay sprinkled between the tombstones. The graves were much further apart than at the cemeteries in Brisbane, as though even in death people from Gympie prioritised land.

I tried jogging around the neighbourhood on the first morning, but at work that day learned of the local ice epidemic and just how many muggings there had been in the previous month, by kids as young as fourteen. So I amended my track to stay nearer the development. It was a blessing in disguise: I saw rabbits and wallabies later in the week and when I burst through the web of a giant golden orb spider, sparkling with morning dew, I wrestled the sticky net out of my hair and wiped my hands on the cold wet grass, and some of the life returned to me. I was catching some kind of breath. Finally getting some fresh air. I only vomited once or twice that fortnight.

⌒

On that first morning we were preparing for a dangerous operation causing death sentence, and Megan and I were emailing again. Driving-related offences are tough because people's actions are always accidents but the stakes are so high. Unlike the terrors of most crime—where you listen in court and worry it might happen to you—dangerous ops are terrifying because you could also possibly do one yourself. Megan had worked on a few of these trials in the year already and by email reported the same fears I did.

On a stretch of road between two properties, less than an hour's drive from the Gympie courthouse, a young German man had driven with two friends in the car. He was sober—the designated driver—but it was late at night, and in a distraction that the court would later classify as negligence, he reverted to driving the way he had learned, on his country's side of the road. Being out in the bush, with barely any signs to remind him he was on the other side of the planet, he rounded a bend and collided, front-on, with a vehicle. The woman in that car, driving on the correct side of the road, was a mother in her forties on her way home to her kids.

Judge took a long adjournment before resuming the court to sentence the young German man to a period of imprisonment instead of a fully suspended sentence. Judge spoke softly, and proceedings were carried out more formally than I'd experienced all that year. I understood that the sense of finality that came with this matter, distinct from all the others, represented the fact that a life had ended. Dangerous ops were the only offence causing death that could be dealt with at the District Court level, rather than being referred straight up to the Supreme Court.

The young man's mother had travelled over from Germany, and she wept in the public seating area. Four people from the deceased's family also came to watch, and they wept too. I took exacting minutes, leaving a perfect record of proceedings, focusing on my small court rituals to build a buffer between myself and the raw pain on display that might otherwise uncontrollably tumble forward.

Negligence—in the legal sense—is a remarkably tricky concept. At once an aspiration that we hold each other to an objective standard of care yet simultaneously an acknowledgement that we can all disappoint one another without meaning to. Sometimes catastrophically. Negligence is a fancy way of saying 'not good enough'. A pointed index finger reminding people they can't stomp through life with reckless indifference to how their actions might affect others.

Just that weekend I'd read some adoring letters to the editor in *The Australian*. Old and politically incorrect people whined about this new age of accountability: casual ableism, cultural appropriation, subconscious gender bias—all bad things that people get 'called out' for all the time, all things that people refuse to accept

responsibility for when the act or utterance wasn't done with deliberate or conscious malice. Hands get thrown in the air—'It's up to
you to take offence!', 'I didn't mean it like that!' I wished that all
of these letter writers had done legal studies at high school, like
some schools do, and learned about how in our power and privilege
also comes responsibility.

Sentencing someone for a negligent act is also difficult
because one of the main aims of any criminal sentence—specific
deterrence—isn't as applicable. That German boy was going to gaol
for reasons of general deterrence; a reminder to the rest of us that
driving a car comes with responsibility to match the potential for
damage. A giant metal machine had crushed a mother's bones, and
now her family wept in court. Of course it's frightening to consider
that without constant vigilance you might be responsible for evil
actions despite not considering yourself to be a 'bad' person.

Many years before becoming an associate, when I first began to
reckon with the memory of being molested, I became afraid that I
would one day inflict the same strange torture on someone else. This
was also around the time I was learning—properly learning—about
sex, and Samuel's acts came to my mind in flashes. I saw babies
being changed in bathroom stalls at shopping centres and terrified
myself into premonitions about awful things I might do to them. In
trying desperately to understand my abuser I had projected myself
into his experience and gone too far in attempting to humanise him.
I thought the event wouldn't make sense to me until I discovered
what would have to happen in my own life to make me capable of
such callousness.

After reading a little about the cycle of abuse—and this was
years before the pretext call where Samuel said he was abused—I
was convinced that the ugliness done to me had come to rest in
me, and that it would leak out against some unsuspecting victim
unless I was constantly vigilant. I thought, for a long time, that if

I didn't monitor myself I might somehow negligently continue the cycle; that Samuel's act had somehow initiated me into a category of humans who were timebombs for further acts of cruelty. Something had been deposited in me and would sit there, forever trying to breach the surface of my consciousness, to release a heinous act.

How else was I supposed to get through Christmas with Samuel sitting on the floor beside me and the tree, among my loving and generous family? How else could I have been alright inviting him to my eighteenth birthday party so that my brother had a friend there? I told myself: *He mustn't be a bad person otherwise everyone else would see him and hate him too. The thing he did wasn't malicious, just negligent.* For a long time—from childhood until the year of my associateship—it was me who needed to shift my thinking to accommodate him and his crime into my life as a young woman.

Out there in Gympie, the morning after that German boy was sentenced, jogging among the headstones, I grappled with those old fears. At some point in the past few years between twenty and twenty-three I had realised that I wouldn't ever molest a young boy, and the thought alone seemed absurd. The thought of being sexually attracted to a prepubescent boy made me recoil, let alone acting on an associated desire without his consent. But I still felt that deposit inside me and worried that without attention it would calcify. I pushed myself up the hill and dug deeper. Why was I attracted to men but not boys, and where did I draw that line? I would have sex with someone younger than me, yes. I would have sex with someone who was eighteen or seventeen, maybe, if they seemed quite mature and were initiating contact. To go to sixteen, the legal age of consent in Queensland, was a stretch. I thought of what boys were like at that age and, now that I was older, the gap seemed insurmountable. What was I missing?

Rising over the crest of the golf course took my heart rate up to 184, and I pictured myself kissing Vincent. He was the control test—the man guaranteed to fill me with desire. Why would I leap into bed with him, but not with fifteen-year-old him? *Drill down, girl.* I ran harder. *Why did Samuel want to touch you when you were a child? Why don't you feel attracted to young people? What's the difference between you?* I clutched my chest, a stitch forming, and thought about when I felt the most sexy: when I was being chased, when I was pursued and receiving constant reassurances of my desirability. Maybe I would sleep with a very young man if he chased me hard enough, if I felt wholly convinced that he resolutely desired me. But even with an eighteen- or 21-year-old, I wouldn't coerce. I don't think I'd be attracted to a young man if he had drunk enough to compromise his decision-making capacity. The two were connected—some kind of agency was missing. A mental component that connected age and consent, and therefore attraction, for me.

I charged forward, pushing through the pain, my throat wheezing for breath, through the final few hundred metres home. I imagined myself touching a boy, imagined Samuel touching me, and I understood them to be different things. My shoes hit the gravel outside the front door of my strange, temporary home and I fell to my knees, gasping, willing myself to picture an image of me as an abuser, pushing myself to imagine that as a desire, but it did not come.

I rolled onto my back and felt the cold, sharp stones on my skin; the sky was such a bright blue it made my eyes water. I couldn't ever do what Samuel had done. I was incapable of being gratified by someone afraid and unwilling. I didn't want that. I felt sure I would never want that. It wasn't even a question of putting my own pleasure above someone else's—it was a case of mutual exclusivity. The other human being afraid and confused would immediately cancel out my arousal. If I were on a trampoline in the back of a friend's yard, with the opportunity to gratify myself with no consequences, at the cost of betraying the sanctity of another human being's bodily autonomy, I would not do what Samuel had done.

In this way, he and I were fundamentally different. I registered that there are three distinct elements required for a person to act the way he did: he wanted to molest me, he didn't fear consequences for doing so, and he didn't care about my life. I might never understand why someone finds a particularly young person attractive, but it was a mistake to think that Samuel's dealings with me existed in a vacuum. Every act of sexual abuse is either deliberately or negligently cruel: each involves a terrified victim whose life experience an abuser completely devalues. I could never overcome that harm; I could never, not even negligently, inflict that kind of damage.

I felt myself lightened, or somehow unchained. Samuel hadn't created any irrepressible bond between us. It was only my own fears unilaterally keeping that imagined connection alive. He had deposited an experience into my lifetime, and that experience was now a memory I couldn't forget, but it wasn't an unknowable, mysterious, evil thing. There was space inside me for it to live alongside all my other memories and thoughts and feelings. I would never beat the demon, I could not exorcise it, I would simply learn to live above it.

That morning I felt myself not only connected to my body, but more within it. I lay there on the gravel, my breath rising in puffs, steam coming off my body, newly comfortable.

It seemed fitting, in some sick way, after my rumination on responsibility and victimhood, that our next big sentence in Gympie would be for child exploitation material. Again with the almost-always men having the almost-always same excuses. Defence danced around what they wished they could say: that he didn't really *do it*. He just *looked at it*.

Megan had a case once where a man—the head of a big, reputable company—had printed out pictures of children as young as three being raped, printed out pictures of his own stepchildren, and cut out the faces of his stepchildren, stuck them to the bodies of children being raped, and then printed his own face and stuck it on the man in the pictures, and masturbated to the unique collages. His defence barrister went all the way, making the submission that his client had gone to such lengths in order to relieve himself and not 'risk' acting on such desires with the stepchildren in real life.

Megan and I spoke for a long time about the moral and philosophical implications of this case. It was basically the most extreme example of the defence of every person charged with possessing CEM—that it was better they did it to images of kids, rather than actual kids. Each one argued they were special or unique, that their case was different, that their predilections didn't have a big effect on the supply-and-demand chain of the production and dissemination of such content. Judge had a drafted response that he tweaked a little for every CEM sentence that came along, such was their lack of originality.

Commonwealth prosecutors had to be flown in to deal with the cases, and special task forces were set up to deal with investigations. People weren't allowed to work in certain departments for more than a few years.

'One of them told a friend of mine that in his three years there he watched a kid growing up through the videos,' Megan told me once. 'That they just couldn't find where these particular videos were being made, and they saw these kids over and over again, getting older and older.'

I groaned and rubbed my eyes, hard.

'Judge says we're putting the wrong people in gaol,' Megan added.

Another associate, Rita, was there with us. 'I saw some CEM once where they were eating a baby,' she said. 'Well, I didn't *see* it myself, you know, because of the envelope, but that's what it was.'

Megan and I were speechless.

The prosecutor handed up a folder to the old bailiff that included a 'representative mix' of the thousands of images they'd found on the defendant's hard drives.

The bailiff went to pass it to me but Judge interrupted. 'Straight to me, please,' he said, reaching out, and the court seemed to hold its breath as he took a moment to open the envelope and consider its contents. We all hung our heads.

'Have you reviewed this sample?' Judge asked the barrister.

'I have not, your Honour, and I would prefer not to, unless your Honour requests I do so. I trust my learned friend's selection of the materials as being representative and I'm prepared to make oral submissions on the nature of the content.'

How bad would it have to be, that your own barrister doesn't want to look at what you've done? We all sat quietly for another moment while I heard Judge flipping through the photos behind me.

'Yes,' Judge said, and I turned and accepted the envelope he was passing down to me. It was physically heavy: an uncomfortable weight. I placed it in front of me, and put its identifying sticker on the front of it, and was overcome with curiosity, so I turned it over. Then relief flooded through me when I saw Judge had already sealed it.

Dad had once told me that when he'd been on the scene of a car accident, he'd noticed that traffic didn't get bad because one lane was blocked, traffic quickly backed up because every driver who went past slowed to get a good look at the mangled vehicles and bodies. I was one of those pathetic, gross people, like everyone else.

Whether I looked in the envelope or not didn't make much difference, all of us there in the courtroom still had to hear almost an hour of horrific descriptions of the images this man had down-loaded. What was worse: seeing the images and having them seared on your mind, or having them described to you, one after the other, allowing time for your mind to fill in the gaps, to imagine the terror, to grapple with the whys and whos that screamed out from the gaps in the story?

The defendant's barrister said that the defendant only liked the 'non-violent stuff' and the stuff where the girls looked around sixteen, and when it 'didn't look like there was no consent', but I didn't think anyone was convinced. He would masturbate two or three times a day, swapping material with other people around the world via an image-sharing database in Russia. There was an international network of 151 users and 55,185 files. He was forty-something, never married, no children. There was a feeling in the courtroom while we all listened that I can only describe as a moral mugginess: instead of moisture in the air it was a reminder of how shit humans can be, and we were all swimming around in it, trying to take showers but still stinking of it at the end of the day.

The barrister read out an email in which the defendant wrote of comparing and sharing files with someone else in his network, and of opening a folder and looking at the images. He said to the correspondent, *Nah, these ones are too young for me.*

I glanced across to the man in the dock and saw him flinch. *I like ten and up, budding boobies*, he had written. He was shaking his head, grimacing. Was he actually disgusted with himself or was this a show? Had he been disgusted while he was downloading and sharing the pictures or had our public airing of his actions given rise to his shame? The security officer to the left of the dock had the corners of his mouth turned down too, his hands clasped tight in front of him. I was glad I didn't have to be that near the defendant.

'This is the kind of conduct that fosters and encourages the feeding of the industry,' Judge said in his sentencing, and the man went to gaol.

'I think maybe I'm more upset about this stuff than I am about the actual physical offending sentences,' I said to Judge when we were packing up for the day. 'Why is that?'

'I think part of it is the sheer volume of the material. This guy had thousands of those images,' he said, 'and they all do, and they try to say that it's less serious, or maybe they think that it's less serious, because it's not "really" them.'

'At least they seem to plead?' I said, trying to look at the positive side.

'Well, how could they not?' he replied. 'It's all sitting there on their computer. What are they going to do, say that someone else downloaded it all and collected it all, over years, on their computers, without them knowing?'

'I am really creeped out by how he kept his records, too,' I said, and to that Judge just nodded—what could he say?

The defendant had listed files and folders with special names to refer to the different ages of the children. Some folders only contained photos and videos of particular children, some of these so full that there could be no doubt he actively sought out material they individually featured in. It plagued my mind—were some children more sought-after than others within these networks? Were there trends and patterns for what kind of material was most popular?

The prosecutor had read out some of a search history that the defendant hadn't realised was being logged, and his predilections were cruel and unusual, and they were also specific. He sat in the dock and didn't look up once until he was called upon to stand in front of Judge to receive his sentence. I searched his face. How could you have known, if you met him somewhere else, that he was this kind of man?

I thought a lot about Judge's words while out there in Gympie: *How could they not plead guilty?* If only there were a way to get to that stage with person-to-person offending. If some day, somehow, we could get to a point where sentences, instead of trials, were the norm for all sex offenders.

In Queensland if something illegal is found on your computer, it's as if someone was speeding in your car—or, more accurately, it's as though the cops have found drugs in your house. The law presumes you have control over your house, and your car, and therefore presumes you were the one speeding, or that you had possession of the drugs, unless you present an adequate alibi or find the guilty party to front up to court. It's odd and rather illuminating that people become so outraged when the prospect of positive consent requirements for sexual acts might be legislated. 'You can't shift the presumption of innocence!' they kick and scream, but we already do, in lots of different areas of the law, all the time. We all know and agree that to drive a car is to have control over a monumentally dangerous thing, and if something goes wrong and somebody gets hurt, we ask, 'Who had control over that thing?' and we find the owner and say, 'This is your responsibility, prove it wasn't.' Driving and sex are both privileges granted at certain ages, both can do irreparable damage when done recklessly, but only driving requires tests, checkpoints and licences.

I don't understand why the government—at schools and through public education programs—doesn't teach people about consent the way we teach them about drink-driving. After all, overconsumption of alcohol often leads to horrific consequences in both activities. Why can a man be charged with negligent, reckless driving after getting himself drunk, but he can argue that the same level of voluntary intoxication led him to honestly and mistakenly believe a woman consented to intercourse, and be acquitted of a rape charge accordingly?

'Hypothetically,' I said to Megan once, 'a man could drink-drive with a woman in the passenger's seat, and crash the car, and they are both on the side of the road, and he could rape her while she's unconscious, and then go to court and use the alcohol as a defence for the rape, saying he mistakenly thought she consented, while it is used against him for the dangerous driving.'

'Yep.'

'And a wreck of a car is evidence, but the wrecked body of a woman isn't, because women lie.'

'Yep.'

⌒

Rebecca was the solicitor for one matter in our second week at Gympie. A man was charged with sexual assault and wouldn't plead guilty, and so we had it listed for trial on the Tuesday. Things were odd, though. Everything on the court and prosecution side was ready to go, and then we found out the defendant, Mr Lang, had experienced a seizure. Things got put on hold for about an hour. Some paramedics attended and informed counsel that it wasn't a seizure but a panic attack. I received a note through the bailiff a further thirty minutes later: *Mr Lang has been given medication and conferenced again. He now understands his instructions. Ready.*

Mr Lang was extremely worried he'd be going to gaol. He sat in the dock with such confusion on his face and I watched as he bit his lips furiously. I read over his report: oxygen deprived at birth, over ten siblings, abusive father. He had seizures and panic attacks regularly and couldn't read or write. For a moment I thought to myself, *Well of course he's in court, what a start in life*, but then I started wondering what Judge would do with him. If a person's drink is spiked and they involuntarily imbibe a substance that renders them unable to control their actions or realise the incorrectness of their actions, they can't be held culpable. But what of people born with foetal alcohol syndrome? Low intelligence and behavioural problems are two of the most common side-effects for those born with their entire life spiked. Where did this defendant's responsibility for his actions fall? What would be the use of or reason for punishing him too severely?

Then I heard the prosecutor repeat what the defendant had said at the time of the offending. 'You've had the rest, now have the best,' he told her, blocking her exit and groping her, forcing her to kiss him. He had waited to make his move until she was at home alone with her newborn baby. The woman said she was now having difficulty being intimate with her husband, that this man had made her feel unsafe in her home.

Defence put forward a 'gentle giant' plot line: the defendant just 'didn't know his own strength' or just 'didn't understand'. This reminded me of a case I'd studied in law school, about a man who was quite far along on the autism spectrum whose counsel successfully argued that because of his condition he couldn't read the facial expressions or noises the complainant was making to communicate to him that she didn't consent to intercourse, and he raped her and was acquitted because he had an honest and reasonable belief that she did consent. But how did that hold up to evidence about how women on the spectrum are diagnosed significantly less frequently than men because all women are raised to *have to* interpret social cues a lot more than men? Women on the spectrum are held to higher standards of learned emotional intelligence than men.

Were men like this defendant in Gympie getting away with assaulting women because nobody expected any better of them? Wasn't that just offensive to everyone?

'I'm very sorry for what I've done,' he said, and my anger faltered. He was thirty-eight, lived alone, and made a tiny income as a gardener. Would he ever have the opportunity to be consensually intimate with a woman? Was he lonely? He was so big—huge hands, extremely tall, a slim body but an oddly square head.

Judge used the word 'attacked' during the sentence. 'It was entirely understandable that she was revolted by your behaviour,' he said to the defendant. 'Do you understand that?'

I looked at his lowered shoulders, his head hung in shame. He nodded. My heart was a tennis ball being hit across the court from 'good guy' to 'bad guy', never landing.

⌒

Judge was keen to get through as many matters as possible so we listed another trial the next day, but the defendant pleaded guilty right after the jurors were empanelled. The defence barrister had used every single one of his eight challenges on the women's names I pulled from the barrel, so the result was two women and ten men. I still couldn't believe defence were allowed to do that, and I was happy when the defendant pleaded guilty so we didn't have to proceed with such an unbalanced panel. At sentence we heard from the prosecutor that the defendant had just broken up with his girlfriend and didn't have a place to live on the night he climbed in the bedroom window of another young woman, who was sleeping, and tried to pull off her pants.

When she was wrestling him off her and her brother ran into the room to get the intruder out, the defendant yelled at her, 'You are the only girls I know in town and you're doing this to me, you dogs!'

How entitled to their bodies did he think he was? In his mind, was this the equivalent of yelling at the local IGA for not being open when he wanted, because it was the only supermarket in town he knew of? And to him, was a woman a 'dog' automatically when she said 'no' to sex with him? What if the brother hadn't run in? She would have been raped with no witnesses, might not have gone to court, might not have got any justice.

The rest of Gympie was relatively straightforward. Michelle Payne won the Melbourne Cup, and I had a lively discussion with Judge about how I could be simultaneously happy for her and loathing of horseracing generally.

Judge and I went to dinner with Rebecca, the visiting prosecutors, and some of the local solicitors. I felt a subtle twinge when I saw her and Judge interact again. It was a reminder that my time with him would be ending soon, and I would miss his company.

The prospect of no longer working in the District Court was exciting but also frightening. I knew I was getting addicted to the feeling of significance inherent in my work. Addicted in the true sense of the word, too—I had a higher tolerance for horrific details, and the rush of awaiting and taking a verdict was fading.

Not many other jobs would give me the opportunity to examine life and liberty on a daily basis, but seeing Rebecca was good timing. We had a quick chat about her work and lifestyle, and I was instantly and freshly reassured that going into law—especially going into defence—wasn't for me.

'How are you going with PLTs?' she asked, and when I groaned she gave me a knowing smile.

'Nearly done,' I nodded, 'and that's about the only positive thing about it.'

We laughed.

I would finish up as an associate, get admitted, and take Samuel to court. The rest of my life would just have to fall into place.

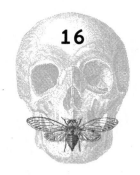

16

I WENT FROM GYMPIE STRAIGHT to Vincent's house on the Friday afternoon. I found him in his bedroom and pulled him into a hug and
toppled us over onto the bed, laughing.

'Why do you always go away from me?' I asked him, joking.

'Babe,' he said in a faux-low-movie-star voice, 'you know I have
to travel around the Australian outback dispensing justice.' And we
laughed again.

I woke the next morning to my phone ringing, and before I had
even opened my eyes I was panicking it would be Samuel. I gently
crawled over Vincent, silenced my phone, and stared at the screen:
a mobile number I didn't have saved. I knew it was him, somehow,
and watched the phone in horror, feeling it vibrate in my palm to
the beat of the ringtone, the light flashing, illuminating my face
in the otherwise dark room.

Finally the vibrations stopped, and I waited. I stared down at
the little grenade. I was perched on the edge of the mattress, every
muscle in my body poised, blood pumping in my ears, minutes
passing. *Bzzzz'd.* It went off and I jumped, absurdly—like waiting for
the toaster and being startled even when you know it's going to *pop.*

'You have one new voicemail.'

I forgot where I was and hit *play,* and my premonition came
true with such force and volume that it was as though the strength

of my fear had willed it into existence. Samuel's voice boomed out into the room, rupturing the peaceful, loving silence Vincent and I had been resting in, blissfully, ignorantly, until that moment.

I listened. Samuel was back in Australia and wanted to know if I wanted to meet up and talk about things. At the end was a casual apology and an offer to buy me a drink. As soon as the message finished I hit #3—Delete.

'Was that him?' Vincent asked me, half asleep.

'Yeah,' I replied, putting the phone on the ground, pushing it away with my foot.

'What did he want?'

'He just apologised again, and he asked me if I want to meet up for a drink to talk about it,' I said, confused.

'Ugh,' Vincent groaned into his pillow, 'come back to sleep,' and he pulled me under the covers, but I didn't get back to sleep. I felt invaded, as if I'd failed somehow and allowed Samuel into our bed, and I panicked that Vincent wouldn't be able to forget it, that he might be repulsed by me like I felt repulsed by myself. *Who wants some broken, dirty thing for a lover?*

Later in the day I remembered the usefulness of the evidence I had destroyed and was furious at myself. I knew better than that. I'd seen so many trials, proofread so many sentences, studied so many cases, and I'd destroyed my own evidence. Jessica's testimony about flushing the tampon full of evidence down the toilet came back to me, along with the memory that neither of her trials resulted in a guilty verdict.

I sent Sean a message to tell him that Samuel was back in the country, and I waited. We all think we'll know what we'll do, if it happens to us, but in The Freeze it's different.

Life went on. Some days were better than others. It was another hot summer with skirts cutting into my waist. I saw my mum and asked her that we not talk about it. I went to work and made the most of the time Judge and I had together, picking his brain about this and that. I got to know my housemates a little better, smoking cigarettes on our rotting back deck, looking out over fiery Queensland sunsets.

I went on a judges-and-associates golf day. It cost well over a hundred dollars and Judge didn't want to go, so I got paired with a different judge who was quite nice. I turned up in a floral tea dress, not realising that many people consider golf to be a 'sport' that requires specific 'activewear'—namely a Polo Ralph Lauren shirt, preferably in a pastel shade reminiscent of gelati. And chinos. Chinos everywhere.

'Well, that's the most exciting golfing attire I've ever seen,' the judge said to me, one eyebrow raised so high it would have hit his hairline if he had one.

'Ah yes, well, I only ever golf in my finest,' I replied with a fake curtsey.

The event was yet another affirmation that I didn't belong in that world. The lunch that took place afterwards was similar fare to what had been served at one of my cousin's weddings—the most important day of their young adult life and one they saved for over a year to put on—and there I was eating it, rather carelessly, with a bunch of twenty-somethings all pretending they weren't wearing the same thing and me pretending I looked different deliberately. Fancy wine flowed and so I drank it. My most vivid memory of the whole day is of kicking my shoes off, in a quiet moment away from everyone, and watching some rainbow lorikeets and feeling the cool breeze in between my toes.

'How was it?' Judge asked me the following Monday.

'I liked driving the golf buggy,' I replied with a shrug, and we exchanged a knowing smile.

~

A call came through one afternoon when I was bustling around my room after work, kicking my heels off and unzipping an impossibly tight pencil skirt.

'Hi, it's Sean from Dutton Park Police, have you got a moment?'

'Sure do,' I replied, sitting at my desk and grabbing my notepad and pen.

'So we sent a couple of officers to knock on his door, so now he knows what's up.'

'Right.'

'So the first thing is, I suppose, to look out for yourself. It's very rare, but sometimes we get an accused who will try to find or contact the victim,' he said, and I didn't mention Vincent's scare. 'Like I said, that's very rare, but it's definitely a good idea to make sure you're locking the house properly and, you know, just keeping an eye out for anyone who might be following you or anything.'

'Right.'

'But I've also received some correspondence indicating that Samuel has hired a solicitor and briefed a barrister.'

'Oh,' I said, confused, 'but they know he admitted it on the pretext call, right?'

'Yep, but, ah, basically they've come back and said that he was ten.'

'What?'

'Ten when it happened, when he did it.'

'Huh?'

'I know, yeah.'

'That's ridiculous!' I said.

'They're saying that the incident occurred when Samuel's family had just moved to the neighbourhood, and that he was ten.'

'Well, that's just impossible. He's at least six years older than me, and I was in my primary school uniform. I would have had to have been four for what he's saying to be true! I don't think I could have even really remembered anything that happened when I was four!'

'Yeah, look, I think they're just trying it on and, at this stage, without you having any strong evidence about the date you say it took place, I don't have much to say back to them.'

I was furious. 'And this couldn't possibly have anything to do with the fact that ten is the last age at which an individual can't be held criminally culpable, can it?' I said, almost spitting with sarcasm.

Sean outlined what was to happen in the coming months and told me to brace for a bit of a fight. It seemed as if Samuel and his lawyers knew they couldn't fight the fact that the offending occurred, so all they could do was to dispute the year it occurred. I tried to see the positive side—they were scraping the bottom of the barrel. I hung up the phone, a little sad but mostly infuriated. Something inside me, in my belly, fired up for a fight. I thought for a moment that perhaps I wasn't a Freeze kind of person anymore, that maybe I really could take him on. I thought back to Maggie, how she'd frozen in the model aeroplanes room but then fought back in the van, and then how she testified in court, and I thought maybe I could learn to be strong like her. That maybe, after all these years, I was on even ground, that with my education and my job and my partner and my family, I could fight for myself.

⌁

Nobody tells you that if you want to press charges against the man who molested you, you still have to go to work, get jobs done and interact with people as though you're a normal human being—more difficult than that, even: that you are your normal self. You can't put your life on pause and tap out while you ride out the bad waves. You'll still drop the roast you just made, and miss your bus, and run out of toilet paper. And all the small things make you furious because, goddamnit, can't the universe see you have some bigger fish to fry? I had good days, sometimes a few in a row, and then I would get very drunk and vomit up dinners, or cut myself, sometimes both depending on what new bullshit trial Judge and I were sitting in that week.

My psychologist appointments were rare because I couldn't find slots to fit around work very often. I was also nervous about having to disclose my mental health care when I went for admission to the legal profession in a few months' time: a section in the paperwork is dedicated to things you have to put on the record that might affect your 'suitability' to practise law, and that's where you disclose your criminal convictions, Centrelink frauds, speeding fines, and whether or not you have any mental illnesses. I didn't even know who I could ask about this process without making it pretty damn obvious that I was on, or was considering going on, a mental health plan. In the meantime my weight yo-yoed and I bought lots of cheap white wine and extra bandaids. Once I bought myself flowers and wine and bandaids on the way home from work, all together, and laughed out loud, at a crowded pedestrian crossing, about what a cliché I was.

It's a realisation most of us have at some point in our young adult lives, that there's no guidebook for the important stuff. When you most want to stride out from under the wings of your parents, you will simultaneously long for their guidance and reassurance like never before. In the worst moments of those nights I thought of my mum, and how I could burn down everything around me and that she would still come help me if I just picked up the phone. Like most of my female friends, I rarely fought with my father and often fought with my mother, but we all knew that when the chips were down our mums would be the first to run into the blaze after us.

Sometimes I wondered if I could ever be a mother like that, the way you had to, and whether I could bring a girl into a world where she had a one in five chance of someone molesting her. Some of the evenings I spent alone were touch-and-go, and my mum didn't even know she was the one who got me through. I never called anyone. I didn't know how long the whole process would take and I didn't want to use up favours too early in the game.

⌢

'I have something for you,' Judge said to me one morning, and handed me two printed pieces of paper. It was the draft for an update to the legislation for domestic violence adding strangulation as a specific offence, as recommended in Quentin Bryce's report.

'Oh, for me! You shouldn't have!' I replied, and we laughed, but my smile was genuine.

In the seven months after non-lethal strangulation became a separate criminal offence in Queensland in April 2016 when the law was eventually passed, *The Courier-Mail* reported that more than five hundred allegations of non-lethal strangulation had been made.

That morning had significance for me as well. I liked that Judge had printed that memorandum off for me. I appreciated that he knew I cared, that it would make me feel good to see that. It was a sign that he knew me properly, and perhaps even respected me.

⌢

I took the printouts with me when I met Dad for a coffee—to tell him of the process as much as to gloat. I was happy for about five minutes before becoming sad again about the fact that the legislation was even necessary. I told him I was afraid, that at work baddies were all around and on the street they were all around. He said that in our jobs lots of people burn out because all they see is the worst cross-section of society. He said the baddies really are a minority and that the overwhelming majority of people in the world are good and nice.

'You only see the 5 per cent,' he said.

'Five per cent!? One in twenty people hurts another person?'

'Well, no, I just mean, not many.'

'One in twenty is a lot!'

'It's not one in twenty.'

'Well then, what is it!?' I asked loudly, and tears came to my eyes. 'How many people are actually criminals?' I gestured around the cafe.

He went quiet for a bit. He didn't have an answer for me. 'Are you still talking to someone?' he sort-of asked.

I thought I had been talking to someone.

⸺

When I slept I had nightmares about sex abuse and assault. Horrific things that I woke up feeling ashamed of. In these dreams, sometimes things would happen to me, or I would witness them happening to a woman near me. Other times I was floating around a scene, invisible at the sidelines, watching. I never recognised the people's faces but each of them was different—a never-ending cascade of boys and girls, plenty of different women, and a plethora of men I'd never seen before. It made me nervous that I'd been wrong about myself in Gympie, and I worried that the nightmares coming from within were a signifier of the horror that sat within me somewhere, that my daytime brain was a pathetic bandaid over the pus, slipping off my rotting, slimy core when I closed my eyes. If Vincent was sleeping with me he would cut the nightmares short by shaking me awake when he heard me crying or screaming.

One night I was walking through a primary school that looked like my own, but I was invisible to everyone, just watching. I saw a man leading a boy away by the hand and I followed them to the bush nearby. The man was tall and broad-shouldered, and he had brown hair and a short beard. He was wearing a relaxed hunting outfit, like recreational hunters I'd seen in the North American woods. The bush we were in was dry but thick with gum saplings, and it must have been autumn because the ground was covered in foliage of classic Australian greys and browns. The man and boy snapped twigs and rustled dry leaves as they walked along but I floated by, unseen. The boy was Asian and had a neat haircut, and he never looked at the man. He didn't even look around, he just watched the ground ahead and showed no emotion. His feet were moving, sure, but I could recognise The Freeze anywhere. I watched as they reached a rise in the gully and the man laid the boy down on his back, and the man straddled the boy's face and raped his mouth until the boy vomited and sat up with a bloody nose. I did nothing. I watched the man pull a full bottle of Bundaberg Rum out of his khaki backpack and stick the neck of the bottle into the boy's mouth like a pacifier, and as the man directed the boy's arms to hold the bottle for himself, and the boy complied, glassy-eyed, not even crying, the man started raping the boy's anus, first slowly, then more and more aggressively. I looked at the boy's face once more, but I didn't recognise him, and then I woke up.

It was dawn and Vincent was sleeping deeply beside me, our heads almost touching. I began to cry. Would I contaminate him? How could I have created such a filthy thing and brought it into our bed? I didn't know those people, I'd never even heard a case where a man did something like that to a boy. And why hadn't I done anything? How could I have just watched that—had I really been there? None of it made sense if there wasn't an ugly thing inside me. Had it left and returned? Half asleep that night, I imagined it was getting excited, reaching its tentacles out and hooking them up around my brain, squeezing my eyeballs. I couldn't keep it down.

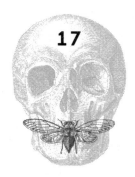

17

I HAD A WEEK OFF work and visited my friend Anna in Melbourne. She was in a new theatre show called *The Living Museum of Erotic Women* and I wanted to support her, and to just drink and smoke and try to chill the fuck out. She'd written an incredible monologue for one part of the show that she performed naked, and in another part she pulled a tape measure out of her vagina—it was epic. I also had to tell her about Samuel in person, for some complicated reasons. Anna had been abused by her stepfather when she was a child. She had also slept with Samuel while I was overseas on exchange in 2011.

'Oh my god, I'm so sorry to hear this,' she said, when I told her about it all, 'and thank you for telling me.'

'I'm just so sorry I didn't say anything when you dated him. I just wasn't ready to even deal with it myself, and I was on the other side of the planet, and when I found out you'd already slept with him I just figured it was too late, and . . . ahhh, these are just excuses, I'm so sorry.'

'You don't have to be sorry for anything,' she said. 'I completely understand.'

'Thank you,' I said, and wiped a little tear off my cheek.

'To be honest, I'm not surprised.'

'What do you mean?'

'I never slept with him because I really wanted to,' she told me. 'I mean, it wasn't rape, but he absolutely manipulated me. It was during the floods, and he told me he was really struggling and vulnerable because his family home had gone under and he'd lost everything, and that if I was intimate with him he'd feel better, and he put this relentless pressure on me. I just kind of gave in after a while.'

'Oh no, I'm so sorry to hear that.'

'I'm just grossed out!' she said, and we laughed a little, and hugged for a long time.

'I was really worried Vincent would treat me differently,' I said, 'but I think it's okay.'

'Yeah, I know what you mean. I'm not ashamed of what happened to me, and you know me, I'm okay to talk about it now, but mostly I just hate the thought that people will start making assumptions about my psychology.'

꒰ꜜ

I walked home alone after her show later that night. Google Maps told me the walk would take forty minutes, and I felt like stretching my legs, but as the sun set I realised I was going past a long stretch of cemetery without lighting. I took my headphones out of my ears just in time to hear a car screech past me, and a man leaned out of the window and screamed at me, 'FAT BITCH!' And four other men in the car laughed and hooted.

I told Anna about it later when we were at her place together.

'You should be more careful,' she said, and I was about to remark that it wasn't like her to wag her finger at me, but she continued, 'Jill Meagher was taken from nearby here.'

We sat in silence for a bit, so much between us not needing to be spoken. We both knew we shouldn't have to change our behaviours, but we also knew better than most that the monsters were men and the men were real.

'People keep telling me to just compartmentalise my life,' I said, pouring us each another glass of wine, 'but I can't even walk down the fucking road without being forcibly reminded that the rapists I see in court are the same as the rapists out on the street.'

'I don't know how you do that job, babe,' she said, reaching out and patting my knee, 'you're amazing.'

I smiled at her. 'No, *you're* amazing! That show was amazing! Tell me all about it.'

And she did, and we had a blast.

⌒

Back at work, Judge asked me about Melbourne.

'I had a wonderful time, thank you!' I said.

'What kind of theatre does your friend do?' he asked.

I paused, cocked my head a little and smiled. 'Experimental.'

'Got it,' he said, and went back to his work.

⌒

My brother's thirtieth rolled around and everyone got together for a party.

'Where's Samuel?' one of his mates asked, and I tried to act casual.

Someone else replied, 'Oh you know him, always bailing,' and everyone else laughed.

One of the reasons I didn't tell anyone about Samuel's behaviour was that for a long time he was one of only two real friends my brother had. I'd always been worried that losing Samuel would hurt Arron deeply. I cracked another beer and grabbed a handful of chips, thinking that I was racking up quite the tally of things to feel guilty about.

Someone at the table asked me what I did, and once I'd explained my job they launched into a monologue about the Baden-Clay case.

The trial had gripped the nation. A man was accused of killing his wife and dumping the body, and he had scratches on his face and had been having an affair, pleaded not guilty to murder, but was convicted by a jury. The conviction was then overturned by the Court of Appeal. Many *Courier-Mail* readers were outraged about the 'low' sentence and then the appeal. I was pleased that people seemed suddenly to care about victims of domestic violence, but I was also getting fed up with so much attention going to that one case. I felt as though every matter Judge and I heard deserved prime-time coverage. I was also fed up with people demanding more from the courts and from the legal system—many of the questions a case like Baden-Clay raised were social, not legal ones. I tried to explain my frustration to the person at the party but was definitely bringing the mood down.

Why was murder the serious thing? Why did people care so much more about it? Murder could happen in one day. A few hours is enough to show intent to kill, and you can kill a person who is nearly dead and it's still murder because of the eggshell skull rule. But what about decades-long sexual abuse that eventually causes suicide? I remembered that photo of schoolkids from ABC News—the one with the faces blacked out. At least some Church victims were getting cameras and reporters. What about all the women I saw in court, though? I'd read and seen so many victim impact statements where abuse survivors outlined multiple suicide attempts. How many suicides meant that nobody was ever taken to court for homicide? How many times were a man's actions buried with the corpse of his girlfriend's daughter?

~

That weekend I got a call from Sean. Samuel's solicitor was asking if I would consider an 'out of court resolution'.

'What does that even mean?' I asked.

'It would be a joint half-day counselling session,' Sean explained. 'You would speak to a psychologist, then he would, and then you would speak to the psychologist together.'

'Right.'

'And he would pay for it.'

'How generous.'

'But you need to know that if you accept this, the condition is that the psychologist could never be called as a witness.'

'Riiiight,' I replied. 'Well, I'm not really interested in any of that.'

'The solicitors said this would be an advisable course of action because of the "staleness of the matter".'

I tried not to scoff. Stale to whom? 'No. I want this on his record.'

For all I knew he'd been weaselling his way out of this bullshit for years. Maybe, at least, if I put up a fight, he would plead guilty the next time someone came forward. Whenever she did, whoever and wherever she was, I did it for *her* as much as for myself.

One Sunday Vincent and I went to Tuttu and Poppa's for lunch. Mum, Dad, Arron and his girlfriend were also there to celebrate three November birthdays.

I sat with Tuttu having a cigarette out the back of their house, pretending to be chirpy while I stared at their Hills hoist. Laundry was flapping on it, bright white against a bright blue sky. She had started getting sick and we were all still pretending it wasn't a big deal. Her cigarettes were killing her, but I was glad to be smoking with her. Having a smoke with Tuttu in front of my family was worlds colliding. Nobody else smoked and Mum gave me a stern look when she passed by, but she couldn't scold me without hitting Tuttu in the crosshairs so I was safe. I remember asking my parents once when I was young, 'Why would you pay someone else to kill you slowly?' But that was before I had a reason to want an excuse to stare into the distance with a relaxing substance for fifteen minutes at a time. When I sat with Tuttu smoking, I could bitch about men and mock the fancy people at work. When we sat together looking out in the same direction, doing something but not really—a catalyst to be there but no pressure for any particular result—in those smokos we became friends. We would only have a dozen such moments together.

As Vincent and I were driving home, we spoke about Tuttu getting sick and what we wanted to do with our lives. It was the kind of conversation that can't begin on its own. The kind of thought processes that you only engage in when forced to by an external event—births, deaths and marriages. When we got back to my place and lay down together I told him how much he meant to me and that sometimes I could feel him swimming in my heart.

'I think I'll love you forever,' I said to him.

'Yeah, of course, we're going to get old and fat together,' he replied, without hesitation, and kissed me more.

The next month we moved into a share-house room together.

⌒

Summer meant it was house-party season in Brisbane. One Saturday I was by a pool talking about the wage gap with a woman I'd just met, and we exchanged some funny workplace stories. Hours later that evening she pushed through the dancefloor and found me again, and outside by the pool in the cool breeze she told me that she was raped by her first-ever boyfriend.

'I'm so sorry,' I said, touching her arm.

'I don't even know why I'm telling you this now, we're at a party, I'm sorry.'

'Don't be sorry, we can talk about it as much or as little as you want. Are you okay?'

'Oh, *ugh*, it was ages ago now, I'm not even sad anymore, I'm just fucking angry. Like, I don't even think he would realise how shitty what he did was. Maybe he doesn't even know it was rape. And I feel guilty wondering if he did it to other girls because I didn't call him out about it, you know?'

'I know,' I said, nodding.

I didn't tell her this, but she reminded me of one time when I was walking around Yeronga; for some reason, Samuel and I were alone together, going from his house to ours, or perhaps vice versa.

'So, you got a boyfriend yet?' he asked without prompting.

'Ah.' I shrugged and half-nodded, lying to impress him.

'Ha! Playing it cool! Nice one, nice one.' He clapped. 'Have you, you know, given it up yet?' He nudged me in the ribs, hard, with his elbow.

'Nah,' I said.

'Yeah, good one, there's no rush,' he said, nodding, as though he was seriously considering the situation, 'and if you think he's getting impatient you can always just give him a—' And he made a gesture in the air of sucking a dick, and a guttural *pop* with his tongue in his mouth, and grinned at me.

At the time it just felt cool that he was even talking to me, the ugly little desperate thing. Now I look back and see a creep exploiting a young girl's blatant innocence.

⌒

During those six months, when I started to tell close friends whom I trusted, so many stories came out of the woodwork. People I'd known for decades listened patiently to me, hugged me, then took their turn to tell me about their own rapes and assaults. I wrote to Hanna—a girl I'd become best friends with while on exchange years earlier—about it, and she wrote back telling me that she had almost been molested as a child by a school groundskeeper in her hometown in Finland, and she had the man arrested and dozens of other girls emerged with stories of his abuse. *How interesting,* she wrote to me, *that we lived together for so long and went through so much, but didn't know this about each other.*

I had nightmares about running into Samuel around Brisbane. Sometimes I froze, sometimes I punched him, sometimes he apologised and sometimes he said cruel things. Every time I woke up furious. Why was nothing up to me? Why was nothing in my control? Who gave him permission to haunt me at night in the beautiful bedroom I shared with my lover? His prying fingers everywhere. I thought of him when I plucked my washing from the line, and when I jogged and the fat of my inner thighs rubbed together. When I was out walking and a car pulled up alongside me, for a moment I would always be most terrified that he was the driver. Why was I letting him in? How could I stop it?

When I was drunk and alone I wondered if I was the ugliest of all the girls and women Samuel had abused. Perhaps he would plead guilty if I was more beautiful. If, upon looking at me, people could understand why he 'couldn't help himself'. That summer, when I was still vomiting sometimes, I wondered if my ugliness made Samuel embarrassed to admit he did what he did. *I was more beautiful when I was a child.* I remembered I was cute—I'd seen photos. Would those images of that adorable little girl with those golden pigtails, in the bright blue checked school uniform, help the jury find Samuel guilty? 'See!' I could say to them. 'I didn't make it up! You may think I'm fat and ugly now, but I was a perfect child then! A sweet thing. Something a subconscious part of you didn't fear and loathe.'

⌒

For my first few appointments at Headspace, my psychologist just sat there and listened. The words were pouring out. She'd ask a single question about my life and I would speak for twenty minutes. She expressed shock when I said some things, sadness when I said

others, and when I paused and wrung my hands she would wait
in silence for as long as I needed to find the right word. I kept it
together for those first few sessions, trying to play it cool or somehow
keep things low-key, then one afternoon she asked if we could talk
about Vincent more.

'Sure,' I said before adding, 'actually, I *would* kind of rather
talk a bit about him. He's my future but all the investigation stuff
is my past.'

'I have in my notes here that you said one of the reasons you
wanted to come to these sessions was because you wanted someone
to talk to about the investigation, because you didn't want to talk to
Vincent about it too much, because you didn't want him to think
of you like that or see you in that way. Is that still how you feel?'

'Well yeah,' I shrugged, 'I want him to, like, desire me and I
think that's normal. I want him to see me sexually and as, like,
his partner.'

'Can you tell me what you mean by not wanting him to think
of you in *that way*?' she asked gently, and I paused.

'Like a victim? I want him to think of who I am now, not the
thing that happened to me. Spoiled or something.'

'This isn't necessarily the case for you, but often people who
have lived through abuse say they feel a dirtiness or shame about
what happened, and they don't want to reveal that to other people.'
I sat silently. 'Do you think maybe that you don't want to talk to him
about it because *you* think it's somehow not okay? That it makes
you undesirable?'

I took a deep breath in, and as I tried to exhale I started crying,
and I cried for a long time. She had looked into me and seen the
ugly thing curled up there.

'I know that I didn't deserve what happened or ask for it, but,'
I tapped my fingers on my chest, 'there is something in there.'

She said that we needed to work on my self-esteem. She said that we needed to get me feeling good about myself so that I didn't rely on other people to affirm my worth.

The next day I made lunch for me and Vincent, and he remarked that my bowl of pasta was quite large, and I had a panic attack. In hindsight that's a little bit funny, but I was crying and crying. I told him I hated my body because I was getting fatter and fatter, and he seemed to become frustrated by that, and he left my side.

But a few minutes later, when he saw me crying, he came and held me.

'Where is this coming from?' he asked. 'You were so happy a minute ago.'

'I feel like I have an ugly thing inside me, and it doesn't matter what I do. Even if I did get skinny, I'll always be ugly!' He kissed me and protested, but I tried to tell him what I felt: 'I feel like people can see it when they look at me, when I walk down the street.' I was frantic.

'See what?'

'The ugly thing.'

'There's nothing there. No ugly thing, you are beautiful.'

I wouldn't look at him, I felt so ashamed.

He put his hand under my chin, firmly, and made me look at him.

'The thing that happened to me,' I said. 'It's inside me all the time. And I don't want to talk to you about it because then you'll see the ugly thing too.'

'There is no ugly thing inside you. There's nothing there. You can talk to me whenever you want, as much as you want. You are beautiful.'

We stood in the kitchen together, him holding me and holding me up, for a long time, until I let go first.

Vincent and I drove to the police station one night at ten for me to make an addendum statement. My mum had remembered that a primary school friend of mine, Dylan, had broken his nose while playing on the trampoline, and that after the accident we moved it to a different area of the backyard with fewer bricks and more grass around it. The infamous nose break happened in the year 2000, and that put Samuel at a minimum of fifteen years old. It was weeks since I'd made my complaint and Samuel knew how old he was that afternoon, and he'd still sent the lawyers in with the only defence they could scrounge up—that he was only a child himself. I was furious at him.

On the drive over to the station, Vincent ate Maltesers and we spoke about lovely, silly things, and I tried to hide how elated I was that he kept his hand on my thigh like he usually did when we drove anywhere together.

We arrived ten minutes early and had a cigarette, joking that it wasn't the right place to flick our butts when we couldn't see a bin. As we walked up the cement ramp to the square concrete building I thought back to the last time I was there, shaking after the pretext phone call, my mother practically carrying me out to the car. Sean met me inside and he looked tired. I was surprised that I didn't really recognise his face despite having met him twice, for several hours each time. I tried to remember first meeting him but it made my shaking worse so I turned my mind back to the present.

'Thank you for making the time to see me again,' I said.

'Oh no, not at all, thanks for coming in so late,' he replied, explaining he was working nights.

Vincent took out his phone and sat down to wait at reception, and Sean and I went upstairs. We sat in a small room with a small computer and began the frustrating process of recording a statement. I remembered how the anger had boiled up inside me the first time I was there, when I'd repeated myself for the fourth time as Sean typed agonisingly slowly with his index fingers. I was much more calm this time. I wasn't being forced to relive the memory now. It felt more like an unpleasant elephant in the room.

We spoke about what would happen next, and Sean minced his words as he tried to ask me if I'd be willing to go to trial. 'I just need to know if there are any alternative resolutions that you'd be happy with?' he asked.

'Like what?'

'Like, a letter, or some kind of reconciliation meeting, or something like that.'

I pictured Samuel sitting at a desk, bashing out some piece-of-shit apology in ten minutes then going for a beer.

'No,' I said. 'I mean, for one thing, he admitted on the phone to me that he did it, and then hired two lawyers to try to weasel his way out of it. He's obviously not the least bit remorseful. And two, he said I wasn't the only one. At least this way if any other girls ever come forward they won't be the first. It'll be on his record.'

'Good,' Sean said and nodded. He was too professional or perhaps just too tired to smile, but I knew enough—from observing my father—to know that on some level Sean was pleased. 'I just needed to make sure I knew what your feelings were before I marched ahead with things.'

'Of course,' I said calmly as I held my hands together under the table to stop them shaking. 'I'll take this as far as it needs to go.'

'I mean, it's a bit *off*—his lawyers sent us a letter basically accusing us of only going ahead with your complaint because of your father's connection to the police and his work at this station.'

'What!?'

'I know. They said the matter isn't in the public interest, that proceeding with such a small and historical matter isn't worth the time or the resources, so we must have some ulterior motive.'

In the car on the way home I told Vincent about the lawyers' letter.

'What incompetent arseholes,' I said, speeding up to get through an orange light, still shaking.

'I know, right? Way to get a ton of cops to pay attention to the case and make sure they do everything *right*.'

'I hope his lawyers are that fucking stupid about the rest of this case.'

'I hope they're bleeding him dry.' Vincent smiled at me and put his hand on my thigh again.

'I'm gonna take this motherfucker down,' I said, driving across the Story Bridge.

I put my foot right down on the accelerator, going over the limit, and as the lights of the city fanned out in front of us I felt the fire come back to my belly. I wondered if this new argument would be raised in court—that the allegation was insubstantial and that it was only investigated and pushed through 'because of the complainant's father's relationship to the police'. What a classic loser move: something happens he doesn't like and so he automatically claims a conspiracy against him. Which was worse: if he believed that, or if he was just seeing what might get him off the hook? I held the car fast and steady, and the thumping of the wheels over the steel beams of the Story Bridge reverberated through me like drums of war. *Ba-dum ba-dum*. Perhaps eggshell skull worked both ways. *Ba-dum ba-dum*. You have to take your victim how they come. *Ba-dum ba-dum*. Samuel was just the unlucky dipshit who'd picked the daughter of a gnarly cop who refused to back down. *Ba-dum ba-dum*. Back then I was small, and now I was strong. *Ba-dum ba-dum*.

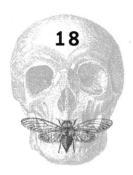

18

I HAD COME BACK TO the courts in January 2016 fresh after the Christmas break, hoping to leave on a high note, but our last trial together as judge and associate was a downer. In the elevator after I'd taken the not guilty verdicts, I turned and said to him, 'Not for the first time in our year together, Judge, I don't think he's necessarily guilty of this offence, but he's definitely guilty of being a dickhead.'

He laughed.

He took me out for lunch and we ate a fancy dish that had fried black ants on it. I had written him a letter saying all the things I knew I'd get teary about if I tried to enunciate them in front of him. We promised each other we'd stay in touch, and I promised him I'd eventually finish my PLT and get admitted.

I hung up my robes and took one last look at them, saying goodbye to all that prestige. I sensed some analogy there, that they never really fit me, but I couldn't find it, so just switched off the lights and went for a beer with Megan. Over the summer she and her boyfriend had decided they'd move to Sydney together when her contract ended.

'So this is goodbye?' I said dramatically, but I also felt forlorn.

'Nah, come see me in Sydney, and I'll be back to visit my family here too.'

'I'll hold you to that,' I nodded seriously, and held my beer up, and we clinked pints again. 'And what is Lizzie going to do?'

'She found out she got a job at some government agency on Monday.'

'Oh, thank God!' I tipped my head back in relief.

'I know. She'll find a little sweet spot in the public service somewhere, with nice people in the office, and she'll be fine.'

'She'll be fine, you'll be great, and I'll be—' I paused, 'here.'

⌒

I called Sean to ask for an update because over a month had passed since I had made my addendum statement.

'Rest assured, he will be charged. His solicitor indicated their intention is to take it to trial if he might have been fourteen, but plead if he was definitely fifteen. So first we need to wait for those hospital records proving the year Dylan broke his nose.'

'Right, okay, sure.'

'We're expecting him to just fall on his sword,' Sean said. 'His solicitors are going to tell him to plead, and hopefully he'll listen to them.'

'Yeah, I agree,' I said, nodding. It was going to be fine. I had other things on my mind.

⌒

I stared at the Hills hoist as I delivered my eulogy for Tuttu in my grandparents' back garden. The autumn was wet and so the gardens were lush. I spoke about the natural world being understood as a series of actions, and equal and opposite reactions. We mourned for the loss of the woman in relation to how deeply we loved her. The pain we felt at her passing was a testament to the happiness she brought us in life, the missing and longing a reminder of how lucky we were to have her with us. It was the ultimate risk we all took, as humans, when we took love into our lives.

My mother and I held each other, and I felt something shift that fortnight. I went from being the youngest of three women to the second of two. I was a young woman delivering a eulogy, not a girl whose birth was the most recent significant family event. Next it would be my turn to deliver a child or disappoint those around me by conscientiously objecting.

I stared up at the Hills hoist and felt all the waves colliding at a giant break. Who would bring a child to this place?

The following week my dad drove us in a clean rental car from Adelaide out to the Barossa Valley. We were in South Australia for Tuttu's second funeral and Mum had suggested an overnight trip to the vineyards. It was going to be great—the four of us having some solid family time and chilling out together. We would sleep in one cheap motel room with beds for each of us. The weather was perfect: a crisp breeze with strong, clear sunshine.

Arron and I were having a pretend-argument in the back seat when my phone started vibrating beside me. A private number—a warning sign. I didn't pick up, just watched the display. A voice-mail—another warning sign. Only one person calls me from a private number and leaves a voicemail. The text message came a few minutes later from Sean Thompson: *Please call.*

I knew it was bad news. I could tell by the words he had used—having spent so long reading over and over our text history, trying to find extra information, trying to find any hint of annoyance or disappointment, or maybe optimism. This time it was obvious: something had happened and something was wrong. I fell silent. A few minutes passed, and Arron asked if I was alright.

'Just a little carsick,' I replied, smiling, wondering how long until we stopped. Wondering if it was something Sean needed to tell me urgently. Planning when I could make the phone call out of earshot. I couldn't hide subtle mood swings from Mum, she knew me too well, but if I was lucky she'd be too wrapped in her own grief to notice mine.

Nearly an hour of driving passed and I didn't have to fake nausea anymore—I'd had kilometres of rolling hillside and smooth highway to consider the worst-case scenarios. Had I said something wrong and the pretext phone call was no longer admissible? Had Dylan given a witness statement and the dates didn't line up with my account? Had Sean decided my matter simply wasn't worth pursuing?

'How's Poppa doing?' Mum asked. 'How does he seem?'

I looked to Arron to answer; he gave a half-shrug.

'Sad, but okay,' I said. 'I dunno, I guess he is how you'd expect. Nothing good, but nothing alarming?' I didn't know what she wanted me to say. He and Tuttu had been together since they were seventeen and sixteen, and Poppa was about eighty. I couldn't even fathom how much life happens over ten adult years, let alone sixty. Every time I thought I was processing Tuttu's death and coming to some closure, I'd look at Poppa and my heart would break again.

Dad remarked that a servo was up ahead on the right. I suggested he stop for petrol in case we didn't see another station for a while, and took my opportunity as soon as he pulled in by the bowsers. I got out of the car and walked about twenty metres to where some gum trees and scrub were at the edge of the concrete.

'Hi Sean, I'm just returning your call,' I said, trying to shield the receiver from the loud trucks rushing past me on the road.

'Hi, yeah, thanks for calling me back,' he said, and now I could hear it wasn't good news. He went on to tell me that Samuel's lawyers had just suggested that regardless of the timing of the offending, they would challenge the charges, because they'd re-listened to the pretext call and thought it wasn't very 'strong'. Sean was calling because he was obliged to ask me if I still wanted to proceed with the matter or if I'd consider round tables or letters of apology.

'It's completely up to you,' said Sean, 'but I just want to make sure that we're still acting according to how you want things to go. We want to know what your motivations and intentions are. What do you want to get out of this?'

I thought of *her*. She was somewhere out there in the world, pretending to be fine, struggling to come to terms with an ugly thing inside of her. What did I want to get out of this? Justice.

'Nope, fuck that,' I said into the phone, 'sorry, I mean, I will take this as far as it goes. What I want is for him to be held accountable for his actions.'

'Okay, sure.'

'And also, juries love pretext phone calls! I know how all this shit works! No. I'm not backing down here. He's had all this time to just admit what he's done, and he's been dragging it out just because he can, and just, no. He picked the wrong girl.'

'Well look, I've relayed to his lawyers that your recollection of the events is compelling and that, with the strength of your testimony and the call recording, you have a very strong case,' Sean said, backing me up.

Tears came to my eyes again. I knew he didn't mean it as a compliment, but I felt flattered in an odd way. Sean's confidence in me was a signal that I was strong—and maybe strong enough—for this. I thanked him for calling and updating me. I presumed he would have told me if anything was significantly amiss in Dylan's statement.

I stepped behind one big old gum tree, out of sight of Mum in the front seat of the car, and slapped my face a few times, taking deep breaths in and out. This was the first day of happiness my family had had together in months. Someone we all loved had just died. *Today isn't about you.* I told myself this wasn't the time to bring it up, and that there was no reason to mention anything until I knew if there would be a trial.

I kept it together for about ten minutes back on the road until I couldn't. The tears came pouring out and I pretended they weren't, but I couldn't stop them, so I sat quietly and stared out the car window.

Mum noticed first and asked Dad to pull the car over. 'What's wrong, lovey?' she asked, reaching out her arm to me, nothing but love and concern in her face.

'I thought if we proved he was fifteen he would plead guilty!' I was wailing. 'But now Sean says they're going to trial no matter what!' My mouth was gaping open, a gurgling noise coming out, and I was bashing my fists hard against my thighs.

My dad reached over and held my hand but I couldn't look at him. I couldn't look at anyone. The ugly thing inside me had come alive, Samuel had woken it up again, and now it was disturbing my family: uncontainable, inappropriate.

'You don't get to keep shitting on someone's life!' I screamed at my lap, smacking myself, rocking.

My family were perfect. They asked me if I still wanted to go to the wineries; they told me a few nasty things they'd like to do to Samuel; they told me they loved me, and that we could talk about it or not talk about it. I cried a little longer then spent the following forty-eight hours trying every wine I could find. We didn't talk about it anymore and we all had a nice time. I kept it together for the rest of our time in the Barossa.

⌒

When we got back to Adelaide, Arron and I hung out together to get a break from some of the relatives. That's when I told him that Anna had also been abused when she was a child, and what she had said about Samuel manipulating her. Arron told me that

Samuel's current partner had been sexually assaulted in the past as well, by another man.

'I don't know if it was when she was a kid or when she was older, but she told Sam once that she's had something like that happen,' he said.

'For fuck's sake,' I sighed, wondering how she'd feel when she found out about what Samuel did to me. 'You know,' I said to Arron, 'I'm lucky he's such a piece of shit.'

'Huh?' He looked confused.

'People believe me. They either aren't or won't be surprised, because he's selfish and tries to scam people and is a shit friend. Imagine if people thought he was a lovely, top bloke. Can you imagine what they'd say about how I was ruining his life?'

'But not if he pleads guilty or if the jury says he's guilty.'

'Even then, Arron, if he was a caring son and a loving partner— or imagine if people thought he was a good dad—it wouldn't matter what a jury said, people would still, on some level, hold me account-able for ruining his life.'

'You think so?' Arron asked.

'I know so. I'm still the one bringing up something that happened over a decade ago. Most people think I'm doing okay. It's like I'm a drama queen or an attention-seeker already. Imagine if I was ruining some family man's reputation? Imagine if he had a blue card and worked with kids and I ruined his career? It doesn't matter if a jury says he did it, people will still see me as the cause of what comes next.'

'People suck.' He sighed.

'In an ironic way, I'm lucky he's such a turd.' I smiled and we laughed.

We were parked outside the house of one of our elderly relatives who lived by the beach. In the silence between us I listened to the waves crashing, trying to count in my head the number of women

I knew who had been assaulted. In every circle there were several, and barely any had ever reported their experiences, but when I spoke to them they encouraged me. I felt supported by them, raised up by this silent mass of victims, but I also felt them all on my shoulders. Perhaps if I was strong enough they would know it was possible to survive the re-victimisation. Were they watching me? Looking to see if my relationships faltered or if I started drinking? If Samuel took things to court and got acquitted, it would send a message to all the women around me—ripples in a pond affirming their sense that people wouldn't believe them. That justice was not for them.

But what if I won? How many women could I tell? How loudly could I announce such a victory? Less than one in three Australian women who are sexually assaulted ever go to the police. What if we all went at once?

I resolved then, in South Australia by the ocean, the night before my grandmother's second funeral, that if I won I would tell anyone who would listen. I would put it on Facebook, I would feast, maybe I'd throw a big party. I knew how good it would feel to win because I had dreamed it so many times. I knew the tears of joy, the sunshine on my face as I stepped out of the courts building, because my brain kept reminding me while I was asleep and dreaming, because I had the memory of George in Warwick, that the feeling of closure was worth the risk.

⌐⌐

Before the conversation in the car with Arron, I'd thought a lot about how, if Samuel pleaded guilty or was found guilty, I could make his life hell. I daydreamed about it, like a fantasy of retribution. I thought about it on a whim if I was having a cigarette and was left to my own thoughts, or when I was in the shower or about to fall asleep. For a few weeks I thought it was just a natural part of my grieving process: I had come to terms with what had happened but wasn't quite ready to let it go. It was also an imaginary way for me to regain agency over this story that had come to be such a defining facet of my life.

I wondered if Tuttu had perhaps felt the same way about her cancer—that her time and love and future were dictated by an external cruelty. Something that could grow and change whenever it pleased, and that we just had to follow along its unknown trajectory, accepting the havoc it wreaked on our lives. I felt grateful, though, that at least my 'cancer' had a name and a face I could punch in daydreams.

But after the conversation with my brother in the car, I was reminded that what I chose to do about Samuel, what effect my claim might have on his life, really could be at my fingertips. This was a dangerously hopeful idea to consider, given I still didn't know if he would contest the matter in court, and I knew that he could be acquitted, and I would risk defamation if I spoke out. But I thought about it because I wanted to know what kind of woman I was. What I would do if the ball was finally in my court.

I wanted all of his friends to know. They already suspected his latest rift with Arron was more significant than ever before, and potentially involved something illegal. None of them had expressed surprise when Arron told them Samuel was no longer welcome in his house.

I wanted his current partner to know. There was a high probability Samuel was hiding the information from her, even after she'd told him that she had been abused once, but I found it difficult to separate my desire to ruin his life from my hopes to inform her. Was their relationship even my business? When I considered that my desire to tell her might be petty and selfish, I remembered what Anna had told me: that she hadn't wanted to have sex with Samuel, but that he manipulated her. He found her weakness and he exploited it. It couldn't be a coincidence that his current partner had also been abused. Then again, so many of us have. What was the likelihood that he was a loving and supportive partner to her as she tried to come to terms with her own abuse? What further damage would I be doing to a woman whose specific pain I ought to understand and empathise with?

But I knew my heart was in the right place for this one because I kept hearing his voice through the telephone: *you weren't the only one.*

Maybe I could talk to Arron and his girlfriend once everything was over, tell them to pass the word on to friends of theirs with younger sisters. Give my mobile number to anyone who had questions. Word would spread quickly among all those men, and perhaps they would remember off-colour jokes Samuel had made. Times when they'd seen him do things at parties. Maybe they would see his face and think of him as a normal man they know, and see my face as a normal woman they know, and it would help people realise that these things happen. That their words and actions have consequences.

I wanted to tell Samuel's parents partly because of another important thing he'd told me on the phone—that he had been abused by an older family member. They didn't know that a cruel person might have been eating at their dinner table with them over the years; that their son's reprehensible behaviour ought not be condemned until fully understood as a continuation of the cycle of abuse. That their sentence for him might be mitigated, the way it might be in court. I couldn't have told my parents a day or an hour earlier than I had, though—I came to them when I was ready and braced for impact. Had someone forced me into that situation I might never have recovered. But I'd also never hurt another and used my past as an excuse. I could understand Samuel and empathise with him as a victim, but I would never sympathise with him as an abuser.

I could do all or none of these things. I felt a responsibility to the other women out there, the ones like me, to warn them about him. To shout and point at this crocodile gliding past them underwater. Perhaps if he pleaded guilty and spared me the trauma of a trial I would be more understanding, but he'd already insulted me by trying to duck and weave out of the charges with legal loopholes. That letter he and his lawyers had sent to the police was unforgiveable. He had no legitimate remorse. If he pleaded it would only be because his expensive lawyers managed to convince him it was in *his* best interests.

Sean warned me on the phone that I wouldn't be happy with the sentence Samuel would receive even if I succeeded in court.

'I'm prepared for that,' I replied.

'Yeah, I thought you might have already suspected that, but I just want you to be ready for it, and if you're doing all this to see him punished, it might not happen.'

There it was again: Sean wondering why I was doing this, as though neither of us worked for the Department of Justice or had taken oaths to protect and serve.

So, was my desire to tell the world of Samuel's crime a kind of vigilante justice? Would the law not punish him adequately? Did I not have faith in the system to take care of the matter of justice?

No, no I did not.

⌒

It took another month, from my conversation with Sean at the roadside in April of 2016, for Samuel's solicitors to find a time in their schedules for him to be brought in and finally interviewed. Pending his answers, he'd be charged. It was all still a little up in the air. I got the distinct impression that it could all get chucked in the bin at any time. I was texting and calling Sean for updates, and he seemed to say different things each time, getting my hopes up then shooting them down, and there was always a reason he hadn't followed up with the lawyers. Samuel's barrister was an ex-cop and had been in the business for decades.

'This barrister probably knows more than I do, to be honest,' Sean said to me. I didn't know how he intended me to take that— most likely he wasn't doing a lot of thinking and the words were just dribbling from his chin like usual. But, regardless, I believed him. At least I knew I was outgunned.

Judge and I organised a time to catch up for lunch when work was supposed to be quiet for him, and I got dressed properly because we had planned to go to a fancy restaurant. But on my way to the city to meet him I got a call from his new associate—some defence barrister had messed up his closing address and so Judge would have to address the error in his summing up that afternoon to avoid a mistrial. Lunch would be sandwiches and about 15–20 minutes.

'I'm so sorry we'll be rushed today,' Judge said after we hugged as old friends.

'No problem!' I said brightly, but it was a problem. I had to tell him about the trial, and I wasn't yet used to telling anyone about anything to do with it all. We went to the cafe across the road from the courts and lined up behind the long lunch rush queue. We were chatting about the news and how my freelance writing was going, but then I glanced at my watch—over 5 minutes already gone. I had to get it out. Couldn't come all this way and chicken out.

'I wanted to meet up with you to let you know—' but was interrupted by the woman taking our order. 'Ah, yes, a long black thank you.' I turned to Judge and spoke quietly but clearly as the woman punched our orders into the computer. 'I thought I should tell you that I was offended against, sexually, I mean, when I was a child, and I've made a police complaint.'

'Here's your change, sir!' The woman at the counter put some coins into his outstretched hand, and he paused before retracting it slowly.

'Oh, I didn't know.' He put his wallet in his pocket and adjusted his glasses, 'let's take a seat.'

'That's okay,' I replied, and we sat down, 'nobody did. I mean, that's the problem, right? We don't talk about it.'

'Of course. This must be very difficult for you.'

'It's been a long time,' I shrugged, 'mostly I just realised last year that he's the same as all the rest of them, and that so am I, and someone really ought to put something on his record. I did a pretext call and he said there were other girls, but none of them have come forward yet, so I think it's important I don't back down.'

'This is brave of you. You would know—more than most—how taxing this process might be for you.'

'Yes. Unfortunately no blissful ignorance over here.'

'And you did a pretext, and it went well, but he isn't pleading?'

'Correct.'

'Well, they all think they can get away with it.'

'I think he's dragging it out, seeing if I'll give up.'

'Well, unfortunately, so many do.'

'Yes. But, I suppose, I just wanted to let you know because it may be in the courts in a little while, and also that, well, it was a contributing factor to why I didn't really feel . . .' I wrung my hands under the table, 'inclined to go straight into a law job after our year together. I felt like I disappointed you when I didn't go to practice, but I just, I couldn't, at least not without dealing with this thing first.'

He seemed surprised and smiled softly. 'I never felt disappointed in you.'

A waiter dropped off our sandwiches and I quickly dabbed my eyes with my serviette.

'Well, that's all the serious stuff then, and we've still got five minutes!' I laughed a little, 'tell me, what's up in Judge-town? What's news?'

⌁

Every day that month before Samuel's police interview, I fantasised about him telling Sean he would plead guilty. The relief in that daydream was overwhelming. I whipped myself into a state where I thought there was no possible chance he would take me to trial. He'd paid for good lawyers and his lawyers would tell him to plead and he would listen to them. I asked my dad about the process and he said that if Samuel was charged, it should take three weeks from that date for him to appear in Magistrates Court. I pictured myself in the back of the courtroom among the public, Samuel not knowing I was watching.

'Guilty, your Honour,' he would say, standing there, and he would cry. And in my daydreaming of that moment I would cry too, first with the imagined relief, and then with the real despair. The hopelessness that accompanies a complete lack of control.

It ended up taking six months for him to be charged properly and to appear in the Magistrates Court. In that time I cried a lot. My psychologist gave me an exercise to do whenever I got upset, to try to halt my normally inevitable spiral of self-loathing. I sat on the front deck of my share house when nobody else was home, watching parents pick their kids up from school; the girls in their checked dresses, like mine, blue and white on the black trampoline. 'I am anxious,' I would say, naming my feeling out loud. 'I am having the feeling that I am anxious,' I'd say next, separating the feeling from myself. 'The feeling that I am anxious is making me feel like I should die,' attributing the thoughts that flowed from the feelings. Sometimes it worked and I would finish, 'This is an awful thing that is happening to me, and it is taking me time to deal with it, and that is okay.'

In those six months I think I appeared normal to most people I spent time with. I attended two literary festivals, one interstate and one overseas; I spent time with family at home; and I cooked dinner with Vincent while sipping cold beers. I saw friends and did my laundry. I would call or text Sean for updates, and he would reply that things just took time. Samuel's lawyers were making things difficult. I needed to be patient. The rest of life carried on and I just sort of let it carry me along too.

Now I'm glad I did. If I'd paused everything, waiting for Samuel to take responsibility for his actions, for the matter to resolve, I would have lost over two years of my life.

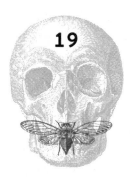

19

THE SECOND WEEK OF NOVEMBER in 2016 was always going to be a tough one. The world was worried about the US election on Wednesday, and I was worried about Friday: the date Samuel, his solicitor and his barrister would meet with Sean to talk about his intention to fight or plead guilty.

On Wednesday morning I was desperately showing Vincent web pages that suggested Hillary Clinton might still pull through. He shot each one down.

'What does this tell people who assault women?' I asked him when we were standing in front of the TV in our share house, stuck on ABC News 24.

'That people in the rust belt want their jobs back and for some reason they think Trump can give that to them.'

'You know what I mean.'

'I know,' he said shrugging, and we slumped down onto the couch 'but for people who are poor this isn't about gender equality or race relations, it's just about their jobs.'

'But being a decent human being shouldn't be optional. I understand that economic policy is extremely important, but surely the basic belief in human equality can't be sacrificed for *anything*. It's not a point of comparison between candidates, it's supposed to be a prerequisite. I don't understand. I feel like this is connected to Friday.'

Vincent started to interrupt me but I pushed through a fleeting worry I would sound hysterical. 'I'm not an idiot,' I said, 'I know that one won't *cause* the other, but I feel like they're connected—no, I *know* they're connected. The same attitudes that just got Trump elected to the highest office in America are the same attitudes that made Samuel think he could go around molesting girls and get away with it. Because obviously you can!' I sat up in my chair and yelled at the television, pointing. 'He did! And somewhere Samuel is watching this, and he will hear this thing, this attitude in the wind, saying he can do whatever the fuck he wants to women and nothing can touch him. That he could be the prime minister! I don't know what to do, Vincent. What can I do?'

He reached out to me again and I collapsed back into the couch, into his arms. 'You're already doing it,' he said, kissing my forehead, 'you're fighting him.'

I couldn't tell if the dread in my belly was nervousness or an intuition, but I sat still for a long while as dozens of angles of Trump's grinning orange face washed over the screen. His wrinkly hands waved in front of cheering crowds and I imagined those hands 'grabbing' the 'pussies' of terrified women, those stubby fingers pushing past the underpants of frozen girls. The ABC broadcasters were trying to mask their disappointment while taking an appropriately grave tone, as though they didn't know how to calm viewers in a politically neutral way.

I had to go into the city that day for some errands, but it was a particularly muggy afternoon in Brisbane and I was sweating before I even left the house to walk to the bus stop. Everyone seemed to be down somehow. All the people I passed had been caught off guard and reminded of the true ugliness in humanity. It was as if we'd all just found a border collie hit by a car and left for dead in the street. It was the feeling I'd had at the end of most days in court, that the aircon was circulating the dead skin cells of paedophiles

so that I couldn't help but taste and inhale them. That afternoon
in November the progressive people of the Western world tried to
tell ourselves we didn't need to take responsibility for the result.
We pretended the heat wasn't hell, that we weren't both suffering
and implicated.

The moisture in the air didn't even break with the usual sweet
and spectacular south-east Queensland afternoon storm. It hung
in the streets, and it swirled and gathered around my brain, and
the 199 bus drove by me before I realised I'd forgotten to hail it,
but I didn't have the energy to lift an arm. If another person hadn't
come by to hail the next bus I might have sat at that stop for hours,
waiting for rain to break the heat, and it wouldn't have come.

Later that night my housemates and I all sat on our deck, having
beers with some mutual friends, and we were talking about Trump.

'This guy just started at my work,' one of our mates, Steven,
said, 'and he's been accused of a rape. I can't even remember how I
know, but he's like a friend of a friend of a friend, and yeah, the girl
dropped out before it went to trial. So now he's just going about his
life like normal, I guess, and he's starting at my office next week.'

'Shit, dude,' I said unhelpfully, taking a gulp of my beer.

'I guess there's nothing I can do?' he said, but lilting up at the
end, like a question.

'I dunno. What would you do if he made a move on one of
your friends?'

'I suppose maybe I'd tell her? I dunno.'

'I dunno either.'

'New beer?'

'Yeah, great, thanks.'

The minutes between Wednesday and Friday dragged out. At first I fought the unpredictable waves of anxiety and tried to keep myself busy, but by Thursday afternoon I was sitting on the front deck of our old Queenslander smoking cigarette after cigarette, sweating and feeling sick from the increase in nicotine and gradual arrival of heatstroke. Paralysis nightmares kept me from sleeping both nights, and I kept being slapped with news broadcasts of Trump. Yet again I had the overwhelming sense that everything was happening *to* me, that control or independence or even basic bodily autonomy were just an illusion. That my body and mind and voice had been irrevocably compromised, and that even if they were somehow still unsullied, they could be robbed from me at any moment. I saw friends and filed invoices for copywriting gigs. I went to Coles just to push a trolley around and gaze at the bright colours, being sure not to pick expensive ingredients that I prayed I had the fortitude to vomit up anyway. I chatted to my mum on the phone but didn't tell her of the significance of Friday.

There was nothing for me to do but wait until I was told what my future looked like. Nothing to do until I was told whether or not my trauma mattered, or if it was agreed upon by others that it had even occurred.

The call came while I was waiting for the bus home on Adelaide Street in the middle of the city. Men in hi-vis jackets were putting up the large Christmas tree in King George Square and a mother was chatting happily to her tiny daughter about the coming school holidays. My mobile was sweaty in my hand and when I heard it vibrate I fumbled with it, extricating myself from the crowd by the bus stop and swiping the screen that showed *Private Number.*

'Hello?' I answered, blocking my other ear with my finger, walking to a shady spot with nobody in earshot.

'It's Sean Thompson here.'

'Hi Sean, thanks for calling, how's it going?'

'Yeah, look,' he began, and my stomach dropped out of my body. It was the moment you realise your wallet isn't in your bag. The moment you go to open your front door and realise the lock is busted. 'I've just finished the interview with Samuel and it's looking pretty clear that he's going to fight the charges.'

I backed into the wall of City Hall as my knees buckled. 'I see.'

'He arrived with his solicitor and his barrister, and they all seemed quite surprised that we were pushing ahead with the charges.'

'What do you mean?'

'They're still saying he was a child when the events took place and that it's not in the public interest to proceed.'

'So even with Dylan's statement he's still saying he was ten?'

'Well, they're arguing he was twelve, and that there's no evidence that the trampoline wasn't always being moved to different parts of the backyard.'

'Right.'

'He also became . . .' Sean paused. 'Samuel, that is, became,' he was choosing his words, 'quite animated. When I informed him that there would be two separate charges of indecent treatment based on the acts you allege occurred that afternoon—and the specifics of the second charge, with it being clearly more severe.'

'But my statement never changed!' I blurted out.

'Yes,' he said, 'but they were surprised. When I told them that stuff, about the two separate charges, his barrister asked me to leave the interview room to let them discuss the matter with Samuel.'

'And when you went back in?'

'His position is quite firm.' There was no optimism in Sean's voice. 'I think you need to prepare yourself for a long fight.' I put my head between my knees and tried to take deep breaths, but I thought

I might vomit. Sean reminded me, again, of how excellent Samuel's barrister was, and spoke a little more about needing another statement from someone, maybe my mum, about the trampoline. He seemed to be pre-emptively curbing my impatience. Apologising for delays he hadn't even let manifest yet.

'So what happens now?' I cut him off.

'It's listed for the first mention in the Magistrates Court on Monday twenty-first of November,' he said, 'but there will likely be a few mentions before things start happening. We'll need to finalise all the evidence before we put it together in a brief and hand it over to the DPP, then it'll be in their hands, and things will take a while on that side as well.'

Why!? I wanted to scream at him. Why was everyone telling me to be patient? It was the simplest matter that could come across their desks: I responded instantly, I never wavered in my intentions, and we had the pretext phone call. Samuel had said I wasn't the only one! Didn't they want to get him on record too?

'Can you call me after the mention and let me know what's happening?' I asked calmly.

'Of course, absolutely. I'll be in touch that afternoon and I'll let you know if there's any news in the meantime.'

'Okay, thanks, Sean.'

'No worries, talk soon.'

I hung up and my phone slipped from my hand into my bag, and the bell tower above me began to strike its midday notes. The low, long clangs reverberated down the building and rang in my ears. They came slowly and I rocked back and forth to them, jamming my ears with the insides of my knees, squeezing my eyes shut.

It was broad daylight and I was in my home city with hundreds of happy Christmas shoppers bustling around, but I felt Samuel's eyes on me, I felt sure that if I looked up I might see him walking toward me through the mall.

I rocked until I realised the bells had stopped minutes ago, and then I found my notebook in my bag, scribbling down the basics of what Sean had told me before it all dribbled out of my mind. I could feel something coming, a storm rolling into my brain. I shifted onto my hands and knees, on the ground, and pulled myself up against the wall, and I put on my sunglasses and returned to the bus stop. The woman and her child were still there chatting happily. I wanted my own mother.

The bus arrived and I took a seat at the back and felt a different fear returning: the possibility that I was wrong. That I *was* a stupid little bitch. That Samuel had been a child and that I might be ruining his life as well as my own. That what he'd said on the phone to me was true—by pursuing this matter I was bringing ruin to everyone, instead of just dealing with it myself. The bus bumbled along its usual route as I sat in terror. I started to imagine being cross-examined, the super-smart barrister's questions barrelling at me, accusing me of being boy-crazy and deranged. My breathing was shallow and I was pinching my thighs as hard as I could through my jeans, trying to keep my mind inside my body.

When I went to get off at my stop, the step from the bus to the pavement was higher than I thought; I hadn't been looking, and the jolt broke whatever tiny membrane of togetherness I'd been clutching, and I panicked. Some switch flipped and normal functions shut down. It was only three blocks to my home but it took me over twenty minutes to get there. All my senses were telling me I was underwater—my muscles weren't responding, I was wading instead of walking, my hearing was muffled and my vision was blurry, my eyes wouldn't open properly and the sun burned them, and I couldn't catch my breath. People passed me and I could tell they were staring but they said nothing; people saw me shuffling by from the fronts of their houses and said nothing. I gripped each tree and each parked car I passed for support, lurching between them, stumbling over roots and driveways with my fingers splayed, reaching forward but as though I was drugged.

I didn't look up, even to cross the road, when I finally reached the corner of my street. I leaned against the high fences of the neighbours' houses and a whining noise came out of me as I dragged myself along the final few metres. I pushed open my gate and as I stepped through it I fell to the ground and wailed. I had expected relief at finally making it home, but instead I realised there was just nowhere else to go. That I wasn't safe in the house where I lived, that I couldn't do anything to avoid the coming trial. The hot concrete burned my face and hands, and I was glad for it. How many times would I have to realise that I carried this matter within me? No time I waited for and no place I waded to would deliver me from the feeling of his hands on me and the years of shame I had let fester. How many revelations of powerlessness did I have to endure? My cheek and chin, and the pads on my fingers were singed, and the wails kept pouring out of my mouth from somewhere within. Snot dripped onto the cement too, sizzling in the sun. I was watching my paralysed self, it was like a night terror, but I was wishing I was asleep instead of wishing I could wake up, my body more separate from myself than ever before.

A figure blocked the sun above me and spoke my name, and arms reached down to lift me, carrying me up the stairs and into the house. He took my bag and sat me on the couch and I cried. He kissed my forehead and held me in his arms and I cried. He asked me questions and said things to me, and I only repeated, 'I'm so scared.' Time passed and he brought me a glass of water. More time passed and he sat with me, and when I finally heard his voice asking me what I wanted and I replied, 'I want to die', he kissed me more and hugged me more, and I wondered, not for the first or last time, where I'd be if I came home to an empty house.

Later in the day when I had calmed down, we sat together on the deck smoking and I explained what I actually knew. I took out my notebook and saw I'd written more in it when I was on the bus. It was scribble. *Now he's saying he was twelve. But first he said he was ten. He would have to be twelve for me to be in my school uniform.*

'He's just picking dates and defences that suit him,' I said to Vincent.

'It's nice to know he's sweating,' he replied.

'Yeah. I have a feeling "quite animated" was an understatement. He's such a fucking shithead, I bet he really lost it. But I don't understand why they were surprised that there would be two separate counts. I can't believe Sean didn't tell them that from the beginning. It's in my statement, that he did two things to me, and the second was way worse.'

'Yeah, that's weird.'

'I asked Sean, and he said he was "pretty sure" he told them that earlier, but he mustn't have, right? They'd remember that. Jesus.'

'You've got the whole system on your side now, though. The cogs are turning and they're turning against him.'

'But he's got that gun ex-cop for a barrister. He makes me frightened.'

'Yeah, but you have—'

'I have Sean!'

'Mighty Sean!' Vincent said in a funny announcer's voice.

'My knight in shining armour!' I exclaimed in my best damsel-in-distress impression, and we both laughed. 'Well, soon he'll have to turn it all over to the DPP and then I might get someone good.'

'True.'

'And at least now it's in court, Sean can't just drag his fucking heels with nobody on his back, you know? If people want delays now, they have to ask the magistrate for an adjournment and give a reason. They can't just ignore my calls.'

'Yep.' We both fell into silence for a moment. 'How're you doing?' Vincent asked.

'I dunno. I'm worried they'll cross-examine me about being a feminist because of things I've said and written online, and I just can't believe he's not pleading. I really can't. I know you might think it's silly, but it feels like Trump again. Like nobody thought the nightmare would become real. I feel like I've been sideswiped. Like a fucking deer in the headlights or something, like such an idiot. And that they were all so shocked to hear he was really being charged!? Like, what the fuck? The most awful thing that's ever happened to me, that is actually illegal, is frivolous and vexatious? How the fuck am I supposed to feel about that? They're basically telling me my life and my experiences don't matter. That Samuel is being caught up in something silly, that he shouldn't have to be bothered by this.' I paused to take a drag. 'I guess I start doing okay every time I start getting angry instead of sad again. But I'm really frightened.'

'You were looking straight through me for a while there,' he said.

'What a diva, huh?' I smiled and butted out my cigarette.

⌒

The next morning Vincent walked with me down the street to get a coffee.

'You know in *Lord of the Rings*,' I said, 'when Gandalf the Grey dies but then he comes back as Gandalf the White, and he's even more badass and is, like, the most powerful motherfucker ever?'

'Yeah.'

'That's gonna be me after this,' I said.

'True,' he replied and nodded.

'If I can get through this I'm fucking invincible. If I can make it through this trial, regardless of how it goes, I'll be untouchable. Seriously, nothing could be worse than this. I'll ride out of that courthouse on a giant eagle.'

~~

I organised to meet my parents for coffee and an update. I needed to explain the process, then ask them to call Sean and go give him an extra statement about the trampoline. When they arrived at the cafe we exchanged hugs and kisses and chatted about silly little things, as though we'd silently agreed to place our orders before we got down to business. I remember thinking how strange it was, all these ways we separated things as being civilised or appropriate. I was short with them that morning. Dad kept interrupting me and defending Sean when I complained about his delays, and Mum had to scold him and tell him to actually listen to what I was saying, but then Dad and I would speak about the legal stuff and Mum would get confused and interject with simple, angry questions.

'I don't understand why he's not in gaol!' she said, almost too loudly. 'He already said he did it, didn't he?'

'I told you, Mum, he's not arguing the acts took place, he's arguing when they took place, and he's saying he was too young to know what he was doing.'

'But he's so much older than you,' she pushed on, and I sighed loudly, letting Dad take over and explain things to her again.

I resented having to relay everything to them—what a big deal it always was, to tell them about the stages of the investigation—but I also resented that they didn't know I only told them about a fraction of the trips and calls and messages I made. I didn't know what I wanted from them. I managed to convince Dad that having patience was one thing, but Sean's incompetence was quite another. It was bugging me that Samuel and his lawyers would be 'surprised' that he was being charged with two counts. I thought maybe he wouldn't have fought so much, so early on, if he knew that I remembered the fully depraved extent of his actions. Sean should have told Samuel the particulars of what he was being charged for.

'The other thing you have to be prepared for,' Dad said, looking at me, 'is that once your file gets handed over to the DPP, they get to choose what happens.'

'I know, they might not even proceed with it.'

'But even if they do go ahead, the first thing that barrister is going to do is call the prosecutor and try to make a deal.'

'Oh shit.' I felt like one of my few scraps of surety had been snatched back from me.

'Yep.'

Mum interjected. 'What do you mean?'

'They can make a deal to reduce the charge, or agree on a younger age, or anything, and they don't have to ask for my permission,' I said, shocked that I could forget that part of the process. Perhaps I had thought that my case was somehow special or different because of my work and expertise, but there I was, again reminded that I was at the mercy of the system like any other complainant.

'How can they do that?' Mum asked.

'Because it's not Me versus Samuel anymore. I'm not the one bringing the charge. It's the Crown. The state is the one fighting him.'

'I've seen some prosecutors,' Dad said, 'who constantly communicate with the victim and make sure they know what the victim wants. But I've seen others who will be standing in court with a defence barrister, and defence will offer them a deal, and they'll take it on the spot without even making a phone call.'

Mum was perplexed. 'Why!?'

'Because then they don't have to do all the work,' I said with a sad smile, realising yet again that trying to exercise control over my situation was futile. 'Accepting a guilty plea is easier than running a trial.'

'So what can we do?' she asked, and I told her that it would help if she went to the station and provided an addendum statement, clarifying the time when the trampoline was moved.

'Don't think about what I want, or what effect it has on me, Mum,' I said to her, trying to be stern but bordering on condescension. 'Where do you really remember the trampoline moving to and from?'

'It was far out the back,' she said, determined, 'then Dylan broke his nose, and we moved it to the grassy area so it would be safer.' She nodded, concluding, and a waitress came to take our cups. 'I remember,' Mum added, handing her cup up and smiling at the young woman, 'because we had to move the old Hills hoist to fit it there.'

I stared at her, gripping my empty cup after the waitress left the table, fending off confusing physiological responses to this new piece of information. It was a silly detail, a thing of no significance to literally anyone else in the world but me. *How does this all fit together?* I thought, very confused. *Why does this mean something?*

But that's the shit thing I know now about PTSD symptoms: they're not special. Shivers and panics aren't Lassie telling you some boy is trapped in a well, or pointers to clues you'd really known all along and just couldn't string together. You don't have special powers and your panic attacks aren't here to help.

We chatted about nicer things for a little while before Mum and Dad left, agreeing to go straight to the police station to give that extra statement to Sean. I couldn't give him an excuse to drag things along.

⌒

Every duck on my side was lined up in a neat row. Everything would be ready for that mention later in November, and when it got to court I might start seeing progress, my matter might really start to get somewhere. The date was in my diary but I couldn't have forgotten it even if I tried.

The final week went by, and when the Monday hit I waited by the phone from 8.30 a.m. By midday I was busting and held my phone in my hand as I peed. Two p.m. arrived and I rolled another cigarette, keeping my eyes on my phone, constantly checking it was still on 'loud', but Sean never called.

I texted him late in the afternoon, politely asking what Samuel's lawyers had said, what the outcome of the mention had been.

The matter was mentioned and has been adjourned to 19/12/16 for another mention. I don't think we will get any result before Christmas but we should know what his intentions are on the next court date.

And so I got sad again, and then I got mad again, and waited another month until the 19th of December.

The lead-up to Christmas in Brisbane was the same relaxed affair as always, but it bustled around me without sweeping me up. I went and bought wrapping paper and tape and made a crappy joke about Michael Bublé to the teenager at the checkout and he didn't get it, so I called Anna. She told me about her job as one of Santa's elves in a shopping centre. 'It's the perfect fucking example of the wage gap,' she raged down the line. 'We do the same hours, but we're the ones who have to deal with the kids and operate the photography equipment, and he gets three times the cash for just sitting on his arse!'

'Dude, that's fucked!'

'I know! And our contracts say we have to wear makeup— foundation and mascara and lipstick—and makeup is so fucking expensive, and we don't get money for that.'

'Makeup is *so* expensive, I think about that all the time.'

'And he gets his whole costume provided but we have to bring our own stockings and socks and shoes.'

'This sounds really shit, dude, I'm sorry.'

'Argh, what can you do, hey?'

'Unionise?' We both laughed.

'Unionised elves, sure, we'll revolt against Saint Nick. Seriously, though, this one is pretty gross. He's really gender-specific with the toys, shaming little boys who want a ring and scolding little girls who want a truck.'

'Fuck that,' I groaned. 'Come on.'

'I know. I've even made a formal complaint about him because of how he behaved to one little Asian girl. He made some joke about being made in Japan.'

'What!?'

'I know.'

'Well, in other shit news, I still don't know what's happening with the court case. Sean—the cop in charge of my matter—keeps saying it's fine, then it's not, then it's fine, and then it's not again. For ages I kept trusting what he was saying, just thinking that I wasn't the one who couldn't keep up, but now I think Sean just isn't that good at his job. It's been so long, and I got him on the phone saying he did it. What the fuck more do they want?'

'Oh babe, I'm so sorry to hear this.'

'I should give you a content warning,' we laughed, 'sorry. I just—I know you get it. I don't really have anyone else who gets it.'

'You can call me any time you want, as much as you want.'

'Thank you.'

'You've got Vincent there, though, right? He's good about it all?'

'Yeah, he's great, he just . . . I dunno. When I talk about this stuff to a man I feel like I'm *complaining*, but really I just want to talk about it so I can process it.'

'I know what you mean. Even if they don't say anything.'

I sat on a bench in Queen Street Mall and watched people pass by, chatting to Anna about some happier things before we wished each other a Merry Christmas and said goodbye. An ad for Tiffany & Co. flapped in front of me, the baby blue background sitting dull against the Queensland summer sky; the skinny blonde pictured was blushing at a new engagement ring, a man gazing up at her. I thought that the summer was melting it all together, but then I remembered I had felt the same back in April. When would I break through? When would the dust settle and the future become clear again?

⌒

'I'm going to the Magistrates Court on Monday,' I said to Vincent back home later that day.

'Can I come?' he asked.

I didn't know why I didn't want him there, but he must have sensed it when I paused before responding. I knew why I wanted to go—because I couldn't trust Sean to call me and tell me what happened. Because I understood the language they might use—because I understood the reasons a solicitor might ask for an adjournment. I knew what 'my client is reconsidering his position' meant, and I knew what 'we're waiting for the full brief before submitting a no-case submission' meant, and that those two reasons for an adjournment had potentially colossal and opposite implications.

'I won't be upset like last time, when I fell down in the yard, but I'd like you to be there when I get home.'

'Okey-dokey.' He shrugged, and I tried not to feel bad for having told him what I actually wanted.

That night in the shower, as I leaned my head back against the tiles, I realised I wasn't crying because of what Samuel had done to me, I was crying because of what he was still doing to me. The 're-victimisation' process for me wasn't about the sexual abuse, it was about the continued abuse of power. On that Friday afternoon when Sean had called and I found out that Samuel's lawyers were still pushing back, hard, and I was asked, yet again, if I really wanted to proceed, and asked why, I'd felt totally power-less. On the trampoline again. Samuel in control again. He was taking up my time, my energy, my life. Calls about the case invaded my beautiful home. Reminders about the next mention invaded my mind when I slept. So long as the legal process continued I would be the complainant—and every two, three or four weeks, I would be reminded of that. Reminded that I was just the girl, reminded of being pushed onto my back, belly-up, frozen.

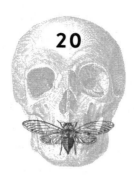

20

I WALKED TOWARD THE MAGISTRATES Court building down the street that morning and regretted going alone. I didn't know if Samuel would be there and so in my panic I saw him everywhere. It was safest not to stop anywhere for a coffee even though I'd arrived fifteen minutes early for that reason. I didn't risk straying into the newsagent to browse the magazines because he could pop in to buy some gum. I imagined how outraged I'd be if he won a scratch-it and got rich, and I let that thought upset me.

As I waited for the lights to change I reflexively glanced over to my old workplace further down the block and saw half a dozen well-dressed young people with fresh coffees walking into the courts building. How far away and absurd that version of me seemed. I longed for one of them to turn around and wave at me, even though they were hundreds of metres away. I craved some kind of recognition from them, a sign that I was still special somehow, different. But it suddenly occurred to me that I didn't want anyone from the previous year to recognise me.

When the lights changed I took long strides to break from the pack and get off the street into the building. Without thinking I started to walk straight past the metal detectors like staff do, but had to slot back into line, sheepishly, for my bag to be scanned. I had no power in that forum anymore. It wasn't for me to pick up a phone to move a matter or request a file. Less than a year ago, in January, I'd been the voice and representative of one of the most important and respected figures in the justice system, but how tiny I felt without those robes! I had been flung out into the cold with all the other normal people and Jesus Fucking Christ I had even more respect for them now. I had made a complaint, I was a complainant, and the man I accused was presumed innocent, and so by necessity I was doubted. Proper process required important people to disbelieve and discredit me. Did I imagine the security guard pausing for a long time on my bag? Should I have worn more demure clothes? I was starting to doubt whether I should have gone there at all, but then I saw it. Up on the television screens in the cool foyer, hundreds of names were listed but his name jumped out at me like my own would have: *Samuel Levins.*

A bolt shot up from my gut into my heart like a big, rough kick up the backside, and I was smiling. I hadn't programmed those television monitors. I never typed his name into the system or scheduled his matter for that specific morning. His name had been put there by people who were paid to get to the bottom of this business, and the true bottom of this was that he was guilty. All I had to do was not back down.

I spun on my heel, grabbed my bag from the tray and headed for the elevators, and while I waited for one to arrive I imagined the doors opening and him standing in front of me—or worse, that he would get into the elevator after me and the doors would close us in together, alone. The panic attack symptoms crept up into my body. *All you have to do,* I said to myself, taking a deep breath in, *is not back down.* I breathed out, and the doors closed on me, alone in the elevator.

The courtrooms Judge and I worked in were always solemn places, mostly very quiet. People didn't speak unless they were being addressed by Judge or it was their turn, and they would be careful to whisper quietly to each other only when absolutely necessary. In the District Court you heard when people rustled papers or shifted in their chairs. I could hear my typing on the keyboard, and if someone had a cold you would know from the sniffling. By contrast, Magistrates Court was Central Station at peak hour. People were coming in and out all the time, talking with each other, asking counsel questions. Four people from the DPP were on one side, and dozens of solicitors and barristers were coming and going on the other. People from the public wandered in with their families, asking each other if they were in the right place, sitting down and standing up. I didn't know if I'd be able to hear someone mention Samuel's name.

A phone went off and I felt myself growing angry. Didn't anyone take any of this seriously? I sat on the edge of my chair, straining forward with one ear out. From what I could hear of the cases being mentioned, most solicitors were telling the magistrate that they'd be away through December into the first half of January. I felt gutted. How could they take so much leave when people were waiting for them? I thought back to Judge in Southport and Warwick, challenging solicitors when they requested adjournments, and I longed for all the professionals in the room to be more like him. I wanted everyone to be more like him. To be competent and expeditious. To make me feel as if they actually knew what they were doing.

After the first hour of waiting in the back of the courtroom with the rest of the public, I had relaxed in the confidence that Samuel himself wouldn't be appearing. After the third hour of waiting I was just extremely bored. His matter—my matter—was called second-last. The solicitor who stood up and approached the bench was young with broad shoulders, blond hair, a bright blue suit, and a fancy leather portfolio case that matched his expensive, freshly polished R.M. Williams boots: exactly the kind of private school boy Samuel used to talk big about knocking the teeth out of. Now

Samuel was employing the young heir-adonis, and it wouldn't have been cheap. I grinned at the thought of it. I had seen the solicitor comparing photos on his phone, pictures from the weekend, with another young man while they were waiting. I wondered what his hourly rate was and how much he was being paid to wait there while I took time away from my own freelance work for nothing.

The magistrate called for the matter to begin, and the process started with the solicitor making a standard request for his client to be excused from appearing, but it was cut short.

'It looks like your client did not sign his bail undertaking at his last appearance,' the magistrate interrupted, flipping through a stapled pile of papers. 'He'll have to get to court and make an appearance before close of business today or I'll have to put a warrant out for his arrest.'

It was like *I* had won the million-dollar scratch-it. I almost clapped my hands together.

'Would your Honour excuse me from the bench so I can step outside and call my client?'

'Well, yes, you'd better,' she replied, 'those are the rules.'

And I beamed as the solicitor ducked out, and I was beaming for the thirty-five minutes it took for him to race back into the courtroom.

'My client said he signed the bail undertaking and returned it via post as he was advised to do, your Honour.'

The magistrate searched through her papers for about a minute. 'Oh, here it is, yes,' she said, pulling a document out from the file. 'I apologise. It had been filed incorrectly, but it is here.'

'May I be excused to phone my client again, your Honour? He's started the drive here from the coast.'

'Of course.'

I was still grinning. That hiccup alone was well worth a four-hour wait.

When the matter was finally, actually mentioned, it was only to order that a full brief of evidence be provided to defence by January, ready for another mention date in February. I was disappointed: I had presumed the magistrate at the very first mention—the one I'd had to text Sean asking about—had already directed Sean to provide defence with the brief of evidence, but it seemed that nothing at all had happened that day.

I called Vincent as I walked to the bus stop and told him what had happened, trying to focus on the positive. 'Imagine that!' I said in a sarcastic voice. 'Imagine how he must have felt, to have his day interrupted by a shit thing he has no control over,' and we laughed.

'The big cogs are turning now,' Vincent said, 'and they're turning against him. He must be shitting himself.'

I decided not to mention how I'd been shitting myself waiting for the elevator doors to close that morning. On the bus home I pictured Samuel getting into his car, swearing the way he must have when he'd finally realised he was being charged—when he became 'quite animated' but also 'extremely unpleasant'. Did he have to make excuses to his employer? Had he had to cancel lunch with his girlfriend? Was this his first experience with the fumbling yet insistent arm of the law?

'Are you alright?' Vincent had asked me on the phone.

'Yeah, yeah, definitely,' I'd said, and it was true. I was sitting on the same bus, just one seat behind where I had been after receiving Sean's phone call the Friday after Trump got elected, and for the second time that morning I felt completely changed from my previous self. I looked down into the empty chair and I felt pity for that girl, that *old* me, but also a well of pride. How the fuck had I got on that bus that day?

Walking home I picked a hibiscus from a bush growing over someone's fence where just weeks before I could barely put one foot in front of the other. How had I spent twenty minutes walking down that small stretch of footpath? I tucked the flower behind my ear and looked along the street that seemed so short and sweet and normal again. There wouldn't be a single galvanising moment, I realised: I was already stronger. I knew I wouldn't back down. I wouldn't be afraid of Samuel for the rest of my life, and this had something to do with the fact that he was now afraid of me. I skipped down that street with a pink flower in my hair, purple sneakers on my feet, and my yellow skirt ballooning and deflating at my thighs. How terrifying I would have looked to him if he'd driven past.

Christmas was six days later. When I was in my first couple of years of university, I had struggled to ask my parents for Samuel not to be invited to Christmas.

'Why is Samuel coming?' I asked.

'Because his family isn't here at the moment,' Mum replied. I made a face. 'Oh, come on now, don't be so selfish, he's Arron's friend, and everyone should have somewhere to go for Christmas.' She left the room. End of discussion. It reminded me of George telling the Court how he had asked his mum to get her boyfriend to leave.

I think back to this often. How horrible a child I must have been, that my own mother presumed selfishness where I just couldn't enunciate my need for self-preservation. Back then I didn't even have the words to explain why I hated him so much, why he made my skin crawl. Who would believe me if I tried to say that he 'looked at me funny'? I would be a Drama Queen. Boy-crazy again.

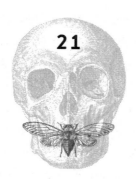

21

IN THE 113 YEARS OF the Australian High Court there had only ever been five women justices, and on 30 January 2017 Australia was going to get its first ever woman Chief Justice of the High Court. My Facebook feed exploded with my law friends sharing articles covered in celebratory emojis. In Queensland only seven of the twenty-seven Supreme Court justices were women, and only nine of the forty-one District Court judges.

I was doing talks on the radio and at writing festivals where people—mostly men—asked me if we just had to be patient: all these young women graduates would just take a little time to work their way up to the top. I thought back to the first barrister I ever worked for and how I'd only been his secretary for a fortnight when he told me of his perception of the 'feminisation' of the legal profession. He had seemed concerned, and I was just so shocked and so grateful for the job I didn't respond.

I thought I'd been doing alright, but the nerves came in a huge wave the night before the next mention. Or rather, the anxiety dumped on me while I was chopping onions and my tear ducts took their cue to release the tidal waves they'd been valiantly containing. When Vincent asked me if I wanted him to come with me, I knew

I shouldn't say yes, but I did, and I thanked him and he held me in the kitchen as my nose dribbled on his shirt. I had been hoping he would remember and offer to come with me all week, but he hadn't brought it up and neither had I.

'I'm just so afraid Samuel will get into the elevator after me and the doors will shut,' I said between sobs. 'Also, I'm chopping onions.'

The next morning we dressed neatly, put some paperbacks into my handbag, and took the bus into the city together.

'This doesn't count as a date,' I said to him with a stern look and he kissed my cheek.

The Magistrates Court was bustling as usual, and we passed through security and gazed up at the monitors to find Samuel's name.

'There,' I pointed, '*LEVINS—Court 20*, let's go.'

We got in the elevator and the doors closed on just the two of us.

Court felt funny with Vincent by my side. Videolinks were scheduled with various prisons, but all the times had been bungled so random men were wandering in and out of the sight of the camera while asking the judge why they'd been pulled in.

'Nobody told me I had court today,' one Caucasian man said, dropping down onto the chair like a sack of potatoes, leaning back and spreading his legs out.

'Are you Van Nguyen?' the magistrate asked.

'Nope!' he shouted and shrugged.

'I see, well, you are not the man we need to speak to. So you may go.'

We watched on the TV screen as the man in the jumpsuit got up, turned around and banged on the door. 'Oi! You got the wrong bloke!'

Vincent and I stifled giggles.

'What were you telling me,' I whispered to him, 'about the mammoth cogs of justice turning on my behalf?'

Time passed and we both got out our books. I looked up each time the prosecutor began the words 'Would your Honour take the matter of—' and after another hour they spoke the name 'Levins', and my ears pricked and I sat up straight. Vincent felt me shift and put his book down. A barrister was at the bar table and it made me hopeful—things were more likely to happen when the barristers were there, rather than just the solicitors or a stand-in town agent.

'The brief of evidence provided last week was incomplete,' Samuel's barrister, Carter, said. I tensed. He was tall and fair-haired, a blond-turning-grey, and his face was soft.

'Well, according to the arresting officer it was complete,' the prosecutor replied.

They went on for a couple more rounds—reminiscent of a play-ground game of 'is-so', 'is-not'—until the magistrate interrupted. 'Adjourned for another four weeks.'

I was furious and bowed to the court before barging through the heavy double doors and storming out toward the elevators.

Carter had also asked for Samuel's presence to be excused at the next court date, meaning that not only had nothing happened just then, but that nothing was going to happen on the next court date either. There was no way he would enter a plea if he didn't even plan to show up.

'I thought I was done having to deal with that man's complete incompetence,' I fumed. 'How is he still fucking things up?'

'Who?' Vincent asked, catching up to me.

'Sean! He literally cannot do his job properly. Why isn't the brief complete? I'm a human being, this is my life, this is another four weeks of my life.'

'Yeah, he really sucks, doesn't he.'

'I can't believe this. I want to punch Sean more than I want to punch Samuel.' I was itchy with anger.

'Want me to buy some cigarettes?' Vincent asked. We'd been talking about quitting.

'Yes please,' I replied, exhaling. 'I'm allowed to smoke today.'

'Yes, yes you are.'

⁓

We got coffees along with the cigarettes and sat on a cement retaining wall in the city smoking, talking about how funny Magistrates Court is.

'Mags hears 90-something per cent of all criminal matters,' I said. 'I think Judge had something to do with that policy. Making sure they can deal with way more at that level. I guess it just makes things a little jumbled sometimes.'

'I can't believe I have to do property and commercial law in PLT but nobody has to do criminal law,' Vincent said. 'Most people, in a normal life, if they come into contact with the law or the courts it'll be Mags Court and they need to know the basics of criminal offences.'

'Chickpeas,' I said.

'Huh?'

'They teach you the areas of law where the money is.' I took a drag, watching the suits pass us to-and-fro. 'You get a lot more money in one conveyancing gig than in repping a dozen shitty little DUIs. It's chickpeas—the whole industry is chickpeas.'

'True.'

'That's why I have Sean. And three weeks after three weeks after three weeks. I'm not the chickpeas, and there's nothing I can do about it.'

I called Sean when we got home. I wanted to ask about the source of the delay. I needed to know if the issue was just some small admin thing, or if there was more actual legwork to do. Had he just forgotten to photocopy some pages in defence's copy of the folder, or made a few too many typos? Or had he overlooked a critical witness or bungled interviews? Perhaps all of the above.

He didn't pick up so I left a message and decided to just try to get on with my life.

⌒

Vincent and I had some beers on the deck, chatting, and later, when I undid the buttons on his shirt we started kissing. When he told me I was beautiful I believed him. That was the first day I really felt as though I could keep living—properly living not placeholder living—while this chapter was still open and unfinished. When I lay in Vincent's arms, naked in bed, and we joked about how sweaty we were, I was genuinely happy, not fake-it-until-you-make-it happy. The wound hadn't healed but it didn't inhibit happiness the way it had for the past year.

Vincent coming to court with me forced me to acknowledge some level of continuity. The legal case wasn't severable; I was the same person there and at home. It couldn't be cauterised. The duality was the new reality, and I would never have seen that for myself alone. I was molested as a child and still grew into a sexual woman. In seeing myself through his eyes, through those rose-tinted glasses, even four years into our relationship, I found a sense of contentedness that wasn't predicated on closure. Every single day, Vincent was the reason I didn't put things on pause in that chapter of my life. How could I have put him, or my love for him, on pause? How different everything would have looked without him. How bleak.

Weeks later I remarked that I was grateful he was still attracted to me even now I was 'flabby'.

'I think I like you even more when you're flabby,' he said, kissing me and putting his hands on me. I grumbled. 'Not that you're even close to actually being flabby,' he clarified and paused, 'I think maybe this is the size you're supposed to be, and everything else is just you starving yourself.' Then he kissed me and left the room.

A few weeks later we moved into our new home, a unit with just the two of us, and a few weeks after that I found him at his computer and said to him, 'This is the first place I've ever lived in, or even stayed in for more than a few nights, in my whole life, where I haven't vomited up a single dinner.'

'Wow.'

I nodded. 'I'm happy here.'

'This is a happy house.'

'Our happy house.'

It was an old square house split into two long, rectangular units, each about three metres wide, and the paint job was awful, and there were chooks out the back that belonged to our neighbours, and I was in love with it. I printed out a photo of Vincent and me at Officeworks—a picture of us kissing at my graduation—and put it in an Ikea frame and hung it on the wall over the old kitchen sink.

One afternoon, shortly after we'd moved in, when Vincent was out with friends, I walked outside and into the backyard. Palm trees swayed in the February breeze and the chooks clucked, and in the space between the back of the house and the chook pen, the spot on the grass where I stood, I reached up and spun the wire arms of the Hills hoist. It was the biggest one I'd ever seen. The wire was strong against my fingertips, and it was heavy but it didn't have the rusty squeak I was expecting. I thought back to that first case I had proofread for Judge two years earlier and wondered where that girl was now. I spun the iron arms again and sat on the grass, squinting up into the sun as the shadows passed over my limbs. Which girl was I wondering about? The girl who had been tied to the Hills hoist, or the other girls Samuel had interfered with, or my old self? What had we all done in two years? Were they all still alive? I longed to reach out to them, closing my eyes, and imagined extending my thoughts to hit theirs somehow. I thought: *You can do it.*

⌒

At the next court date in the first week of March, I wore a plain black dress and when I approached the bench to ask about the matter of Levins they offered me the file, presuming I was Samuel's counsel. I got bumped between courtrooms three times, panicking on each trip that in the brief time it took me to get from one courtroom to the other I would miss the mention. The third time I approached the bench and asked about Levins, a different young man tried to give me the file.

'Oh, you're the victim?' he said, confused.

'The complainant,' I said, correcting him.

Eventually, after several hours, the matter was heard last because Samuel's representatives just hadn't shown up. A man arrived and announced himself as the town agent: a cheap stand-in for the actual barrister. The prosecutor announced the matter and it was all over in under two minutes. Some of the holes in the brief had been filled, a couple of others hadn't; they were waiting on the investigating officer to file the rest of the evidence. In my handwritten notes, *FUCK YOU SEAN* punctures the paper.

'Adjourned for two weeks,' the magistrate announced. What a win! Two weeks instead of four felt like a triumph. 'Nine a.m. on Monday 20 March.'

I flipped through to the date in my diary: *Admission.*

I wouldn't be able to attend the next Magistrates Court mention because I would be across the grassy lawn in the Supreme Court being admitted as a lawyer. The coincidence surpassed irony and landed in absurdity.

On the bus home I thought about the paperwork I still had to file, and some deadlines, and about what I would have for dinner.

I felt some small, pleasant surprise when my *go* card had more money than I'd expected, and so when the clock tower struck its long notes I marvelled at just how recently I had crumpled on the same streets. The thought of progress pleased me even more. I was disappointed, but my optimism for an outcome was shifting and hardening into something else. Each adjournment came with less let-down, less stress. Life was less and less parcelled into four-week arcs of hope and disappointment and denial.

⌒

One morning the following week when I needed to drop some paperwork into the Supreme Court registry for my application to be a lawyer, I saw a flurry of cameras and people milling around outside the building.

'What's all this about?' I asked a man standing behind the news truck.

'The bikie who killed his girlfriend just got sentenced,' he replied.

I kept my head down and passed the crowds. Women were speaking in front of cheap-looking banners, and the men had wiry beards and sunglasses. While I waited for my number to be called inside at the registry, I read about the bikie story on my phone.

The couple had been driving when the man grabbed the steering wheel from the passenger's seat and crashed the car into the side of the road, then left the vehicle, went around to her side of the wreckage, and punched her until she died.

I found it difficult to imagine how someone could ever be that angry. I had good reason to be angry: I had been wronged, and the man who wronged me continued to prolong my pain, and apart from smacking my own legs during the family trip to the Barossa, the only time I had ever so much as raised my voice was alone in the car out in the sticks once, banging my fists on the steering wheel with nobody around.

Comments on the article questioned why he'd done it. People always want to know why. Defence barristers tiptoe around the question: 'Why on earth would he do this?' and the tough thing for the prosecutors is that it's rarely an easy story like stolen money or a love triangle. People of sound mind do horrible things because they want to, because they're not worried about the consequences, and because they place their wants and needs above those of others. There is no great conspiracy.

Samuel didn't molest me *because* someone touched him when he was young. He didn't molest me *because* of anything external to himself. He did it because in that moment on that trampoline he wanted to, and because he completely disregarded my thoughts and feelings on the matter. The first part is easy. I know why he wanted to: sexual exploration and gratification. The cycle of abuse may have been a contributing factor to his desire to interfere with me but it didn't force his hand. What was far more troubling and mysterious was his reckoning with the latter part of the equation: me. Why didn't he think about how it would affect me? To molest a child is to completely disregard their humanity. Their personal and physical autonomy. To commit irreparable damage to a still-soft, still-forming mind.

I also read the sentencing submissions of the bikie murder case on my phone. The man was 'sorry'. Samuel was 'sorry' too. Neither would be sorry if they hadn't been caught, for the same justification they'd used, perhaps subconsciously, to act in a wholly selfish manner in the first place—it is rare that we behave truly abhorrently to people we consider our equals. The law allows us to hit our dogs and our children because they fall under our dominion. We are in control of them. The language of 'necessary discipline' applied to women until very recently too.

I looked out the window to the right of me, to Roma Street Parkland. Race was an extra layer difficult for me to fathom. Where was she now, that Aboriginal woman whose community resented her speaking to the police after she'd been brutally raped? What monumental strength she must have shown.

⌒

The paperwork went through and—much to Judge's relief—my admission date rolled around. I was putting lipstick on in the mirror and stepping through the process that would take place at court, calming my nerves. It was such a different kind of nervousness, but it was still in my belly—excited nerves instead of dread. Butterflies. Part of me was tempted to duck across to the Magistrates Court first in case my matter was mentioned before I needed to run to the Supreme Court at 10 a.m., but I was almost certain my matter wouldn't be heard within the first hour of the day. My presence wouldn't make a difference anyway: Vincent was the only one who knew about the scheduling overlap, and he'd offered to sit at the mention in my place.

'No way,' I'd said, kissing him. 'One of these things is much more important than the other. I want you in my life at the good bits.'

I looked good and I felt good. When Judge arrived to where my family and I waited outside the Banco Court, we hugged and I introduced him to my brother and grandfather, as he already knew my mother, father and partner. They were all there for me.

It was an achievement to be going for admission in the first session of the day because they're arranged in order of graduating grade point averages, and I felt like a big deal. My name was read aloud and I was referenced as Judge's previous associate, and we nodded at each other across the room in front of the crowd, and I felt proud of myself. After the swearing-in ceremony my family and I went to morning tea together with Judge and the woman who had moved my admission. It was custom that the newly minted lawyer take everyone out as a sign of gratitude for their support over the years.

'So how will you write about today?' Judge asked me as we all walked past the Magistrates Court to a cab rank, and I laughed louder than I should have.

I wanted to tell him about the absurdity of it all. That my matter might be being heard at that exact moment, in a building I could reach out and touch. I wanted to tell him that I felt proud of myself for being able to enjoy the day despite the thought that Samuel might have more reason than usual to be in that area of the city. And I hadn't told anyone my secret nervousness that Samuel would somehow find my application for admission and oppose it, as any member of the public is entitled to do. I'd played out in my mind, in the days prior, what would happen if he showed up at court to make a scene, 'objecting' like you can do at a wedding.

'With much champagne,' I said to Judge, and we all laughed.

Sometimes it's easiest to let them underestimate you.

The next day I called Sean to find out what I'd missed. I didn't really expect much from him, and those expectations were met.

'I don't understand why Samuel's dragging this out so much,' I said to Sean, after he gave me the short update.

'Yeah, look, I think he would have just been expecting it all to have gone away by now.'

'And he's deliberately found a barrister who used to be a cop. It's so fucking, I don't know, it's—'

'He's a bit of a prick, actually,' Sean said.

'Carter?'

'Yeah, well, I mean, I should say, he's not the friendliest gentleman barrister I've had to deal with.'

I laughed loudly, and Sean and I exchanged pleasantries before saying goodbye. At least he was honest.

I put the phone down and picked up my certificate of admission. It had been spitting rain on the way home, and a blotch sat at the bottom right-hand side of the big red seal on the page. The night before I'd felt disappointed by the imperfection, but with time to reflect I'd decided it was fitting. I didn't fit in that scene—something was a little amiss—but I'd still get the paper framed. I could have been a hotshot lawyer if I'd wanted to, and that thought alone was enough permission for me to leave it behind.

⌒

One day the next month I got a letter in the mail with a government seal. It was an information pack about being the 'victim of a crime' in Queensland. It had the phone number of my victim liaison officer, Rhys, and so I called it thinking he might have more information than Sean. He said that after all the Magistrates Court stuff, if the DPP decided to continue with the matter, it would take several months for things to reach the District Court.

'How long is a long time?' I asked.

'Our guidelines are to aim for four months from committal, but it can take up to six months for us to create the indictment to then be presented.'

I thanked him for his time, hung up, and screamed into a cushion for a while.

⌒

The next mention was listed for 10 April, and I didn't ask Vincent to come with me until the night before. We were in the kitchen doing dinner dishes.

'Do you think he's going to plead?' he asked me with a tone that suggested he didn't understand why I wanted his company all of a sudden.

'No, I've given up on thinking about that anytime soon. He's not even going to be arraigned until it gets up to the District Court. But I think he might be there. Some stuff Sean told me on the phone made me think that tomorrow they're going to list it for a committal hearing.'

'Right.' He put a wet dish down on the drying rack slowly but wouldn't look at me.

'Which makes me think he might be there. Or that at least his actual barrister will be there.'

'Sure.'

'Which is why I'm a bit nervous about it, I guess.' I was wringing the tea towel in my hands.

'Okay, well, I have an oral presentation for my thesis at 2 p.m. that I need to prepare for in the morning,' he said, trailing off slightly.

'Of course, yeah, it's my fault for asking you so late.'

He held me for a long time, kissing my face, and when he left the room I stood in the same position until my feet hurt, and then I poured myself a large, warm glass of the Jameson my brother had given me as an admission present, and sat with it in the bottom of the shower. I thought a lot about vomiting, touching my fingers to my lips, but I didn't. When the hot water ran out I turned the taps off and lay in the tub until the Jameson ran out. When I was finally shivering from the cold I got up, swaying, dried myself, lay in bed, and thought a lot about cutting, but didn't. I could have—I had closed the bedroom door and taken sewing scissors with me, and I'd poured myself more Jameson. Vincent was at the other end of the unit gaming online with friends. I wrote awful things about myself in my journal and cried. *How can you be so disgusting and fat? You are taking up time and resources from people who really need the system. This is all one big ego exercise.*

I woke the next morning, went for a run, skipped breakfast, and said goodbye to Vincent. It was the first really cold morning of the year.

'Keep me posted?' he asked.

'Sure,' I replied, but I was thinking: *Fuck you. How often do I ask? I would never leave you like this.* There was no guidebook for either of us.

⌒

I got off the bus, walked into the building and stepped into the elevator. No Samuel. I got out of the elevator, scanned the waiting room, went into Courtroom 20, approached the bar. No Samuel.

'Good morning, I'm the complainant in the matter of Levins,' I said to the clerk. This wasn't my first rodeo and by then I even knew the number of the other courtroom my matter might have been moved to. 'Can you please tell me if the mention will be here or in Courtroom 19?'

'Ahh . . .' She looked at me with confusion.

'I've been here a few times now and I know sometimes files get pinballed between 19 and 20,' I said, shrugging.

'Umm . . .' She flipped through her papers, and I saw his name, and pointed it out to her. 'Well, I don't have anything written here,' she replied.

'So it'll be here? In 20?'

'I think so.'

'Can you please let me know if it changes?'

'I don't know,' she replied and began to turn her body away from me, but I stayed there, unblinking, so she couldn't really ignore me. 'Sorry, it's my first day. I'll try.'

I smiled at her and sat down, full of frustrated nerves about the possibility of missing the mention. Two hours passed with nothing. Someone said 'Levan' and my heart leapt, but that was followed by another hour of nothing. The magistrate announced they'd move on to the legal aid matters—a clear indication that all of the privately funded matters had been dealt with.

I jumped to my feet, pushing through to the bar table. 'Excuse me, has the Levins matter been mentioned?' I asked the clerk in a stage whisper.

She shuffled through her papers and then found the file. 'No, it's still here,' she said, confused, and we both looked down at it for a moment. 'I'll ask for you.'

Within ten minutes the magistrate called for a short adjournment. I saw the clerk speaking with her senior and approached them. The senior was a very broad-shouldered woman with dark hair and intimidating curtness; I liked her immediately.

'Nobody for this matter has arrived,' the senior said to me.

'Yes, I can see that. What happens if nobody from his side turns up today?' I asked.

'We just adjourn it and get another mention date.' She shrugged and again started to turn away from me, but again I didn't move.

I looked straight at her face. 'So they can have a listed court date, and not turn up, and nothing happens?'

She turned back to me and paused for a moment, and I saw her lips purse as though she was trying to stop herself saying something, and instead she turned to the clerk. 'Do you have your phone on you?'

'Yes,' the clerk replied.

'Call them and see where they are.'

I smiled. 'Thank you,' I said, and she nodded.

Ten minutes later I ran into the clerk in the ladies' bathroom and she explained, while we washed our hands, that after multiple calls and a voicemail, she had learned that the town agent for the matter had forgotten about the mention, and that he was now on his way.

Court resumed and the legal aid matters continued for another twenty minutes. As I waited in the back of Courtroom 20, I scrolled

through my social media accounts and wondered where *she* was—
the other girl—what she looked like and if she'd gone on to seem
normal too. At the edge of my vision I saw a woman in a black
suit run in, grab a file, and start to dash back out. I didn't want to
make a scene but I couldn't risk missing this mention.

'Excuse me!' I said in a very loud whisper, and began pushing past
people's knees to get to the edge of the row, following the woman
out the double doors, remembering to bow to the Magistrate—as
is customary—at the last moment.

Out in the waiting area I caught up to her. 'Is that the Levins
matter?' I asked.

'Yes,' she replied, not stopping.

'And we're going to Court 19 now? The solicitor is here?'

'The town agent,' she corrected me, 'yes.'

We bowed and entered, and I saw a man sitting at the bar, on
his mobile phone. In the ten minutes we waited for the magistrate
to arrive he jiggled his foot incessantly.

'Silence, all stand.'

The mention was over in two minutes.

The town agent mispronounced both the name of the defendant
and the name of the solicitor's office he was working for. He said
defence wanted to cross-examine a witness.

DPP requested a date two months away for an application to
cross-examine. The court wasn't available on that date. They spoke
about July. Everyone agreed that 12 July would be best. 'Listed for
12 July for an application to cross-examine. Appearance required.
Adjourned.' The magistrate stood up. 'Silence, all stand.'

⌒

I sat there at the back of the court, slapped in the face. *Again! You
idiot!* Nervous for nothing. Not only was Samuel not there, but his

solicitor hadn't bothered coming and had paid for a cheap town agent to take his place, and *even that agent had forgotten.* Nobody gave a fuck about me sitting there. I could have missed the whole thing if I'd waited for people to tell me what was happening. And then—the worst bit—there would be three more months of waiting.

The town agent walked out and I looked at his face. I could have reached out and shoved him, but he seemed pathetic to me. He was incapable of doing his own job.

I approached the bar and waited for several minutes until someone from the prosecution side saw me.

'Can I help you?' she asked.

'Yes, please, I'm the complainant in that last matter, Levins, the one that was listed for an application to cross-examine, and I was hoping someone could tell me what that means? What's happening?'

'Oh.' The two prosecutors at the bar table looked between each other, confused, and one started flipping through papers. 'The file says that defence made a request to cross-examine a witness, and the DPP rejected that request, so now the matter is listed for an application in front of the court.'

'Right,' I said, 'so this new date we have, that's not for a cross-examination. That's just the application to see if the magistrate will allow a cross-examination?'

She nodded. 'Yes.'

'And which witness was it? Can you tell me? Am I even allowed to know that?'

She spoke back into her folders. 'How about I get someone to call you?'

⌒

It was hot by the time I walked out of the building. I called the number of the Brisbane DPP.

'Good afternoon,' I said and introduced myself, 'my matter was just mentioned this morning and I was hoping to speak to someone about what happened?'

They put me through to the victim liaison officer, Rhys.

'You want to know what happened in court this morning?' he asked.

'No, I was there in court this morning, I know what happened, but things were mentioned this morning that I wasn't aware of, and I'd like to speak with someone about my case, if I can—if I'm allowed.'

'Well, I might just get the legal officer to call you back when she has time.'

'Oh, sure.'

'Was that everything?'

'Yes.'

He hung up. I stood still for a little while, watching the people come and go around me. A bus rushed by on the road very close to me and I almost thought I didn't see myself in the reflection of the windows. I was a small ghost.

A text came through from Vincent: *How'd you go?*

I was still angry at him. *If you cared you would have come!* I wanted to reply. *Stop doing things in halves! I need to know if you're here for me or not.* But now I was angry at everyone. What could I do?

How could I keep living until July?

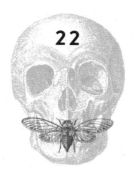

22

I'M NOT SURE WHEN THE seed of thought—the thought that my matter wasn't that important—finally took root. I'd been told it in many ways, by many different mouths. I had fought against that chorus for so long, trying to find pride in the perseverance, gaining strength from the act of opposition, determination breeding determination.

Sean called me and said he'd received an email from the DPP requesting more information about a few different things. It should have been straightforward but Sean stayed on the phone. I had questions about the delays, and he started talking to me about the process from his end, saying that the police didn't know if they 'should or shouldn't have charged Samuel based on the evidence' and that they 'were on the fence and then thought, *You know what, let's just run with it*'.

Those things were so hard to hear. I don't think he realised how brutal he was being.

Sean called again a few weeks later and said, 'His solicitors have sent through a list of things they're seeking. Over twenty things.'

'Huh? What twenty things?'

'It looks like they're preparing to cross-examine all the witnesses with the intent of getting the matter thrown out, or taking it to a full trial. I'll need you to come in and make another addendum statement.'

I banged my little fists against my thighs.

'It seems they're just trying to make the whole process as difficult as possible, in the hopes that we'll drop it.'

I wanted to ask him: *Will you?*

After I put the phone down I sat on the edge of the bathtub for a long time. Vincent had headphones on in the other room. With nobody to perform for, I realised my feelings were more complex than just tears or frustration. I sat, perched and cold, approaching the discomfort, peeling back the shows I'd put on. How did I truly feel? How would I think and feel without an audience? Things I could never be certain about, but felt sure of, emerged. I underlined a note I had made—that Sean said they'd pressed charges because of my 'reliability as a witness'. He meant that I was the right kind of complainant: white, educated, articulate. I felt a suspicion that Samuel really might not have been charged if my father hadn't been a police officer. Things were dragging on and I was draining resources for a one-off, historical matter.

Another thing I felt sure of: I pitied Samuel. Almost two decades later his behaviour as a teenager was haunting him, and no matter what he paid or said, I wouldn't go away. Malevolent, persistent spirit. I stood and washed my face, quelling the dread again, and looked at myself in the mirror. Why was I doing this to him? Really?

It wasn't *just* him in the same way it wasn't *just* me. It was because I was sick of men *like* him. Because I'd seen them all, each as unoriginal in their selfishness as the next. Because they needed to be taught a lesson. Because the harder he pushed back and the more money he spent on lawyers, the more he proved his own inability to take responsibility for his actions. Because he'd let those words slip from his mouth: that I wasn't the only one. Because the girl he'd molested had grown into a furious feminist, and that just made him plain unlucky, and that was just too bad for him, because that's eggshell skull.

⌒

I went back to the police station to make the addendum statement by myself. A sunny skyline opened up as I hopped off the bus and I was listening to good music, and I felt okay. When I walked in the sliding doors, I saw ghosts of myself coming and going from the building: first being stoic with my father, then falling into my mother's arms, then putting on a brave face with Vincent, and finally, there and then, alone and average.

I read over my initial statement and realised how much detail was missing—I must have been so exhausted and overwhelmed. Sean's two-fingered typing technique hadn't improved.

⌒

I got another letter from the DPP dated the week of the last mention: 'The purpose of the committal hearing is for a magistrate to determine whether there is enough evidence for a trial to be held in the District Court at Brisbane.'

The letter was signed by Kirsty—a new, different victim liasion officer.

The envelope also included a printout of a flowchart depicting the stages all criminal matters go through. The chart had about fifteen levels, and on most of them there was a line from the bubble out to the edge with a possibility saying 'Dismissed' or 'Discontinued', and then no more lines from that bubble. One of the bubbles had been highlighted in yellow for me—I was pretty early on in the flowchart, and there were still half a dozen major potential movements for my matter to go through. I wondered what it would look like to a non-lawyer.

On the opposite side of the chart there was a 'commonly used terms' sheet. 'Discontinued' was defined and finished with: 'Our office will contact you before this occurs.' I knew from my research work that case attrition is highest at the police stage: fewer than one in five sex offences reported to the police result in charges being laid and criminal proceedings being instigated. The flowchart should have included some stats after the first 'Police/Investigation' level saying, 'Make it past here and you're in the top 20 per cent, gold star'. The second most likely stage is where I was at—where the DPP can decide at any moment that they don't think it's worth proceeding. My perceived credibility was critical to a prosecutor's estimation of the probability of success at trial. It would be good for my image if I showed up to each court date, well dressed and well spoken. I hadn't been injured physically and Samuel wasn't a stranger who'd jumped out at me from the bushes, so to a jury my matter might not look terribly 'convincing'.

I didn't think I was too nervous, but then I couldn't stop putting makeup on. There had been four or five mentions in the Magistrates Court, but this one, on 12 July, would be the first one where Samuel's appearance was required.

'Should we go soon?' Vincent asked me, ten minutes after we both knew we should have left, standing in the doorway to the bathroom. I had to look good. I had to look beautiful. So much, and yet nothing at all, hung on it. It was seeing an ex or walking into a school reunion. Caring so much only proved you weren't over it. Over him. I blow-dried my hair.

We walked down the street to the bus stop.

'Thank you for coming with me,' I said to Vincent, and as a sensation of guilt arrived in my belly—that I was wasting his time when he was so busy with his doctorate, and on such a gross thing—it was replaced almost instantly with fury.

The anger arrived in my chest so quickly I only just managed not to direct it at Vincent, instead kicking a seed pod violently. It skidded once then hit some rich turf on the side of the pavement and sat, unaffected, and I could have screamed at it. I longed to throw my handbag across the street, to slap and strangle someone, anyone, and then to smack my head onto the rough bark of a tree until it bled and I cracked my skull. I fantasised about the impact of a high-speed vehicle and a body—my body—being flung across a busy intersection. Then I was tapping my *go* card and a bus driver smiled at me, saying something pleasant, and when the bus lurched forward and I reached up an arm to grab hold of a support bar, I smelled how much I had been sweating already. *Just breathe.*

'Do you need some water?' Vincent asked me, the side of our bodies touching.

'It's fine,' I replied curtly, but as I breathed and let go of the anger the strength left me, and I was blinking away tears.

My phone was vibrating and lighting up, Mum and Dad wondering where I was. They had been waiting for us. More guilt.

We got off the bus and walked the final two blocks to the court-house; a freezing wind tunnel formed between high-rises and whipped my hair around my face. I lowered my head, trying to imagine I was ploughing through the weather, ploughing through it all, but the strength wouldn't come. The anger wouldn't well up inside.

When we made it through the security check, Dad saw me. 'Ah, here she is,' he said cheerfully, and my mother looked up from her seat, smiling, and they both opened their arms to embrace me, and I started crying.

'Ohhhh, hey, what's the matter, lovey?' Mum asked, holding me, patting my back.

'I'm scared,' I said, my face pressed into her neck, and my father's arms closed around us. They smelled like home.

When we disentangled Mum found a tissue from her bag and I saw she had tears in her eyes as well. The tissue was very soft, not the generic-brand ones Vincent and I bought, and I touched it to my face. It smelled like home as well. Vincent and my father shook hands, that age-old absurdity for men to avoid an embrace, and said good morning to each other. Then we set off, with Dad giving directions to the elevators, to the right floor, to the courtroom, and all the while my eyes darted around us, searching for Samuel's face or gait. I tuned out of my family's conversation and listened for his voice. When I conjured it in memory, it came from down the phone line of the pretext call.

'Yeah,' his voice replayed, 'and you weren't the only one.'

Then we were outside the courtroom. My family turned to look at me, waiting for a sign. People bustled around us: barristers, solicitors, police officers, prosecutors, volunteer support staff. Wheelie bags knocked against seats and phones went off.

'Hey mate.' A barrister waved to Vincent, strolling past confidently with his wig in his hand. I recognised him from one of our house parties months ago.

'Hey,' Vincent replied with a smile, and the man almost paused to chat, but then in a flash I saw recognition on his face. 'Catch up with you later.'

There was to be no real demarcation of the battleground then, I figured. I couldn't build walls between the court occurrences and the rest of my life. I had brought my safety blanket into the fire, and in doing so sacrificed any final opportunity to make a clean break from the wretched mess. I looked at the faces of the people I loved and regretted having asked them to come, dirtying all our lives. I wouldn't have cried if I was alone—I knew that much—I was always weakest when I was with them. A true self revealed under the looking glass of their unconditional love.

'I don't see him here,' I said, glancing to Dad for guidance.

He shrugged. 'Let's just go in then, I guess,' and moved toward the double doors.

The small courtroom's standing space was packed with professionals but all the seats were empty, so I picked a row and moved right to the end.

'What if he doesn't come?' I whispered to Vincent next to me as we sat down. I was thinking about how much the taxi into the city had cost my parents, because parking would be too expensive, and then how much they'd paid for coffee and breakfast while they waited for me. My mother would be calculating it whether she wanted to or not: middle-class habits die hard. 'Why isn't he here?' I asked the same question differently.

'Just wait and see,' Vincent said, and shrugged.

Minutes passed, my stomach clenching every time the courtroom door opened, my ears straining until they finally picked up a thread.

'The matter of Levins?' someone said, and I looked up and saw Samuel's barrister, Carter. The prosecutor took a moment looking through his stack of cases, and the barrister smiled patiently. I saw freshly printed pages in his hand, covered in writing and stapled, and he had a heavy compact leather case wheeling behind him. The instant realisation that he was prepared—well prepared—and the length of what he had prepared for made my stomach constrict so quickly that my throat tightened and my body shifted in my seat.

'What's up?' Vincent asked.

'What *is* all that stuff?' I asked him back, nodding to the barrister, panicking. 'Why has he got so much fucking stuff?'

But I knew the answer to my own bleating. A barrister doesn't need pages of notes and a folder of materials if his client is entering a guilty plea. The day was just beginning, and I wouldn't be spared a fight. Until then I hadn't realised just how much hope I had held that the day would end in rejoicing. I still clung to the memory of the dream I'd had over a year earlier—the one of my family embracing in the sunshine after Samuel pleaded guilty. I thought that moment might have come simply because it was so overdue.

'Silence, all stand,' the clerk called out, interrupting my demoralised panic, and the room obliged, but not for long. People came in and out, whispering loudly, exchanging briefs and handshakes. The magistrate made her way through a huge stack of matters, hearing what counsel had to say about time estimates and intentions for proceedings, and allocating the matters to different courtrooms and magistrates.

I kept my eyes locked on Samuel's expensive champion, searching him for an indication of evil, but all I saw was professionalism. I stewed in the fear it gave me.

He must have seen his moment, and stepped up to the bar table. 'Your Honour, might I raise the matter of Levins?' he asked.

'Levins, Levins, Levins,' she repeated, moving folders from one pile to another, 'ah yes, what's happening with this matter?'

'An application to cross-examine, your Honour,' he replied. 'My estimate would be forty-five minutes.'

'Very well,' she said, making a note for the clerk and allocating us a different courtroom, announcing it and moving on.

I stood up to leave, and Vincent and my parents followed my lead, and the barrister saw us as he turned from the bar table, and he assessed us quickly then left through the doors first, hurrying ahead. We moved to the elevators and he was already gone.

On a higher level with only two courtrooms, things were much quieter—silent, even—and we spotted the right number above yet another set of double doors. This time we didn't pause. I pushed them open and saw Samuel sitting there in the front row, his head bowed in concentrated conversation with his solicitor, and I turned on my heel and picked a line among the empty rows on the prosecutor's side of the room. The four of us filed in and sat down.

Carter saw us and something came across his face. He turned to Samuel, raised his eyebrows in a questioning expression, jabbing his head in our direction. Samuel turned, looking over his shoulder at us, and quickly turned back around, and nodded. We sat six rows behind him and on his right, and I knew all our eight eyes were burning down onto his neck. Adrenalin rushed through me. It was a fundamental shifting of shame, and as it lifted from me and settled on Samuel I felt what I could only describe as a surge. A chest-beating, wings-expanding battle cry.

The barrister grimaced and I knew then that I had tasted blood. Something of the strength of character I thought would only come once the whole ordeal was over, some sense of invincibility, of absolution, arrived inside me.

Aside from the people he paid, Samuel's side of the courtroom was empty. No parents, no friends, no partner. I was armoured, flanked, and bolstered with love. What he sought to keep hidden was being dragged into the light.

My champion emerged a moment later and her name was Sarah. She walked up to our row with the confidence of a busy person, and when she shook my hand I liked her immediately.

She looked right at my face and smiled. 'You must be Miss and Mrs Lee?' she asked.

'Yes,' Mum and I answered.

'My name is Sarah. I'm from the DPP and I'll be handling your file. Unfortunately I'll need both of you to wait outside today. As counsel and I will be discussing witness statements, they would be able to argue that your evidence had been compromised if you heard what we were talking about.'

I felt the wings I'd just grown get clipped, a bullet to the beating chest. How could I have been so stupid? Of course I wasn't allowed to listen to the pre-trial arguments for *my own* damn trial.

'Of course,' I replied with a smile, moving past Vincent to the edge of the row, 'we'll just wait outside then?'

'Yes, and Mr Lee, I presume,' Sarah addressed my dad, 'you're not going to be called as a witness so you can stay, but you can't speak to either your daughter or Mrs Lee about the proceedings.'

Dad nodded and went to stand up, but I stopped him. 'Can you and Vincent please stay here and let me know if anything procedural happens? Any new dates and stuff?' And they agreed.

Mum and I took a seat outside.

'It's so frustrating!' I said, my teeth clenched. 'I just feel like there's nothing I can do. I'm not even allowed to listen.'

'I know,' she said, and held my hand, making small strokes on it with her thumb like she'd done whenever I was sick as a child. 'At the police station when we last went there for the extra statement, Sean kept asking me what I thought you wanted to get out of all this, why you'd go through all this.'

'I just want something on his record,' I said, annoyed. How many times would Sean ask? I wanted him to do his fucking job and get some fucking justice.

We waited for ages. The whole thing ended up taking well over four hours, and Vincent popped out to tell us that the magistrate was displeased with Carter's original 45-minute estimate. Vincent went back inside to the courtroom and Dad came out to go to the bathroom and get a coffee, then came back and swapped with Vincent again. I felt completely useless. Every time the courtroom door opened, my gut fell through to the floor.

Mum ran out of random things to say. 'You know I'm just waff-ling,' she said, 'to keep us both distracted.'

'Thank you.' I smiled at her, before dropping the expression and returning my gaze to where it was trained on the double doors.

Finally Sarah came out and asked if Mum would be available on a certain date, and she said 'yes' and Sarah disappeared again. Everything fell away and all I heard was my heart beating—the blood pumping in my ears. Five minutes later she re-emerged and ushered us into a small conference room. It had a band of clear glass at the bottom, the rest was frosted, and I watched the feet go past until I saw Samuel's shoes appear on the right, take steps, and disappear to the left. He was gone.

'Well,' Sarah said, 'some of these barristers will try to get away with as much as they can when they're not in front of a jury, but overall I'd say today went well for us.'

I found out that Carter's first application was to cross-examine me on the entirety of my statement, and that the magistrate rejected his request immediately. Sarah asked me and Mum all kinds of questions, and seemed both frustrated and happy by our answers. As we knew, the only question truly being asked was in what year the offending had occurred. I repeated what I'd told Sean about the trampoline, and Mum mentioned that Dylan's broken nose was fixed at a Mater children's hospital.

'Why isn't any of this in the brief!?' Sarah said, sounding exasperated.

'We've told Sean all of this,' Mum said, confused, 'a few times, I think.'

'Well, if everything you just told me was provided to me in the brief, today probably wouldn't have even been necessary.'

'That's good news, though—I mean, for me, right?' I asked.

'Absolutely,' she replied. 'Your mum is the only one who needs to answer any questions before we present an indictment, and the magistrate has ordered that she can only be asked certain things about the timing and dates, nothing else.'

We met Vincent and Dad outside, and decided to all go for lunch together.

'We're only here today because Sean can't do his fucking job,' I said to Vincent.

'What's new?' he replied as we walked out through security into the light.

'At first I was angry, but then I was thinking, how much do you think Samuel paid for today?'

'A few thousand at least, I'd say,' he replied, 'to prepare all that material, then to be in submissions for so many hours.'

'And it was all a waste!' I said. I squeezed his hand and grinned, and he kissed me, and the four of us got dumplings.

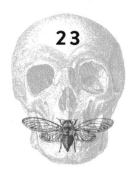

23

MY WHOLE FAMILY WAS IN Noosa for our annual winter beach trip the weekend before the pre-trial hearing on 31 July. Vincent and I went for a walk through the national park nearby, as we had done each year, and I was glad that twelve months ago when I was last there nobody knew that Samuel still wouldn't have pleaded guilty an entire year later, or I might have given up. I tried to pretend the impending Monday wasn't tainting the weekend.

'I'm nervous,' Mum said on Sunday night when nobody else was around. She wouldn't bring it up in front of the boys.

'*You're* nervous?' I replied, irritated.

'Well, you don't have to do any talking,' she jabbed back.

'I'm going for a walk.'

I looked out at the ocean and wondered if the following day might end it all, or if I would return to Noosa, a whole year later, still churning and snappy. The unit had new couches and new wi-fi: a time stamp. What would change next winter? Maybe the local coffee stand would finally take debit cards, and maybe my mother would be nervous about having to give evidence at a trial in the District Court.

The next morning the four of us—Mum, Dad, Vincent and I—went up in the elevator and found the right courtroom together.

'Want to sit over there, facing out the window?' Mum asked me, pointing to the far side of the floor.

'No, I want to sit right here, where I can see everything,' I replied, and dropped my bags. A small interview room was annexed to the courtroom we'd been allocated, and I'd seen Samuel's shoes through the non-frosted section of the glass near the floor. I may have been locked out of the courtroom, but I was determined to make my presence known.

Mum was clearly still nervous. Vincent and Dad went into the courtroom, and when Sarah arrived a moment later she told us to wait there, and that she'd come out to get Mum 'in a minute'. The 'minute' was more like twenty, and Mum was fidgeting and talking a lot. She said something about how I should be grateful that Vincent was coming along to all the court dates. Finally Sarah emerged and walked toward us, and Mum stood up.

'Do you take an oath or affirmation?' Sarah asked her.

'What?'

'Do you swear on the Bible, or just make a promise?' she clarified, but Mum's panic was blocking her ears.

'To who?' She looked at me, frightened.

'You have to promise to tell the truth when you go in,' I said, touching her arm. 'And do you want the religious version or the non-religious version?'

'Oh, non-religious,' she said.

I smiled and nodded at her, watched them walk away together, then slumped back into my chair and waited. A television in the corner showed a white man with a gross neck beard going around Japan, eating their hottest chillies and making grotesque gestures, surrounded by beautiful Japanese women applauding. After every challenge that he completed, a big stamp of words would slam onto the screen, 'Man versus Heat', with a sound effect like weights dropping. Everything seemed incredibly absurd.

The pre-trial hearing only took about fifteen minutes. Everyone came out of the double doors at once, and I saw Samuel leaving quickly, his hands in his pockets. He looked a bit like the man in the chilli show—like shit.

'Well, that went really well,' Sarah said to all of us standing in a semicircle.

Vincent grabbed and squeezed my hand and smiled at me.

'But Samuel didn't enter a plea?' I asked. I had thought if it went 'well' enough, he might just plead on the spot.

'No, the matter has been transferred up to the District Court. It'll take me about three months before I have time to do the paperwork to present an indictment, and then it'll get given a date for trial.'

I exhaled. 'Okay.'

'But today couldn't have gone any better,' Sarah turned to Mum, 'you did really well.'

'Thank you,' she said.

⟡

The four of us went for coffee afterwards, and Mum and Dad told us about how the police had tried to organise drones to fly around the neighbourhood of the family home to get aerial photos of the spaces in the backyard, where the trampoline had been, but had been so disorganised that they failed, twice. People hadn't shown up, things hadn't worked.

'Was it Sean?' I asked.

'Yes,' Dad said, 'once just him and someone else, and the actual drones never arrived, and the next time there were about six other officers. It was ridiculous.'

'And were the photos used in court?'

'No!'

Vincent and I said goodbye to my parents and went to the shops to buy socks. At lunchtime we made our way to the food court and were stepping off an escalator when Vincent grabbed my hand. 'Samuel, nine o'clock, change direction, this way.'

And we turned right and walked outside, all the way to our bus stop.

'Did he see us?' I asked when we were safe on the bus.

'No.'

'What was he eating?'

'Sushi.'

'Did he look happy?'

'No.'

'What did he look like?'

'I dunno.'

'Come on.'

'He looked like a miserable man who's been rightly accused of molesting a child, and who has just spent another few thousand dollars fighting an inevitable outcome, and then has to go eat some sushi for lunch.'

'He was alone?'

'Yes.'

'Good. Did I tell you my parents got a Christmas card from his parents last year?'

'What?'

'I know, he hasn't told anyone.'

⌒

I got another letter from the DPP three weeks later. The same flowchart and list of definitions, but this time the bubble one step further was highlighted. The next bubble was 'indictment presented', but then there was a bubble below it saying 'mentions' before the flowchart split into two—'Not Guilty Plea/No Plea' compared to 'Guilty Plea'. I got confused. How could he not enter a plea at all if the indictment had been presented? How many times would I need to be reminded, in new or different ways, that the stuff I'd seen as an associate was the very end of the long journey?

I remembered the research I'd been doing into sex offenders and dug up the statistics sheet from the ABS. Seventy per cent of people accused of criminal offences plead guilty, but the number drops to about 30 per cent for sex offences. Each step of the flowchart is risky for a complainant. This time the letter said: 'If an indictment is presented . . . It is important to note that it could be some time before this matter is listed for a significant court event. . . We will advise you once a date has been set and if or when you are required to attend court.'

Then, on a total whim a few weeks later, 22 August, I called the number on the letter and asked for Kirsty, and was informed that I had a new victim liaison officer: Dan was my third. Was it normal to go through three VLOs? I didn't know anything about why they were changing. Dan was out at lunch.

When he called me back I was walking around Coles, and he told me the good news that the indictment against Samuel was being presented on 5 September, a full month ahead of schedule. I was ecstatic for a split second, then my stomach sank—Vincent and I had scheduled a week away to celebrate our fifth anniversary.

I asked Dan if someone would be in touch with me about the outcome of the indictment being presented, or if I should attend myself, and he said he'd make sure a letter got posted to me. I scoffed silently. As soon as he'd said the date a new little egg timer had started in my mind. There was no way I was going to wait until a letter *maybe* arrived in the post weeks later, if at all, to find out what happened.

I would have been livid if Vincent had asked to cut our time away in half, but when I called him on the phone to tell him the news he immediately offered that we drive back to attend the indictment. I felt as if I had to choose between him and Samuel: between my past and my future.

'Well, either he pleads guilty and we go out and have the biggest bender of our entire lives, on me,' I said down the line, 'or he says "not guilty", and I'm glad I didn't interrupt our holiday for bad news.' I was walking along the makeup and razor blades aisle.

'Yeah, sounds great, it's totally up to you,' Vincent replied.

'Even if he pleaded guilty, it would be listed for sentence on a separate date anyways, and I'd definitely go to that. I think this is fine.'

I wondered exactly how long it had been since I'd made my first complaint, and when I got home I dug through some paperwork. I found statement number one, taken when I was twenty-three, on 22 September 2015. The whole ugly mess was a month shy of its second birthday. A two-year-old human can speak a few words and dress themselves—Samuel still hadn't even had to enter a plea.

Kingscliff was beautiful. Vincent and I just slept in, had sex, watched Netflix, ate, had beers, watched more Netflix, ate more, and went to bed. It was a dream until I got the phone call from Dan on the fifth.

'Yes, the indictment was presented this morning, and the trial against Mr Levins has been listed as Trial Number One on Monday December the eleventh in the District Court at Brisbane.'

'Thank you,' I said. 'Oh, and Dan, do you have in your notes that I was previously a judge's associate?'

'Oh,' he replied, and paused, probably scrolling through something on his screen, 'I'll let the legal officer know.'

'Great, thanks, they'll need to be careful about which judge the trial is allocated to.'

'No worries. Got it.'

I hung up, but still had worries. I'd mentioned that information to both my previous victim liaison officers. Didn't I have a file? It was an upsetting phone call. I had really thought that after how well the pre-trial hearing had gone, Samuel might just plead guilty at the presentation of the charges against him. Was I being optimistic or just naive, holding out hope he would plead at every step?

Weeks later, in October, I called to check up on Sean. I knew that he still had to do some tasks to make sure everything was ready to go to trial, and I needed him to know I was counting on him.

'Everything at this stage is going ahead,' he said. 'The DPP were pretty surprised he didn't plead, given his counsel indicated that if the matter was committed up to the District Court they would take "a certain course of action", but yeah, he still might just plead on the Monday morning, you know, that happens, and hopefully this will all be over before Christmas. I suspect that's a happy—well, not happy, but that's a good thing for you.'

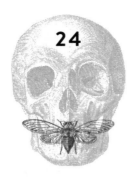

24

ALL I HAD TO DO was not step in front of a bus for about four more weeks.

Sean came to my house to serve me with my subpoena. 'I suppose I don't need to explain anything to you about being summoned to court,' he said, standing wide-legged in my tiny kitchen. He handed me a pile of papers. I noticed they were held together with one of the little silver clips I used to find at home as a child when I rummaged through my father's things, looking for loose change to buy lollies. I nodded and smiled as Sean spoke, and offered him a glass of water, while I tapped the clip with my fingernail.

'So you know it's the eleventh of December?' he asked.

'Couldn't forget it if I tried, mate,' I replied.

'Yeah, of course, righto. And your birthday is the thirteenth, isn't it?'

'Yep. And nothing new has come up?'

'No, no. It's the same as before. No idea why this is a trial, but.' He shrugged to finish the sentence.

After he left I looked through the papers briefly then went to finish doing the dishes but turned the tap on too hard. Water hit the open side of a spoon and splashed up onto my face, and the shock of it set me off. I threw the plate I was holding into the sink and stormed into the bedroom, grabbing a clean bath towel and screaming into it. The yelling turned into crying, and then Vincent was holding me for a long time.

⌒

Every time my mobile rang my stomach clenched up because I presumed it would be news about the trial. It rarely was—until the week before the trial, when it always was. Tuesday was a call from Judge, checking in with me, and helping me to make sure that none of the judges who I'd worked or interacted with would be allocated to the matter. On the Wednesday a call came through from a clerk at the DPP, asking if I was available the very next day to go into their office. I told them I was.

It made me anxious to think of how late they'd left contacting me; maybe they had finally called because there was a problem.

Going in the next day meant I had to write my victim impact statement that night. I should have drafted it weeks earlier, but the task was immensely frustrating and I'd abandoned it several times. In the document I needed to outline the ways I had suffered and how the offending had negatively affected my life, but in reality I was proud of how I'd spent most of my time trying to rise above it all. It felt exhausting to put into words how sad the whole thing had made me—right down to the vomiting and the self-harm—in order to try to make a judge understand. And in the end, if Samuel wasn't convicted, the statement would just be thrown in the rubbish with no one reading it.

⌒

I met the prosecutor, Raymond, and the young clerk, Adeline, the next afternoon in the DPP's building in the city. We made small talk about the weather in the noisy old elevators on our way to a meeting room. They both seemed like no-nonsense people, and I was reassured by the huge document folder tucked under Raymond's arm, covered in Post-its and bulging with pages and dividers. *That's me in there.* Raymond was relaxed but authoritative, and Adeline was quick and attentive.

'Well,' Raymond said to me after the door to the meeting room shut behind us, 'thank you for coming in. I suppose there's a lot about this process I don't need to explain to you.'

'Yes, I'm okay with most of the court stuff.'

'I'm going to be honest with you,' he said, and I held my breath, 'I can't make any guarantees, but this is one of the strongest cases I've seen all year. I'm not expecting any surprises.'

'Oh, thank you, thank you, good, thank you.' I put my face in my hands with relief.

'I'm not even sure why this is a trial.'

'People keep saying that, yes.' I made a flourishing sweep with my right arm and announced with a fake smile, 'And yet here we are.'

We spoke for a few minutes about the history of the matter, and then planned where and when to meet on the Monday morning— and how I should prepare. I lost the sassiness. It was all getting very close.

'I do have one last question,' I said. 'Do you think he'll give evidence?'

'Yes,' Raymond said.

'Should we be worried about that?'

'I don't think so.'

'But I don't know why he's fighting this, unless he has something up his sleeve?'

'He just seems like that kind of man.' He shrugged and shut his folder. 'I'm seeing more and more men like him, who think they can stand up in court and bullshit their way out of things. But they can't.'

I sat still for a moment, dumbstruck at Raymond's candour. Then my face broke into a grin. I thought back to Pullman making up the story about chasing a rat and trying to catch it with his bare hands. Pullman had gone down. It was nice to hear someone in the industry—especially a man—talk about the patterns in the defendants I'd seen.

⌒

The next morning Sean called at eight just to make sure everything was okay. Then I got a call from Arron at lunchtime when I was at a small takeaway restaurant

'I've just found out that Samuel has contacted a bunch of our old mutual friends and asked them to give evidence for him.'

'Fuck,' I said quietly, and started sweating. My mind pinballed through the people Samuel could have called, racing from face to face of their old friends, searching my memories for the ace Samuel had up his sleeve.

'Sorry to tell you on the phone.' Arron sounded sad. 'I just thought you should know as soon as possible.'

'And what did they say?'

'At least one told him to go jump, but another one said yes.'

'Fuck!' I said again, louder, and left the restaurant, people staring. 'Thank you, I'd better call some people.'

'Good luck.'

After I'd hung up, I dialled the DPP. I was pacing around on the street outside, holding the phone against my ear with my shoulder, cracking all my fingers.

'Yeah, that's not surprising,' Raymond said calmly. 'Samuel doesn't realise that giving evidence means being open to cross-examination, though, and I'm ready for him.'

But I was still afraid of Samuel's barrister. His lawyers knew the whole prosecution case against him, and we had no idea what they were going to get up and say. I wouldn't know until I'd finished giving my evidence.

It also made me upset to think of Samuel calling people up to say I was a liar. He was *still* going to such lengths to fight me, and I felt insulted. What might he say about me in the witness stand? What if he called me boy-crazy? What if he got one of his mates to agree that I was just some attention-seeking little bitch?

The night before the trial was truly hell. I was reading and re-reading my police statements, which meant reliving the incident with a deliberate, slow, meticulous accuracy. Stop, rewind—that hand there, my dress there, he said this, I did that. Slow down, play. Again. *Again!* I searched for gaps or inconsistencies and reassured myself of my memories.

But I didn't practise responses to questions. My evidence would have to appear as natural as possible. I rehearsed saying the affirmation I'd have to swear when I arrived in the courtroom, although I'd heard it so many times during my year as an associate that I knew it by heart. I'd never thought it would be me saying it.

You wake up on the morning of your trial and you're trying to have a shower, and the hot water conks out like it always does in your cheap old unit, and you yell at the taps, 'Don't you know what's happening today!?' But the hot water system doesn't know. The iron doesn't know when it spits calcium and dirty water over your white blouse. And what do you wear to court anyway? How do you do your hair? Which shade of lipstick says 'please believe me'?

I emerged from the bathroom and Vincent smiled.

'Pretty enough to look at, but not so pretty that I might be lying?' I asked him.

'Nailed it.'

In the back of the taxi on the way into the city I had the overwhelming sense of being limbless, or carried. Detatched. With underwater ears.

Outside Vincent held my hand and I could barely feel it. I let him lead me. We walked across the grass in front of the courts building, the Kusama mural staring at me, unblinking. It was hot and burningly bright outside—the way I would always remember that place—the way it was when I arrived on my first day of work. Had Samuel arrived yet? Had he wondered if the eyes were looking at him?

We stepped past the glass doors and went through security. The click of my heels on the marble sounded familiar, and the smell of the building's air-conditioning brought back memories, but it was an alien place. I had changed so much that it did not recognise me.

'Courtroom 24, level seven,' I said to Vincent from memory, in a monotone.

Mum and Dad were waiting for us in the open space outside all the courtrooms, and Sean was there too. I hugged my parents and shook hands with Sean.

Raymond and Adeline arrived, and I went over to them. 'Like I said,' Raymond told me, seeming relaxed, 'no surprises.' I nodded.

There was nothing for me to do but wait. Wait without passing out or jumping off the balcony. Mum did a great job at encouraging general chatter, and Dad went to get coffees. About an hour later a door off the side of the room opened and strangers flowed in, about fifty of them, then walked into the back of Courtroom 24.

'Those are the jurors,' I said to Mum.

'All of them!? I have to talk in front of all of those people?'

'No, no—twelve people will be picked out randomly from that group, and the rest move on.'

I thought of the associate on the other side, calling the names out of the barrel, and wondered who would be challenged and who would be empanelled. Which twelve people would be deciding my fate? I didn't tell anyone—not even Vincent—that I had still been hoping Samuel would plead guilty on the morning of the trial. The empanelment of the jury signified that he was waving a red flag, not a white one. I felt silly for having been optimistic.

'They challenged all the women,' Sean said, after emerging from the courtroom about twenty minutes later. I just laughed and shook my head. A bitter laugh. 'But there are still four,' he added.

'Still four?' I asked quickly.

'Yep, it was pretty funny, actually. It was so obvious what they were doing, but the associate just kept pulling out women's names and they ran out of challenges.'

'So long as there are more than two,' I said to Vincent, and he squeezed my hand, 'they might feel confident enough to speak their minds during deliberations.'

⌒

There was another period of waiting.

'What's happening now?' Mum asked me.

'The judge is welcoming the jury and explaining their job to them, and telling them what they can and can't do. Like, they're not allowed to tell other people what they hear, or look me up on the internet or try to do any investigating themselves.'

'Otherwise what?'

'It'll be declared a mistrial, and we'll all have to go back to the beginning, with a new jury.' I stared at her. 'And I don't know if I can do that.'

Everyone went quiet for a bit, and then I heard my name called. Adeline was standing by the door to the courtroom. 'We're ready for you.'

My hands started shaking and I felt the pressure of tears behind my eyes. *Not yet*, I told myself, *just get through it*. I pulled open the frosted glass doors and the courtroom appeared before me: light-filled, silent, attentive, poised to receive. I bowed to the judge at the threshold of the room, not recognising his face, and caught the eye of the associate. Her face was expressionless. All her thoughts imperceptible. The bailiff stood by the witness box and I walked towards her, trying to stand up straight, my hands clasped together to try to stop the shaking.

'Do you solemnly and sincerely affirm and declare that the evidence you give here today will be the truth, the whole truth, and nothing but the truth?' she asked.

'I do.' I sat down and glanced over to Samuel. *Do you?*

The jurors were seated against the far wall opposite me, two rows of six: a wall of everyday Australians bestowed with the divine power of truth-seeing.

Raymond stood up. 'Can you please state your full name for the record?' he asked me, and it began.

His questions led me perfectly. We stepped through the dates of my childhood, photos of the family home, Samuel's presence in our lives. The easy parts.

'And, you know why we're here today,' he said, his tone changing. 'Can you please tell the court about the incident with Samuel?'

I spoke firmly and clearly, but my body was revolting against my mind. My shoulders clenched up. I couldn't make eye contact with anyone. I felt short of breath, and when I tried to gesture, to demonstrate Samuel's actions to the jury, I struggled to speak and move simultaneously. The underwater ears were extreme. My stomach, by that point, was full of razors.

I got to the end of the retelling, and Raymond had to ask a couple of follow-up questions about placement, about fingers, about whether the sun was up or down.

'Your Honour, I'd now like to play the pretext phone call,' he said to the judge.

'How long does it go for?'

'About forty-five minutes, your Honour.'

'Well, we'll take a morning tea-break and then come back to it,' the judge said and stood up.

'Silence, all stand,' the bailiff quickly declared, and I stood, panicking, and looked to Raymond for guidance, but he was shuffling papers, and so I looked across to Samuel in the dock, and he was talking to his solicitor.

The bailiff appeared beside me. 'You can wait outside if you'd prefer,' she said softly with a sad smile, gesturing to the door. I smoothed my skirt and walked right past Samuel and out of the room. Everyone was standing there, waiting for me.

'Haven't finished yet,' I said to them. 'Morning tea-break. Then pretext, then cross-examination.'

Vincent hugged me. I couldn't stomach a coffee. Couldn't make small talk anymore. I sat and watched the palm trees of Roma Street Parkland sway under the stark sunlight for twenty minutes.

'The waiting is always the worst bit,' Vincent said, and I just nodded.

⌇

When court resumed, finally, I went back in and we were about to get started when they found they couldn't get the CD with the recording on it to play through the courtroom speakers. We adjourned for another five minutes and I imagined what would happen if it didn't work. We'd adjourn for the rest of the day, and I'd have to come back for cross-examination the next morning. I gripped the handles on the chair and watched the seconds tick by on the courtroom clock.

'We've sorted it out,' the bailiff whispered to the associate after a couple more minutes, and I felt a rush of relief. *Just get it done.*

The judge came back in, the jury came back in, and we all listened to the CD. I winced at the sound of my voice—it was much louder than Samuel's, because of the way the audio was recorded, and it was shrill and fake. I'd made myself come across so casual and chirpy, and now my nerves and wet eyes in court seemed fake.

'Yeah, that's awesome, dude!' my voice replied to something he'd said. 'Yeah, cool, I'm doing great!' I tried not to squirm in my seat too much.

In the final third of the recording, when Samuel was giving me waves of unsolicited business advice and gloating about his latest investment scheme—after he'd admitted the offending and said I wasn't the only one—and his responses were lengthy and mine had shrunk to single words here and there, I heard some sniffling in the tiny gaps between his sentences, and it made me furious. The fire returned to my belly, pushing the nervous churning aside, and in my mind I reached back in time to myself in that room, to that terrified young woman who had run straight into the fire, and I thought, *You can do it.* And I saw her sitting there, silently crying between her chipper responses, and I imagined her saying it back to me, *You can do it too.*

But then the recording ended and Carter stood up, and the cross-examination began.

⌣

In the year leading up to the trial, I'd been reassured by the thought that the only real question to be answered was about the date of the offending. I had told Anna and Vincent that Samuel's admissions in the pretext meant he wasn't denying the offending itself. The legal officer at the Magistrates Court pre-trial hearing even told me that age was the only question. Just that weekend I'd said to myself, *At least the jury won't think I'm making it all up.*

But then, in court, a few questions into Carter's cross-examination, he said, 'I put it to you that nothing else happened after Samuel touched you the first time.'

'What?'

'I put it to you that Samuel only ever touched you with his finger, and only once, and that's what he was referring to on the phone.'

'No!'

'And that the second allegation is a fabrication.'

'No, I remember it.'

Carter's questions continued. Couldn't Samuel have gone to a more secluded part of the yard if he wanted to do something so serious? Couldn't he have waited until nightfall? Hadn't my brother only just gone inside the house?

Then the questions moved to my memory of the dates, and of the location of the trampoline, and went on and on and on.

Finally the judge interrupted. 'I don't mean to rush you at all, Mr Carter, but we do need to break for lunch soon. How much longer will you be?'

My chest was in a vice. I couldn't go out and come back again. Not there.

'Only five or ten minutes, your Honour,' Carter replied.

'Well then, I'm sure Ms Lee would prefer to finish?' the judge said, looking to me.

'Yes, please.'

And with that nudge, that endpoint in sight, I made it through.

~

I pushed out the courtroom doors and burst into tears.

'Are you finished?' Vincent asked me.

'It's done.'

Raymond came out a couple of minutes later. I hadn't finished crying. He gestured to a small private conference room and asked, 'Can the two of us have a chat?' I must have looked terrified.

'I'm sure it's fine,' Vincent said, pushing me gently on the shoulder. I followed Raymond into the conference room and closed the door behind me.

'Right,' he said, 'that went just about as well as it could have.'

'But he's denying the second count!'

Raymond shrugged. 'It just makes him look like a liar. The details of your account have never changed. I don't see why the jury would think you lied about the second count. No, it's fine. You should be very proud of yourself.'

⟿

Mum, Dad, Vincent and I left the courts building together to go for lunch, and I caught sight of Samuel across the grass at The Coffee Club beside the Kusama mural. Vincent had his arm around me on one side, and my mother was holding my hand on the other side, and my dad was close behind us. Samuel was alone but for his solicitor—the man he was paying thousands of dollars.

We went to a small restaurant nearby but I couldn't eat anything. I just had a cold, sweet apple juice.

⟿

After the lunchbreak my mum gave evidence, and then Dylan arrived and gave evidence, and then Sean went in. Hours ticked by and in my mind I was replaying, already, moments from the cross-examination.

In the mid-afternoon the prosecution case closed and the court took another short break. When it resumed I waited, my eyes trained on the door; I was holding out hope Samuel wouldn't give evidence. No such luck.

'He literally can't go any lower,' I said to Vincent another hour later. 'He's denying the second count *and* he's running a defence.'

At half past four the judge called for an adjournment and sent everyone home. Raymond, Adeline and Sean came out of the courtroom and we all stood over to one side as Samuel and his team exited.

'He's a very combative witness,' Sean said to me, 'answering questions with questions. He doesn't come across very well.'

'Really?' I asked, everyone listening now.

'Raymond asked him something and his reply was, "That's a personal question, I don't have to answer that."'

We all murmured in anger and disgust.

'And you're allowed to listen,' I said to Sean, 'even though you're a witness for the prosecution?'

Raymond answered, 'Yes, sorry, I presumed you knew—you're allowed to listen now that the prosecution case is closed. I'm in the middle of cross-examining Samuel, so you can catch the end of it tomorrow morning.'

I nodded. 'Good.'

⌒

Vincent and I got a beer on our way home. With my part done I was feeling a bit better, or at least like I'd done my best. We spoke about who Samuel could possibly call on to give evidence for him, and I talked about how I could have lied.

'I could have said all kinds of things. I could have said that I remembered he did it after 9/11, and then he would have been on trial as a seventeen-year-old and sentenced as an adult. I could have said I remembered my second dog, Snoopy, playing with us, and Samuel would have been seventeen. I could have said I somehow definitely remembered being in Grade Seven, making me twelve and him eighteen. I could have lied in so many different ways to get him held accountable at an older age.' I took a gulp of my beer. 'But at least I know that I was honest and did my best, and that if he gets acquitted it won't be me who failed, it will be the system failing me.'

I woke up the next morning a lot angrier because I was a lot more scared.

'You've done the hard part,' Vincent kept saying, but it was a different kind of scared. The day before I'd been afraid of having to give evidence and be cross-examined. Now I was afraid that Samuel would be acquitted.

We arrived at the courts building a few minutes early and went straight inside, up the elevators and into the courtroom, where we took seats in the corner at the back. I had a straight line of vision to the dock where Samuel would soon be sitting, and also to the witness box where he was due to finish being cross-examined. He entered a couple of minutes later, not looking at me, and when he sat down I stared at the back of his neck. *I put you there.* At least if he got off I'd have the satisfaction of seeing him relinquish control to the justice department during the trial.

Mum and Dad arrived, then Sean, then all the counsel, and it started again.

Carter kept glancing at me. Right before the judge was about to return, I saw him go over to Raymond. 'I've never seen this before—shouldn't she have to wait outside?' he asked, frustrated, or perhaps nervous. I didn't know I was allowed to watch because I had never seen a complainant do it before. Carter mustn't have either. I didn't hear Raymond's reply, but he was still calm and Carter was not, and I did not flinch from his gaze.

'Samuel got to sit there and listen while he called me a liar,' I whispered to Vincent. 'Now it's my turn.'

⌁

Samuel's lawyers had probably advised him to be a bit calmer, but it was obvious that he was angry underneath. I sat up straight and put on a calm, unaffected face, and stared right at him. He didn't look at me. Raymond was challenging him on his claims that he'd had no idea that his actions were 'wrong'.

'If you didn't know what you were doing was wrong, why did you wait until Arron had left, until you were alone with the complainant?'

'I don't know.'

'And on the phone you said you'd been in trouble at school previously for touching girls' underpants. Are you telling the court that even after those incidents and being called into the principal's office for them, you still didn't understand that touching a little girl in that area was wrong?'

'No.'

'You didn't know it was wrong?'

'Well, inappropriate, maybe.'

'Inappropriate, maybe?'

I got the sense Raymond was keeping Samuel in the box for as long as he could, letting the jury see as much of him as they could. It was always a good sign to see a prosecutor feel comfortable with a defendant giving evidence.

When they'd finished, Samuel's sister called into court from where she lived in the UK. She stated her name for the record, then confirmed the address of where she'd always lived with Samuel and their parents in Yeronga.

Carter asked her just one question. 'Did Samuel ever act in an inappropriate, sexual way with you?'

'No,' she replied.

'Thank you, Ms Levins,' he said.

Raymond stood up. 'No questions, your Honour.'

And the call was disconnected.

'The final defence witness, your Honour, is Mr Joshua Forbes,' Carter said, and I shifted in my seat. Josh had been Samuel's friend, and he'd visited our house several times to hang out with Arron, but I thought that was when the boys were all *much* older. I was in high school by then, I thought.

Josh's evidence was about the trampoline. He said it was 'always moving around', and I started sweating. He was undermining the only thing we had to pinpoint a date—and therefore age—for Samuel.

In cross-examination, Raymond only asked Josh a single question. 'Could it be the case that the trampoline was moved in the years much later than 2000?'

'That's possible,' Josh replied, and then it was time for the closing addresses.

⟶

Because Samuel had given evidence, the prosecution got to address the jury last. Carter made a show of that being a big deal as it meant he had no right of reply.

'It's not a crime to be a bit of a big-noter,' he said about the pretext call. 'And I don't know, but I suspect that my learned friend will tell you that Samuel is lying about he himself being abused.'

I shook my head. We would never. Every time Samuel went lower, we went higher.

What made me nervous was how much emphasis Carter put on the delay in the proceedings. The old 'what took her so long?' and 'why is she only coming forward now?' He kept repeating that 'reasonable doubt' was at an incredibly high standard as well, reminding the jurors that they had a witness who said that the trampoline was always moving around. Samuel had admitted to the first count occurring, but again Carter said it had happened when Samuel was just a child himself, and that it wasn't too serious. The second count, which was serious, couldn't have been the actions of a child, and therefore I was lying about it.

In Raymond's closing address, he told the jury there were three main reasons they should convict. 'First and foremost, because Ms Lee is an honest, reliable and compelling witness. Her account of the incident has not changed once. Not at all in the past two years of proceedings. She has given you no reason to question her credibility or reliability.'

I held back tears, feeling proud of myself. One of the jurors looked over to me, and I put on my associate's face again. Calm, unreadable. Vincent squeezed my hand.

The judge took a twenty-minute adjournment and then returned and summed up the case to the jury. It was relatively short, but in its even-handedness it struck me as unjust—like when homophobes are allowed to debate marriage equality on television. The judge's presentation of Samuel's arguments as alternatives to mine lent them a legitimacy they didn't deserve. His testimony, so full of lies and evasion, was 'his version', as though mine was just 'my version' and not the truth.

'Now I will ask you to consider your verdict,' the judge concluded, and my whole body twitched.

The twelve of them stood up and walked out, and I watched each one, longing more than I ever had before to hear what was being said in that small room.

My family met outside the courtroom. The judge had said he wouldn't take a verdict between 1 p.m. and 2.15 p.m. It was 12.45 p.m.

'The only time I saw a guilty verdict in less than an hour,' I whispered to Vincent, 'was in Gladstone that time I called you, and Judge told me if a verdict comes back too quickly it's because it's an acquittal. So I suppose we should wait here until one o'clock, just in case.'

Raymond came out of the courtroom and paused, so Vincent and I went over to him.

'That was a great summing-up,' I said.

'Thank you,' he replied. 'It's in the jury's hands now, but I do feel positive.'

'Yeah, Samuel didn't come across particularly well in the box,' Vincent said.

'Yesterday I asked him about his business, or tried to find out what it was he actually did for a living. He talked about having an interest in some investment company, but it turned out he didn't really have any ownership in that company. And when I asked him what skills and experience he brought to the company, he said, "My energy."'

Vincent and I burst out laughing.

'Lunch then?' Dad called over to us.

'Sure,' I replied.

Then I saw Samuel walk past confidently, and I looked down. My heart was beating so hard that my shirt was moving.

I picked the only vegetarian dish on the menu, something with rice, thinking of what might be easiest to bring back up if necessary and not wanting to waste any meat. I put the food in my mouth and moved it around in there. Even though my mobile was on loud, I kept it on the table beside me and checked it every few minutes. The knot in my stomach didn't leave a lot of space for food, so Dad finished my meal when I pushed my plate away. I rested my forehead on the table, groaning, and took Vincent's hand.

'I can't handle this,' I said.

'The hard part is over.'

But my body was twitching, shaking. I jiggled my foot incessantly and wrung my hands. The small travel can of deodorant I'd brought was nearly finished. As we left the restaurant a bus rushed past me, loud and stinky.

'Just a few more hours, right?' I asked Vincent.

'Right.'

We were back up near the courtroom at 2 p.m.

'The worst thing about waiting for a verdict,' Sean said, 'is that you don't even know how long you'll be waiting for.'

I paced around, then sat down, then went to the bathroom, then had a glass of water. The minutes ticked by, my mind devouring itself, descending into desperate hypothesising.

Sean and Dad were sharing cop stories. Sean was saying that he had applied to be moved to the fraud squad because in the past two years he'd had to work several murder investigations, and he had two small children at home. I saw him then, for a brief, clear moment, as someone who had been trying his best, and I was newly awash with guilt for my derision of him.

I walked over to where Vincent was sitting. 'How are people supposed to do this? I'd prefer for him to be found not guilty than for the jury to be hung. Or if they convict on count one but not count two, he'd be able to appeal the first conviction, and then we'd be back again. I couldn't do this again. I can't do this.'

Vincent held me and kissed my forehead.

'What are you thinking about the deliberation time?' he asked.

'It's a good sign that it's been over an hour, but I'll be worried if we get to 4 p.m. That would mean one or more of them can't agree with each other.'

More pacing. More staring angrily, then sadly, then in fear out the window at Roma Street Parkland. More cop stories from Sean and Dad. More chatter about Christmas plans from Mum. All the while feeling as though someone was shaving slices off my stomach lining.

It had been just under three hours when I got the phone call from Adeline. I was worried she would say they had a note, which would mean a question or a problem, but mercifully she told me, 'There's a verdict.'

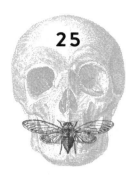

25

ALMOST EVERYONE WAS READY WITHIN five minutes, but Carter asked for an extra 'three minutes' for the solicitor to arrive. My body was out of my control. I sat down beside Vincent, and he put his whole right arm around my waist, pulling me in, holding my left hand with his, and I could feel how sweaty he was and how fast his heart was beating. The minutes ticked by—three passed, five passed—and just as the solicitor entered the courtroom, the bailiff stood up.

'Silence, all stand,' she announced.

The judge came in and took his seat, and the associate followed him, still nothing on her face.

'We have a verdict,' the judge said. 'Please, Madam Bailiff, get the jury in.'

In the silence of the room I heard my blood pounding in my ears.

'I'm so scared,' I whispered to Vincent, and then his body shuddered, a ragged breath in, and I tried not to cry.

Hot anger rushed over me as the jurors filed in. *Who are you to say if I'm a liar!?* I dug my fingernails into my right palm, clenching my fist. They stood in a line facing outward so I couldn't see their faces from where I sat.

The associate got to her feet. 'Members of the jury,' she said, and the rest of her question was already in my mind, memorised, 'have you reached your verdict?'

'Yes,' the speaker said.

I started crying, couldn't help it, couldn't stop it.

'Do you find the defendant guilty or not guilty of count one, indecent treatment of a child?'

'Guilty.'

'So says your speaker, so say you all?'

'Yes,' they all chorused.

'And do you find the defendant guilty or not guilty of count two, indecent treatment of a child?'

I looked up to the ceiling, holding my breath, tears splashing onto my forearms.

'Guilty.'

'So says your speaker, so say you all?'

'Yes,' they chorused again, and I began the second chapter of my life.

I let the feelings come in waves while the business of the court continued around me. The sadness, the anger and the pride: it all rushed in like a flash flood, washing out the lingering worries and fears, taking the ants and the bindi-eyes with it, the sheer force of my relief catching me off guard.

'We did it,' I whispered, holding Vincent so tight, my tears all over us.

'You did it,' he replied.

⌒

We moved straight to sentencing submissions. Raymond handed up my victim impact statement to the judge, who took several minutes to read it. Four or five jurors filed into the back of the courtroom and I felt them looking at me but tried to avoid eye contact.

'I would like to refer your Honour to the final paragraph, and keep my submissions on the complainant's suffering brief,' Raymond said.

I thought of that final paragraph.

I do not want to read this letter aloud in court because I do not want Mr Levins to understand the particulars of the pain he has caused me, as his actions over the past two years have sufficiently convinced me that he is the kind of man who might appreciate hearing details of my suffering. I only wish to convey that I understand how severe many matters are that pass through the District Court, and that although the facts of Mr Levins' offending were not nearly as severe as many, they have had a severe impact on my life. It is not for Mr Levins to decide how serious his offending was. In our legal system defendants must 'take their victims as they find them'.

The only time I thought I saw a hint of something cross the associate's face was when Carter stood up and made his sentencing submissions. Samuel's lawyers were asking for probation instead of a wholly suspended sentence, so that Samuel wouldn't have a conviction recorded and could therefore still apply for a Blue Card to work with children or the elderly. My jaw dropped and the associate looked at me, and I thought I saw her eye twitch, just a little.

The judge ripped into Carter about that submission being 'inappropriate'. I thought that was a nice use of the word, given how defence had used it over the preceding forty-eight hours.

'I will adjourn for a short time to consider my sentence,' the judge announced. 'In the meantime, the defendant shall be remanded in custody.'

Two security officers, who'd been standing at the edge of the dock, ushered Samuel from the courtroom into a side door that led to the cells under the building.

'Way down in the basement, with all the other criminals,' I whispered to Vincent as my family and I took the opportunity to stand up and hug each other. Sean came over and we all shook his hand. Mum handed me some fresh tissues. I sent Judge a text:

Guilty on both counts. Conviction recorded. We got him. And he replied within minutes, wishing me a happy birthday for the next day and adding, *Your courage has been vindicated.*

When court resumed, Samuel was accompanied back in by the officers. He was asked to remain on his feet as the judge delivered his sentencing remarks.

'I am sufficiently convinced that you have showed absolutely no remorse, and that even after making admissions against your own interest in a pretext phone call, you refused to accept responsibility for your actions, and caused the complainant significant distress in bringing this matter to trial. I must also add,' and he paused, looking at Samuel, 'that you came to trial with a defence that was doomed from the start, and which was clearly fabricated to fit with what you had already admitted to in the pretext call.'

Samuel received a total of nine months' imprisonment, but the term was wholly suspended and the conviction was to be recorded. So while he didn't have to do any time, it would be on his record forever. It was all I'd ever wanted.

⌒

Outside court I thanked Raymond, Adeline and Sean, saying goodbye to them, then took the remaining four of us for a drink in a nearby restaurant.

'This is where I came with Judge when we ate black ants!' I said to Mum.

She asked me to explain what Samuel's sentence meant, and so I let her know about the irony of his situation.

'It's because he fought me so hard, and for so long, that he's got a criminal conviction now. When he came up against me, the harder he pushed and the more I refused to back down, the worse he was making things for himself in the end.'

And that's eggshell skull.

⌐⌐

The next morning I woke up to Vincent kissing my forehead.

'Happy birthday,' he said.

'Oh, a double-guilty, you shouldn't have!' I said, stretching out in the sunlight. 'Plus a conviction recorded! What more could a girl want!?'

And we laughed together.

⌐⌐

As I was washing my hair on the day after my birthday, the thought popped into my mind, as it had sporadically over the past two years, *When is the next mention?* And then I remembered the trial, and the feeling I'd had when the jurors walked back into the courtroom to deliver their verdict, and even though it was the right one I was flooded with panic and had to sit down to catch my breath in the bottom of the shower.

That Friday I had a small party for my close friends in the backyard and named it 'Bri's Birthday and Justice Brews', and when everyone had arrived I popped some champagne and told them what had been happening over the past two years.

'Some of you knew and some of you didn't, but I couldn't have done it without you all.' I only cried a tiny bit. 'And Vincent hates public displays of emotion, but he *loves* French champagne!' Everyone laughed and I called him over and thanked him and told him I loved him. 'This kind of stuff happens because people don't talk about it, so I mainly want to tell you all that I'm okay to talk about it—and if any of you or anyone you know ever wants to talk about it, the feelings or the process or anything, then I'm right here. Call me any time.'

I had hung fairy lights over the entire Hills hoist. As the sun set they shone brighter, twinkling, and we all stood around laughing and drinking until the wee hours. The night smelled like mosquito coils and was warm but not too hot, and lots of people hugged me.

A friend who used to work as a clerk for the DPP was asking me about the trial, and if I was okay, and we started comparing notes on how the system treats women. She had left the industry because she'd seen one too many complainants shattered. 'I had the most heinous pre-trial hearing once,' she said.

'No you didn't, I did,' I interrupted, thinking of the very first judgment I'd had to proofread for Judge, 'but you go first.'

'Well, mine involved a girl being tied to a Hills hoist, and—'

'No way! That was mine!'

'What?'

'That was my judge! Who allowed the similar fact to be admissible at trial. What happened? How did the trial go?'

'We got him!'

'We got him!' I shouted, and someone nearby heard me, and they shouted too, 'We got him!' And everyone cheered.

I went up into the house to get more ice and looked down at the party from the second-storey window. It was so beautiful. I stood still and put my hands to my face like I was holding a camera. I blinked, taking a picture in my mind. I felt incredibly, wholly safe. Entirely surrounded by friends and family. Happy and triumphant.

SO WHAT DO YOU DO in the days and weeks that follow? When you're hanging out the washing on those rusty steel lines and your arms lock up, and you're dizzy under the hot summer sun. When your knees buckle and you rest your forehead on scalding concrete while you catch your breath. When every man who yells at you on the street is pushing you onto your back again, and every grabby hand at a party makes you feel belly-up and frozen again.

What do you do in the months and years that follow? When winning the battle has only opened your eyes to the breadth of the war.

You cry and you cry, and when you're done crying, you wipe your eyes, and slap your cheeks, and you get angry, and you get to work.

ACKNOWLEDGEMENTS

WITH A MEMOIR LIKE THIS there are a lot of people you need to thank. The book spans over three years of my young adult life, and I'm incredibly grateful to so many people whose generosity towards me and my work saw me through several particularly dark times. This acknowledgment is very important to me.

Firstly, to my mother: you won't know until you read this book just how much your love kept me alive. I go through this life having complete faith in your love for me. Dad, I'm sorry I talk so negatively about your stoicism and yet we all lean so heavily upon it. Thank you for teaching me about justice. And thank you to my big brother—you were, and continue to be, a wonderful brother.

Judge! Thank you for letting me write this book! Thank you for being a bastion of hope for me during that tumultuous year. If more people in the legal industry were like you, books like this wouldn't need to be written. I will always respect and admire you.

To the many friends I cannot name—I have told you in person how much you mean to me. I'll try to say it more often.

To my agent, Grace, who championed me back when none of us knew how *Eggy* would turn out: your unwavering support has been so reassuring. You make this work so fun, and I look forward to our long, champagne-filled future together. Jane, Best Publisher in the World, when I met you I said to Grace, 'I want her to be my publisher because that's the kind of woman I want to be.' Having the two of you at my back is like a badass attack formation from which I can do anything.

Genevieve, Kate, and Julia—please don't tell anyone what this book looked like before you saw it and edited it so wonderfully. Thank you to my excellent publicist, Louise, and everyone else at Allen & Unwin for being so consistently delightful to work with. Five stars. Would recommend.

As part of the Kat Muscat Fellowship I was able to meet and spend time with the Muscat family, and I want to thank them for the professional opportunities the fellowship gave me, but also for how much they encouraged me. I truly hope this work embodies the defiance Kat stood for. I thought of her often.

As part of that fellowship I also got to spend time with mentors: Liam Pieper and Krissy Kneen. You were integral to so many steps of this manuscript coming together. Thank you for continuing to mentor me even now, so many years later.

I must also thank *Griffith Review* for naming me as a 2017 Fellow and publishing an early excerpt of *Eggshell Skull*.

And finally, to 'Vincent'. I love you so much it's like sometimes I'm going to explode! You are my favourite person in the world. If I had done all this without you I'd be a husk of a human. We both rode out of that court on giant eagles and my 26th birthday with you was the best day of my life. I hope we are together forever.

26 IWM, Women's Work Collection, (WWC), Army 3/19, '*QMAAC Internal Report: Post-war Employment of Women*'.

27 *The Times*, 24/4/1919l.

28 Throughout the inter-war years the Ministry of Labour attempted to boost the number of women working in domestic service by funding residential 'Homecraft courses' run by the Central Committee for Women's Employment on the understanding that participants signed a written undertaking to enter service afterwards. D. Beddoe, *Back to Home and Duty: Women Between the Wars, 1918–1939*, London: Pandora, 1989, p. 63.

29 *Daily Sketch*, 5/3/1919.

30 *Old Comrades Association Gazette*, Vol. 6, December 1920, p. 8.

31 *Daily Telegraph*, 11/1/1919.

32 See for example 'Women and the War – How they are Working Mischief', *Daily Call*, 19/11/1914, 'The Girl in the Street – Women's Campaign Against New Evil', *Daily Express*, 3/11/1914. For detailed discussion of the attacks on female morality see Susan R. Grayzel, *Women's Identities at War: Gender, Motherhood and Politics in Britain and France During the First World War*, Chapel Hill, NC: University of North Carolina Press, 1999, 'Chapter Four: Women's Wild Oats: Sexuality and the Social Order', pp. 121–156.

33 *Pall Mall Gazette*, 6/3/1916.

34 *Saturday Review*, 11/1/1919.

35 Ibid., 9/11/1918.

36 C. Gasquoine Hartley, *Women's Wild Oats: Essays on the Refixing of Moral Standards*, London: T. Werner Laurie, 1919, p. 23.

37 Hartley, *Women's Wild Oats*, p. 54. Susan Kingsley Kent discusses this movement in some depth, arguing that a widespread shift away from attacking separate sphere ideology to a general acceptance of different roles for women and men helped to bring about a demise of British feminism in the inter-war years. S. Kingsley Kent, 'The Politics of Sexual Difference: World War One and the Demise of British Feminism', *Journal of British Studies*, 27 July 1988, pp. 232–253.

38 TNA, WO162/54, *Overseas Settlement of QMAAC Members*.

39 IWM, WWC, Army 3/19, '*QMAAC: Requirements on Demobilisation*'.

40 J. M. Winter, *The Great War and the British People*, Basingstoke: Macmillan, 1985, p. 267.

41 *Daily Chronicle*, 20/1/1919.

42 TNA, WO162/54.

43 *Report of the Overseas Settlement Committee for Year Ended 31 December 1919*, London: HMSO, 1920, p. 8.

44 TNA, WO162/54.

45 Ibid.

46 Lady Londonderry's proposed Household Service Section of the Women's Legion recommended a minimum annual salary of £50 for a housekeeper in London, a suggestion which was criticised as extortionately expensive by many employers. *Daily Telegraph*, 22/1/1919.

47 TNA, WO162/54.

48 *Report of the British Government Overseas Settlement Mission to Canada*, London: HMSO, 1919, p. 6, col. 8.

49 *QMAAC Old Comrades Association Gazette*, Vol. 6, December 1920.

50 *Report of the British Government Overseas Settlement Mission to Canada*, 1919, p. 13, col. 52.

51 TNA, Minstry of Reconstruction (RECO), *The Mission of the British Army*, Reconstruction Problems 37, HMSO: London, 1919.

52 NAM, WRAC, Helen Gwynne-Vaughan Papers, *Memorandum*, 9401–253–83.

53 NAM, WRAC, Helen Gwynne-Vaughan Papers, *Minutes of First Meeting, Women's Reserve Committee*, War Office, 1920, 9401-253-75, p. 16.

54 NAM WRAC, Helen Gwynne-Vaughan Papers, 1920, 9401-253-75, p. 3.

55 NAM, WRAC, Helen Gwynne-Vaughan Papers, *Report of the Women's Reserve Committee*, War Office, 1920, 9401-253-72.

56 J. M. Keynes, 'The Revision of the Treaty', London: 1922, republished in *The Collected Writings of J.M. Keynes: Vol. 3*, Basingstoke: Macmillan, 1971, pp. 4–5.

57 For detailed discussion of British policy in this period, see P. Towle, 'British Security and Disarmament Policy in Europe in the 1920s' in R. Altman, A. M. Burke and M. Howard (eds) *The Quest for Stability: Problems of West European Security 1918–1957*, Oxford: The German Historical Institute, Oxford University Press, 1993, pp. 127–153.

58 E. Kier, *Imagining War: French and British Military Doctrine Between the Wars*, Princeton, NJ: Princeton University Press, 1999, p. 115.

59 NAM, WRAC, *QMAAC Old Comrades Association, Minutes of Council Meetings*, 29/6/1926, 9401-145-2.

60 NAM, WRAC, *Vere Brodie Papers*, 9801-261.

61 For more discussion see Grayzel, *Women's Identities at War*, A. Gregory, *The Silence of Memory: Armistice Day 1914–1946*, Oxford: Berg, 1994, J.M. Winter, *Sites of Memory, Sites of Mourning: The Great War in European Cultural History*, Cambridge: Cambridge University Press, 1995.

62 NAM, WRAC, *President's Report to Annual General Meeting, 1927*, 9401-145-2.

63 NAM, WRAC, *QMAAC OCA Minutes*, 18/7/1929, 9401-145-2.

64 IWM, DD, *Papers of Miss A. M. Gammell: FANY Ambulance Car Corps News Sheet*, January 1932.

65 IWM, DD *Gammell Papers, FANY News Sheet*, December 1934.

66 Figures from G. Braybon and P. Summerfield, *Out of the Cage: Women's Experiences in the Two World Wars*, London: Pandora, 1987, p. 146. For discussion of inter-war feminism in Britain, see C. Beaumont, 'The Women's Movement, Politics and Citizenship 1918–1950s' in I. Zweiniger-Bargielowska (ed.) *Women in Twentieth Century Britain*, London: Longman, 2001, pp. 262–277.

67 B. Liddell-Hart, *Europe in Arms*, London: Faber & Faber, 1937, p. 1.

68 For discussion of this see M. Ceadel, 'Popular Fiction and the Next War 1918–1939' in F. Gloversmith (ed.) *Class, Culture and Social Change: A New View of the 1930s*, Brighton: Harvester, 1980.

69 Kier, *Imagining Warfare*, p. 115.

70 A. Calder, *The People's War: Britain 1939–1945*, London: Jonathan Cape, 1969, p. 24.

71 Ibid., p. 24.

72 V. Woolf, *Three Guineas*, London: Hogarth Press, 1938. For a survey of women in the British peace movement see J. Liddington, *The Long Road to Greenham: Feminism and Anti-Militarism in Britain Since 1820*, London: Virago, 1989.

73 *The Times*, 15/12/1933.

74 Ibid., 9/11/1933.

75 Ibid., 25/1/1935.

76 TNA, WO32/10650, *Women's Reserve 1933–1936*, December 1933.

77 TNA, WO32/10650, January 1934.

78 Ibid.

79 Ibid.

80 TNA, WO/10650, 27/5/1935.

81 TNA, WO32/10650, 27/5/1935.

82 TNA, AIR2/2694, *Committee of Imperial Defence Sub-Committee of the Man-Power Sub Committee*, Meeting, 3/10/1935.

83 Angus Calder claims that it was widely believed that 600,000 civilians would be killed and 1 million 200 thousand seriously injured by aerial bombardment in the first days of a war. Calder, *The People's War*, p. 22.

84 Kier, *Imagining Warfare*, p. 130.

85 TNA, AIR2/2694, Meeting, 10/10/1935.

86 Ibid., 19/2/1936.

87 TNA, AIR2/2694, Home Office Memo: 'Estimate of the numbers of women required in the first three months of a national emergency', 25/1/1936. The Home Office figures did not include estimates for domestic staff in general hospitals.

88 TNA, AIR2/2694, Home Office Memo: 'Estimate of the numbers of women required in the first three months of a national emergency', 25/1/1936.
89 TNA, AIR2/2694, Letter to Secretary of Committee of Imperial Defence, 18/2/1936.
90 Cited in Izzard, *A Heroine in Her Time*, pp. 232–233.
91 TNA, WO32/4502, *Women's Legion – Formation of OTS (1936–1944)*, 12/2/1937.
92 TNA, WO32/4502, 5/2/1936.
93 *Emergency Service Recruiting Leaflet* London: Emergency Service, 1936.
94 H. Gwynne-Vaughan, *Service with the Army*, London: Hutchinson, 1942, p. 81.
95 TNA WO32/10651, *Women's Legion 1937–1939*.
96 TNA AIR2/2694, *Emergency Service Enrolment Form*.
97 NAM, WRAC Archive, Helen Gwynne Vaughan papers, 9401-253-159-274.
98 Calder, *The People's War*, p. 22.
99 *Hansard, House of Commons*, 5th Series, Vol. 332, col. 177.
100 Calder, *The People's War*, p. 31.
101 TNA WO32/10652, *Women's Reserve 1937–1938*, 5/1/1938.
102 IWM, DD, *Gamell Papers*, FANY News Sheet, January 1939: Annual Company Reports.
103 NAM, WRAC Archive, 9701-145-1, 28/4/1938.
104 TNA, 10651, 11/4/1938.
105 TNA, WO10652, 'Memo on the Utilization of Women's Services in National Defence', 19/3/1938.
106 S. Kingsley Kent, 'The Politics of Sexual Difference', p. 234.
107 TNA, WO32/10651, 23/7/1937.
108 Ibid., 11/4/1938.
109 TNA, WO32/10652, 6/5/1938.
110 Ibid., 20/5/1938.

6 'The Gentle Sex': the ATS in the Second World War

1   For the definitive work on this, see A. Calder, *The People's War: Britain 1939–1945*, London: Jonathan Cape, 1969.
2   J. S. Haldane, *A.R.P.*, London: Left Book Club, 1938, pp. 99–100.
3   C. Gledhill and G. Swanson, 'Gender and Sexuality in Second World War Films – A Feminist Approach' in G. Hurd (ed.) *National Fictions: World War Two in British Films and Televisions*, London: BFI, 1984.
4   *Picture Post*, 15/6/1940.
5   *Woman's Own*, 4/5/1940.
6   Ibid., 13/4/1940.
7   Imperial War Museum (IWM), Department of Art, Catalogues and Posters, PST 0726 and ART 15707, undated.
8   *Woman's Own*, 14/10/1939.
9   S. Jameson, 'In Courage Keep Your Heart' in 'Woman's Journal', Autumn 1939, cited in J. Waller and M. Vaughan Rees, *Women in Wartime: The Role of Women's Magazines*, London: McDonald optima, 1987, p. 14.
10 P. Summerfield, *Women Workers in the Second World War: Production and Patriarchy in Conflict*, London: Croom Helm, 1984.
11 The National Archive (TNA), Department of Labour and National Service (LAB), LAB 76/3, *Women's Auxiliary Services*, J. L. Brooke-Wavell, 1956, p. 4.
12 TNA, War Office (WO) WO32/10652, *Women's Reserve 1937–1938*.
13 TNA, LAB 76/3, p. 3.
14 E. Bigland, *Britain's Other Army: The Story of the ATS*, London: Nicholson & Watson, 1946, p. 10.
15 TNA, WO 32/10651, *Women's Legion 1937–1939*.
16 Ibid.
17 M. Gwynne-Vaughan, *Service With The Army*, London: Hutchinson, 1942, p. 130.

18 J. Hammerton, *History of the Second Great War*, London: Amalgamated Press, 1945, n.d.
19 TNA, LAB 76/3, p. 5.
20 E. Kier, *Imagining War: French and British Military Doctrine Between the Wars*, Princeton, NJ: Princeton University Press, 1999, p. 129.
21 C. Harris, *Women at War in Uniform 1939–1945*, Stroud: Sutton Publishing, 2003, p. 16.
22 Gwynne-Vaughan, *Service With The Army*, p. 94.
23 *Report of the Committee on Amenities and Welfare Conditions in the Three Women's Services*, London: HMSO, 1942, p. 7, para. 27.
24 TNA, WO 32/4705, *ATS Uniform and Badges – Draft*, 14/9/1938.
25 Gwynne-Vaughan, *Service With The Army*, p. 102.
26 *The New Statesman and Nation*, 6/12/1941.
27 Imperial War Museum (IWM), Documents Department (DD) Box 87/19/1, *Papers of the Honourable Miss L. E. Lawson*.
28 IWM, DD, Box 97/25/1, *Marian Mills: Women Soldiers: A Memoir of the ATS*.
29 M-O, TC 32, Box 32/1/G, *Printed Material on the Women's Services. Auxiliary Territorial Service Recruitment Pamphlet* 7/11/1941.
30 M-O, TC 32, Box 32/2/D, *Unsigned Letter to Sir John Wardlow Milne MP*, 12/11/1941.
31 M-O, TC 32, Box 32/2/D, *Rough Report of Miss Groombridge's Visit to the ATS*, 6/6/1941.
32 J. B. Priestley *British Women Go To War*, London: Collins, 1943, p. 23.
33 Ibid., pp. 25, p. 30.
34 L. Whateley, *As Thoughts Survive*, London: Hutchinson, 1949, p. 20.
35 M-O, TC32, Box 32/2/D, *The ATS and You: By a Newly Appointed Officer*, 6/3/1941.
36 TNA, LAB 76/3, p. 26.
37 *Evening News*, 15/11/1941.
38 *Daily Sketch*, 18/7/1941, *Evening Standard*, 12/7/1941.
39 M-O, TC32, Box 2, File 2/A, *Undated notes headed 'M.G.'s article "Modern Woman"'*.
40 C. Moriarty, 'Abram Games: An Essay on His Work and its Context' in N. Games, C. Moriarty and J. Rose, *Abram Games, Graphic Designer: Maximum Meaning, Minimum Means*, Aldershot: Lund Humphries, 2003, p. 60.
41 A. Lant, *Blackout: Reinventing Women for Wartime British Cinema*, Princeton, NJ: Princeton University Press, 1991, p. 84.
42 This transition can be seen in a variety of sites, including women's magazines such as *Woman* and *Woman's Own* and in Ministry of Information propaganda, which increasingly tended to demonise the sexual, glamorous woman as a specific threat to the war effort. This process is discussed in depth by Lant, 1991, pp. 68–75.
43 *The Star*, 3/10/1941.
44 *Hansard, House of Commons* 5th Series. Vol. 370, March–April 1941, Woman-Power Debate, col. 354.
45 *Hansard*, Vol. 370, col. 321.
46 Ibid., cols 351, 325, and 353.
47 P. Tinkler, *Constructing Girlhood. Popular Magazines for Girls Growing Up in England 1920–1950*, London: Taylor & Francis, 1995, p. 121.
48 P. Summerfield, *Reconstructing Women's Wartime Lives: Discourse and Subjectivity in Oral Histories of the Second World War* Manchester: Manchester University Press, 1998, p. 45.
49 Whateley, *As Thoughts Survive*, pp. 25, 19.
50 Ibid., p. 39.
51 *Evening Standard*, 25/9/1941.
52 V. Douie, *Daughters of Britain: An Account of the Work of British Women During the Second World War*, Oxford: Vincent Baxter Press, 1949, p. 26.
53 *Punch*, 4/6/1941.
54 TNA, WO365/159, ATS: *Reports of Recruiting*.
55 TNA, LAB 76/3, p. 23.

56 M-O, TC32, Box 32/2/A *Street Questionnaire Replies to 4 Questions on Women and War Service, Central London*. Of the women interviewed in this survey, only 8 per cent were willing to join the ATS.

57 M-O, File Report (FR) 955, *Attitudes to Women in the ATS*, 8/11/1941.

58 Sylvia Townsend Warner, 'Fifty Girls Who Shouldn't' in *Our Time*, No. 9, December 1941, p. 13.

59 Cited in S. Rose, 'Girls and G.I.s: Race, Sex and Diplomacy in Second World War Britain', *The International History Review*, Vol. XIX, No. 1, February 1997, pp. 146–160.

60 TNA, LAB 76/3, p. 29.

61 Ibid., p. 31.

62 *Hansard, House of Commons*. Vol. 376, 1941–1942, November–December 1941. Debate on Maximum National Effort, col. 1026.

63 *Hansard*, Vol. 376, col. 1036.

64 TNA, LAB 76/3, p. 108.

65 *Hansard*, Vol. 376, col. 1037.

66 Ibid., cols 1419–1420.

67 Ibid., col. 1420.

68 Ibid., cols 1079–1080.

69 Ibid., col. 1065.

70 Ibid., col. 1442.

71 Ibid., col. 1087.

72 Ibid., col. 1088.

73 Ibid., col. 1448.

74 Ibid.

75 TNA, WO365/159, ATS: *Reports of Recruiting*.

76 For figures giving the numbers occupied in different areas of work in the ATS, see PRO, WO365/221, *ATS Strengths*.

77 Joubert Committee on Anti-Aircraft Reorganisation, March 1941, cited in PRO, LAB76/3, p. 22.

78 General Sir Frederick Pile, *Ack Ack. Britain's Defence Against Air Attack During the Second World War*, London: Harrap, 1949, p. 186.

79 Ibid., p. 226.

80 Ibid., p. 187.

81 Ibid., p. 192.

82 J. Bourke, *An Intimate History of Killing: Face to Face Killing in Twentieth Century warfare*, London: Granta, 1999, p. 328, V. Douie, *Daughters of Britain*, p. 34.

83 Pile, *Ack Ack*, p. 186.

84 G. De Groot, 'Combatants or Non-Combatants? Women in Mixed Anti-Aircraft Batteries During the Second World War', *RUSI Journal*, October 1995, p. 67.

85 Pile, *Ack Ack*, p. 378. Winston Churchill had already warned Grigg, the Secretary of State for War that the conditions women on anti-aircraft sites would be living in 'are very bad and rough', and cautioned him that 'a great responsibility lies on you as Secretary of State to see that all these young women are not treated roughly'. TNA, WO208/5137, *ATS Policy Problems*.

86 D. Parkin, 'Women in the Armed Services 1940–1945' in R. Samuel (ed.) *Patriotism: The Making and Unmaking of British National Identity: Vol. II, Minorities and Outsiders*, London: Routledge & Kegan Paul, 1989, p. 169.

87 Pile, *Ack Ack*.

88 E. Taylor, *Women Who Went to War 1939–1945*, London: Grafton, 1988, p. 88.

89 IWM, DD Box 95/27/1, *No Medals for Us*, B. Holbrook, unpublished memoir, p. 122.

90 TNA, WO208/5137, *ATS Policy Problems 1939–1945*.

91 IWM, DD Box 97/25/1, p. 6.

92 Ibid., p. 19.

93   IWM, DD Box 95/27/1, p. 8.
94   Ibid., p. 117.
95   *The Times*, 11/12/1941.
96   *Hansard*, Vol. 376, col. 1750.
97   *Report of the Committee on Amenities and Welfare Conditions in the Three Women's Services*, London: HMSO, 1942, p. 5.
98   M-O, *File Report* 952: *ATS Campaign*, 7/11/1941.
99   *Report of the Committee on Amenities and Welfare Conditions in the Three Women's Services*, p. 7.
100 Ibid., pp. 37–43.
101 R. Howard, *In Search of My Father: A Portrait of Leslie Howard*, London: Kimber, 1981, p. 125, cited in Lant, *Blackout*, p. 93.
102 J. Richards and D. Sheridan (eds) *Mass-Observation at the Movies*, London: Routledge & Kegan Paul, 1987, p. 220.
103 TNA, WO32/10653, *Women's Services: Women's Organisations (Military) in the Dominions and Colonies*.
104 Ibid.
105 B. Bousquet and C. Douglas, *West Indian Women at War: British Racism in World War Two*, London: Lawrence & Wishart, 1991, p. 2.
106 R. Terry, *Women in Khaki: The Story of the British Woman Soldier*, Reading: Columbus, 1988, p. 135.
107 See, for example, *Woman's Own*, 3/4/1942, *Woman*: 16/1/1943, 16/5/1945.
108 *Woman's Own*, 11/12/1942, 13/4/1940.
109 S. Bidwell, *The WRAC*, London: Leo Cooper, 1977, p. 107.
110 Ibid., pp. 107–115.
111 IWM, DD Box 89/4/1, *Letters from Sybella Stiles, Head Driver, MTC*.
112 IWM, DD Box 87/19/1, *Letters from the Honourable Miss L.E. Lawson*.
113 NAM, WRAC Collection, *M. Doherty: The Best Years of My Life*, 9802-66-1.
114 P. Summerfield, 'My Dress for an Army Uniform: Gender Instabilities in the Two World Wars', *Inaugural Lecture, University of Lancaster*, 30/4/1977, Women's Library, London Metropolitan University, 940:308.2, p. 6.
115 J. Bourke, *The Second World War*, Oxford: Oxford University Press, 2001, p. 121.
116 G. Braybon and P. Summerfield, *Out of the Cage: Women's Experiences in the Two World Wars*, London: Pandora, 1987, p. 2.
117 TNA, WO32/10663, cited in P. Goodman, *Women, Sexuality and War*, Basingstoke: Palgrave, 2002, p. 88.
118 Whateley, *As Thoughts Survive*, p. 163.
119 Ibid., p. 136.
120 Ibid., p. 188.
121 Douie, *Daughters of Britain*, p. 42.
122 Ibid., p. 42.
123 *Hansard*, Vol. 406, November–December 1944 , col. 1957.
124 Ibid., col. 1958.
125 *Hansard*, Vol. 407, January–February 1945, ATS Overseas Service Debate, cols 845 and 865.
126 *Hansard*, Vol. 407, cols 871, and 880.
127 Whateley, *As Thoughts Survive*, p. 157.
128 A. Calder, *The People's War*, p. 528.
129 Cited in J. Waller and M. Vaughan-Rees, *Women in Wartime*, p. 125.
130 'The Family and Neighbourhood', *British Way and Purpose*, 13, December 1943.
131 N. S. Wilson, *Education in the Forces: The Civilian Context*, The Year Book of Education, 1949, p. 94.
132 T. H. Hawkins and L. F. J. Brumble, *Adult Education: The Record of the British Army*, London: Macmillan, 1947, p. 149.
133 W. E. Williams, 'A Woman's Place', *Current Affairs*, ABCA, 1944, No. 61, p. 2.

134 Major General A.J.K. Piggott, 'Show Me The Way To Go Home', *Current Affairs*, ABCA, 23/9/1944, No. 78, p. 17.
135 Wilson, *Education in the Forces*, p. 94.
136 Terry, *Women in Khaki*, p. 164.

7 'Gentle in manner, resolute in deed': women in the postwar army

1 E. Thompson, 'My Post-War Aims', *Woman's Magazine*, November 1944, in J. Waller and M. Vaughan Rees, *Women in Wartime. The Role of Women's Magazines*, London: McDonald Optima, 1987, p. 124.
2 Sir William Beveridge, *Social Insurance and Allied Services: Report by Sir William* Beveridge, London: HMSO, 1942, p. 53.
3 Beveridge, 1942, p. 53.
4 S. Bruley, *Women in Britain Since 1900*, Basingstoke: Macmillan, 1999, p. 120.
5 Ibid., p. 120.
6 R. Titmuss, *Essays on the Welfare State*, London: Allen & Unwin, 1958, p. 90.
7 J. C. Spence, *The Purpose of the Family: A Guide to the Care of Children*, London: National Children's Home, 1946, p. 50, Women's Group on Public Welfare, 'The Neglected Child', 1948, cited in J. Lewis, *Women in Britain Since 1945*, Oxford: Blackwell, 1992, p. 23.
8 J. Bowlby, *Forty Four Juvenile Thieves: their Characters and Home Life*, Bailliere: Tindall & Cox, 1946, *Maternal Care and Mental Health*, Geneva: World Health Organisation, 1951.
9 D. Riley, *War in the Nursery: Theories of the Child and Mother*, London: Virago, 1983.
10 P. Summerfield, *Reconstructing Women's Wartime Lives: Discourse and Subjectivity in Oral Histories of the Second World War*, Manchester: Manchester University Press, 1998, p. 260.
11 Mass-Observation, *The Journey Home: A Mass-Observation Report on the Problems of Demobilisation*, London: John Murray, 1944, p. 55, *Woman and Beauty*, 1944, cited in Waller and Vaughan-Reeves, *Women in Wartime*, p. 125. For further contemporary discussion of the impact women's wartime experience would have on their postwar lives see M. Goldsmith, *Women at War*, London: Lindsay Drummond, 1943, P. Scott, *They Made Invasion Possible*, London: Hutchinson, 1944. The M. P. Edith Summerskill regularly expressed the view that the war had opened up new opportunities for women, particularly for those who had chosen to join one of the uniformed services. For example see E. Summerskill, *Women Fall In: A Guide to Women's Work in Wartime*, London: Hutchinson, 1941 in which she argued that 'the ATS offers opportunities that many girls have been longing for in peacetime', p. 24.
12 *Woman's Journal*, March 1944, cited in Waller and Vaughan-Reeves, *Women in Wartime*, p. 126.
13 'Has the War Really Changed Our Women?', *Sunday Graphic*, 1944, article reprinted in *When Peace Broke Out*, London: HMSO, 1994, p. 100.
14 A. Lant, *Blackout: Reinventing Women for Wartime British Cinema*, Princeton, NJ: Princeton University Press, 1991, p. 204.
15 *Hansard*, 5th Series, Vol. 404, November 1944, Debate on Manpower (Release from Forces), col. 1989. This debate is discussed in more detail in J. Swindells, 'Coming Home to Heaven: Manpower and Myth in 1944 Britain', *Women's History Review*, Vol. 4, No. 2, 1994, pp. 223–234.
16 *Hansard*, Vol. 404, col. 2034.
17 Ibid., col. 1988.
18 *Regulations for Release from the Army*, London: HMSO, 1943, p. 43. Women who had been serving overseas received an extra £5.00 clothing grant.
19 *Hansard*, Vol. 404, col. 1988.
20 The National Archives, (TNA) War Office (WO) 365/221, *ATS Strengths 1941–1944*. For numbers of women in the forces at the end of the war, see table 2.
21 TNA, WO365/159, *ATS: Reports of Recruiting. Progress Reports Since National Registration Act 19/4/1941*.

22 TNA, Ministry of Labour (LAB) 76/3, *Women's Auxiliary Services*, J. L. Brooke-Waddell, 1956, p. 73.
23 Ibid., p. 82.
24 Ibid., p. 84.
25 *Hansard*, Vol. 410, April–May 1945, cols 955–956.
26 E. Wilson, *Only Half-Way to Paradise: Women in Post-War Britain 1945–1968*, London: Tavistock, 1980, p. 23. Wilson notes however that this number had fallen to 200,000 by 1961, despite the formation of an Institute of Houseworkers in 1947 as part of the Labour government's attempts to introduce proper training, wages and conditions of service to domestic employment.
27 *Regulations for Release From the Army 1945*, London: HMSO, 1945, p. 5.
28 TNA, LAB 44/198, *Demobilisation: Questions and Answers*, p. 10.
29 TNA, LAB 76/3, p. 84.
30 TNA, LAB 44/198, p. 17.
31 Imperial War Museum (IWM), Department of Documents (DD) Box 97/25/1 Marian Mills, *Women Soldiers: A Memoir of the ATS*, Unpublished memoir, 1991, p. 44.
32 E. S. Turner, 'Ballade of the Forgotten Gun-Site', *Punch*, 13/9/1944.
33 J. Laffin, *Women in Battle*, London: Abelard-Schuman, 1967, p. 185.
34 'Woman's Own', January 1945, article reprinted in *When Peace Broke Out*, p. 5.
35 'Good Housekeeping' 1945, article reprinted in B. Braithwaite, N. Walsh and G. Davies (eds) *The Home Front: The Best of Good Housekeeping 1939–1945*, London: Ebury Press, 1987, pp. 189–190.
36 *Hansard*, Vol. 407, January–February 1945, ATS Overseas Service Debate, col. 862.
37 TNA, WO32/11161, *Relations Between Allied Occupying Forces and Inhabitants of Germany*.
38 Ibid.
39 Ibid.
40 Ibid.
41 *Hansard*, Vol. 448, March 1948, col. 1021.
42 TNA, WO205/387, *Occupation of Germany: Employment of Allied Civilians and Women's Services*.
43 TNA, WO32/11161.
44 TNA, WO32/11407, *Allied Behaviour in Germany During Occupation*.
45 Ibid.
46 At times this was made explicit. See for example the article 'ATS Girls Annoyed by Frauleins at Dance' in the *Sunday Pictorial* during October 1945 which described an incident at Luneberg, Germany. Women from the ATS complained that British Officers were taking German women, whom they called 'pieces of frat', dancing at the Officer's Club. The article compares the German civilian women with the 'good-looking' ATS, and concludes that the ATS were at a disadvantage because they were compelled to wear uniform to dances rather than civilian dress, implying that uniformed women were less attractive to the troops, and less 'feminine' than civilian women. Article reprinted in *When Peace Broke Out*, p. 119.
47 TNA, WO32/11407.
48 Ibid.
49 TNA, CAB130/3, cited in P. Hennessy, *The Secret State: Whitehall and the Cold War*, London: Penguin, 2002, p. 46.
50 M. Dockrill, *British Defence Since 1945*, Oxford: Blackwell, 1988, p. 35.
51 TNA, LAB 8/1087, *Memo on the Subject of Compulsory National Service for Women During the Post-War Period*.
52 Ibid.
53 *Yorkshire Post*, 10/10/1946.
54 TNA, LAB 8/1087.
55 Ibid.
56 *Hansard*, Vol. 435, March–April 1947, col. 1727.

57 *Hansard*, Vol. 435, cols 1729–1730.

58 Ibid., col. 1757.

59 Ibid., col. 1730.

60 TNA, LAB 8/1087.

61 L. Whateley, cited in S. Bidwell, *The WRAC*, London: Leo Cooper, 1972, p. 136.

62 *Hansard*, Vol. 423, May–June 1946, col. 1338.

63 A side effect of this decision was its impact on the unofficial women's military organisations such as the First Aid Nursing Yeomanry (FANY) which was informed in 1947 by the Army Council that it was 'unable to allot a role for the Women's Transport Corps (FANY) in the Post-War Army'. Cited in H. Popham, *The Story of the Women's Transport Corps (FANY)*, London: Leo Cooper, 1984, p. 117.

64 TNA, Ministry of Information (INF), 2/85, *ATS 1943–1947*.

65 *Hansard*, Vol. 430, November 1946, col. 860.

66 TNA, WO32/12159, *Modification of the Army Act to Make it Applicable to the Regular Women's Services*. The new corps narrowly avoided the title Royal Auxiliary Territorial Service, with the acronym RATS.

67 TNA, INF2/185.

68 National Army Museum (NAM), WRAC Papers, 9802–42, Eva Buckingham, *Service Life at Home and Abroad*.

69 TNA, WO32/12159. As the WRNS retained their civilian status, their position was not considered to be a problem in this discussion.

70 Ibid.

71 Ibid.

72 Ibid.

73 Ibid.

74 Ibid.

75 Ibid.

76 P. Summerfield, 'The Home Guard and the Memory of the British War Effort', paper given at *Britain and the Home Front Conference*, University of Portsmouth, 13 April 2005.

77 TNA, WO32/13689, *Non-Combatant Role of the WRAC and Military Nursing Corps in War*, 1949.

78 TNA, WO32/13173, *Defensive Role of the WRAC in War*, 1948.

79 TNA, WO32/13689.

80 TNA, WO32/13173.

81 TNA, WO32/13689. The description of 'little Olga' is presumably a reference to women in the Soviet Union who had served as combatants in the Air Force, in Air Defence and as partisans during the Second World War although, ironically, gender distinctions were in the process of being reinforced by the introduction of a strongly pro-natalist family policy in the postwar Soviet Union. See B. Alpern Engel, 'The Womanly Face of War: Soviet Women Remember World War II' in N. Dombrowski (ed.) *Women and War in the Twentieth Century: Enlisted with or Without Consent*, New York: Garland Publishing, 1999.

82 TNA, WO32/13689.

83 Ibid.

84 TNA WO32/13173 and WO32/13689.

85 TNA WO32/13173 and WO32/12689.

86 For a discussion of the chivalrous ideal in British popular culture, see M. Paris, *Warrior Nation: Images of War in British Popular Culture 1850–2000*, London: Reaktion Books, 2000. For wartime imagery which represented women as sexualised victims of war see S. Gubar, 'This is my Rifle, This is my Gun: World War Two and the Blitz on Women', in M. Higonnet, J. Jenson, S. Michel and M Collins Weitz (eds) *Behind the Lines: Gender and the Two World Wars*, New Haven, CT: Yale University Press, 1987, pp. 227–259.

87 TNA, WO32/13689.

88 D. Barker, *Soldiering On: An Unofficial Portrait of the British Army*, London: Andre Deutsch, 1981, p. 180.

89 NAM, WRAC 9710–163, *Minutes of the Committee on Post-War Dress for QAIMNS and WRAC*, Mass-Observation (M-O), File Report 1083, *Summary of Report on ATS Campaign*, 2/2/1942.
90 TNA, WO32/13699, *Report of the Committee on Post-War Dress for QARANC and WRAC*, 1949.
91 *Daily Express*, 8/11/1940.
92 M-O, Topic Collection 32, Women in Wartime, Box 2, File 2H, *ATS Survey: Women's Attitudes*, November 1941.
93 TNA, WO32/13699.
94 NAM, WRAC 9710–163, TNA WO32/13699.
95 NAM, WRAC 9710–163.
96 Ibid.
97 Ibid.
98 S. Bidwell, *The WRAC*, p. 138.
99 TNA, INF2/86, *ATS/WRAC Recruiting Campaign 1948–1949*.
100 A slightly later campaign demonstrates this point even more clearly. A drawing of a smiling woman was used in several adverts which stressed both an underlying feminism and contrasted the opportunities for adventure and travel offered by the WRAC with the lack of these in other available jobs. Strap lines included: 'Yes, I showed that big brother of mine', 'Yes Dad, I'm in the Army now' and 'there are few other jobs that offer a girl the chance of foreign travel'. TNA, INF2/86.
101 TNA, WO32/12166, *ATS: Maintenance of Women's Services*, 1948.
102 Ibid.
103 As discussed in the previous chapter Grigg agreed in 1943 that a small number of black women could serve with the ATS in Britain but commented in a letter to Oliver Stanley the Colonial Secretary, who had pushed for a change in policy that 'I don't at all like your West Indian ATS ideas'. Bousquet and Douglas argue that Grigg only agreed to this because the United States were proposing to send black members of the US Women's Army Corps to serve in Britain. B. Bousquet and C. Douglas, *West Indian Women at War: British Racism in World War Two*, London: Lawrence & Wishart, 1991, p. 103.
104 TNA, WO32/12166.
105 Ibid.
106 For more on the experience of black women in postwar Britain, and the construction of national identity as white, see W. Webster, *Imagining Home: Gender 'Race' and National Identity 1945–64*, London: UCL Press, 1998.
107 P. Thane, 'Women Since 1945' in P. Johnson (ed.) *20th Century Britain: Economic, Social and Cultural Change*, London: Longman, 1994, p. 395.
108 *Hansard*, Vol. 448, March 1948, col. 1021.
109 TNA, WO32/13168, *WRAC Corps Warrant Action*.
110 Ibid.
111 This pattern was to continue in the postwar years and was justified by women's non-combatant status. For example, in the army pay awards of 1979, men were awarded an average rise of 10 per cent whilst women were awarded 5 per cent. D. Barker, *Soldiering On*, p. 184.
112 E. Nolan, Director of WRAC 1973–1977, cited in R. Terry, *Women in Khaki: The Story of the British Woman Soldier*, London: Columbus, 1988, p. 191.

Conclusion

1 C. Enloe, *Does Khaki Become You? The Militarization of Women's Lives*, London: Pandora Press, 1983, p. 212.
2 *Parson's Weekly*, 29/9/1917.
3 M. Botchkareva, *Yashka: My Life as a Peasant and Exile (as set down by Isaac Don Levine)*, London: Constable, 1919, p. 76.

4 National Army Museum (NAM) WRAC Collection, Accession number 9401-253-20, *Gwynne Vaughan Papers, undated letter from Chalmers-Watson to Gwynne Vaughan*, Mass-Observation (M-O) File Report (FR) 955, Attitudes to Women in the ATS, 1941.

5 *The Globe*, 19/9/1917, M-O, Topic Collection 32, Box 32/1/E, *Women in the Forces.*

6 *Ladies Pictorial*, 21/8/1915.

7 The National Archives (TNA), *War Office (WO) 32/5252, Women's Army Auxiliary Corps: Uniform of Officers*, M. Garber, *Vested Interests: Cross Dressing and Cultural Anxiety*, New York: Routledge, 1992, p. 55.

8 *Answers*, 26/1/1918.

9 Women's Library, 940.308.2, P. Summerfield, *My Dress for an Army Uniform: Gender Instabilities in the Two World Wars*, Inaugural Lecture, University of Leicester, 30/4/1997, p. 15.

10 TNA, WO32/9423, cited in P. Summerfield, 'She Wants A Gun, Not a Dishcloth! Gender, Service and Citizenship in Britain in the Second World War' in G. De Groot and C. Peniston-Bird (eds) *A Soldier and a Woman: Sexual Integration in the Military*, Harlow: Longman, 2000, p. 125.

11 Penny Summerfield has written about the disjuncture between feminist historians 'readings of historical records and women's individual memories of their experiences during wartime. P. Summerfield, *Reconstructing Women's Wartime Lives*, Manchester: Manchester University Press, 1998.

12 C. Dandeker, 'New Times for the Military: Some Sociological Remarks on the Changing Role and Structure of the Armed Forces of the Advanced Societies', *British Journal of Sociology*, Vol. 45, No. 4, 1994, p. 639.

13 *Hansard*, 6th Series, Vol. 299, House of Commons, July–October 1997, col. 616.

14 *Hansard*, col. 728–729.

15 Ibid., col. 616.

16 Ibid., cols 620 and 779.

17 Ibid., cols 797–798.

18 Ibid., cols 738 and 779.

19 Employment of Women in the Armed Forces Steering Group, *Women in the Armed Forces*, London: Minstry of Defence, 2002, p. 2.

20 Employment of Women in the Armed Forces Steering Group, *Women in the Armed Forces*, p. 3.

21 Ibid., pp. 3 and 5.

Bibliography

Archival sources

Imperial War Museum

Department of Art, Catalogues and Posters
Department of Documents
Department of Printed Books
Women's Work Collection (Army, Press Cuttings 1914–1918, Volunteer Corps)

Mass-Observation Archive, University of Sussex

Mass-Observation File Reports (FR 952, FR 955, FR 1083)
Topic Collection 32 'Women in Wartime'

The National Archives

Cabinet Office Records (CAB 130)
Home Office Records (HO 185)
Ministry of Information Records (INF 2)
Ministry of Labour Records (LAB 8, LAB 44, LAB 76)
Ministry of Reconstruction Records (RECO 1)
Royal Air Force Records (AIR 2)
War Office Records (WO32, WO162, WO205, WO365)

The National Army Museum

Women's Royal Army Corps Collection

The Women's Library, London Metropolitan University

Eleanor Rathbone Personal Papers (7/ELR)
Records of the Society for Overseas Settlement of British Women 1917–1964 (1/SOS)

Newspapers and magazines

Britannia
British Way and Purpose
Chicago Tribune
Common Cause
Contemporary Review
Current Affairs
English Review
The Gentlewoman
The Herald
Ladies Pictorial
The New Statesman and Nation
Nineteenth Century and After
Our Time
Picture Post
Punch
The Spectator
The Sphere
The Times
The Vigilance Record
The Vote
Woman
Woman Worker
Women and War
Women's International League for Peace and Freedom Monthly Newsheet
Women's Own
Women's Volunteer Reserve Magazine

Official publications and parliamentary papers

Beveridge, W., *Social Insurance and Allied Services: Report by Sir William Beveridge*, London: HMSO, 1942

Central Office of Information, 'An Investigation into the Attitudes of Women, the General Public and ATS Personnel to the Auxiliary Territorial Service', *Wartime Social Survey*, New Series no. 5, October 1941

Central Statistical Office, *Fighting With Figures. A Statistical Digest of the Second World War*, London: HMSO, 1995

Hansard, House of Commons, 5th Series 5 July–29 July 1915, Vol. 73, National Registration Bill, Second Reading

Hansard, House of Commons, 5th Series 21 March–2 May 1916, Vol. 81, Oral Answers

Hansard, House of Commons, 5th Series 26 March–27 April 1917, Vol. 92, Franchise and Electoral Reform Debate

Hansard, House of Commons, 5th Series 21 February–11 March 1938, Vol. 332, Oral Answers

Hansard, House of Commons, 5th Series 18 March–10 April 1941, Vol. 370, Woman-Power Debate

Hansard, House of Commons, 5th Series 12 November–19 December 1941, Vol. 376, Debate on Maximum National Effort

Hansard, House of Commons, 5th Series 24 October–28 November 1944, Vol. 404, Debate on Manpower (Release from Forces)

Hansard, House of Commons, 5th Series 29 November–21 December 1944, Vol. 406, ATS Overseas Service

Hansard, House of Commons, 5th Series 16 January–9 February 1945, Vol. 407, ATS Overseas Service Debate

Hansard, House of Commons, 5th Series 17 April–18 May 1945, Vol. 410, Oral Answers

Hansard, House of Commons, 5th Series 12–29 November 1946, Vol. 430, Women's Auxiliary Services (Continuance)

Hansard, House of Commons, 5th Series 1–25 March 1948, Vol. 448, Supply: Army Estimates

Hansard, House of Commons, 6th Series 28 July–30 October 1997, Vol. 299, Defence Policy

Hansard, House of Lords, 5th Series 27 November 1917–28 January 1918, Vol. 27, November 1917-January 1918, Representation of the People Bill

Ministry of Defence, *Front Line First: The Defence Costs Study*, London: HMSO, 1994

Ministry of Defence, *Women in the Armed Forces*, London: HMSO, 2002

Ministry of Labour, *Report of the Commission of Enquiry into the Women's Army Auxiliary Corps in France*, London: HMSO, 1918

Ministry of Labour, *Report of the British Government Overseas Settlement Mission to Canada*, London: HMSO, 1919

Ministry of Labour, *Report of the Overseas Settlement Committee for year Ended 31 December 1919*, London: HMSO, 1920

Ministry of Reconstruction, *The Mission of the British Army*, Reconstruction Problems 37, London: HMSO, 1919

Regulations for Release from the Army, London: HMSO, 1943

Report of the Committee on Amenities and Welfare Conditions in the Three Women's Services, London: HMSO, 1942

The War Office, *Regulations for the ATS*, London: HMSO, 1941

Unpublished theses, lectures and papers

Sheridan, D., *Challenge and Containment in Women's Lives in the Military During the Second World War*, unpublished MA Thesis, University of Sussex, 1988

Summerfield, P., *My Dress for an Army Uniform: Gender Instabilities in the Two World Wars*, Inaugural Lecture, University of Leicester, 30/4/1997, Women's Library, Accession no. 940.308.2

—— 'The Home Guard and the Memory of the British War Effort', Conference Paper *Britain and the Home Front Conference*, University of Portsmouth, April 2005

General bibliography

Addis, E., V. Russo and L. Sebesta (eds) *Women Soldiers: Images and Realities*, London: Macmillan, 1994

Addison, P., *The Road to 1945: British Politics and the Second World War*, London: Quartet, 1977

Adie, K., *Corsets to Camouflage: Women and War*, Hodder & Stoughton in association with the Imperial War Museum, London, 2003

Alberti, J., *Beyond Suffrage: Feminists in War and Peace 1914–1928*, London: Macmillan, 1989

Allatt, P., 'Men and War: Status, Class and the Social Reproduction of Masculinity' in E. Garminikow, D. H. J. Morgan, J. Purvis and D. Taylorson (eds) *The Public and the Private*, London: Heinemann Educational Books, 1983

Allen, M., 'The Domestic Ideal and the Mobilisation of Woman-Power in World War II', *Women's Studies International Forum*, Vol. 6, No. 4, 1983

Alpern Engle, B., 'The Womanly Face of War: Soviet Women Remember World War Two' in N. Dombrowski (ed.) *Women and War in the Twentieth Century: Enlisted With or Without Consent*, New York: Garland Publishing, 1999

Altman, A., A. M. Burke and M. Howard (eds) *The Quest for Stability: Problems Of West European Society 1918–1957*, Oxford: The German Historical institute, Oxford University Press, 1993

Anon, *WAAC: The Women's Story of the War*, London: T. Werner Laurie, 1930

Ashworth, T., *Trench Warfare 1914–1918: The Live and Let Live System*, London: Macmillan, 1980

Baden-Powell, R., *Scouting For Boys*, London: Pearson, 1908

——*Girl Guides: A Suggestion for Character Training for Girls*, London: Bishopgate Press, 1909

Barker, D., *Soldiering On: An Unofficial Portrait of the British Army*, London: Andre Deutsch, 1981

Barton, E. and M. Cody, *Eve in Khaki*, London: Nelson, 1918

Beauchamp, P., *Fanny Went to War*, London: Routledge and Kegan Paul, 1940

Beauman, N., ' "It Is Not the Place of Women to Talk of Mud" Some Responses by British Women Novelists to World War One' in D. Goldman (ed.) *Women and World War One: The Written Response*, Basingstoke: Macmillan, 1993

Beaumont, C., 'The Women's Movement, Politics and Citizenship 1918–1950s' in I. Zweiniger-Bargielowska (ed.) *Women in Twentieth Century Britain*, London: Longman, 2001

Beckett, I. and K. Simpson (eds) *A Nation in Arms: A Social Study of the British Army in the First World War*, Manchester: Manchester University Press, 1985

Beddoe, D., *Back to Home and Duty: Women Between the Wars 1918–1939*, London: Pandora, 1989

Bennett, Y., 'Vera Brittain and the Peace Pledge Union' in R. Roach Pierson (ed.) *Women and Peace: Theoretical, Historical and Practical Perspectives*, London: Croom Helm, 1987

Bet-El, I. R., 'Men and Soldiers: British Conscripts, Concepts of Masculinity and the Great War' in B. Melman (ed.) *Borderlines: Genders and Identities in War and Peace*, New York: Routledge, 1998

Biddle, M., *The Women of England*, Cambridge (USA): Riverside Press, 1941

Bidwell, S., *The WRAC*, London: Leo Cooper, 1977

Bigland, E., *Britain's Other Army: The Story of the ATS*, London: Nicholson & Watson, 1946

Billington, M. Frances, *The Roll Call of Serving Women: A Record of Women's Work for Sufferers and Combatants in the Great War*, London: The Religious Tract Society, 1915

Blythe, R., *The Age of Illusion: Some Glimpses of Britain Between the Wars 1919–1940*, Oxford: Oxford University Press, 1963

Botchkareva, M., *Yashka: My Life as a Peasant and Exile* (as set down by Isaac Don Levine), London: Constable, 1919

Bourke, J., *Dismembering the Male: Men's Bodies, Britain and the Great War*, London: Reaktion Books, 1996

——*An Intimate History of Killing: Face to Face Killing in Twentieth Century Warfare*, London: Granta, 1999

——*The Second World War*, Oxford: Oxford University Press, 2001

Bousquet, B. and C. Douglas, *West Indian Women at War: British Racism in World War II*, London: Lawrence & Wishart, 1991

Bowlby, J., *Forty Four Juvenile Thieves: their Characters and Home Life*, Bailliere: Tindall & Cox, 1946

——*Maternal Care and Mental Health*, Geneva: World Health Organisation, 1951

Braine, J., *Room at the Top*, London: Penguin, 1957

Braithwaite, B., N. Walsh and G. Davies (eds) *The Home Front: The Best of Good Housekeeping 1939–1945*, London: Ebury Press, 1987

Braybon, G., *Women Workers in the First World War: The British Experience*, London: Croom Helm, 1981

——(ed.) *Evidence, History and the Great War*, Oxford: Berghahn Books, 2003

Braybon, G. and P. Summerfield, *Out of the Cage: Women's Experiences in Two World Wars*, London: Pandora, 1987

——'Winners or Losers: Women's Symbolic Role in the War Story' in G. Braybon (ed.) *Evidence, History and the Great War: Historians and the Impact of 1914–1918*, Oxford: Berghahn Books, 2003

Brittain, V., *Testament of Youth: An Autobiographical Study of the Years 1900–1925*, London: Virago, 1978, first published London: Victor Gollancz, 1935

——*Chronicle of Youth: War Diary 1913–1917*, A. Bishop and T. Smart (eds) London: Victor Gollancz, 1981

Brooke, R., *The Collected Poems of Rupert Brooke*, London: Sidgwick & Jackson, 1918

Brown, M., *The Imperial War Museum Book of 1918: Year of Victory*, London: Sidgwick & Jackson, 1998

——*Put That Light Out! Britain's Civil Defence Services at War 1939–1945*, Stroud: Sutton, 1999

Bruley, S., *Women in Britain Since 1900*, Basingstoke: Macmillan, 1999

Bryant, L., *Six Months in Red Russia*, New York: George H. Doran, 1918

Burton, E., *What of the Women? A Study of Women in Wartime*, London: Muller, 1941

Butler, J., *Gender Trouble: Feminism and the Subversion of Identity*, London: Routledge, 1990

Calder, A., *The People's War: Britain 1939–1945*, London: Jonathan Cape, 1969

——*The Myth of the Blitz*, London: Jonathan Cape, 1991

Campbell, D., 'Women in Combat: The World War II Experience in the United States, Great Britain, Germany and the Soviet Union', *Journal of Military History*, 57, 1993

Cantwell, J. D., *Images of War: British Posters 1929–45*, London: HMSO, 1989

Carter, A., 'Should Women Be Soldiers or Pacifists?' in L.A. Lorentzen and J. Turpin (eds) *The Women and War Reader*, New York: New York University Press, 1998

Cavadini, A., *This Was the ATS*, n.p. 1946

Ceadel, M. 'Popular Fiction and the Next War 1918–1939' in F. Gloversmith (ed.) *Class, Culture and Social Change: A New View of the 1930s*, Brighton: Harvester, 1980

——*Thinking About Peace and War*, Oxford: Oxford University Press, 1987

Clapham, I., *Towards Sex Freedom*, London: John Lane, 1935

Cole, G. D. H., *Workshop Organization*, Oxford: Clarendon Press, 1923

Colleclough, M., *Women's Legion 1916–1920*, London: Spearman, 1940

Collins, C. R., *Army Women's Handbook*, New York: McGraw Hill, 1942

Colls, R. and P. Dodds (eds) *Englishness: Politics and Culture 1880–1920*, Kent: Croom Helm, 1986

Condell, D. and J. Liddiard, *Working for Peace? Images of Women in the First World War, 1914–1918*, London: Routledge and Kegan Paul, 1987

Cooke, M., *Women and the War Story*, Berkeley, CA: University of California Press, 1996

Cooke, M. and A. Wollacott (eds) *Gendering War Talk*, Princeton, NJ: Princeton University Press, 1993

Cooper, H. C., A. A. Munich and S. M. Squire, (eds) *Arms and the Woman: War, Gender and Literary Representation*, Chapel Hill, NC: University of North Carolina Press, 1989

Costello, J., *Love, Sex and War: Changing Values 1939–1945*, London: William Collins, 1985

Cotterell, A., *She Walks in Battledress – The Day's Work in the ATS*, London: Christopher, 1942

Cowper, Colonel J., *A Short History of the Queen Mary's Army Auxiliary Corps*, Aldershot: WRAC Association, 1957

Crang, J., *The British Army and the People's War*, Manchester: Manchester University Press, 2000

—— 'The British Army as a Social Institution 1939–1945' in H. Strachan (ed.) *The British Army, Manpower and Society: Towards 2000*, London: Frank Cass, 2000

Cunningham, H., *The Volunteer Force: A Social and Political History 1859–1908*, London: Croom Helm, 1975

Dagget, M. Potter, *Women Wanted: The Story Written in Blood Red Letters on the Horizon of the Great World War*, London: Hodder & Staughton, 1918

D'Amico, F., 'Feminist Perspectives on Women Warriors' in L. A. Lorentzen and J. Turpin (eds) *The Women and War Reader*, New York: New York University Press, 1998

Dandeker, C., 'New Times for the Military: Some Sociological Remarks on the Changing Role and Structure of the Armed Forces of the Advanced Societies', *British Journal of Sociology*, Vol. 45, No. 4, 1994

—— 'A Farewell to Arms? The Military and the Nation-State in a Changing World' in J. Burk (ed.) *The Adaptive Military: Armed Forces in a Turbulent World*, New Brunswick: Transaction Publishers, 1998

—— 'Don't Ask, Don't Tell and Don't Pursue: Is a Pragmatic Solution the Way Forward for the Armed Services in Today's Society?', Royal United Services Institute (*RUSI) Journal*, June 1999

Darracott, J. (ed.), *The First World War in Posters*, New York: Dover, 1974

Davies, M. Llewelyn, *Maternity: Letters from Working Mothers*, London: Virago, 1978, first published 1915

Davin, A., 'Imperialism and Motherhood', *History Workshop Journal*, Vol. 5, 1978

Dawson, G., *Soldier Heroes: British Adventure, Empire and the Imagining of Masculinity*, London: Routledge, 1994

Degan, M. L., *The History of the Women's Peace Movement*, New York: Garland Publishing, 1972

De Groot, G. J., 'Combatants or Non-Combatants? Women in Mixed Anti-Aircraft Batteries During the Second World War', *RUSI Journal*, October 1995

—— *Blighty: British Society in the Era of the Great War*, London: Longman, 1996

De Groot, G. J., 'Whose Finger on the Trigger? Mixed Anti-Aircraft Batteries and the Female Combat Taboo', *War in History*, Vol. 4, 1997

——'Arms and the Woman' in G. De Groot and C. Penniston-Bird (eds) *A Soldier and A Woman: Sexual Integration in the Military*, Harlow: Longman, 2000

——'Lipstick on her Nipples, Cordite in her Hair: Sex and Romance Among British Servicewomen During the Second World War' in G. De Groot and C. Penniston-Bird (eds) *A Soldier and A Woman: Sexual Integration in the Military*, Harlow: Longman, 2000

De Groot, G. and C. Penniston-Bird (eds) *A Soldier and A Woman: Sexual Integration in the Military*, Harlow: Longman, 2000

Dockrill, M., *British Defence Since 1945*, Oxford: Blackwell, 1988

Dombrowski, N., 'Soldiers, Saints or Sacrificial Lambs? Women's Relationship to Combat and the Fortification of the Home Front in the Twentieth Century' in N. Dombrowski, (ed.) *Women and War in the Twentieth Century*, New York: Garland 1999

——(ed.) *Women and War in the Twentieth Century*, New York: Garland 1999

Douie, V., *Daughters of Britain: An Account of the Work of British Women During the Second World War*, Oxford: Vincent Baxter Press, 1949

Drummond, J., *Blue for a Girl: the Story of the WRNS*, London: Allen, 1960

Dworkin, A., *Pornography: Men Possessing Women*, London: The Women's Press, 1987

Dyhouse, C., *Girls Growing Up In Victorian and Edwardian England*, London: Routledge and Kegan Paul, 1981

Ehrenreich, B., *Blood Rites: Origins and History of the Passions of War*, New York: Henry Holt & Co., 1997

Elshtain, J. Bethke, *Women and War*, New York: Basic Book, 1987

Enloe, C., *Does Khaki Become You? The Militarization of Women's Lives*, London: Pandora, 1983

——*The Morning After: Sexual Politics at the End of the Cold War*, Berkeley, CA: University of California Press, 1993

——*Maneuvers: The International Politics of Militarizing Women's Lives*, Berkeley, CA: University of California Press, 2000

Ewing, E., *Women in Uniform Through the Centuries*, London: Batsford, 1975

Fayderman, L., *Surpassing the Love of Men: Romantic Friendship and Love Between Women from the Renaissance to the Present*, New York: Morrow, 1981

Fenner, L., 'Either You Need These Women Or You Do Not: Informing the Debate on Military Issues and Citizenship', *Gender Issues*, Vol. 16, No. 3, 1998

Finch, J. and P. Summerfield, 'Social Reconstruction and the Emergence of Companionate Marriage, 1945–49' in D. Clark (ed.) *Marriage, Domestic Life and Social Change. Writings for Jacqueline Burgoyne*, London: Routledge, 1991

Flint, R. W., *Marinetti: Selected Writings*, London: Secker & Warburg, 1971

French, D., ' "You Cannot Hate the Bastard Who is Trying to Kill You . . ." Combat and Ideology in the British Army in the War Against Germany 1939–1945', *Twentieth Century British History*, Vol. 11, 2000

Furse, Dame K., *Hearts and Pomegranates: The Story of Forty Five Years: 1875–1920*, London: Peter Davies, 1940

Fussell, P., *The Great War and Modern Memory*, Oxford: Oxford University Press, 1975

——(ed.) *The Bloody Game: An Anthology of Modern War*, London: Scribners, 1991

Games, N., C. Moriarty and J. Rose, *Abram Games, Graphic Designer: Maximum Meaning, Minimum Means*, Aldershot: Lund Humphries, 2003

Garber, M., *Vested Interests: Cross Dressing and Cultural Anxiety*, New York: Routledge, 1992

Geraghty, C., 'Disguises and Betrayals: Negotiating Nationality and Femininity in Three Wartime Films' in C. Gledhill and G. Swanson (eds) *Nationalizing Femininity: Culture, Sexuality and British Cinema in the Second World War*, Manchester: Manchester University Press, 1996

Gilbert, M., *The Second World War*, London: Wiedenfield & Nicholson, 1989

—— *The First World War*, London: Wiedenfield & Nicholson, 1994

Gledhill, C. and G. Swanson 'Gender and Sexuality in Second World War Films – A Feminist Approach' in G. Hurd (ed.) *National Fictions: World War Two in British Films and Television*, London: BFI, 1984

—— (eds) *Nationalizing Femininity*, Manchester: Manchester University Press 1996

Goldman, N. (ed.) *Female Soldiers: Combatants or Non-Combatants? Historical and Contemporary Perspectives*, West Port, CT: Greenwood Press, 1982

Goldman, N. and R. Stites, 'Great Britain and the World Wars' in N. Goldman (ed.) *Female Soldiers: Combatants or Non-Combatants ? Historical and Contemporary Perspectives*, West Port, CT: Greenwood Press, 1982

Goldsmith, M., *Women at War*, London: Lindsay Drummond, 1943

Goldstein, J., *War and Gender: How Gender Shapes the War System and Vice Versa*, Cambridge: Cambridge University Press, 2001

Goodman, P., *Women, War and Sexuality*, Basingstoke: Palgrave, 2002

Gould, J., 'Women's Military Services in First World War Britain' in M. Higonnet, J. Jenson, S. Michel and M. Weitz (eds) *Behind the Lines: Gender and the Two World Wars*, New Haven, CT: Yale University Press, 1987

Grayzel, S., ' "The Outward and Visible Sign of Her Patriotism": Women, Uniforms and National Service During the First World War', *Twentieth Century British History*, Vol. 8, no. 2, 1997

—— 'The Enemy Within: The Problem of British Women's Sexuality During the First World War' in N. Dombrowski (ed.) *Women and War in the Twentieth Century*, New York, 1999

—— *Women's Identities at War: Gender, Motherhood and Politics in Britain and France During the First World War*, Chapel Hill, NC: University of North Carolina Press, 1999

—— 'Liberating Women? Examining Gender, Morality and Sexuality in First World War Britain and France' in G. Braybon (ed.) *Evidence, History and the Great War*, Oxford: Berghahn Books, 2003

Gregory, A., *The Silence of Memory: Armistice Day 1914–1946*, Oxford: Berg, 1994

—— 'British "War Enthusiasm": A Reassessment' in G. Braybon (ed.) *Evidence, History and the Great War: Historians and the Impact of 1914–1918*, Oxford: Berghahn Books, 2003

Gribble, F., *Women in War*, London: Sampson, Low, Marston & Co., 1916

Gubar, S., 'This is My Rifle, This is My Gun: World War Two and the Blitz on Women' in M. Higonnet, J. Jenson, S. Michel and M. Weitz (eds) *Behind the Lines: Gender and the Two World Wars*, New Haven, CT: Yale University Press, 1987

Gullace, N., 'White Feathers and Wounded Men: Female Patriotism and the Memory of the Great War', *Journal of British Studies*, Vol. 36, No. 2, 1997

Gwynne-Vaughan, H., *Service With the Army*, London: Hutchinson, 1942

Haldane, J. S., *A.R.P.*, London: Left Book Club, 1938

Hall, G. Stanley, *Adolescence: Its Psychology and its Relations to Physiology, Anthropology, Sociology, Sex, Crime, Religion and Education*, New York: Appleton, 1904

Hall, R., *The Well of Loneliness*, London: Virago, 1982, first published London, 1928

Hall, S., 'The "Social Eye" of Picture Post', *Working Papers in Cultural Studies 2*, Centre for Contemporary Cultural Studies: University of Birmingham, 1972

Hamilton, C., *William – An Englishman*, London: Persephone, 1999, first published London: Skeffington & Son, 1919

Hammerton, J., *History of the Second Great War*, London: Amalgamated Press, 1945

Harper, S., 'The Representation of Women in British Feature Film 1939–1945' in P. Taylor (ed.) *Britain and the Cinema in the Second World War*, London: Macmillan, 1988

——— 'The Years of Total War: Propaganda and Entertainment' in C. Gledhill and G. Swanson (eds) *Nationalizing Femininity*, Manchester: Manchester University Press, 1996

Harris, C., *Women at War in Uniform 1939–1945*, Stroud: Sutton Publishing, 2003

Harris, R., 'The Child of the Barbarian: Rape, Race and Nationalism in France During the First World War', *Past and Present*, Vol. 141, 1993

Harrisson, T., *Living Through the Blitz*, London: William Collins, 1976

Hartley, C. Gasquoine, *Women's Wild Oats: Essays on the Refixing of Moral Standards*, London: T. Werner-Laurie, 1919

Hartley, J., *Millions Like Us: British Women's Fiction of the Second World War*, London: Virago, 1997

Haste, C., *Keep the Home Fires Burning: Propaganda in the First World War*, London: Allen Lane, 1977

Hawkins, T. H. and Brumble, L. F. J., *Adult Education: The Record of the British Army*, London: Macmillan, 1947

Hendrix, S. N., 'In the Army: Women, Camp Followers and Gender Roles in the British Army in the French and Indian Wars 1755–1765' in G. De Groot and C. Penniston-Bird (eds) *A Soldier and A Woman: Sexual Integration in the Military*, Harlow: Longman 2000

Hennessy, P., *The Secret State: Whitehall and the Cold War*, London: Penguin, 2002

Hicks Stiehm, J., *Arms and the Enlisted Woman*, Philadelphia, PA: Temple University Press, 1989

Higonnet, M. R., 'Not So Quiet in No Woman's Land' in M. Cooke and A. Wollacott (eds) *Gendering War Talk*, Princeton, NJ: Princeton University Press, 1993

Higonnet, M. R. and P. L. R. Higonnet, 'The Double Helix' in M. Higonnet, J. Jenson, S. Michel and M. Weitz (eds) *Behind the Lines: Gender and the Two World War*, New Haven, CT: Yale University Press, 1987

Higonnet, M. R., J. Jenson, S. Michel and M. Weitz (eds) *Behind the Lines*, New Haven, CT: Yale University Press, 1987

Hinton, J., *Women, Social Leadership and the Second World War: Continuities of Class*, Oxford: Oxford University Press, 2002

Hirschfield, Dr M., *The Sexual History of the World War*, New York: Panarge Press, 1937

Holm, Major General J., *Women in the Military: An Unfinished Revolution*, California: Presidio, 1982

Holton, S. S., *Feminism and Democracy: Women's Suffrage and Reform Politics in Britain 1900–1918*, Cambridge: Cambridge University Press, 1986

Homer, *The Iliad*, trans. R. Fitzgerald, Oxford: Oxford University Press, 1984

Howard, K., *Sex Problems of the Returning Soldier*, Manchester: Sydney Pemberton, 1945

Howard, R., *In Search of My Father: A Portrait of Lesley Howard*, London: Kimber, 1981

Hymowitz, C. and M. Wiseman, *A History of Women in America*, New York: Bantam, 1978

Hynes, S., *A War Imagined: The First World War and English Culture*, London: Bodley Head, 1990

——(ed.) *The Soldier's Tale: Bearing Witness to Modern War*, New York: Penguin, 1997

Izraeli, D., 'Gendering Military Service in the Israeli Defence Service' in G. De Groot and C. Penniston-Bird (eds) *A Soldier and A Woman: Sexual Integration in the Military*, Harlow: Longman, 2000

Izzard, M., *A Heroine in Her Time: A Life of Dame Helen Gwynne-Vaughan 1879–1967*, London: Macmillan, 1969

Jeffrey, K., 'The Post-War Army' in I. Beckett and K. Simpson (eds) *A Nation in Arms: A Social Study of the British Army in the First World War*, Manchester: Manchester University Press, 1985

Jeffreys, S., *The Spinster and Her Enemies. Feminism and Sexuality 1880–1930*, London: Pandora, 1985

Jesse, F. Tennyson, *The Sword of Deborah: First Hand Impressions of the British Women's Army in France*, London: Richard Clay & Sons, 1918

Johnson, P., (ed.) *Twentieth Century Britain: Economic, Social and Cultural Change*, London: Longman, 1994

Jones, Squadron Leader E.G., 'Women in Combat – Historical Quirk or the Future Cutting Edge?', *RUSI Journal*, Vol. 139, 1993

Kamester, M. and J. Vellacott (eds) *Militarism Versus Feminism: Writings on Women and War*, London: Virago, 1987

Keegan, J., *A History of Warfare*, London: Hutchinson, 1993

——*The First World War*, London: Pimlico, 1999

Kent, S. Kingsley, 'The Politics of Sexual Difference: World War One and the Demise of Feminism', *Journal of British Studies*, Vol. 27, 1988

——*Making Peace: The Reconstruction of Gender in Interwar Britain*, Princeton, NJ: Princeton University Press, 1993

Keynes, J. M. *The Collected Writings of J.M. Keynes: Vol. 3*, Basingstoke: Macmillan, 1971

Kier, E., *Imagining War: French and British Military Doctrine Between the Wars*, Princeton, NJ: Princeton University Press, 1999

Kirkham, P., 'Beauty and Duty: Keeping Up the (Home) Front' in P. Kirkham and D. Thom (eds) *War Culture: Social Change and Changing Experience in World War Two Britain*, London: Lawrence & Wishart, 1995

——'Fashioning the Feminine: Dress, Appearance and Femininity in Wartime Britain', in C. Gledhill and G. Swanson (eds) *Nationalizing Femininity*, Manchester: Manchester University Press, 1996

Laffin, J., *Women in Battle*, London: Abelard-Schuman, 1967

Lamm, D., 'Emily Goes to War: Explaining the Recruitment to the Women's Army Auxiliary Corps' in B. Melman (ed.) *Borderlines: Genders and Identities in War and Peace*, New York: Routledge, 1998

Lant, A., *Blackout: Reinventing Women for Wartime British Cinema*, Princeton, NJ: Princeton University Press, 1991

Lawrence, J., 'The First World War and its Aftermath' in P. Johnson (ed.) *Twentieth Century Britain: Economic, Social and Cultural Change*, Harlow: Longman, 1994

Le Quex, W., *German Atrocities: A Record of Shameless Deeds*, London: n.p., 1914

Lewis, J., *Women in England 1870–1950: Sexual Divisions and Social Change*, Sussex: Wheatsheaf, 1984

Lewis, J., *Women in Britain Since 1945*, Oxford: Blackwell, 1992

Liddell-Hart, B., *Europe in Arms*, London: Faber & Faber, 1937

Liddington, J., *The Long Road to Greenham: Feminism and Anti-Militarism in Britain Since 1820*, London: Virago, 1989

Light, A., *Forever England: Femininity, Literature and Conservatism Between the Wars*, London: Routledge, 1991

Londonderry, Marchioness of, *Retrospect*, London: Frederick Muller, 1938

Lorentzen, L. A. and J., Turpin, *The Women and War Reader*, New York: New York University Press, 1998

Lowe, R., 'The Second World War, Consensus, and the Foundations of the Welfare State', *Twentieth Century British History*, Vol. 1, 1990

McClaren, B., *Women of the War*, London: Hodder & Stoughton, 1917

Macdonald, S., P. Holden and S. Ardener (eds) *Images of Women in Peace and War*, Basingstoke: Macmillan, 1987

Mackay, J., and P. Thane, 'The Englishwoman' in P. Colls and R. Dodd (eds) *Englishness: Politics and Culture 1880–1920*, Kent, 1986

Mansfield, S., *The Rites of War: An Analysis of Institutionalized Warfare*, London: Bellew, 1991

Marinetti, F. T., 'The Founding and Future of Futurism' in R. W. Flint (ed.) *Marinetti: Selected Writings*, London, 1971

Marshall, C., 'Women and War' in M. Kamester and J. Vellacott (eds) *Militarism Versus Feminism: Writings on Women and Wars*, London: Virago, 1987, first published 1915

Martel, G. (ed.) *The World War Two Reader*, London: Routledge, 2004

Marwick, A.,*The Deluge: British Society and the First World War*, London: Macmillan, 1991, first published 1965

—— *War and Social Change in the Twentieth Century*, London: Macmillan, 1974

—— *Women at War 1914–1918*, London: Croom Helm, 1977

Mason, U. Stuart, *The Wrens 1917–1977: A History of the Women's Royal Naval Service*, Reading: Educational Explorers, 1977

Mass-Observation, *The Journey Home: A Mass-Observation Report on the Problems of Demobilisation*, London: John Murray, 1944

Maynard, M. and J. Purvis (eds) *Researching Women's Lives from a Feminist Perspective*, London: Taylor & Francis, 1994

Melman, B., *Women and the Popular Imagination in the 1920s: Flappers and Nymphs*, Basingstoke: Macmillan, 1988

—— (ed.) *Borderlines*, New York: Routledge, 1998

Miles, E., *Untold Tales of Wartime London*, London: Cecil Palmer, 1930

Miller, L., 'Not Just Weapons of the Weak: Gender Harassment as a Form of Protest for Army Men', *Social Psychology Quarterly*, Vol. 60, No. 1, 1997

Minns, R., *Bombers and Mash: The Domestic Front 1939–1945*, London: Virago, 1980

Mitchell, D., *Women on the Warpath: The Story of the Women of the First World War*, London: Cape, 1966

Morgan, D. and M. Evans, *The Battle for Britain. Citizenship and Ideology in the Second World War*, London: Routledge, 1993

Moriarty, C., 'Abram Games: An Essay on His Work and its Context' in N. Games, C. Moriarty and J. Rose, *Abram Games, Graphic Designer: Maximum Meaning, Minimum Means*, Aldershot: Lund Humphries, 2003

Muir, K., *Arms and the Woman*, London: Coronet, 1992

Murray, E., *Women's Value in Wartime*, Women's Freedom League, n.p., 1917

Myrdal, A. and V. Klein, *Women's Two Roles. Home and Work*, London: Routledge & Kegan Paul, 1956

Nicholson, M., *What Did You Do in the War Mummy? Women in World War Two*, London: Chatto & Windus, 1995

Noakes, L., *War and the British: Gender and National Identity 1939–1991*, London: I.B. Tauris, 1998

—— 'Gender, War and Memory: A Review Essay', *Journal of Contemporary History*, Vol. 4, October 2001

—— 'War and Peace' in I. Zweiniger-Bargielowska (ed.) *Women in Twentieth Century Britain*, Harlow: Longman, 2001

Obelkevitch, J. and P. Catterall (eds) *Understanding Post-War British Society*, London: Routledge, 1994

Oldfield, S., *Women Against the Iron Fist: Alternatives to Militarism 1900–1989*, Oxford: Blackwell, 1989

Oram, A., ' "Bombs Don't Discriminate!" Women's Political Activism in the Second World War' in C. Gledhill and G. Swanson (eds) *Nationalising Femininity*, Manchester: Manchester University Press, 1996

Ouditt, S., *Fighting Forces, Writing Women: Identity and Ideology in the First World War*, London: Routledge, 1994

Pankhurst, E., *My Own Story*, London: Eveleigh Nash, 1914

Pankhurst, E. S., *The Suffragette Movement: An Intimate Portrait of Persons and Ideals*, London: Longman, Green, 1931

Paris, M., *Warrior Nation: Images of War in British Popular Culture 1850–2000*, London: Reaktion Books, 2000

Parkin, D., 'Women in the Armed Services 1940–1945' in R. Samuel (ed.) *Patriotism: the Making and Unmaking of British National Identity: Vol. II, Minorities and Outsiders*, London: Routledge & Kegan Paul, 1989

Payne, C., *Women: After the War and Now*, London: Unwin, 1914

Pederson, S., 'Gender, Welfare and Citizenship in Britain During the Great War', *American Historical Review*, 4, 1990

Peniston-Bird, C., 'Ambiguity, Contradiction and Possibility' in G. De Groot and C. Peniston-Bird (eds) *A Soldier and a Woman*, Harlow: Longman, 2000

—— 'Classifying the Body in the Second World War: British Men in and Out of Uniform', *Body and Society*, 9, 2003

Pierson, R. Roach (ed.) *Women and Peace: Theoretical, Historical and Practical Perspectives*, London: Croom Helm, 1987

Pile, General Sir F., *Ack Ack. Britain's Defence Against Air Attack During the Second World War*, London: Harrap, 1949

Plain, G., *Women's Fiction of the Second World War: Gender, Power and Resistance*, Edinburgh: Edinburgh University Press, 1996

Popham, H., *The Story of the Women's Transport Service*, London: Leo Cooper, 1984

Priestley, J. B., *British Women Go To War*, London: Collins, 1943

Pugh, M., *Women and the Women's Movement in Britain 1914–1999*, London: Macmillan, 2000, first published 1992

Purvis, J., 'Deeds, Not Words: Daily Life in the Women's Social and Political Union in Edwardian Britain' in J. Purvis and S. Stanley Holton (eds) *Votes for Women*, London: Routledge, 2000

—— (ed.) *Women's History: Britain 1850–1945*, London: Routledge, 2000

—— *Emmeline Pankhurst: A Biography*, London: Routledge, 2002

Ratazzi, P. (ed.) *Little ATS Anthology: The First Girl Writers in Battledress*, n.p: Staples, n.d.

Richards, J. (ed.), *Imperialism and Juvenile Literature*, Manchester: Manchester University Press, 1989

Richards, J. and D. Sheridan (eds) *Mass-Observation at the Movies*, London: Routledge & Kegan Paul, 1987

Riley, D., *War in the Nursery: Theories of the Child and the Mother*, London: Virago, 1983

——— 'Some Peculiarities of Social Policy Concerning Women in Wartime and Postwar Britain' in M. R. Higonnet, J. Jenson, S. Michel and M. Collins Weitz (eds) *Behind the Lines*, New Haven, 1987

Roberts, K., 'Gender, Class and Patriotism: Women's Paramilitary Units in First World War Britain', *International History Review*, Vol. 19, No. 1, 1997

Robinson, V., *Sisters in Arms: How Female Gunners Defended Britain Against the Luftwaffe*, London: Harper Collins, 1996

Roper, M. and J. Tosh, *Manful Assertions: Masculinities in Britain Since 1800*, London: Routledge, 1991

Rose, S., 'Girls and G.I.s: Race, Sex and Diplomacy in Second World War Britain', *The International History Review*, Vol. 19, No. 1, 1997

Rublack, U., 'Wench and Maiden: Women, War and the Pictorial Function of the Feminine in German Cities in the Early Modern Period', *History Workshop Journal*, Vol. 44, 1997

Ruck, B., *Khaki and Kisses*, London: Hutchinson, 1915

Samuel, R. (ed.), *Patriotism: The Making and Unmaking of British National Identity*, Vols *1–3*, London: Routledge, 1988, 1989

Sanders, M. and P. Taylor, *British Propaganda During the First World War*, London: Macmillan, 1982

Sandes, F., *An Englishwoman Sergeant in the Serbian Army*, London: Hodder & Stoughton, 1918

——— *The Autobiography of a Woman Soldier: A Brief Record of Adventure with the Serbian Army 1916–1919*, London: H.F.G. Witherby, 1927

Scott, J., 'Gender: A Useful Category of Historical Analysis' in J.W. Scott (ed.) *Feminism and History*, Oxford: Oxford University Press, 1988

Scott, P., *British Women in War*, London: Hutchinson, 1940

——— *They Made Invasion Possible*, London: Hutchinson, 1944

Segal, L., *Is the Future Female? Troubled Thoughts on Contemporary Feminism*, London: Virago, 1987

Shaw, M., *Post-Military Society: Militarization, Demilitarization and War at the End of the Twentieth Century*, Philadelphia, PA: Temple University Press, 1991

Sheridan, D., 'Ambivalent Memories: Women and the 1939–1945 War in Britain', *Oral History*, Vol. 18, No. 1, 1990

Sinclair, A. (ed.) *The War Decade: An Anthology of the 1940s*, London: Hamilton, 1989

Smith, H. L., 'The Effect of the War on the Status of Women' in H. L. Smith (ed.) *War and Social Change. British Society in the Second World War*, Manchester: Manchester University Press, 1988

——— (ed.) *British Feminism in the Twentieth Century*, Aldershot: Edward Elgar, 1990

Smith, H. Z. (pseud.) *Not So Quiet: Stepdaughters of War*, London: A.E. Marriott, 1930

Spence, J. C., *The Purpose of the Family: A Guide to the Care of Children*, London: National Children's Home, 1946

Springhall, J., 'The Boy Scouts, Class and Militarism in Relation to British Youth Movements', *International Review of Social History*, Vol. 16, No. 2, 1971, *Women's History Review*, 8, No. 4, 1999

Stafford, A., *Army Without Banners*, London: Collins, 1942

Stone, T., 'Creating a (Gendered?) Military Identity in the Women's Auxiliary Air Force in Great Britain in the Second World War', *Women's History Review*, Vol. 8, No. 4, 1999

Summerfield, P., *Women Workers in the Second World War: Production and Patriarchy in Conflict*, London: Croom Helm, 1984

—— 'Women in Britain Since 1945: Companionate Marriage and the Double Burden' in J. Obelkevich and P. Catterall (eds) *Understanding Post-War British Society*, London 1994

—— *Reconstructing Women's Wartime Lives: Discourse and Subjectivity in Oral Histories of the Second World War*, Manchester: Manchester University press, 1998

—— 'She Wants A Gun, Not a Dishcloth! Gender, Service and Citizenship in Britain in the Second World War' in G. De Groot and C. Peniston-Bird (eds) *A Soldier and a Woman: Sexual Intregration in the Military*, Harlow, 2000

Summers, A., 'Militarism in Britain before the First World War', *History Workshop Journal*, Vol. 2, 1976

—— *Angels and Citizens: British Women as Military Nurses 1854–1914*, London: Routledge & Kegan Paul, 1988

Summerskill, E., *Women Fall In: A Guide to Women's Work in Wartime*, London: Hutchinson, 1941

—— *A Woman's World*, London: Heinemann, 1967

Swindells, J., 'Coming Home to Heaven: Manpower and Myth in 1944 Britain', *Women's History Review*, Vol. 4, No. 2, 1995

Taylor, E., *Women Who Went to War 1938–1946*, London: Grafton, 1989

Tennyson, A., *Poems of Tennyson*, Oxford: Oxford University Press, 1917

Terry, R., *Women in Khaki: The Story of the British Woman Soldier*, London: Columbus, 1988

Thane, P., 'Women Since 1945' in P. Johnson (ed.) *20th Century Britain: Economic, Social and Cultural Change*, London: Longman, 1994

—— 'The British Imperial State and the Construction of National Identities' in B. Melman (ed.) *Borderlines: Genders and Identities in War and Peace 1870–1930*, London: Routledge, 1998

Thewelweit, K., *Male Fantasies. Volume One: Women, Floods, Bodies, History*, London: Polity, 1987

Thom, D., *Nice Girls and Rude Girls: Women Workers in World War One*, London: I.B. Tauris, 1998

—— 'Making Spectaculars: Museums and How We Remember Gender in Wartime' in G. Braybon (ed.) *Evidence, History and the Great War*, Oxford: Berghahn Books, 2003

Tinkler, P., *Constructing Girlhood. Popular Magazines for Girls Growing Up in England 1920–1950*, London: Taylor & Francis, 1995

Titmuss, R., *Essays on the Welfare State*, London: Allen & Unwin, 1958

Towle, P., 'British Security and Disarmament Policy in Europe in the 1920s' in R. Altman, A. M. Burke and M. Howard (eds) *The Quest for Stability: Problem of west European Society 1918–1957*, Oxford: The German Historical Institute, Oxford University Press, 1993

Tweedie, A., *Women and Soldiers*, London: Bodley Head, 1918

Tylee, C., *The Great War and Women's Consciousness: Images of Militarism and Womanhood in Women's Writings 1914–1964*, Iowa City: University of Iowa Press, 1990

Vicinus, M., *Independent Women: Work and Community for Single Women 1850–1920*, London: Virago, 1985

Wade, E., *The World Guide Chief, Olave, Lady Baden-Powell*, London: Hutchinson, 1957

Waller, J. and M. Vaughan Rees, *Women in Wartime: The Role of Women's Magazines*, London: McDonald Optima, 1987

—— *Women in Uniform 1939–1945*, London: McDonald Optima, 1989

Ward, I., *F.A.N.Y. Invicta*, London: Hutchinson, 1955

Ward, P., ' "Women of Britain say Go": Women's Patriotism in the First World War', *Twentieth Century British History*, Vol. 12, No. 1, 2001

Warner, W., *Monuments and Maidens: The Allegory of the Female Form*, London: Picador, 1985

Watson, J., 'Khaki Girls, VADs and Tommy's Sisters: Gender and Class in First World War Britain', *The International History Review*, Vol. XIX, No. 1, 1997

Webster, W., *Imagining Home: Gender 'Race' and National Identity 1945–64*, London: UCL Press, 1998

Weil, S., *The Iliad or the Poem of Force*, trans. M. McCarthy, Wallingord: Pendle Hill Paperbacks, 1956, first published 1940/1941

Whateley, L., *As Thoughts Survive*, London: Hutchinson, 1949

Wheelwright, J., *Amazons and Military Maids: Women Who Dressed as Men in the Pursuit of Life, Liberty and Happiness*, London: Pandora, 1989

—— *The Fatal Lover: Mata Hari and the Myth of Women in Espionage*, London: Collins Brown, 1992

Wilkinson, M., 'The Women's Work Collection at the Imperial War Museum', *Imperial War Museum Review*, Vol. 6, 1991

Wilson, E., *Only Half-Way to Paradise: Women in Post-War Britain 1945–1968*, London: Tavistock, 1980

Wilson, N. S., *Education in the Forces: The Civilian Context*, The Year Book of Education, n.p., 1949

Winship, J., 'Nation Before Family: *Woman*, the National Home Weekly, 1945–1953' in *Formations of Nation and People*, London: Routledge & Kegan Paul, 1984

—— 'Women's Magazines: Times of War and Management of the Self in *Woman's Own*', in C. Gledhill and G. Swanson (eds) *Nationalising Femininity*, Manchester: Manchester University Press, 1996

Winter, J. M., *The Great War and the British People*, Basingstoke: Macmillan, 1985

—— *The Experience of World War One*, Oxford: Oxford University Press, 1986

—— *Sites of Memory, Sites of Mourning: The Great War in European Cultural History*, Cambridge: Cambridge University Press, 1995

Woolf, V., *Three Guineas*, London: Hogarth Press, 1938

Woollacott, A., ' "Khaki Fever" and its Control: Gender, Class, Age and Sexual Morality on the British Homefront in the First World War', *Journal of Contemporary History*, Vol. 29, 1994

Zweiniger-Bargielowska, I., *Women in Twentieth Century Britain*, Harlow: Longman, 2001

Index

Note: Page numbers in italics indicate figures.

208   *Index*

Routledge History

Women's History, Britain 1700–1850: An Introduction
Edited by Hannah Barker and Elaine Chalus

In this broad-ranging and well-balanced collection of essays by established experts and dynamic new scholars, Hannah Barker and Elaine Chalus present a comprehensive history of British women in the eighteenth and nineteenth centuries. Combining new research with discussions of current secondary literature, the contributors examine areas as diverse as the enlightenment, politics, religion, education, sexuality, family, work, poverty and consumption.

A captivating overview of women and their lives, this book is an essential purchase for the study of women's history. With its delight in detail and the wealth of women's experiences that it reveals, it will also appeal to any reader with an interest in the topic.

Hbk 0–415–29176–3
Pbk 0–415–29177–1

Women's History, Britain 1850–1945: An Introduction
Edited by June Purvis

This edited collection includes chapters, written by experts in their field, on the suffrage movement, race and empire, industrialisation, the impact of war and women's literature, health, the family, education, sexuality, work and politics. Each contribution provides an overview of the main issues and debates within each area and offers suggestions for further reading. This book not only provides an invaluable introduction to every aspect of women's participation in the political, social and economic history of Britain, but also brings the reader up to date with current historical thinking on the study of women's history itself. This is an invaluable and concise overview of an essential area of historical and contemporary study.

Pbk 0–415–23889–7

Available at all good bookshops
For ordering and further information please visit:
www.routledge.com

WOMEN AND WORK
IN BRITAIN SINCE 1840

Gerry Holloway

Women and Work in Britain since 1840
Gerry Holloway

With suggestions for research topics, an annotated bibliography to aid further research and a chronology of important events which places the subject in a broader historical context, Gerry Holloway considers how factors such as class, age, marital status, race and locality, along with wider economic and political issues, have affected women's job opportunities and status.

Key themes and issues that run through the book include:

- continuity and change and women's employment;
- the sexual division of labour;
- women as a cheap labour force;
- women's perceived primary role of motherhood;
- women and trade unions;
- equality versus difference – the key feminist debate;
- women's education and training.

Students of women's studies, gender studies and history will find this a fascinating and invaluable addition to their reading material.

Hbk 0–415–25910–X
Pbk 0–415–25911–8

Outspoken Women: An Anthology of Women's Writing on Sex, 1870–1969
Lesley Hall

This anthology brings together the non-fictional writings of British women on sexual attitudes and behaviour nearly a hundred years prior to 'second wave' feminism. Studying the period from the supposedly prudish Victorian era, to the sexual revolution of the 1960s, this comprehensive study reveals a neglected tradition of British women's writing.

The excerpts analysed here come from polemics, works of advice, surveys, essays and belles-lettres, and the authors, both famous and lesser known figures, provide a diverse range of perspectives, and include social Darwinists, sexologists, psychoanalysts, VD campaigners, as well as women writing about their own lives and experiences, providing an engaging examination of a fascinating subject.

Hbk 0–415–25371–3
Pbk 0–415–25372–1